Party in the Street

The Antiwar Movement and the Democratic Party after 9/11

Party in the Street explores the interaction between political parties and social movements in the United States. Examining the collapse of the post-9/11 antiwar movement against the wars in Iraq and Afghanistan, this book focuses on activism and protest in the United States. It argues that the electoral success of the Democratic Party and President Barack Obama, as well as antipathy toward President George W. Bush, played a greater role in this collapse than did changes in foreign policy. It shows that how people identify with social movements and political parties matters a great deal, and it considers the Tea Party and Occupy Wall Street as comparison cases.

MICHAEL T. HEANEY is Assistant Professor of Organizational Studies and Political Science at the University of Michigan, Ann Arbor. He has previously served as a Postdoctoral Fellow at the Center for the Study of American Politics at the Institution for Social and Policy Studies, Yale University, and as the William A. Steiger Fellow in the Congressional Fellowship Program at the American Political Science Association. His research has received funding from the National Science Foundation and has been published in a wide array of academic journals, such as the *American Political Science Review*, the *American Journal of Sociology*, *Social Networks*, and *Perspectives on Politics*.

FABIO ROJAS is Associate Professor of Sociology at Indiana University, Bloomington. He previously served as a Robert Wood Johnson Foundation Scholar in Health Policy Research at the University of Michigan. Rojas's research has been published in a wide array of academic journals, such as the *American Journal of Sociology*, the *Academy of Management Journal*, *Social Forces*, and the *Journal of Black Studies*. His first book, *From Black Power to Black Studies: How a Radical Social Movement Became an Academic Discipline*, was published in 2007. He blogs regularly at orgtheory.net.

Advance Praise for *Party in the Street*

"The blockbuster finding in *Party in the Street* is its careful documentation of the role of political partisanship in first filling the ranks of the antiwar movement in the early 2000s and then emptying it out again after partisan control of the presidency shifted in 2009. More broadly, the book provides a theoretically and empirically rich account of the interplay of movement mobilization and partisan political mobilization."

– Pamela Oliver, Chair of Sociology, University of Wisconsin–Madison

"In *Party in the Street*, Heaney and Rojas show how overlapping movement and partisan identities shape political activism and the ebb and flow of social movements themselves. Focusing on the puzzle of activism in the post-9/11 antiwar movement, the authors offer a unique and compelling theoretical framework and marshal an impressive array of empirical evidence, ranging from organizational and legislative networks to movement event data. Taking excellent advantage of the unique opportunity to study a movement as it unfolded, the authors not only engage in participant observation but they field well-designed survey instruments to protesters as well – no small feat! – producing unprecedented insight into the conflicting motivations and goals of movement activists. The result is a distinctive accounting of the dynamics of various political identities that helps us understand the political fortunes of both social movements and political parties in the United States."

– Christina Wolbrecht, Department of Political Science, University of Notre Dame

CAMBRIDGE STUDIES IN CONTENTIOUS POLITICS

Editors

Mark Beissinger *Princeton University*
Jack A. Goldstone *George Mason University*
Michael Hanagan *Vassar College*
Doug McAdam *Stanford University and Center for Advanced Study in the Behavioral Sciences*
Suzanne Staggenborg *University of Pittsburgh*
Sidney Tarrow *Cornell University*
Charles Tilly (d. 2008) *Columbia University*
Elisabeth J. Wood *Yale University*
Deborah Yashar *Princeton University*

(continued after the index)

Party in the Street

The Antiwar Movement and the Democratic Party after 9/11

MICHAEL T. HEANEY
University of Michigan, Ann Arbor

FABIO ROJAS
Indiana University, Bloomington

CAMBRIDGE
UNIVERSITY PRESS

CAMBRIDGE
UNIVERSITY PRESS

32 Avenue of the Americas, New York, NY 10013-2473, USA

Cambridge University Press is part of the University of Cambridge.

It furthers the University's mission by disseminating knowledge in the pursuit of education, learning, and research at the highest international levels of excellence.

www.cambridge.org
Information on this title: www.cambridge.org/9781107448803

© Michael T. Heaney and Fabio Rojas 2015

First published 2015

Printed in the United States of America

A catalog record for this publication is available from the British Library.

ISBN 978-1-107-08540-4 Hardback
ISBN 978-1-107-44880-3 Paperback

For
Marilyn Olin
A great teacher

Contents

Tables

Figures

Abbreviations

9/11	The terrorist attacks of September 11, 2001
AARP	(formerly) American Association of Retired Persons
AASS	American Anti-Slavery Society
ACORN	Association of Community Organizations for Reform Now
AFL	American Federation of Labor
AFL-CIO	American Federation of Labor–Congress of Industrial Organizations
AIDS	Acquired Immune Deficiency Syndrome
ANSWER	Act Now to Stop War and End Racism
CPA	Coalition Provisional Authority
CSUSIME	Coalition to Stop U.S. Intervention in the Middle East
DNC	Democratic National Convention
IMF	International Monetary Fund
IVAW	Iraq Veterans Against the War
LBJ	Lyndon Baines Johnson
MGJC	Mobilization for Global Justice Coalition
MTV	Music Television
NAACP	National Association for the Advancement of Colored People
NATO	North Atlantic Treaty Organization
NCPME	National Campaign for Peace in the Middle East
RNC	Republican National Convention
SANE	Committee for a Sane Nuclear Policy
SDS	Students for a Democratic Society
SOFA	Status of Forces Agreement
TEA	Taxed Enough Already
TPP	Tea Party Patriots
UFP	United for Peace
UFPJ	United for Peace and Justice
USA PATRIOT	Uniting (and) Strengthening America (by) Providing Appropriate Tools Required (to) Intercept (and) Obstruct Terrorism
WTO	World Trade Organization

Introduction

January 27, 2007, was an unseasonably warm Saturday in Washington, D.C. With the sun shining and afternoon temperatures reaching 57 degrees Fahrenheit, the weather conditions were perfect for an antiwar march in the nation's capital. The political conditions seemed perfect, too. Only a few months earlier, on November 7, 2006, the Democratic Party had won a decisive victory in the congressional midterm elections. Democrats gained thirty-one seats in the U.S. House of Representatives and six seats in the U.S. Senate, allowing them to control both the House (by a 233–202 margin) and the Senate (by a 51–49 margin) for the first time since 1994 (CNN 2006; Zelney and Zernike 2006). Media accounts of the election widely attributed the outcome to voters' dissatisfaction with President George W. Bush and the Iraq War (see, for example, Dewan 2006).

Leaders in the antiwar movement sought to seize the political opportunity created by the Democrats' return to power. Given the belief that Democrats owed their victory to antiwar sentiment, movement activists hoped to press Democratic leaders into bringing the Iraq War to a quick end. To support this goal, upward of one hundred thousand people gathered at the National Mall for a rally organized by United for Peace and Justice, the nation's largest and broadest antiwar coalition during the presidency of George W. Bush. The rally focused on the slogan "The voters want peace. Tell the new Congress: ACT _NOW_ TO END THE WAR!" (United for Peace and Justice 2007d, emphasis in original). The speakers included elected officials from the Democratic Party, such as U.S. Representatives Dennis Kucinich (D-OH), Maxine Waters (D-CA), and Lynn Woolsey (D-CA); movement leaders, such as the Reverend Jesse Jackson and Medea Benjamin; and celebrities, such as Jane Fonda and Danny Glover, all of whom echoed the view that the 2006 elections were a mandate for peace. As U.S. Representative Lynn Woolsey exclaimed in her remarks, "We have an antidote to this insanity.... It is what _you_ sent _us_ to do last November.

It's called H.R. 508 ... the Bring [the] Troops Home and Iraq Sovereignty Restoration Act" (Woolsey 2007b, emphasis in original).

Organizers followed up on the rally with a Capitol Hill lobby day. Approximately one thousand grassroots activists participated. After receiving a day of basic lobbying training on Sunday, activists swarmed into House and Senate office buildings on Monday, January 29, ready to press their representatives to support a laundry list of pending resolutions and to join the congressional Out of Iraq Caucus. Teams of citizen lobbyists were organized by state and armed with detailed records of representatives' support (or lack thereof) for pending antiwar legislation. The day was a model of the "inside-outside" strategy, in which activists attempt to keep one foot inside political institutions and one foot outside them (Selfa 2008, pp. 160–2). By intentionally combining contentious politics with institutional politics, this strategy aims to leverage the power of movements for policy influence. At the same time, it places movements in a nebulous position that has the potential to undermine their cause as much as, or more than, it helps it (Tarrow 2012).

While many movement leaders and activists emphasized the role of Congress as a whole in ending the Iraq War, others specified a role for the Democratic Party, in particular. For example, Lynn Woolsey gave an interview to MSNBC shortly after Saturday's rally, in which she claimed, "We're hoping to build on the November 7th election when the public spoke loudly [and] told Democrats, 'we want *you* to be the majority because you will change that policy in Iraq and bring our troops home'" (Woolsey 2007a, emphasis in original). From Woolsey's point of view, a victory for the Democratic Party and the cause of peace were one and the same. As a sponsor of antiwar resolutions and a cochair of the Out of Iraq Caucus, Woolsey was one of a handful of Democratic members of Congress who had been working hand in hand with grassroots leaders in the antiwar movement and sympathetic Democrats in Congress in an effort to end the Iraq War. For Woolsey and her allies, the elections, rally, and lobby day were the culmination of many years of hard work.

The alliance between the Democratic Party and the antiwar movement in 2006–2007 underscores the potential for synergy between social movements and political parties. In this case, leaders of a social movement identified an issue, framed it for political discourse, and helped to mobilize supporters from the rank and file of a political party. Leaders of a political party adopted the movement's issue and frames. They promised to address the issue if elected. Mobilization by the movement's supporters boosted the party's success in the election. After the election, party leaders worked together with movement activists to implement the movement's agenda.

To the disappointment of many activists, the alliance between the Democratic Party and the antiwar movement proved to be short lived. The antiwar movement became a mass movement from 2001 to 2006, as Democratic Party loyalty and anti-Bush sentiment provided fuel for the movement. However, the 2006 elections and their immediate aftermath were the high point for party-movement synergy. At exactly the time when antiwar voices were most well poised to exert pressure on Congress, movement leaders stopped sponsoring lobby days. The size of antiwar protests declined. From 2007 to 2009, the largest antiwar rallies shrank from hundreds of thousands of people to thousands, and then to only hundreds. Congress considered antiwar legislation, but mostly failed to pass it. In 2008, the Democrats nominated an antiwar presidential candidate in U.S. Senator Barack Obama (D-IL). But once Obama became president, his policies on war and national security resembled those of his Republican predecessor, President George W. Bush. By 2009, synergy between the Democratic Party and the antiwar movement appeared to have largely evaporated. Thus, there was a decline in antiwar movement activity in three domains – individual, organizational, and legislative. This was not a case of evaporating protest that was compensated by activity at other levels, but an across-the-board reduction in movement activity.

The decline of the antiwar movement in the United States after the January 2007 lobby day poses a puzzle for the study of social movements and political parties. The movement's Democratic allies were on the rise in Congress. The prospects for an antiwar president in 2008 were strong. If ever there was a time when the antiwar movement could have exerted influence over decision makers, this was it. Political scientists, such as Ken Kollman (1998) and Kenneth Goldstein (1999), argue that policy makers tend to be responsive to *outside lobbying* undertaken by social movements when they believe that it is a clear signal of the preferences of their constituents. If elected leaders were inclined to be sympathetic to antiwar appeals, then antiwar activists might have been able to encourage progress on issues such as prohibiting the construction of permanent military bases in Iraq or stopping plans for an escalation of troops. But, rather than intensify its efforts, the movement reduced them. These observations lead us to question the nature of the antiwar-Democratic alliance. What explains the emergence of the alliance and what accounts for its erosion?

Previous scholarship on the dynamics of social movements offers a variety of explanations for the rise and fall of movements. For example, Anthony Downs (1972) points to the importance of issue-attention cycles among the public. Albert Hirschman (1982) emphasizes temporal change in subjective assessments of benefits and costs of activism, which can lead to both engagement and burnout among activists. David Meyer (1990) stresses the opening and closing of political opportunities available to movements. Dennis Chong (1991) highlights the mass psychology of movements, particularly how policy successes can have a demobilizing function for movements (see also Bernstein 2005; Jenkins and Eckert 1986; McAdam 1982; Meyer 2008; Rupp and Taylor 1990; Tarrow 1993). Yet none of these explanations accounts for why the rise to power of a movement's political allies – which presumably opened political opportunities for the movement and raised its chances for success – would lead to a decline in the movement before those allies effected the changes that they had promised.

Our explanation centers on the shifting partisan alignments favoring the Democratic Party. We observe demobilization not in response to a *policy* victory, but in response to a *party* victory. The rising power of the Democratic Party may have convinced many antiwar activists that the war issue would be dealt with satisfactorily, even if they did not keep applying grassroots pressure through an organized social movement (in contrast to what many scholars predict; see, for example, Ganz 2009; McAdam 1982; Skocpol, Liazos, and Ganz 2006). According to this view, after 2006, it was no longer "necessary" to have an antiwar movement in the streets because the Democratic Party *was* the antiwar movement. Starting in 2007, a Democratically controlled Congress could use the power of the purse to defund the Iraq War and force President Bush slowly to withdraw U.S. forces (Stein 2007). If a Democratic Congress was unable to force an end to the war, then, as *Washington Post* columnist David Broder (2007) prophesied, a Democratic president elected in 2008 would.

The explanation that many antiwar activists deferred to the Democratic Party after 2006 requires that we understand why many antiwar activists seemed to trust the Democratic Party. After all, the movement started to decline in the midst of President Bush's escalation of the Iraq War through "the surge" (Bush 2007), when we might have expected protest to grow instead. The decline corresponded with votes by Democrats in Congress to approve a succession of war supplemental appropriation requests made by President Bush. The decline started *before* the Democrats made good on promises to enact legislation to revise the civil liberties provisions of the USA PATRIOT Act, to condemn the doctrine of preemption, or to stop the surge. So, why did many antiwar activists stop fighting before they achieved their goal? How come they did not, instead, intensify their collaboration with their Democratic allies? If antiwar advocates wanted to end war, why did so few of them actively pressure President Obama to do so once he was in office? Why did the movement not grow during the surge in Afghanistan in 2009?

In this book, we aspire to unravel this puzzle by making sense of the relationship between the antiwar movement and the Democratic Party in the United States after the terrorist attacks of September 11, 2001 (hereafter 9/11). To do so, we inquire into the *dual identifications* that many political actors had with the Democratic Party and the antiwar movement. We argue that when the Democrats were out of office and the Republicans were in power, these intersecting identities promoted synergy between the party and the movement. Indeed, the rise of the antiwar movement as a mass movement can be traced to dissatisfaction among many Democratic partisans with the presidency of George W. Bush. Anti-Republican partisanship helped to fuel the growth of the antiwar movement and explains why its mobilization appears to have depended more on changes in partisan control than on substantive adjustments in foreign policies.

More generally, we argue that social movement mobilization is driven to a significant degree by the dynamic interrelationship between social movements and political parties. We posit that the direct identification of political actors (such as grassroots activists, nonprofit organizations, and members of Congress) with political parties and social movements is a critical (though, not the only) factor that drives both mobilization success and failure. Drawing on theories of *intersectionality* (Collins 2000; Combahee River Collective 1995; Crenshaw 1989; Hancock 2007; Strolovitch 2007), we claim that *partisan identification* tends to be stronger and longer-lasting than *movement identification*, which enhances the advantaged status of parties. Thus, *identity shifts* – transitions in how political actors answer the question "Who am I?" – tend to favor parties over movements when identities conflict. In explaining these dynamics, our research adds to the understanding of identity shifts and how they affect the mobilization of social movements.

Partisan identities tend to develop over longer periods and reach a broader segment of the population than do movement identities (Rosenblum 2008). Partisan identities are consistently reinforced by periodic elections in a way that movement identities are not, a tendency that often makes partisans an advantaged subgroup within movements and movement activists a disadvantaged subgroup within parties. Thus, as the Democrats regained control of government, actors' party identifications tended to trump their movement identifications. Rather than staying focused on their position on a single issue – such as their opposition to war – many partisans gave greater attention to other callings from the Democratic Party. As a result, many Democratic activists and war opponents withdrew from the antiwar movement as they felt less threatened by the Bush administration and shifted their attention to other party priorities, such as health care. Once the fuel of partisanship was in short supply, it was difficult for the antiwar movement to sustain itself on a mass level.

The decline of the antiwar movement was not the result of a centralized decision by movement leaders to stop fighting against the war. Rather, it was the product of a multitude of individual decisions made by activists, members of Congress, financial backers, and others as they redirected their energies to other purposes. The collective result was that the antiwar movement found itself unable to attain critical mass at exactly the time when its efforts might have been applied to the greatest political effect. While the Democratic Party was able to leverage antiwar sentiments effectively in promoting its own electoral success, the antiwar movement itself ultimately suffered organizationally from its ties to the Democratic Party.

The case of the antiwar movement and the Democratic Party after 9/11 suggests that the relationship between political parties and the mobilization of social movements is linked to the identities of individual political actors. The distinctive theoretical contribution of our book is to explain more generally how the interplay of partisan and movement identities can provide an account for the dynamics of social movement mobilization.[1] Other scholarship on party-movement interaction, such as the work of Mildred Schwartz (2006; 2010) and Daniel Schlozman (2015), examines how parties and movements as a whole affect one another at the macrolevel but neglects the part played by individuals and organizations within social movements and parties. This book demonstrates how the microlevel behaviors of individual and organizational actors matter for macrolevel patterns of party and movement dynamics.

We argue that the consequences of intersecting movement-party identities can be observed not only in the case of the antiwar movement, but also in movements as diverse as the Tea Party and Occupy Wall Street, both of which exhibited fluctuating overlap between movement supporters and party supporters. For example, after the election of Barack Obama as president of the United States, the threat perceived by conservative activists upon Obama's election quickly translated into Tea Party protests in 2009 and 2010 (Skocpol and Williamson 2012). However, Tea Party rallies dissipated once the Republican Party regained control of the U.S. House of Representatives after the 2010 congressional elections (Shear 2012). Instead, the Tea Party switched its emphasis from outsider tactics (such as protests) to insider tactics (such as lobbying). While Tea Party-Republican ties are somewhat different from antiwar-Democratic ties, the similarities are strong enough to suggest that a more general phenomenon is at work. We suggest that the consequences of party-movement overlap may be amplified when American politics is highly polarized along party lines (Abramowitz 2010; Hacker and Pierson 2005; Hetherington 2009; Masket 2011; Sinclair 2006).

To be clear, this book's primary focus is not on explaining the emergence of an antiwar movement after the terrorist attacks of 9/11 and in the run-up to the Iraq War in March 2003. We think that the explanation for the movement's rise is relatively straightforward. The United States has a long tradition of antiwar activism that extends from the Revolutionary War through all military conflicts in the nation's history (Mann 2010). Antiwar protests after 9/11 were organized by many of the same individuals and organizations that had been active in peace struggles from the Vietnam War of the 1960s and 1970s through the confrontations with Iraq in the 1990s (Woehrle, Coy, and Maney 2008). People opposed war for a mix of reasons, such as concerns about the potential geopolitical implications of U.S. military intervention, general opposition to the policies of the Bush administration, and religiously motivated pacifism. By generating turnout from people with a range of motivations, these

---

[1] We are not claiming that party and movement identities are the only kinds of identities that matter for social movement mobilization. Rather, we maintain that multiple identities matter in the mobilization process. Our analysis focuses on partisan and movement identities because their interaction has important consequences for the mobilization process in a wide variety of political contexts.

protests were able to reach an unprecedented scale – including the largest internationally coordinated protest in all of human history on February 15, 2003 – largely due to the new information environment created by the Internet (Gillan, Pickerill, and Webster 2008). The movement drew on widespread disenchantment with the Bush administration, much of which began with the disputed 2000 presidential election (Craig, Martinez, Gainous, and Kane 2006). Given this underlying movement capacity, the emergence of an antiwar movement after 9/11 seems to have been quite likely.

Moreover, our focus is not on why the antiwar movement failed to prevent – or to end – the wars in Iraq and Afghanistan. We think that the answer to this question is similarly evident: Barriers to policy success for the antiwar movement may have been insurmountable from the start.[2] In general, antiwar movements tend to be less successful in achieving their policy goals than other social movements because they challenge the security interests of state actors and, thus, receive relatively little facilitation from the state (Kriesi, Koopmans, Duyvendak, and Giugni 1995; Marullo and Meyer 2004; Yeo 2011). As a result, antiwar movements rarely prevent nations from going to war. Under the right conditions, movements have the potential to influence public opinion and weaken institutional support for war significantly (Marullo and Meyer 2004). However, the challenges for antiwar activists were especially difficult after 9/11. The war in Afghanistan began almost immediately after 9/11, with little more than token opposition on the streets at that time. The Bush administration had made definitive war plans for Iraq by July 2002 (Holsti 2011), before the antiwar movement had begun in earnest. Once the wars began, the Bush administration had demonstrated a willingness to pay immense domestic political costs to continue the wars (Kriner 2010). In contrast, the antiwar movement had few financial resources and ran on a shoestring budget (Cortright 2004). Under these conditions, the chances that the antiwar movement would have a major influence on war policy in the 2000s appear to have been small from the outset.

Rather than focusing on the policy success or failure of a movement, this book tells the story of the interaction between political parties and social movements in a social space that we call the *party in the street*. Our goal is to illuminate how different types of political actors interface with one another to generate macropolitical outcomes. Thus, we conduct our empirical investigation at multiple levels of analysis to examine the behavior of individual activists, legislators, organizations, coalitions, the Democratic Party, and

---

[2] In focusing on policy success, we are not denying that the antiwar movement was successful along other dimensions. For example, the movement helped to raise the political consciousness of millions of people who participated in demonstrations and other movement activities. These individuals were educated in the movement's goals and values through their participation (Munson 2008). Their training will likely prove useful to future social movements that will draw upon their experiences (Taylor 1989).

the antiwar movement as a whole. In doing so, we treat the organized U.S. domestic opposition to the wars in Iraq and Afghanistan as a single movement, rather than different movements against two separate wars.

Chapter 1 begins this story by developing the concept of the party in the street and situating it in the academic literature on political parties and social movements. Among those who study American politics, there is often a division of labor by those who study parties and movements, with political scientists paying greater attention to parties and sociologists paying closer attention to movements (McAdam and Kloos 2014). However, we explain that parties and movements, in fact, are overlapping fields that ought to be understood explicitly in relation to one another. The resulting concept of the party in the street provides a framework for analyzing the interaction of parties and movements. Next, we consider the historical coevolution of political parties and social movements in the United States. We trace the paths of parties and movements from their origins in the nation's founding to the current period of political polarization. Finally, we consider the specific case of the antiwar movement after 9/11. We discuss the context for this investigation by considering the historical evolution of peace activism in the United States, starting with opposition to the Revolutionary War and ending with the antiwar movement after 9/11. The movement after 9/11, in many ways, evolved from the peace movements that preceded it, especially the movement to end the war in Vietnam. We are careful to compare the movement after 9/11 to the Vietnam antiwar movement, which was the most significant and consequential antiwar movement in American history. Among the important differences between the two, we note that the movement after 9/11 operated in a highly partisan environment, while the polarization during the Vietnam War era was not as partisan in nature.

We elaborate upon the key empirical puzzle of the book in Chapter 2 by mapping the relationships among parties, foreign policies, and the movement. We consider the aphorism that "politics stops at the water's edge" to ask whether the politics and policies surrounding U.S. wars in Iraq and Afghanistan were influenced by partisanship. In examining war policy positions taken by candidates in the 2004 and 2008 elections, we find that Democratic politicians articulated more fervent antiwar positions than did politicians within the Republican Party, even though there were varying positions among politicians in both parties. Exit poll data reveal that politicians in the Democratic Party benefited during electoral contests from the support of antiwar constituencies. However, when we look at the evolution of actual war policies from the Bush to the Obama administrations, we find more continuity than change. The Obama administration shifted emphasis from Iraq to Afghanistan, but these shifts were still only a slight redirection of the trajectory set forth by the Bush administration. Given Obama's continuation of many of Bush's policies, we would have expected the antiwar movement to react with steady or increased levels of protests. Yet, antiwar protests declined during

Obama's presidency, even in the presence of policies that continued war. We argue that, in order to explain this pattern, a new perspective is needed on the relationship between parties and movements.

Chapter 3 aims to resolve the puzzle identified in Chapter 2 by offering a new theoretical perspective on the mechanisms through which fields of political parties and social movements interact. In contrast to most of the previous scholarship on this topic, which treats parties and movements as a whole as the units of analysis, we stress the *multiple identities* of individual actors in mediating this interaction. Political actors embrace multiple identities during their participation in politics. When these identities overlap, they have the potential both to amplify party-movement cooperation (when they reinforce one another) and to undercut party-movement cooperation (when they conflict with one another). Thus, the interplay of multiple identities helps to provide an explanation for the dynamics of the party in the street. Drawing upon scholarship in the *intersectionality* tradition, we hypothesize that partisan identities often trump movement identities during periods of conflict, a tendency that may lead to important *identity shifts* among mobilized actors. A consequence of identity shifts is that political parties are often in a stronger position than movements after the conflict. Thus, our partisan identification theory offers an important explanation for why Democratic electoral success ultimately spelled doom for the antiwar movement.

Chapter 4 investigates the sources of decline in participation by activists in the antiwar movement and the Democratic Party. Drawing upon original field surveys that we collected at antiwar events held between 2004 and 2010, as well as surveys that we conducted of participants at the 2010 United States Social Forum and delegates to the 2008 Democratic National Convention (DNC), we explore the tension between partisan and movement identities. Using these data, we test three sets of hypotheses related to the ideas that partisanship motivates antiwar mobilization, partisan and movement identities trade off against one another, and partisanship shapes activists' worldviews. The findings show that antiwar activists with identities linked to the Democratic Party tended to depart from the antiwar movement earlier than did activists without Democratic identities. Further, the results of the Democratic delegate survey reveal that although Democratic Party members generally held an antiwar point of view, their mobilization for the antiwar cause usually assumed a lower priority than mobilization on many other issues, such as health care. Together, these results suggest that identification with the Democratic Party drew activists away from the antiwar movement once the party attained electoral success. Partisan identities were more likely to trump movement identities than vice versa, when these identities were in conflict. We reach these conclusions after controlling for alternative explanations for individuals' behavior, such as the possibility that differences in ideology may account for activists' opposition to war under all circumstances, as opposed to under specific conditions.

Chapter 5 adopts an organizational lens with which to interpret the dynamics of the party in the street that we document in Chapter 4. Like individuals, organizations have identities that are connected to a greater or lesser extent to political parties. We argue that these organizational identities matter for how and when organizations exerted leadership within the antiwar movement. We find that organizations with Democratic identifications gained more central positions within the network of antiwar organizations as the Democratic Party rose to power, but then tended to lose those positions once Obama became president. These shifting networks affected the operation of leading national coalitions, which were broader and more institutionally focused during the Democratic Party's rise and narrower and more radical during the Obama administration. Finally, organizations with identities that intersected explicitly with the party and the movement tended to shift toward their partisan roots during periods of unified Democratic government. In addition to supporting our argument in this chapter with statistical and archival evidence, we discuss case studies of three organizations that illustrate the contours of our account: United for Peace and Justice, MoveOn, and Black Is Back.

Chapter 6 looks at the movement to oppose war within Congress. Members of Congress such as Lynn Woolsey (D-CA), James McGovern (D-MA), John Murtha (D-PA), Barbara Lee (D-CA), and Maxine Waters (D-CA) worked closely with antiwar lobbyists in an attempt to advance antiwar agendas, especially through the Out of Iraq Caucus and the Out of Afghanistan Caucus. They were largely unsuccessful in doing so. Drawing upon data on the cosponsorship of antiwar legislation, we show how their efforts rose and fell with the fortunes of the Democratic Party. Once Barack Obama became president, the antiwar movement within Congress almost vanished. There was some resurgence of antiwar sentiment during the third year of Obama's first term (2011), but most of this opposition focused on Republicans' concerns with the administration's limited military intervention in Libya, rather than on the larger military commitments in Afghanistan. Within Congress, as well, partisan identities were more likely to trump movement identities than vice versa.

In Chapter 7, we consider the relevance of our argument to movements beyond the antiwar movement, such as the Tea Party and Occupy Wall Street. Our goal is not to produce a comprehensive analysis of these movements, but to examine the ways in which our hypothesized mechanisms might plausibly operate within another context. We argue that the greater the overlap is between the party and the movement, the greater the correspondence is between the movement's mobilization and the electoral cycle, as well as the greater likelihood that movement actors turn to institutionally based political tactics. The Tea Party developed a close relationship with the Republican Party such that it quickly evolved to be an organized faction within the party, rather than a movement outside it. In contrast, the core participants of Occupy Wall Street deliberately eschewed collaboration with their closest major party ally – the Democratic Party – in favor of a militant nonpartisanship. We find that the

Tea Party's mobilization was driven by fluctuations in Republican electoral success, while Occupy Wall Street experienced a steady decline unrelated to elections. Further, the Tea Party evolved toward working inside Republican political institutions, whereas Occupy Wall Street continued to avoid collaboration with the Democratic Party. Thus, variations in the size of the party in the street help to explain movement dynamics.

In the concluding chapter, we consider the implications of our analysis for movements operating in a time of high partisan polarization. We argue that polarization amplifies challenges for the mobilization of social movements. We propose strategies for both political parties and social movements to manage party-movement relations during both highly polarized and less polarized times. Finally, we suggest several directions for future research on the implications of the party in the street for the politics of social movements and political parties.

****

This book has come to fruition over a decade of research, beginning in 2002. Some of the results have been published, in part, in prior journal articles. Versions of the work appear in Michael T. Heaney and Fabio Rojas, "Partisans, Nonpartisans, and the Antiwar Movement in the United States," *American Politics Research,* Vol. 35, No. 4 (July 2007): 431–64; Michael T. Heaney and Fabio Rojas, "The Partisan Dynamics of Contention: Demobilization of the Antiwar Movement in the United States, 2007–2009," *Mobilization: An International Journal,* Vol. 16, No. 1 (March 2011): 45–64; and Michael T. Heaney, "The Partisan Politics of Antiwar Legislation in Congress, 2001–2011," *University of Chicago Legal Forum,* Vol. 2011 (2011): 129–68. We have not reprinted these articles here, but we acknowledge that we have drawn heavily on the ideas contained within them. Parts of the article in the *University of Chicago Legal Forum* are adapted and directly reused here with permission from the *Legal Forum.* We thank the editors at these journals, Jim Gimpel (*American Politics Research*), Sidney Tarrow and Doug McAdam (guest editors for a special issue of *Mobilization*), and Emily Tancer, Ann Wagner, and Tara Tavernia (at the *Legal Forum*) for taking an interest in our ideas and helping to push the project along.

We are deeply indebted to the institutions that have nurtured us and this research over the last decade. Heaney is grateful to the Brookings Institution, where the research began when he was a Special Guest in Governance Studies during 2002–2003. Yale University supported the initial phases of the survey research when he was a postdoctoral fellow in the Center for the Study of American Politics, Institution for Social and Policy Studies, in 2004–2005. The University of Florida continued the funding of the survey research while he was an Assistant Professor there from 2005 to 2009. A congressional fellowship from the American Political Science Association afforded Heaney the opportunity to conduct interviews in Washington, D.C., during 2007–2008. Finally, the University of Michigan enabled this research to be moved to completion while Heaney was an Assistant Professor from 2009 to the present. He is particularly appreciative of research grants provided at Michigan by the Office of the Vice President for Research, the Barger Leadership Institute, the Organizational Studies Program, the Undergraduate Research Opportunity Program, and the College of Literature, Science, and the Arts.

At the Brookings Institution, Heaney is especially grateful to Shubha Chakravarty, who helped to encourage initial interest in this research in 2002. At Yale, he thanks Khalilah Brown-Dean, Justin Fox, Alan Gerber, Donald Green, Jacob Hacker, Ange-Marie Hancock, Greg Huber, David Mayhew, Costas Panagopoulos, and Susan Stokes. At Florida, he benefited from constructive conversations with Michael Martinez, Dan Smith, and Ken Wald. At Michigan, he received instructive feedback from Elizabeth Armstrong, Ted Brader, Bill Clark, Farid Damasio, Jerry Davis, Lisa Disch, Steve Garcia, Elisabeth Gerber, Victoria Johnson, Donald Kinder, Ken Kollman, Barbara Koremenos, Amy Krings, Sandra Levitsky, Walter Mebane, Mark Mizruchi, Candace Moore, Jim Morrow, Dan Myers, Brendan Nyhan, Jason Owen-Smith, Phil Potter, Rick Price, Jana von Stein, Kiyoteru Tsutsui, Mayer Zald, Mariah Zeisberg, as well as participants in the Interdisciplinary Workshop on American Politics, the Interdisciplinary Workshop on Politics and Policy, the Research in Political Science seminar, the Social Movements Workshop, and the Networks Workshop. He presented earlier versions of the research at colloquia held at Indiana University-Bloomington, the University of Maryland-College Park, Michigan State University, The Ohio State University, the University of Wisconsin-Madison, and the University of Chicago.

For Rojas, this research began at Indiana University-Bloomington when he was an Assistant Professor and continued through his promotion to Associate Professor. The Department of Sociology supported this project from start to completion with a series of indispensable research grants. Work on the project moved forward in 2008–2010, while he was a Robert Wood Johnson Foundation Scholar in Health Policy Research at the University of Michigan. He benefited from productive conversations with Tim Bartley, Clem Brooks, Erik Bucy, Tom Gieryn, Jane McCleod, Eliza Pavalko, and Rob Robinson and presented earlier versions of the research at colloquia held at Indiana University and George Mason University. He thanks the cobloggers and readers of orgtheory.net for always providing prompt and useful responses to queries and requests.

For assistance with administrative aspects of this research, we thank Melissa Eljamal, Pam Greene, Susan Platter, Tiffany Purnell, Theresa Ramirez, Debbie Wallen, and Denise Yekulis.

For hospitality during our fieldwork in Washington, D.C., we recognize the Centennial Center for Political Science and Public Affairs of the American Political Science Association. Thanks to Bryan Caplan, Robert Lucas, Frank Mason, Chris Pisares, Jane Silverman, Kate Taylor, and Leora Vegosen for opening their homes to us during visits to Washington, D.C.; Charlotte, North Carolina; and New York, New York.

A number of scholars have taken the time to comment on early drafts of chapters, allowing us to produce a much stronger product. Thanks go to Jeffrey Berry, Paul Frymer, Elizabeth Gerber, Kristin Goss, Matt Grossmann, David Karpf, Ken Kollman, Daniel Kreiss, Amy Krings, Robert Lucas, Suzanne Luft, Doug McAdam, David Meyer, Mark Mizruchi, and six anonymous reviewers. Sidney Tarrow and Rob Mickey read and commented on the entire manuscript in draft form. The manuscript improved immeasurably as the result of a book conference held at the University of Michigan in September 2013, which was generously funded by the College of Literature, Science, and the Arts. We owe a special debt to the participants in the conference: Elizabeth Armstrong, Frank Baumgartner, Lisa Disch, Ken Kollman, and Pam Oliver.

We appreciate the suggestions and assistance that we received from Scott Ainsworth, Michael Brown, Kevin Esterling, Matthew Green, Jennifer Hadden, John Mark Hansen, William Howell, Lorien Jasny, Katie Lavelle, Seth Masket, David McBride, Corrine McConnaughy, Aldon Morris, Clayton Nall, John Padgett, Kathryn Pearson, Eric Schwartz, Sarah Sobieraj, Laura Stoker, Dara Strolovitch, Melody Weinstein, and many others. The number of students who contributed to this work as research assistants is too numerous to list their names here. We acknowledge their work in Appendix A. Our work would not have been possible without the anonymous participation of more than ten thousand respondents to our surveys and interviews. Their contributions were indispensable in generating the insights and results that make up this book.

Lew Bateman and Shaun Vigil at Cambridge University Press did a splendid job managing the review process and guiding the book to publication.

Finally, our greatest debts are owed to our loved ones, who have supported us through this process. Heaney thanks his wife, Suzanne Luft, for tolerating the weekends away from home and late nights spent writing, as well as superb assistance in developing our graphics. Rojas thanks his wife, Liz Pisares, for her unfailing support. Finally, we acknowledge our children, Merlyn, Coltrane, and Margaret – each born over the years of writing this book – who have very different ideas of what it means to party in the street.

The Party in the Street and Its Historical Context

The Republican Party held its quadrennial presidential nominating convention at Madison Square Garden in New York City from August 30 to September 2, 2004. The selection of New York City was a highly symbolic choice. Less than three years earlier, 2,763 people had been killed in New York as a result of coordinated terrorist attacks on September 11, 2001. In siting its convention in New York, the Republican National Committee sought to demonstrate its solidarity with 9/11 victims. The Republicans also hoped to bolster the reelection prospects of their nominee, President George W. Bush, by framing his policies – such as the USA PATRIOT Act, the Homeland Security Act, the invasion of Afghanistan, and the invasion of Iraq – as effective responses to the events of 9/11.

The decision to hold the 2004 Republican National Convention (RNC) in New York was contentious, especially given the liberal leanings of New York's population. It should have come as little surprise to Republicans that their convention was met by massive protests from the general public. For more than a week, New York City was besieged by demonstrations large and small, organized on issues ranging from women's rights to the Iraq War to the human needs of people living in poverty.

One of the anti-RNC demonstrations was a rally sponsored by the New York City Central Labor Council on Wednesday, September 1. Participants gathered on 8th Avenue of Manhattan and stretched from 30th Street to beyond 23rd Street. People were clustered according to local union membership, with colored T-shirts distinguishing the Service Employees International Union, the International Brotherhood of Electric Workers, the United Food and Commercial Workers Union, and many others. Speeches and performances by leaders and celebrities – such as John Sweeney (president of the AFL-CIO, American Federation of Labor-Congress of Industrial Organizations), actor Danny Glover, and singer Steve Earle – were broadcasted on Jumbotrons hanging across the avenue.

Unlike many other protesters outside the convention that week, the participants in the Central Labor Council's rally did not march forward. Rather, they stood in stationary positions as they listened to speeches given from a professionally constructed stage. Other than the fact that the event was held outside, the festivities looked and sounded a lot like a party convention. Given the overwhelming Democratic Party affiliation of those in attendance, it was almost as if the labor movement had brought the Democratic Party out into the street. In observing the juxtaposition of political parties and social movements at this event, we coined the phrase the *party in the street*.

In this chapter, we lay the groundwork for our study by considering how it is possible for social movements and political parties to relate to one another at all. In many ways, movements and parties are very different types of entities, so the ways in which they are connected are not always immediately apparent. We explain how the party in the street is constituted by the intersection of movements and parties. We invoke the party in the street throughout the book as a lens to help interpret the behaviors and outcomes we observe. Having laid this theoretical foundation, we then consider the historical emergence of the party in the street through the coevolution of political parties and social movements. Finally, we consider the history of our specific case by reviewing antiwar activism from the Revolutionary War to the wars in Iraq and Afghanistan. We explain how the antiwar movement after 9/11 built on organized peace activism that preceded it. We also note that the substantial partisanship that we observe in the movement after 9/11 is a relatively new aspect of antiwar activism.

DEFINING POLITICAL PARTIES AND SOCIAL MOVEMENTS

This book explores the question of how the antiwar movement and the Democratic Party related to one another in the years after 9/11. Before we address this question directly, we must first consider how it is possible that a political party and a social movement could be related to one another given the nature and differences of their organizational forms. Neither political parties nor social movements are unified, homogeneous, rational actors. Rather, they are decentralized fields of strategically motivated individuals and organizations. They have porous boundaries. No one political actor can speak authoritatively on behalf of a party or a movement. How is it possible for movements and parties to work together or form alliances under these conditions?

Political parties are coalitions of political actors that seek to control the government by winning elections. They have nominal leaders, such as the chairpersons of the Democratic National Committee and the Republican National Committee. However, these leaders cannot control who become members of a party, what issues they work on, or what positions they take. Along with Marty Cohen and his colleagues (Cohen, Karol, Noel, and Zaller 2008), we view parties as a framework for coalitions of actors to promote their own interests. Party activists often introduce new agendas to party politics. At the same time, party activists learn about issues and politics through their participation in and engagement with party organizations (Layman, Carsey, Green, Herrera, and Cooperman 2010; Wilson 1962). As a result, the efforts of parties vacillate with the shifting strength of coalitions and the changing motivations of activists.

In the United States, candidates win elections by obtaining a plurality of the vote – not necessarily a majority, but the most votes of any candidate – so that political parties have a strong incentive to form the broadest coalitions possible. Under this system, elections are most competitive when there are two major parties that each command the loyalty of close to 50 percent of the electorate (Downs 1957). In this system, parties assemble potential governing coalitions before elections take place. In parliamentary political systems – where control of government is usually determined through negotiation after an election, rather than directly as a result of it – actors with divergent interests may have incentives to form minor parties (Dodd 1976).[1] These minor parties hope to form postelectoral coalitions with larger parties in which they might help to determine the policies of the government. In the United States, however, parties that do not field candidates who are able to win pluralities do not receive any representation and, thus, cannot participate directly in controlling the government.

Social movements are sustained interactions between challengers and authorities in which challengers seek to change some aspect of the social or political world. They are usually more decentralized than political parties. Sometimes parts of a social movement are able to work together cohesively through coalitions (Van Dyke and McCammon 2010). But, at other times, they are fragmented and work at cross-purposes (Balser 1997). One of the reasons why movement actors sometimes clash is that they have other loyalties, identities, and interests that may, at times, be contrary to the goals of the social movement (Coles 1999). For example, individuals who identify as antiwar activists or war opponents may simultaneously identify as environmentalists, mothers, students, workers, homosexuals, Democrats, or any other of a wide number of salient social identities. These identities may at times support, and at other times undermine, the work of individuals toward the movement's goals.

Under some parliamentary systems of government, movements may have strong incentives to organize directly as political parties (Kitschelt 1989; Schwartz 2010). In the United States, however, minor parties face greater obstacles, especially since the turn of the twentieth century (Rosenstone, Behr, and Lazarus 1984; Disch 2002). While movements sometimes seek to work

---

[1] We use the term "minor party" rather than "third party" because "third party" naturalizes the two-party system, which we argue is a political construction. However, our meaning of "minor party" is equivalent to "third party," as the term is commonly used.

with minor parties, they often find work with major parties to be more expeditious. Movement leaders may see major parties as a route to policy, a way to co-opt elected politicians, and a way to leverage overlap between their supporters and the supporters of political parties.

Some readers may wonder about the distinction between *interest groups* and social movements. These concepts are commonly confused because social movements and interest groups are closely interrelated spheres of politics. Interest groups are formal organizations that attempt to influence government decision makers using institutional tactics such as lobbying, campaign contributions, and lawsuits (Baumgartner, Berry, Hojnacki, Kimball, and Leech 2009). Interest groups are usually active parts of social movements. For example, the National Association for the Advancement of Colored People (NAACP) was one of the interest groups that led the civil rights movement of the 1960s. Formal interest groups sometimes evolve out of informal, grassroots organizations, which are very important for the development of social movements (Costain 1981).[2] Interest groups often live on after their originating social movements have transitioned to abeyance (Goss 2006; Taylor 1989) and are typically more centrally controlled than are movements. Social movements are almost always broader in scope than a single interest group, which is typically one of many actors involved in a social movement. Scholars call this broader constellation of organizations the *social movement sector*. It encompasses the decentralized field of contentious politics, including groups that sponsor protests and advocate for social change (McCarthy and Zald 1977).

PARTIES AND MOVEMENTS AS INTERSECTING FIELDS

Political scientist V. O. Key (1942) observed more than seventy years ago that political parties could be conceptualized as having three loosely interconnected parts: the party organization, the party in the electorate, and the party in government (see also Sorauf 1980, p. 8). The party organization includes party officials and employees at the local, state, and national levels. The party in the electorate includes voters who regularly support the party and its

---

[2] We do not draw a sharp distinction here between "interest groups" and "social movement organizations," which we see more as a difference in degree rather than a difference in kind. Social movement organizations are entities that assist social movements in their mobilization and maintenance. Interest groups are organizations that advocate for a cause (or causes) to governmental decision makers. The difference between the two is that social movement organizations need not necessarily try to influence government decision makers directly, while interest groups need not necessarily be affiliated with a specific social movement. But there is extensive overlap between these two categories of organizations. The National Rifle Association, for example, is both an interest group advocating for a set of polices to government decision makers (e.g., few limitations on the purchase of semiautomatic weapons) and an organization that supports the movement for gun rights in the United States.

candidates in elections.[3] The party in government includes elected officials who run for office under the party's label. Each of these parts contributes to the party's operations without formally being able to command the other parts. These different parts of the party are not formal designations, but provide a conceptual framework for how these operationally distinct entities aggregate to a coherent whole. While the parts of a party sometimes work together toward a common goal (e.g., electing a president), at other times they clash with one another in factional disputes over issues, ideology, personality, or other matters that compose the messy world of politics.

Scholars of political parties have expanded Key's typology in recent years to incorporate other types of political actors. Robin Kolodny and David Dulio (2009) point to the growing role of political consultants as evidence that they have emerged as stable components of parties (see also Nyhan and Montgomery 2015). Richard Skinner, Seth Masket, and David Dulio (2012) argue that "527 organizations" – a recently popularized way to make campaign expenditures – reflect and help to define a party's field. Michael Heaney and his colleagues (Heaney, Masket, Miller, and Strolovitch 2012) emphasize the importance of interest groups in understanding the polarization of party networks. These studies reflect a growing consensus among scholars that Key's tripartite perspective is incomplete in today's political world. Instead, we imagine political parties more broadly as loosely interconnected fields of a wide range of heterogeneous actors (see, inter alia, Cohen, Karol, Noel, and Zaller 2008; Goldstone 2004; Monroe 2001; Karol 2009; Noel 2013; Schlozman 2015; Schwartz 1990). According to this perspective, parties are not just made up of entities that formally have a party label, but include people and organizations that work in a regularized way to promote and/or shape the interests of the party. Although it does have formally organized components, the totality of party organization is much more informal than it is formal.

Social movements, too, are organized as decentralized fields (Armstrong 2002; Blee 2002; Fligstein and McAdam 2012). For example, when we think of the civil rights movement in the United States, we may think first of the influential work of Martin Luther King Jr. and his leadership of the Southern Christian Leadership Conference. However, it would be inaccurate to see the civil rights movement as having been unified under the direction of King (Morris 1984). More accurately, the movement should be remembered as having had many parts, some of which clashed with one another. The movement was also led by organizations as diverse as the NAACP, the Student Nonviolent Coordinating Committee, the Congress of Racial Equality, and the Black Panther Party, which espoused an array of ideological perspectives

---

[3] Unlike Key (1942), most other party scholars (e.g., Cohen, Karol, Noel, and Zaller 2008) exclude mass identifiers from inclusion in "the party," formally speaking. From the point of view of our argument, it does not matter whether the boundary of "the party" includes mass identifiers or the line is drawn at party activists.

and tactical approaches (Haines 1995; McAdam 1982). The dynamism of the movement was driven not just by decision making at the top of these organizations, but in the grassroots debates of activists in chapters around the United States (Polletta 2002). The heroes of the movement included college students who put themselves at great personal risk to promote racial equality (McAdam 1988). Outcomes of the movement ranged from greater access to public accommodations to the emergence of black studies programs at colleges and universities (Rojas 2007). While these individuals and organizations were largely unified by the goal of racial justice, they were connected by informal networks rather than by a single formal organization.

We refer to political parties and social movements as *fields* in order to convey that they are made up of actors that are aware of one another, interact with one another, and strategize vis-à-vis one another, even though they are not necessarily part of a single formal organization. According to Neil Fligstein and Doug McAdam (2012, p. 9), fields are made up of actors who "are attuned to and interact with one another on the basis of shared ... understandings about the purpose of the field, relationships to others in the field ... , and the rules governing legitimate action in the field." For example, by saying that the Republican Party is a field, we are saying that it consists of a wide range of actors – such as current and former elected officials, campaign staff, contributors, interest groups, and conservative media – who are aware of one another and recognize they are collectively working to elect Republicans to public office and assist them in their duties while they are there. They know who the power players in the party are (e.g., John Boehner, Mitch McConnell, Karl Rove, Grover Norquist) and who is contending to join these ranks. They know that it would be severely frowned upon for a participant in the field to endorse a Democratic candidate for public office, except under unusual circumstances. However, to say that the Republican Party is a field is not to say that consensus necessarily exists within it. Actors in the Republican Party may disagree on how conservative the party should be (with some preferring that the party hew to the far right and others preferring a big tent that embraces moderation), what its issue positions should be (such as whether or not the party should oppose same-sex marriage), and who its leaders should be (such as whether or not Grover Norquist should play a prominent role). The boundaries of the party have some ambiguity, may be contested, and may change over time, but they are clear enough that most of the field's participants are able to distinguish between routine activity that falls inside or outside of the field.

Society is made up of a large number of fields. These fields do not exist in isolation from one another. Rather, each field interacts and intersects with other fields in its environment (Bourdieu 1977; DiMaggio and Powell 1983; Fligstein and McAdam 2012). This is true in the case of political parties and social movements (McAdam and Tarrow 2013). Individuals and organizations enter politics with goals that may sometimes be pursued simultaneously through parties and movements. For example, the civil rights movement worked cautiously with the Democratic Party – especially the presidential administrations of John F. Kennedy and Lyndon Baines Johnson (LBJ) – as tenuous allies in fighting segregation in the southern United States. At the same time, the movement pursued direct action in restaurants, on public transportation, and in the streets. Some civil rights leaders were elected to office as Democrats, such as John Lewis, who was elected to Congress in 1986 as a representative from Georgia's fifth congressional district. For some segments of these fields, political parties and social movements may be virtually inseparable.

The intersection and interaction of partisan and movement fields sometimes occur seamlessly but, at other times, are fraught with conflict. Parties and movements work well together when they serve each other's instrumental needs. On the one hand, a movement may benefit from working with a party because party involvement may help to educate a movement's activists and motivate them for political action. Since parties have the potential to control the government, they may be able to extend social movements' access to policy levers to achieve some of their goals. Working with parties may also be a way for movements to cultivate, recruit, or co-opt candidates for public office who will do the bidding of the movement later down the line.

On the other hand, a party may benefit from working with a movement because the movement may be closely networked with a particular demographic or issue group in the mass electorate. Thus, the party may be able to use its affiliation with the movement to appeal to that group during the next election, helping to instill a sense of the party's vibrancy in the broader electorate. The party may be able to draw resources directly from the movement in the form of cash donations, volunteer support for get-out-the-vote drives, and other essential party activities. Under some circumstances, the party may even be able to use the movement to do its dirty work while appearing to remain above the fray. For example, organizations connected to the movement may be able to launch venomous attacks against the party's opponents without the party appearing to be involved.

Yet, parties and movements may face conflict because they tend to be defined by different approaches to politics. American political parties strive to control the formal apparatus of government by winning pluralities in democratic elections (Downs 1957). In contrast, social movements organize with a common purpose to change society without necessarily attempting to control the formal institutions of government (Meyer 2007, p. 10). These approaches are not always in sync with one another. Adam Przeworski and John Sprague (1986) argue that social movements generally have great difficulty securing electoral majorities for their causes. As a result, political parties with social movement constituencies usually broaden their platforms to appeal to a wider spectrum of voters. This broadening pulls the party's agenda away from the social movement's goals, which often lie at the radical edges of politics. Thus, the partisan approach creates pressures to moderate issue positions, whereas the issue purity of the movement approach tends to fall short of majority support.

The competing imperatives of parties and movements may lead to tensions between leaders and activists dedicated primarily to the goals of the party and those dedicated primarily to the goals of the movement. On one side of the divide, partisans may be inclined to see movements as ineffective because they insist on policy proposals that are unlikely to garner majority support. Partisans may worry that collaborating with movements may attract radical and undesirable elements into the party's fold, which may create image problems for the party. Even more directly, they may fear that movement activists may become part of the party's establishment, thus shaping its agenda and threatening its electoral viability. Therefore, partisan actors are confronted with dilemmas about whether engaging the movement to tap its energy and resources outweighs the risks that the party will be steered off course by catering too much to the movement.

On the other side of the divide, movement leaders and activists may be inclined to think that partisans are willing to sell out their core values in order to attain political power. If partisans care more about power than values or issues, then the movement leaders and activists may worry that they will be abandoned by the party as soon as doing so is expedient for the party (Harvey 1998). As a result, movement actors fear that their contributions to the party's success will ultimately be co-opted for purposes out of alignment with their own goals (Gitlin 2012, pp. 140–57). Thus, movement actors are confronted with dilemmas about whether engaging the party for its access to power outweighs the risks that movement's goals will be downplayed in the midst of the party's ambitions.

The divergent perspectives of movement and partisan actors are often coupled with strong preferences over which tactics should be deployed to achieve political goals (Jasper 1997, pp. 229–50; Snow and Soule 2009, pp. 171–2). Partisans tend to prefer more institutional tactics, such as voting and lobbying (Heaney and Rojas 2007). Movement actors tend to prefer more confrontational tactics, such as public demonstrations and direct action (Fitzgerald and Rodgers 2000). Of course, some leaders and activists see value in both institutional and confrontational tactics. When they weigh the trade-offs of partisan and movement approaches, they conclude that both are needed to force the changes that they want in the world. These *movement partisans* try to use the institutional power of political parties to advance the goals of the movement and attempt to harness the grassroots energy of social movements to promote the electoral success of the party.

THE CONCEPT OF THE PARTY IN THE STREET

The preceding discussion makes clear that there are both points of congruence and points of incongruence between political parties and social movements. Both fields of political activity are organized as decentralized networks, and they are driven by some of the same types of political goals, but they are divided by their degree of willingness to compromise their issue positions and their preferences over tactics. Thus, we imagine the intersecting fields of political parties and social movements as having three regions. First, there is the mainstream political party. Its participants tend to focus on winning elected offices, are willing to compromise issue positions to attract majority support, and rely on electoral mobilization, lobbying, and campaign spending as their principal political tactics. Second, there is the radical social movement. Its participants tend to focus on advancing their issue positions, are very hesitant to compromise, and rely on demonstrations, direct action, civil disobedience, and (occasionally) violence as their principal political tactics. Third, there is a middle ground, which is composed of actors that want parties and movements to work together. They want parties to fight for their core issues when they can, believing that majorities can be persuaded to join their side, but also recognize that it is better to be in power than to be in the right. They believe that an "inside-outside" strategy, which combines electoral mobilization and lobbying with demonstrations and direct action, is most likely to advance their goals (Selfa 2008, pp. 160–2).

We call the middle ground between parties and movements the *party in the street*. In developing this phrase, we borrow from Key's (1942) tripartite conceptualization of the party as organization, the party in the electorate, and the party in government.[4] We emphasize that movement activity is a vital part of party politics. At the same time, we note that this party activity is generated by mobilized activists – whom James Q. Wilson (1962) calls the *amateurs* of the party – who also have a willingness to use contentious tactics. The party in the street relies on grassroots tactics, though it also recognizes the value of working with institutions. It is a *two-way* street. Actors in parties and movements both expect to benefit (Schlozman 2011). Primarily party-oriented actors may attempt to enlist the party in the street to advance a cause or push the party in the direction in which they would like to see it move. They may do so, in part, by funding organizations to prop up the party in the street or by granting it access to the mainstream party's resourses (such as meeting halls and mailing lists). Primarily movement-oriented actors may look for ways to engender dependence of the party on the movement. They may sponsor primary debates or create voter scorecards to give mainstream partisans incentives to cater to their constituencies. Perhaps the most potent tool that the movement-oriented actors have in their arsenal is the threat to sponsor their own candidates in primaries (Boatright 2013). If unleashed, this tactic may disrupt business as usual within the mainstream political party, forcing it to expend resources during primaries that it would prefer to reserve for competition with the other

---

[4] As we indicate in note 3, it is not critical for our purposes whether the boundaries of the mainstream political parties include mass identifiers or not. The boundary can be drawn either at mass identifiers or at party activities and our arguments still hold.

major party in general elections. The party in the street is a potential source of growth, dynamism, and chaos for both the party and the movement.

Figure 1.1 reflects a number of the key aspects of the party in the street. The radical social movement is represented by the white figure on the left, the mainstream political party is represented by the black figure on the right, and the party in the street is represented by the gray region where the two fields intersect.[5] The vertical dimension indicates where an actor is in the party or movement hierarchy, with elites gravitating toward the top of the figure and rank-and-file participants gravitating toward the bottom of the figure. The horizontal dimension reflects ideology, with more radical actors positioned toward the left and more moderate actors positioned toward the right.

We represent the political party using a larger figure and the social movement using a smaller figure in order to capture the fact that major political parties are usually (but not necessarily) larger than social movements. The party may be larger, in part, because it addresses a wider set of issues than does the movement and, thus, has a broader appeal. The downward slope of the surfaces allows less overlap between the party and the movement at the elite level than among the rank and file. This feature of the diagram suggests that there may be a few elites that join the party in the street – perhaps a handful of members of Congress who are also regular participants in movement events – but the party in the street is more a phenomenon of the rank and file than of the elites.

What constitutes a realistic visualization of the party-movement intersection varies depending on the party-movement pair in question. In some cases, the party and the movement ought to be represented by substantial overlap, while in other cases the overlap may be less extensive. It would make sense to represent the figure with a steeper slope when the party and the movement are more decentralized and a shallower slope when they are more hierarchical. Likewise, it would be plausible to include additional surfaces in the figure if it were important to consider the simultaneous intersection among multiple social movements and one or more political parties.[6]

---

[5] In referring to the parts of a social movement that do not overlap with a major party as "radical," we are assuming that these actors are ideologically to the right of the Republican Party or the left of the Democratic Party. We believe that this assumption holds for the majority of – and certainly the largest – social movements in the United States. However, quite strictly, this assumption need not always hold. For example, a grassroots movement to promote measured fiscal discipline might rest at the center of American politics, between the Democrats and Republicans. Given such cases, our visualization in Figure 1.1 reflects the relationship between most parties and social movements, but not all of them.

[6] For example, in the context of the United States, it would make sense to visualize multiple movements intersecting with the Democratic Party (such as the antiwar movement, the immigration rights movement, the gay rights movement, and the environmental movement) and multiple movements overlapping with the Republican Party (such as the Tea Party movement, the right-to-life movement, the home schooling movement, and the climate change denial movement). Some movements may even overlap with multiple parties. The libertarian movement, for example, has notable overlap with the Republican Party (especially activists fighting to lower taxes and

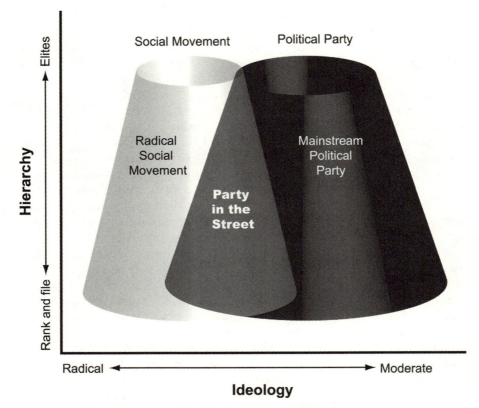

FIGURE 1.1. The Intersection of Political Parties and Social Movements

The visualization of the party in the street in Figure 1.1 allows us to clarify several aspects of our framework. First, we do not argue that a social movement *is* a party in the street.[7] Our framework recognizes that many social movement actors reject partisan politics, as denoted by the white region of the figure. Second, we do not argue that all partisan activities take place in the street or through movement tactics. Our framework recognizes that many partisan actors reject movement politics, as denoted by the black region of the figure.

---

regulation), the Democratic Party (especially activists working to legalize marijuana), and the Libertarian Party (especially activists who want an alternative to the two-party system). Once multiple parties and movements are considered, the system and its dynamics appear much more complicated than we have presented in Figure 1.1. However, we opt for clarity and simplicity in order to illustrate our conception of party-movement relations.

[7] Similarly, we do not intend to imply that all movement activities literally take place "in the street," as we use this term metaphorically. Of course, street demonstrations are an important part of movement politics. Yet, we recognize that movement activities take place in many settings, such as offices, meeting halls, boardrooms, court rooms, and legislative chambers.

Third, we do not claim that there are bright lines between the mainstream political party and the party in the street and the radical social movement. These are fuzzy sets. The translucent boundaries of the figures symbolize the ambiguity in establishing the boundaries between the fields. For example, a member of Congress who sometimes speaks at movement rallies but at other times votes with her party's leadership to oppose the movement's goals may be somewhat part of the party in the street and somewhat part of the mainstream political party. The concept of the party in the street is useful as a way of locating a political actor's behavior in relation to parties and movements, even if the actor does not fall unambiguously into one category or the other.

The concept of the party in the street guides our inquiry as to how political parties and social movements intersect and interact. First, it is important to inquire as to how extensively the party and the movement overlap. The size of the social space occupied by the party in the street may vary considerably depending on the party-movement pair in question. For example, the Tea Party movement in the United States, from 2009 to the present, appears to have functioned largely within the boundaries of the Republican Party (Arceneaux and Nicholson 2012; Bailey, Mummolo, and Noel 2012; Courser 2012; Parker and Barreto 2013; Skocpol and Williamson 2012; Weaver and Scacco 2012). A principal goal of the movement is to insist that the Republican Party remain true to conservative principles, especially with respect to the selection of candidates for public office (Heaney 2012). The Tea Party is an insurgency within the party (Schwartz 2010).

In contrast, the core activists in the Occupy Wall Street movement, from 2011 to the present, mostly have preferred to stay outside the boundaries of the party system. Occupy's core members consistently attacked its closest potential major party ally, the Democratic Party, by claiming that the Democrats are as much a cause of economic inequality as are the Republicans (Fouhy 2011). Occupy activists contested efforts by outside groups affiliated with the Democratic Party (such as MoveOn) to support the movement, lest their support eventually encourage co-optation of the movement (Gitlin 2012, pp. 140–57). Nonetheless, some Democratic leaders, including President Barack Obama, incorporated Occupy Wall Street themes in their messages (Oliphant 2011). In an on-the-ground survey conducted by Costas Panagopoulos (2011), a plurality of Occupy Wall Street participants indicated a willingness to support Democratic candidates in the 2012 elections, a strong minority pledged support for minor-party or no-party candidates, and few indicated support for Republican candidates. These observations suggest that there is some connection between Occupy Wall Street and the Democratic Party, but it appears to be small relative to the connection between the Tea Party and the Republican Party. Investigating the party in the street leads us to ask how these patterns differ depending on the party and movement in question.

A second subject of inquiry is the extent to which party-movement relationships change over time. The nature of the relationship between a party and a movement at any one point is partially a function of the political opportunity structure and polarization of opinion at that time (Kriesi 1995). The emergence of threats or crises may be especially generative of mobilized responses to open opportunities (Hansen 1985). For example, the Tea Party movement sprang up in early 2009, shortly after the inauguration of a Democratic president who was backed by strong Democratic majorities in Congress. Many conservative activists perceived their interests to be threatened. At the same time, many of them perceived the Republican Party to be in a weakened state. These perceptions, coupled with favorable media attention by Fox News and calls for a Tea Party, created opportunities for the grassroots movement to grow rapidly in 2009. With Republican gains in the 2010 midterm elections, many Tea Party activists felt less threatened by the governing regime. By 2012, the form of the Tea Party had changed substantially. It placed less emphasis on directly attacking President Obama and the Democrats and more on influencing the selection of candidates within Republican primaries (Stewart 2012). Tea Party actors had joined the field of established players within Republican politics. Investigating the party in the street motivates us to follow these changing configurations of party-movement interaction.

A third subject of inquiry is the nature of mechanisms by which individuals and organizations attach themselves to a party and/or to a movement, as well as how they choose between these attachments in cases of conflict. If political actors join parties and movements with similar political goals, why do some actors develop stronger attachments to one or another? Why do other actors deliberately embrace the party in the street? For example, many evangelical Protestants who opposed abortion first joined the political fray in the aftermath of the Supreme Court's 1973 decision in the case of *Roe v. Wade* (Allen 2007). While there were opportunities for the prolife movement to join forces with either the Democratic or the Republican Party during the 1970s, the movement had decidedly merged with the Republican Party by the 1980s (Carmines, Gerrity, and Wagner 2010; O'Connor 1996). One of the reasons for this merger was the comparatively hierarchical nature of the Republican Party (in contrast to the less hierarchical Democratic Party), which facilitated the ability of prolife activists to "win" a divisive issue among Republicans in a way that was not as easily accomplished among Democrats (Freeman 1986). Investigating the party in the street draws our attention to these structures that help to sort actors into one field of activity rather than another.

Finally, we wish to underscore that we understand the party in the street as a concrete political entity. It is more than just an abstraction. Activists fighting for the right to life, peace, labor rights, or a return to strict constitutionalism – to take a few contemporary examples – embody vibrant political projects at the intersection of parties and movements. They work as – and become recognized as – hybrid players in the political system. They have the potential to be – and often are – a contentious force for political change.

THE COEVOLUTION OF POLITICAL PARTIES AND SOCIAL MOVEMENTS IN THE UNITED STATES

As we have discussed, political parties and social movements are decentralized fields of action. Our perspective is similar to that offered by scholars who, in recent years, have conceptualized parties and movements as networks (see, for example, Cohen, Karol, Noel, and Zaller 2008; Diani 2009; Hadden 2015; Karol 2009; Monroe 2001; Noel 2013; Schwartz 1990; Zuev 2010). While we recognize that parties and movements are certainly composed of social networks, we invoke the concept of *field* to highlight that their boundaries are defined by the reflection and discussion among interested actors. Identifying parties and movements as fields directs attention to the fact that they are widely recognized areas of institutional life (DiMaggio and Powell 1983). Within fields, actors struggle over resources, positions, and the boundaries that divide fields from one another (Bourdieu 1977). For example, the debate about which party an ideologically moderate politician should belong to is possible because political parties are fields. Should the former U.S. Senators Joe Lieberman (CT) and Arlen Specter (PA) rightly have been considered Democrats, Republicans, or independents, given their ideologically ambiguous policy positions? People who identify with the parties have a sense of what a "true" Democrat or Republican is, and they often try to impose these views on others.

Fields that are closely related and often interact are known as *proximate fields* (Fligstein and McAdam 2012, p. 18). In our case, parties and movements are proximate fields that are interdependent through shared social relationships. Actors in parties control access to resources and opportunities that are valuable to movement actors, and vice versa. As party and movement actors contend with one another over time, they come to be defined in conjunction with one another. The evolved logics of parties depend, in part, on their responses to social movement strategies. Likewise, the evolved logics of movements depend, in part, on the opportunities opened and foreclosed to them by parties (Armstrong and Bernstein 2008; Friedland and Alford 1991). Thus, parties and movements have emerged as the fields that they are today, in part, through their mutual coevolution (Heaney 2010; Padgett and Powell 2012). Through coevolution, there is feedback between parties and movements that creates path dependence (Pierson 2004); once particular organizational structures are established, it is very costly or impossible to return to the previous organizational regime. Examining the coevolution of parties and movements in the United States informs us about why they have come to be seen as alternatives to one another.

The Founding and the Nineteenth Century

Neither political parties nor social movements are mentioned in the Constitution, yet they both have their origins in the early days of the American republic. James Madison's (1982 [1787], pp. 44, 48) seminal analysis of factions never enumerates the forms of these mischievous organizations, yet he had a clear sense that groups would develop around interests such as land, manufacturing, trade, banking, and religion. Madison himself participated in many such groups during his lifetime (Yoho 1995). The Federalist and Republican Parties, which arose in the late 1700s, were the nation's first political parties, even though their supporters did not favor the existence of "parties," per se (Hofstadter 1969, p. 12). The party as a mass organization designed to win elections was invented in 1828 by Martin Van Buren, who forged the Democratic Party in the service of Andrew Jackson's campaign for president (Aldrich 1995, p. 97). By that time, social movements had begun to make their mark, as well. For example, the prohibition movement had gained enough visibility to attract notice by Alexis de Tocqueville (1988 [1840], p. 516) during his travels to the United States in 1831 and 1832, which he would later document in his treatise *Democracy in America*.

Despite the emergence of a "modern" party with the Democratic Party, the United States did not have a fully institutionalized "two-party system" in the nineteenth century. Party coalitions were fragile. Control of government alternated between the Democrats and the Whigs during the middle years of the century, but contention from smaller parties was a genuine threat to major-party dominance. The Liberty Party, the Free Soil Party, and the Know-Nothing Party grew out of social movements against slavery, immigration, and Catholicism (Rosenstone, Bher, and Lazarus 1984). In 1860, the Republican Party was able to assemble a winning coalition out of these minor parties and the remnants of the Whig Party, triggering events that plunged the nation into civil war. After the war, the Greenback Party, the People's Party, and the Prohibition Party tapped into nascent social movements, such as the labor movement, which gained enough momentum to swing the balance of power in numerous elections (Babb 1996; Rosenstone, Bher, and Lazarus 1984). Electoral politics of the nineteenth century was a politics of parties and movements.

The close relationship between parties and movements shaped the strategies of actors in both fields during much of the nineteenth century. For example, the movement for the abolition of slavery began to spread in the United States during the 1820s and 1830s. The American Anti-Slavery Society (AASS) was the most prominent organization in the movement at that time, with the infrastructure of the movement provided largely by chapters at the state and local levels (Johnson 2009). The majority of participating activists relied on tactics aimed at moral suasion: They sought to convince their fellow citizens of the evils of slavery. As slavery became an increasingly contentious issue, some members of the AASS began to press for a greater involvement in institutional politics, prompting a split within the organization. Many activists who preferred a more institutional approach to the fight against slavery left the AASS to form the Liberty and Free Soil Parties. While neither party ever gained more than 2.3 percent of the popular vote (in the election of 1844), a substantial showing in New York by Liberty Party presidential candidate James Birney was arguably enough to throw the margin of victory nationally from Henry Clay (Whig-KY) to James K. Polk (D-TN) (San Francisco Argonaut 1892). In 1860, the strategy of reorganizing fragments of the Liberty and Free Soil Parties would prove to be a critical element of the Republican Party's successful venture to capture the White House.

The case of the abolition movement illustrates the possibilities for party-movement interaction during the nineteenth century.[8] As a social movement grew, some of its supporters were interested in achieving their goals through electoral means. Even though there was some disagreement within the movement about whether the electoral route was a wise one, it was relatively easy for proelectoral factions to seek and achieve support from the electorate. Movement parties were not able to win the presidency on their own, but the support of their constituents often proved pivotal in elections. In observing how the minor parties mobilized support – and in recognizing the possibility that they could make a difference in the outcome of elections – major parties actively courted support from the constituencies identified by the minor party. It was even possible for a coalition of minor parties to displace a major party. The overall milieu was one in which movements had easy access to viable strategies that affected parties, and vice versa.

The Twentieth Century

By the turn of the twentieth century, many social movement actors had grown frustrated with the strategy of seeking political influence through political parties. The partisan realignment of 1896 had reorganized party loyalties nationally such that competitive tension between the Democratic and Republican Parties was replaced by a system of regional one-party dominance (Sundquist 1983). Neither party could be challenged in its regional strongholds (the Northeast and West for Republicans, and the South for Democrats), with the Republicans commanding a convincing majority nationally. Given that each party was practically unchallengeable in its region, the possibilities that social movement–inspired minor parties could tip the balance of power were reduced. With less opportunity to swing the outcome of elections, social movements had diminished leverage over politicians, who had less of a need to pursue votes from movement-based constituencies.

In addition to changes in the electoral alignment of politics, the twentieth century introduced new institutions that worked to the advantage of Democrats and Republicans at the expense of minor-party candidates. The widespread diffusion of the Australian ballot in the United States at the end of the

---

[8] The history of the Free Soil Party and the Know Nothing Party exhibited similar political dynamics to those that we discuss regarding Liberty Party (Desmond 1905; Rayback 1970).

nineteenth and beginning of the twentieth century would prove to be a serious obstacle to minor parties (Evans 1917). By requiring all ballots to be cast secretly, the Australian ballot raised barriers to entry for political parties, which were then required to acquire permission from the state to appear on the ballot. The new ballot laws made it harder for smaller parties to compete in elections because of state thresholds for ballot access. The secret ballot eliminated the ability of parties to distribute party tickets directly to their supporters, making it more challenging for minor parties to educate voters about their slates of candidates. These changes, along with laws that prevented minor parties from fusing their votes with major parties, greatly increased the difficulty for social movements to turn to electoral strategies as a way of pursuing their goals (Disch 2002).

Social movement actors responded to the reduced viability of party-based strategies by inventing new tactics. Elisabeth Clemens (1997) documents how social movements of farmers, workers, and women invented a new organizational form – the citizens' interest group – and turned to nonpartisan lobbying as an alternative to partisan politics. These interest groups bore a resemblance to previous social movement organizations, but they placed a greater emphasis on using tactics that engaged existing governmental institutions (Armstrong 2002, pp. 16–18; Goss 2006; McAdam 1982, p. 25). The adoption of these more institutionalized tactics contributed to the success of movements in overcoming the multiple veto points of the American political system (Banaszak 1996). Concomitant with new organizations and tactics, social movement actors revised their political identities and adjusted their issue foci. Farmers, for example, quickly abandoned their pursuit of agrarian democracy in favor of economic corporatism (Clemens 1997, p. 146). The rise of interest group politics socialized movement actors into new approaches to politics and prompted them to adopt identities linked to interest group organizations.

As the twentieth century progressed, clearer distinctions emerged between the logics of movement politics and the logics of party politics. Movements continued to utilize protests and lobbying. However, the major movements tended to channel their electoral involvement into alliances with, or in opposition to, major party candidates (Schwartz 2006; 2010). The major parties became increasingly adept at blocking the threats posed by minor parties. When minor parties did appear on the ballot, their electoral prospects were often thwarted when major parties co-opted their positions on popular issues (Hirano and Snyder 2007). When non-major-party candidates did gain visibility – such as Henry Wallace and Strom Thurmond in 1948, John Anderson in 1980, Ross Perot in 1992 and 1996, and Ralph Nader from 1996 through 2008 – it was more a result of personal reputation and charisma than a function of party organization. As Steven Rosenstone, Roy Behr, and Edward Lazarus (1984) argue, these campaigns are more accurately understood as "third person" campaigns than as genuine "third party" campaigns.

Consolidation of the two-party system during the twentieth century meant that social movements wielded less influence within party politics than they had in the previous century. Cross-national studies of parties and movements yield results that are consistent with this conclusion. For example, Hanspeter Kriesi and his colleagues (Kriesi, Koopmans, Duyvendak, and Giugni 1995) comparatively analyze parties and new social movements in four Western European nations (France, Germany, the Netherlands, and Switzerland). Among other points, they find that the number of viable political parties was a critical aspect of the political opportunity structure for social movements. To the extent that countries were closer to an open, multiparty system, social movements were more likely to thrive within party coalitions. To the extent that countries were closer to a closed, two-party system, social movements were less likely to thrive within party coalitions.

A discourse about party-movement relationships coevolved along with the changing logics of movement and party politics. Partisan actors, in particular, endeavored to delegitimize efforts by movements to support minor parties. Votes for minor party candidates were decried as "wasted votes." Major parties emphatically warned voters that supporting minor-party candidates could lead to the highly undesirable outcome of aiding the election of a voter's least-preferred candidate. To prevent this outcome, voters must instead cast their vote for "the lesser of two evils." Movement actors were implored to ally with the major party, which promised to fight passionately for the movement's interests. Lisa Disch (2002) argues that the ability of the major parties to inculcate these views in the minds of voters and activists is "the tyranny of the two-party system." Major parties use these arguments to create a sense of their own inevitability, which helps to sustain the duopoly of the Democratic and Republican Parties in the United States. In the 2012 presidential election, for instance, the Democrats and Republicans together captured 98.27 percent of the votes cast for president, with the most successful minor-party challenger (Gary Johnson of the Libertarian Party) winning slightly less than 1 percent of the vote (Federal Election Commission 2013).

To the extent that social movement actors accept the premise of major party inevitability, their constituents are vulnerable to *capture* by one of the major parties. Paul Frymer (1999) stipulates that a constituency is captured when one party – the one that is more ideologically distant from it – is not interested in taking the policy stands that would be necessary to court its votes, such that the other party – the one that is ideologically closer to it – has an incentive to deliberately neglect the constituency's interests. For Frymer, the archetypal case of capture is African Americans and the Democratic Party. He notes that Democratic Party leaders sometimes go so far as to attack African American interests openly in an effort to dissociate the party from blacks in the eyes of more moderate white voters. In instances of capture, party politics effectively demobilizes social movement activism.

Once the possibility of capture is taken into account, the veracity of the wasted votes argument is called into question. While movement actors may not want to see the more distant of the major parties win the election, if they give their unquestioned support to the closer major party, they may likely find their interests neglected just the same. By supporting a minor-party alternative, movements may be able to show the major party the value of their support to the balance of power over a longer period. By forcing major parties to contend for their support, movements have the potential to push major parties away from the logic of only appealing to the median voter (Downs 1957; McAdam and Kloos 2014).

In attempting to challenge two-party hegemony, some movement actors advance a discourse that strives to delegitimize participation in major party activism. Movement activists on the left side of the political spectrum, for example, are prone to refer to the Democratic Party as "the graveyard of social movements" (McLemee 2007; Selfa 2008, p. 116). So the argument goes, the Democratic Party is a graveyard in the sense that movements lose their life once they ally with the Democrats. Proponents of this perspective call attention to how the Democrats co-opt movement energies for the party's needs and, thus, distract movements from pursuing their own agendas. The labor movement, for example, regularly made an all-out push to support Democratic candidates at election time in recent years, but Democrats proved to be ineffective partners once they were in office when promoting the major items on labor's legislative agenda (Francia 2010). In the women's movement, collaboration with the Democratic Party promotes norms within the movement to curtail its own agenda for the good of the party (Banaszak 1996, p. 40; Freeman 1987, p. 241). To respond to this co-optation, some of the more radical activists pushed movements to abandon engagement with the Democratic Party, as well as to avoid other forms of institutional engagement, such as lobbying. Of course, such claims are not exclusive to the left side of the political spectrum. In recent years, numerous leaders in the Christian Right movement have openly questioned whether their alliance with the Republican Party has stymied their ability to exert influence on many public policy issues that they care about passionately (Wilcox and Robinson 2011, pp. 185–7).

The rise of partisan polarization during the last three decades of the twentieth century exacerbated the difficulty for movements to operate independently of political parties. Partisan polarization is a process through which political actors (whether ordinary citizens or political elites) tend to cluster with other members of the same political party in terms of whom they vote for, their views on policy issues, where they live, and how they view the world. Alan Abramowitz and Kyle Saunders (2008) document that this polarization began in the 1970s and grew through the 2000s, especially as southern whites left the Democratic Party to identify with the Republican Party. Among members of Congress, partisan polarization began increasing in the late 1940s; the rate of polarization increased dramatically in the 1970s and has remained high since that time (Voteview 2012). These shifts have occurred as the Democratic Party has come to rely more on urban constituencies and minorities as its social base, and as the Republican Party has become more southern, rural, and white.

With polarization, political actors increasingly view all things political in partisan terms, including movements. As a result, it is more difficult than it once was for movements to make demands and successfully exert pressure on political elites in a way that clearly separates them from parties. The Christian Right movement of the 1990s and 2000s, for example, found itself closely embedded in the Republican Party, even though not all of its issue positions – such as those pertaining to social justice for the least fortunate – aligned perfectly (Wilcox and Robinson 2011). The need to work through the party system spurred changes in the tactics through which movements, such as the Christian Right, advanced their issues politically (Clifton 2004).

The New Century

By the dawn of the twenty-first century, the patterns of relations between parties and movements looked much different than they had two centuries earlier. Rather than operating as fluid arenas that were almost interchangeable at times, parties and movements solidified their boundaries and divided the space of legitimate action. Major parties gained the upper hand over movements, in part, by successfully discouraging movements from supporting minor-party electoral challenges. Major parties developed a "wasted votes" logic that convinced many movement activists to align with major parties. Movement actors grudgingly accepted this logic, lest they help put in power a worse alternative during a period of partisan polarization, even when major parties failed to deliver on their promises, election cycle after election cycle. At the same time, some movement activists promoted a logic that eschews engagement with political institutions altogether or, perhaps, supports endorsing minor parties, such as the Green Party and the Libertarian Party.

Our story of coevolution offers insight into how parties and movements became what they are today, as well as the logics through which they operate. Understanding coevolution allows us to formulate expectations about how parties and movements function in contemporary American politics. Movements are a force that tends to resist the two-party system and, instead, promote participation through noninstitutional tactics or minor parties. Parties, on the other hand, push to have political conflicts resolved by elections. Movement actors are welcome within parties to the extent that they advance the party's goal of winning elections but are otherwise considered a nuisance.

PARTIES AND PEACE ACTIVISM OVER TIME

In this section, we consider the specific case of antiwar activism and its coevolution with political parties. In many ways, the antiwar movement after

9/11 was an original movement that earned an independent place in the history of social movements. At the same time, it built on the activism that preceded it by drawing upon repertoires, frames, organizational infrastructure, and personnel that waited in abeyance from movements past (Taylor 1989). At times, antiwar activism drew on partisan sentiments, but, at other times, it was more driven by issues than by partisanship.

From the Revolution to Vietnam

Citizen dissent against military action has been present during every war fought by the United States. Thousands of loyalists to the British Crown dissented during the Revolutionary War, sometimes earning them the fate of being tarred and feathered, other times costing them their lives (Halstead Van Tyne 1902). Much of the domestic opposition to the War of 1812 was organized by the Federalist Party, which quickly found itself in a position of political irrelevance for the remainder of the decade (Hofstadter 1969; Mann 2010). In the aftermath of the War of 1812, pacifists began to organize their opposition to war by establishing local peace societies throughout New England. Their efforts culminated with the founding of the American Peace Society in New York City in 1828 by William Ladd (Brock 1968). For the remainder of the century, legislators, military officers, and ordinary citizens spoke out against the U.S.-Mexican War, the Civil War, and the Spanish-American War, often at great risk to themselves.

Opposition to war from the Revolution to the Spanish-American War might best be described as "factional" in the Madisonian sense (Madison 1982 [1787]). War opposition was mostly loosely organized, emerging from within political parties and among discontented citizens and politicians. Antiwar politics began to assume a more well-organized character in the aftermath of the Spanish-American War with the formation of the Anti-Imperialist League in 1898, which opposed the acquisition of Cuba, Guam, the Philippines, and Puerto Rico by the United States. The Anti-Imperialist League, which was founded in Boston by businessman Edward Atkinson, claimed 30,000 members and 500,000 contributors by 1899 (Beisner 1970, p. 196). This grassroots league aggressively distributed pamphlets, such as *The Hell of War and Its Penalties,* and had chapters in many of the major cities of the United States (Beisner 1970, p. 196).

A more broad-based antiwar movement developed in the midst of World War I. Pacifist organizations and other war opponents at that time included the Socialist Party, the Industrial Workers of the World, the Women's International League for Peace and Freedom, the Women's Peace Party, the National Civil Liberties Bureau (the precursor to the American Civil Liberties Union), the Fellowship of Reconciliation, the Anti-Enlistment League (the forerunner of the War Resisters League), and the American Friends Service Committee (Austin 2012; Bennett 2003; Fellowship of Reconciliation 1917; Stone 2004).

World War I was an especially difficult time for war resisters as a result of the passage of the Espionage Act of 1917, which criminalized disloyal speech. Approximately nine hundred people spent time in prison under the act before it was repealed in 1921, including Socialist Party presidential nominee Eugene Debs, who served almost three years of a ten-year prison sentence for giving a speech on behalf of others who had been jailed for opposition to the war (Zinn 1997, p. 269).

World War II, sometimes referred to as "The Good War," faced less domestic political opposition than did other wars of the twentieth century. Still, more than forty-two thousand Americans refused to fight in the Second World War (Ehrlich and Tejada-Flores 2000). Some of them registered as conscientious objectors, while others simply did not submit to conscription. Among the most famous of these were the Union Eight, a group of students at Union Theological Seminary in New York who served a year in prison for their refusal in 1940 to register with Selective Service during the first peacetime military draft in the nation's history (Tracy 1996). The historic peace churches, which included the Religious Society of Friends (Quakers), Church of the Brethren, and the Mennonites, played an important role in promoting conscientious objection on a nonpartisan basis during the war, along with the wider peace field that had been growing in the United States since the turn of the twentieth century.

The use of nuclear weapons by the United States at the end of World War II, and the ensuing international competition for the development of nuclear weapons during the cold war, raised the specter of the destruction of humanity as the result of war. The threat of total nuclear war gave rise to an international movement to "ban the bomb" (Katz 1986). A new cadre of organizations joined the peace field around this time as it became increasingly internationalized, such as the Committee for a Sane Nuclear Policy (also known as SANE, in the United States), the Struggle against Atomic Death (in West Germany), and the Campaign for Nuclear Disarmament (in the United Kingdom) (Wittner 2003). Although these organizations offered a well-articulated moral opposition to a changing international environment, they did little to quell the proliferation of nuclear weapons or the growth of nuclear stockpiles.

The Vietnam Antiwar Movement and Its Aftermath

Up to the end of the 1950s, domestic opposition to war had never constituted a mass political movement in the United States. Pacifists and other war opponents had irritated presidents who sought to marshal the nation in times of war, but they had not constituted a serious challenge to the government's ability to raise an army. However, the movement against the war in Vietnam, Laos, and Cambodia (which we hereafter refer to as the Vietnam War) during the 1960s and early 1970s became a major disruptive political force during its era. The massive scale of the protests against the war, the highly contentious – and sometimes violent – nature of the opposition, as well as widespread draft resistance during the war, made the movement a major challenge to the presidential administrations of LBJ and Richard Nixon. The Vietnam antiwar movement stood out from all other antiwar movements such that, for almost thirty years after it ended, any reference to "the antiwar movement" was generally assumed to be a reference to the *Vietnam* antiwar movement.

U.S. military involvement in Vietnam began in the 1950s with the introduction of American military advisers in the region (Herring 2002). American involvement escalated gradually with an expanded troop presence in 1962, then again after the Gulf of Tonkin incident in 1964, until the United States was eventually engaged in a full-fledged war in Vietnam. The war would eventually spill over into Laos and Cambodia during the presidency of Richard Nixon before it finally ended with the fall of Saigon in 1975 (Schulzinger 1997).

Like U.S. military engagement in Vietnam, the Vietnam antiwar movement grew slowly over time. Much of the early opposition to the war arose from committed pacifists affiliated with the peace movement of the 1940s and 1950s. One of the movement's early, visible events occurred when Students for a Democratic Society (SDS) adopted the Port Huron Statement, drafted by Tom Hayden, at its first convention in 1962 (Students for a Democratic Society 1962). While the statement did not focus on the Vietnam War, it provided an overarching critique of American domestic and foreign policies, as well as the way that leftist social movements had attacked these policies. Among other arguments, it proposed a strategy to transform the Democratic Party into a more progressive party. In doing so, the statement helped to provide a rallying cry for a student-led antiwar movement in the coming years.

Demonstrations against the war grew incrementally until 1968, when police-initiated violence against demonstrators outside the DNC in Chicago put the antiwar movement on the world stage (Farber 1988). A new, radical wave of antiwar organizations joined the existing peace field, among the most prominent of which were Clergy and Laymen Concerned about Vietnam, GI's United against the War in Vietnam, SDS, the National Mobilizing Committee to End the War in Vietnam, Vietnam Veterans against the War, and the Vietnam Day Committee. The antiwar movement was fueled even further by the initiation of a draft lottery in 1969, which was highly disruptive to people's lives and widely unpopular. With considerable growth in its ranks, historian Melvin Small (2002, p. 3) estimates that "[by] 1969 there may have been as many as 17,000 national, regional, and local organizations that could be considered in the movement." The antiwar movement continued in earnest through 1973, but declined once it became clear that U.S. policy was to end the war.

As the topic of the Vietnam antiwar movement has already filled many scholarly volumes (see, for example, DeBenedetti 1990; Farber 1988; Garfinkle 1995; Gitlin 1981; Seidman 2010; Small 2002), we do not provide an extensive discussion of that movement in this book. However, we wish to highlight several key points that are essential for contextualizing the antiwar movement of the 2000s.

The Vietnam antiwar movement was not largely driven by partisan loyalties or motivations. Public opinion on the war did not follow a strong partisan trend. Adam Berinsky (2009, p. 119) reports that survey respondents identifying with both the Democratic and Republican Parties concurrently withdrew their support for the war over the 1965 to 1972 period, though partisans registered war support levels that were slightly above average when the president in power was a member of their party. Similarly, movement actors appear to have been driven more by loathing of the Vietnam War than by a desire to elect or defeat any particular candidate or party. The initial escalation of the war began, and the antiwar movement grew substantially, during the presidency of LBJ, a Democrat. Activists did not withhold their vitriol merely because the occupant of the White House was a supporter of civil rights, the war on poverty, and other liberal causes. One of the most famous chants of the movement was "Hey, hey, LBJ, how many kids did you kill today?" (Arnold 1966). The movement suffered some of its harshest repression at the hands of Chicago Mayor Richard J. Daley, also a Democrat, during the 1968 DNC (Lukas 1968). The war and the movement both continued with the election of a Republican president, Richard Nixon, in 1968.

Many movement activists supported some Democratic presidential candidates who were advocates for peace, most visibly Robert Kennedy (in 1968), Eugene McCarthy (in 1968), and George McGovern (in 1972). But this support appears to have owed largely to these candidates' peace positions, rather than merely to their party affiliations. Democratic candidates such as Hubert Humphrey (in 1968), who did not have strong peace bona fides, did not attract devoted constituencies within the antiwar movement.

A key feature of the Vietnam antiwar movement was that it was substantially student/youth driven. Some of the chief grievances of the movement – mounting casualties among young men, the draft, and fairness of determining draft eligibility – had a significant effect on and resonance with youth. Colleges and universities, which were filled with recipients of deferrals and exemptions from the draft, were fertile grounds on which to discuss and criticize national policies on conscription. For these reasons, it is not surprising that much of the movement's initial mobilizing energy arose from nascent student organizations such as SDS (Gitlin 1981).

A number of pivotal events during the Vietnam antiwar movement involved violent confrontations between activists and authorities. Some of these events, such as the May 4, 1970, massacre of student demonstrators by National Guard troops at Kent State University, are among the most unforgettable incidents of the Vietnam War era (Gregory and Lewis 1988). The bombings committed by a radical SDS splinter group, known as the Weathermen, continued to be controversial as late as the 2008 presidential election, with a firestorm arising from Democratic nominee Barack Obama's ties to former weatherman Bill Ayers (Cooper 2008). Violence – whether perpetrated by the authorities or by those in the movement – was often an effective tactic that swayed the direction of congressional policy making in favor of those who perpetuated it (McAdam and Su 2002).

The movement borrowed heavily from nonviolent tactics that were taught by Mohandas Gandhi and adapted effectively to the American context by the civil rights movement. At the same time, the Vietnam antiwar movement offered important examples of tactical innovation. For example, the Moratorium campaign designated specific days and times for ordinary people to refrain from work in order to call attention to the war (Small 1987). These tactics, along with humorous and satirical tactics developed by groups such as the Yippies, helped the movement to penetrate the public consciousness of the era (Farber 1988).

The movement was largely divided on the basis of race, while offering only limited opportunities for leadership by women. African American activists were involved in the Vietnam antiwar movement from the very beginning. Their participation was generally channeled through black-identity organizations, such as the Black Panther Party, the Student Nonviolent Coordinating Committee, and the National Black Anti-War Anti-Draft Union (Westheider 2008, p. 64). Some prominent African Americans became important voices against the war, such as Martin Luther King Jr., who spoke out against the war from 1967 until his assassination in 1968 (Fairclough 1984). However, the antiwar movement was a predominantly white movement, with whites and blacks usually marching separately. Women rarely rose to positions of leadership outside organizations specifically devoted to women's mobilization (such as Women Strike for Peace) (Meyer and Whittier 1994, p. 284). Jane Fonda stands out as an exception but, given her celebrity status, was likely the exception that proves the rule.

Finally, the Vietnam antiwar movement had a significant impact on domestic politics in the United States, but had only an ambiguous effect on actual U.S. policy in Vietnam. The social disorder caused by the antiwar movement was a contributing factor in LBJ's decision to withdraw from the 1968 presidential election, thus assisting the election of Richard Nixon as president in 1968 (DeBenedetti 1990). The movement helped to mobilize public opinion against the draft, specifically, and the war, overall, thus weakening the government's hand in prosecuting the war. However, the movement may have helped to prolong the war by encouraging the North Vietnamese to keep fighting and/or by strengthening the resolve of American conservatives to resist the goals of the hippie-liberal activists (Small 2002, p. 161).

In the aftermath of the Vietnam War, peace activism receded into abeyance for the remainder of the 1970s. Even so, the 1980s saw the revival of the antinuclear movement, which peaked roughly between 1982 and 1984, during the administration of Republican President Ronald Reagan (Meyer 1990). New organizations joined the peace field around this time, such as Plowshares, Women's Action for New Directions, and the Nuclear Weapons Freeze Campaign (which would merge with SANE to form Peace Action in 1987).

Movements against Wars in the Middle East

The antiwar movement reappeared briefly in 1990–1991 to oppose the U.S. operation to expel the Iraqi army from Kuwait. The short duration of the Persian Gulf War (forty-three days), as well as the high levels of public support that it received, afforded the movement little opportunity to blossom (Woehrle, Coy, and Maney 2008). Still, the antiwar coalitions that developed at that time were important in that they became organizational predecessors of major coalitions that would oppose the (much longer) wars in Afghanistan and Iraq during the 2000s. The more radical of the two major coalitions, the Coalition to Stop U.S. Intervention in the Middle East (CSUSIME), was the precursor of the International ANSWER coalition (Act Now to Stop War and End Racism) of the 2000s (Heaney and Rojas 2008). The more moderate of the coalitions, the National Campaign for Peace in the Middle East (NCPME), was the precursor of United for Peace and Justice (UFPJ) during the 2000s (Heaney and Rojas 2008). Antiwar activism resurfaced again, during the administration of Democratic President Bill Clinton, to offer modest resistance to U.S. bombing of Iraq in 1998 and U.S. military intervention in Kosovo in 1998–1999 (Woehrle, Coy, and Maney 2008). There was little indication at the time, however, that major military conflicts and a revitalized antiwar movement would be just over the horizon in the new century.

In the immediate aftermath of 9/11, it was clear that the United States would strike out in response, once it could be determined who was responsible for these horrific events. Given the outpouring of sympathy for the victims of 9/11, however, many social movement actors were unclear on what would be the best and most appropriate way to oppose the expected war. They had to strike a delicate balance between raising critical policy concerns and appearing appropriately patriotic at a time of national tragedy.

At the time of the 9/11 attacks, 117 organizations in the Mobilization for Global Justice Coalition (MGJC) were in the midst of planning a series of actions in Washington, D.C., targeted at the World Bank and the International Monetary Fund (IMF) on September 30, 2001 (Gillham and Edwards 2011). This coalition did not focus on issues of war and peace, but on the economic relationships between the major industrial powers and the developing world. Leaders from many of the organizations in the coalition – especially those with ties to organized labor and domestic reform movements in the United States – worried that going forward with their originally planned mobilization would be seen as in poor taste and disrespectful to those who had died on 9/11. On the other hand, leaders from many organizations closely tied with the anarchist and anti-imperialism movements saw the 9/11 attacks as a product of the capitalistic policies that they had long opposed. From this point of view, September 2001 was exactly the right time to seize attention for their causes.

While most of the organizations in the MGJC chose to abandon their action plans for September 2001, anarchist and anti-imperialist elements of the coalition decided to move forward with their protest plans (Gillham and Edwards 2011). The International Action Center, which was one of the key anti-imperialist organizations in the MGJC, decided to break away from MGJC to take the lead in organizing International ANSWER as an antiwar coalition rooted in the antiimperialist community. According to Brian Becker (2008), ANSWER's national coordinator:

The ANSWER Coalition was really those groups in the anti-globalization movement [also known as the global justice movement] who quickly transitioned and developed an antiwar focus and began mobilizing against the Bush Administration rather than restricting the target to the IMF, the World Bank, and other financial and corporate institutions that had been identified with all of the evils and the injustice perpetrated against working people around the world as a result of this new phase of economic life, capitalist globalization.

In place of the events originally planned by MGJC, International ANSWER sponsored the first significant antiwar protest of the post-9/11 period on September 29, 2001, in Washington, D.C. (International ANSWER 2001). Given high levels of public support for U.S. invasion of Afghanistan, the nascent movement was unable to exert much pressure against military action, which commenced on October 7, 2001.

The antiwar movement began to pick up steam in the latter half of 2002, once the Bush administration's intention to invade Iraq became clear. Much of the initial mobilization took place within the context of other movements. For example, when the Mobilization for Global Justice held a rally against the IMF and the World Bank in Washington, D.C., on September 28, 2002, some organizations used this opportunity to galvanize the antiwar grass roots. An illustration of how this strategy played out in practice is given by Figure 1.2. This photo, taken at the September 28 anti-IMF/World Bank demonstration, shows activists carrying signs printed by the Socialist Worker and the International Socialist Organization. On one side, the signs convey the anti-IMF/World Bank themes intended by the event's organizers, reading "Stop Washington's war on the world's poor! Shut down the WTO, IMF, & World Bank." On the other side, however, they stress an antiwar theme: "No war on Iraq. End the Sanctions." The clear goal was to pull global justice movement activists into the antiwar movement. With these efforts, much of the organizing energy of the global justice movement spilled out into the antiwar movement (Hadden and Tarrow 2007).

Many of the organizations in the peace field, such as the American Friends Service Committee, Peace Action, and the Women's International League for Peace and Freedom, had become frustrated with the initial direction of the antiwar movement. Organizations such as International ANSWER advanced anti-imperialistic arguments against war that seemed, to many, to appeal only to hard-core antiwar activists (Cagan 2008). More moderate peace organizations and Democratic Party allies decided to form a new coalition, originally

FIGURE 1.2. Mobilization for Global Justice Demonstration, Washington, D.C., September 28, 2002 (Photo by Michael T. Heaney)

known as United for Peace. In contrast to that of ANSWER, its focus was primarily on a possible war in Iraq, rather than the war in Afghanistan, which enjoyed wide public support. Leslie Cagan (2008), who served as the coalition's national coordinator until 2008, explained:

We convened [our] first meeting in Washington [D.C.] in October of 2002, and there were representatives there from about 55 organizations, and they were predominantly national organizations at that point. Right from the beginning, we said, we're gonna focus on Iraq because it looks like the Bush administration is committed to going to war, we have to try and stop that war before it starts.... But we also said very clearly that we all know that what's going on in Iraq is not an isolated phenomenon, it's connected to other aspects of US foreign policy and, indeed, to other aspects of US domestic policy.

As its first public event, UFP called for decentralized actions by local peace groups around the country on December 10, 2002.

Shortly after the formation of UFP, the antiwar movement in Europe called for an international day of action against the war in Iraq on February 15, 2003 (Walgrave and Rucht 2010). Changing its name to United for Peace *and Justice,* UFPJ took the lead in coordinating demonstrations in the United States. The coalition against the war began to extend beyond the traditional peace field, including groups such as MoveOn – an organization supporting progressive/ Democratic causes. And the peace field itself grew as activists crafted organizations fitted to the politics of the twenty-first century, such as Code Pink: Women for Peace, Military Families Speak Out, and Win Without War, which was itself a coalition that included many progressive/mainstream organizations, such as the Sierra Club, Rainbow/Push, and the United Methodist Church. Organizations in the movement argued against the war for a variety of reasons, not all of which were necessarily consistent with one another, such as that Iraq played no role in the 9/11 attacks; attacking Iraq would lead to a wider war in the Middle East; thousands of innocent people would die in a war; the United States would lose influence around the world by attacking Iraq; the United States should not invade Iraq without authorization of the United Nations Security Council; and money spent on war would be better spent on meeting domestic needs in the United States.

Organized on the theme "The World Says No to War," February 15 was an almost unimaginable mobilization success. The day reflects the extent to which the antiwar movement had become a genuinely transnational movement. Leslie Cagan (2008) recounts that

[on] February 15th of 2003, we were able to put 500,000 people on the streets of New York, and February 15th, if you're not a New Yorker, you might not realize, it could be pretty cold, and it was pretty cold that day. And we also generated enough interest that there were over four hundred demonstrations around the United States, and our count was there were over nine hundred all around the world. Literally every continent, every corner of the world. The biggest demonstrations happened to be in Europe. I think Rome had the biggest one with two million people there that day, and London had a million people, and Paris had I don't know how many.... [T]he mainstream media reports were that somewhere between ten and thirty million people were out on the streets that day. In the United States, in terms of our work, of course that kind of helped put UFPJ on the map as the largest coalition, and then we grew again after that.

With a touch of hyperbole, Patrick Tyler (2003) of the *New York Times* called the antiwar movement a global "superpower" in analyzing the aftermath of the rallies (see also Cortright 2004). President Bush was less impressed, referring to the worldwide demonstrations as little more than a "focus group" (Democracy NOW! 2003). The president instead gave greater weight to the 59 percent of Americans who supported the invasion than to street protesters, who may have been perceived by some to be outside the mainstream of the country (Jones 2003).

Despite the impressive and unprecedented mobilizations against war, the Bush administration was unmoved. The U.S. invasion of Iraq began on March 19, 2003. While, in many ways, this day was *the* definitive loss for the antiwar movement, it was also a day of beginning for the movement. Having failed to prevent war, many activists began their efforts to bring the troops home. They would unleash diverse tactics in their efforts, from massive protests to quiet vigils, from lobbying days to sit-ins, from newspaper advertising to street theater. The movement functioned as a genuine mass social movement roughly from 2001 through Obama's election as president in 2008, at which time it transitioned to a state of abeyance.

Some readers may wonder whether there is a distinction to be made between the movement against the war in Iraq and the movement against the war in

Afghanistan. We have not made such a distinction; nor do we think that it would be practical or informative to do so. Instead, we group both movements under the umbrella of the antiwar movement after 9/11, just as the movement against the wars in Vietnam, Laos, and Cambodia is generally labeled as the Vietnam antiwar movement. Although the antiwar movement after 9/11 began with opposition to the war in Afghanistan, the same organizations that contested that war joined in opposition to the war in Iraq. As the war in Iraq wound down, many organizations that were created mainly in response to the Iraq War (such as UFPJ) continued on as opponents to the war in Afghanistan. Thus, opposition to the two wars was organizationally and thematically unified. In fact, the Bush administration encouraged this unification because it talked about the two wars as policies in the War on Terror and as responses to the events of 9/11. Moreover, there were strong military connections between the two wars, as many military personnel who served in one theater also served in the other. Organizations such as Iraq Veterans Against the War (IVAW) included Afghanistan veterans among their membership. Thus, although there was a military difference between the two wars, the domestic politics of the two were usually conflated.

Comparing the Movements

In locating the antiwar movement after 9/11 within the history of peace struggles in the United States, the best point of comparison is the Vietnam antiwar movement. These movements were comparable in their breadth of citizen participation and their duration of mobilization. Nonetheless, they differed from one another in important respects. The most relevant of these, given the focus of this book, is the contrasting partisan contexts within which they emerged. Public opinion was polarized according to party to a much greater degree during the 2000s than was the case during the Vietnam War era (Hetherington 2009, p. 442). Polarization was highly consequential in the formation of public opinion on the war. As Gary Jacobson (2010, p. 31) notes, "the Iraq war has divided the American public along party lines far more than any other US military action since the advent of scientific polling back in the 1930s." Americans often took their cues about how to make sense of developments in Iraq from their partisan identifications (Gelpi 2010). We argue that, as a result, the rhythms of the antiwar movement after 9/11 were driven by partisanship much more than was the case during the Vietnam antiwar movement.

The fact that the Vietnam antiwar movement preceded the Iraq-Afghanistan antiwar movement in history is a defining feature of the relationship between these movements. This point may be exceedingly obvious, but we think that its consequences are both nonobvious and significant for the movement after 9/11. The historical sequence of these movements meant that many of the participants of the Vietnam antiwar movement were able to participate in the antiwar movement after 9/11. Indeed, most of the key leaders of the movement after 9/11 had also protested the Vietnam War. For example, both Brian Becker and Leslie Cagan – coordinators of the two most important coalitions after 9/11 – also protested during Vietnam (Becker 2008; Cagan 2008). As a result, the movement after 9/11 was not youth led, as was the movement during Vietnam. SDS was re-formed in 2006, after having faded out of existence in the 1970s. But it failed to reclaim the vanguard role that had been held by its 1960s predecessor. Youth leadership was likely stymied by the presence of a strong cohort of returning Vietnam Era protesters, but it was also obviated by the lower salience of the wars after 9/11 to youth. The abolition of the draft in 1973 and the transition to an all-voluntary military force eliminated what had been one of the central grievances of the Vietnam antiwar movement. With war creating less of a threat to their interests, youth after 9/11 had less reason to be leaders of the movement.

After 9/11, the antiwar movement was almost entirely peaceful and nonviolent in nature, involving few contentious clashes with police, unlike the Vietnam antiwar movement. This reduced contentiousness was characteristic of protest in the era of "the social movement society," when demonstrations and grassroots advocacy were usually seen as a normal element of the political process, rather than a fundamental challenge to the social order (Meyer and Tarrow 1998). These conditions likely lessened the political impact of the movement, as political elites believed that it had less potential for significant disruption and, therefore, was less of a threat to their interests.

The movement after 9/11 borrowed heavily from the tactics of the Vietnam War era, especially the emphasis on spring and fall organizing drives. In many ways, the movement after 9/11 accomplished these mobilization tasks with much greater efficiency than had been the case during the 1960s and 1970s, largely through the instantaneous communication environment created by the rise of the Internet (Gillan, Pickernill, and Webster 2008). Some efforts to mimic the tactics of the 1960s did not work so well. For example, the Iraq Moratorium never approached the same level of acclaim and visibility that the Moratorium had during Vietnam (Iraq Moratorium 2009). Despite its reliance on mobilizing models of the 1960s, the movement after 9/11 did offer important examples of tactical innovation, such as the grassroots lobby days it held from 2003 through 2007. Organizations such as Code Pink and IVAW mastered methods of gaining media attention through street theater and peaceful disruption (Boyd and Mitchell 2012; Goss and Heaney 2010; Leitz 2014). At times, antiwar activists drew effectively upon the innovative tactics that emerged out of the global justice movement – and the Battle of Seattle of 1999, in particular – in which protesters became more adept at circumventing advances in police control of protests (Herbert 2007; Noakes and Gillham 2007; Smith 2001). Still, the movement after 9/11 often found itself limited by a reliance on an outdated repertoire of action from the 1960s.

Over the last decade, the antiwar movement was less divided on the basis of race and gender than had been the case during the Vietnam Era. In contrast to the Vietnam Era, women led peace organizations on par with men, if not to a greater extent than men. After 9/11, peace organizations self-consciously appointed persons of diverse races, ethnicities, nationalities, sexes, and sexual orientations to prominent leadership positions in the movement. However, at the grassroots level, the movement after 9/11 almost entirely failed to attract a substantial constituency among African Americans and other minorities. This failure may be part of the explanation for why the antiwar movement never gained a greater foothold within the Democratic Party.

Finally, the mass movement after 9/11 was less politically consequential than was the Vietnam antiwar movement. Some possible explanations for this difference are the changed nature of war in the twenty-first century, the determination and obstinacy of the Bush administration, the early alignment between the movement after 9/11 and the Democratic Party, as well as the inherent improbability for peace movements to achieve significant, policy-related goals. Even though the movement after 9/11 did not match the Vietnam antiwar movement in terms of political impact, it nonetheless stands out as the second most significant antiwar movement in American history.

Peace activism has confronted the power of political parties throughout American history. At times, antiwar movements have aligned with parties. Nonetheless, foreign policy issues are often outside the boundaries of party politics. In the next chapter, we address the ambiguities that emerged after 9/11 as the party in the street challenged foreign policies on a decidedly partisan basis. Our investigation into this movement, reported in the pages that follow, is revealing of the partisan nature of politics in the early twenty-first century.

2

Partisan Politics at the Water's Edge?

> Partisan politics, for most of us, stopped at the water's edge. I hope that they stay stopped – for the sake of America – regardless of what party is in power. This does not mean that we cannot have earnest, honest, even vehement domestic differences of opinion on foreign policy. It is no curb on free opinion or free speech. But it does mean that they should not root themselves in partisanship. We should ever strive to hammer out a permanent American foreign policy, in basic essentials, which serves all America and deserves the approval of all American-minded parties at all times.
>
> U.S. Senator Arthur Vandenberg (R-MI), January 11, 1947

Senator Arthur Vandenberg (1947) is credited with originating the aphorism "Politics stops at the water's edge." Speaking at the beginning of the cold war in defense of President Harry Truman's internationalism, Vandenberg sought to justify his departure from his long-held position of isolationism in foreign policy. Isolationism no longer seemed politically palatable in the aftermath of World War II with the rise of the United Nations and a greater sense of global interdependence, thus making nonpartisanship a safer political strategy. Following in this tradition, the principal tenets of American foreign policy have tended not to fluctuate as a function of which party is in office (for a contrary view, see Zelizer 2010). Part of the reason for this stability is that foreign policy is driven by state actors that operate largely outside the confines of electoral politics (Mearsheimer 2001; Morgenthau 1948). When foreign policy issues do arise in elections, voters may be likely to give greater weight to domestic policies, which are closer to their immediate concerns, thus reducing the potential partisan gains from refining foreign policy positions (Rattinger 1990).

This book explores the relationship between the party in the street and U.S. policies toward Iraq and Afghanistan. Yet, whether or not U.S. foreign policies are affected by partisan politics is generally disputed. Some foreign policy analysts claim that the politics of the early 2000s were an exception to the general rule that foreign policy issues are not partisan in nature. For example, Peter Beinart (2008) argues that while the war in Afghanistan enjoyed broad bipartisan support, the commencement of the "war on terror" (and the associated war in Iraq) polarized the country and initiated a new era of partisan foreign policy (see also Kupchan and Trubowitz 2007). This perspective sees President Bush's foreign policy as a significant departure from the administrations that preceded it, and as inconsistent with the kind of policy that otherwise would have been implemented by a Democratic presidential administration.

Other foreign policy analysts contend that the war on terror was not as radical a break from the status quo as it seems on the surface (Chaudoin, Milner, and Tingley 2010). In a provocative counterfactual analysis, Frank Harvey (2012) argues that a hypothetical President Al Gore – the Democrat who would have been elected president in 2000 were it not for electoral irregularities in Florida – would likely have waged a war against Iraq, as did President Bush. He bases this argument on a variety of evidence, including the aggressive anti-Iraq policies of the Clinton administration, public statements by Gore while serving as vice president and campaigning for president, and the neoconservative advisers who would likely have joined the Gore administration if he had become president. If, as Harvey contends, the policies of a President Gore would have been very similar to those of President Bush, then it is difficult to sustain the claim that the Bush administration ended a long tradition of nonpartisanship in U.S. foreign policy.[1]

This chapter investigates the relationship between partisanship and U.S. policies in Iraq and Afghanistan. We frame our investigation by considering two competing hypotheses. The "water's edge" hypothesis, $H_{2.1}$, suggests that there should be no systematic difference between Democrats and Republicans on war issues. If there are differences, these should be idiosyncratic, rather than partisan in nature. The partisan policy hypothesis, $H_{2.2}$, suggests alternatively that the parties differ systematically on matters of war and peace.

Whether or not U.S. policy in Iraq and Afghanistan is partisan in nature matters for our interpretation of the party in the street. If, as the water's edge hypothesis suggests, there is no difference between Democrats and Republicans on foreign policy, then it would be difficult to understand why the party in the street would mobilize against war. In this case, opposition to war should be independent of partisan loyalties. If, instead, as the partisan policy hypothesis suggests, there are substantial differences between the parties on foreign policy, then the party in the street is expected to fall in line behind the Democratic Party.

---

[1] For a discussion and critique of Harvey's argument, see the review symposium appearing in the June 2013 issue of *Perspectives on Politics*.

We investigate a variety of types of evidence in this chapter to ascertain the extent to which the Democratic and Republican Parties were divided during the 2000s with respect to their stances on policies toward Iraq and Afghanistan. First, we examine the positions that the parties took during federal elections in the 2000s and assess the extent to which those positions allowed them to attract support from the electorate. Second, we examine the actual policies implemented by the Bush and Obama administrations in Iraq and Afghanistan in order to understand the nature of the similarities and differences between the two administrations. Third, we map out the relationship between changes in those policies and the mobilization of the antiwar movement through street protests.

The findings of our investigation yield some support for both hypotheses. Supporting the partisan policy hypothesis, we find that Democratic candidates were more likely than Republican candidates to take antiwar policy positions in presidential and vice-presidential debates, for which they were rewarded by support from antiwar voters. However, examination of Bush's and Obama's policies in Iraq and Afghanistan points more to continuity than to change, as the water's edge hypothesis anticipates. While there were some differences between the ways the two administrations approached war in the Middle East, these differences do not appear to be fundamentally partisan in nature.

The puzzle of our book becomes clear when we observe that antiwar mobilizations decreased after Democrats achieved electoral victory but before they implemented any notable policy changes. This finding is fully consistent with neither the water's edge hypothesis nor the partisan policy hypothesis. If the water's edge hypothesis is correct, then the level of protest should follow changes in policy, not just changes in party, as we observe. But if the partisan policy hypothesis is correct, then changes in policy should follow changes in party, which we do not observe. Thus, we argue that a new theoretical perspective on parties and movements is needed. In the next chapter we offer this perspective, which is based on the dual identifications that political actors have with movements and political parties. The antiwar movement may have demobilized not necessarily because there was a change in policy, but because some activists may have *perceived* a change in policy linked to party. Partisanship is a filter through which activists judge policies regarding war and peace.

THE ELECTORAL POLITICS OF WAR

In order to understand whether there was a difference between the parties in the 2000s on war issues, we ask two questions. First, did the parties represent themselves differently on war issues during elections? Second, if the parties did attempt to separate themselves on war issues, did voters recognize those differences and reward or punish candidates in accordance with those positions? To address the first question, we examine the statements of presidential and vice-presidential candidates during debates in the 2004 and 2008 elections.

To address the second question, we model voting in federal elections from 2002 to 2008 as a function of antiwar attitudes.

To assess similarities and differences between the parties on war issues, we examined all the statements of candidates for president and vice president in the primary and general election debates in 2004 and 2008. We focus on presidential and vice-presidential candidates because these individuals seek to represent their party as a whole; looking at the statements of these individuals gives us a sense of the range of positions that might plausibly represent a party. We examine both primaries and general elections in recognition of the fact that candidates may speak differently when attempting to reach out to party loyalists (who are likely to be decisive in the primaries) as opposed to swing voters (who are likely to be decisive in the general election). We limit our analysis to 2004 and 2008 because these are the two years in which Iraq and Afghanistan policies were actively discussed by presidential candidates.

We collected all of the transcripts of the primary and general election debates in 2004 and 2008. We analyzed the transcripts of seventeen Democratic primary debates from 2004 and twenty-four Democratic primary debates from 2008. Since George W. Bush sought reelection in 2004 as the incumbent president, there were no Republican debates that year, leaving us with only seventeen Republican primary debates from 2008. There were four general election debates in 2004 and in 2008 (including one vice-presidential debate each year). For each candidate in each debate, we coded the number of times she or he used the word "war," "Iraq," or "Afghanistan." We also coded whether she or he discussed war in "positive" or "negative" terms. "Positive" statements pointed to the potential good that may result from war, such as achieving regime change in a rogue state, introducing democracy to the Middle East, or protecting the rights of women. "Negative" statements pointed to the downsides of war, such as the deaths of innocent civilians, the erosion of America's image around the world, or the staggering financial costs associated with warfare. Finally, we recorded the number of words that a candidate spoke in the debate in order to control for the fact that some candidates might have a greater opportunity to speak than other candidates.

We modeled the differences between candidates in the debates using panel negative binomial regressions on the number of positive statements and the number of negative statements per candidate per debate. Additionally, we estimated regressions on the number of times that candidates raised the issues of war, Iraq, and Afghanistan, regardless of the positions they took. We control for whether the debate was a Democratic primary, Republican primary, or general election debate, held in 2004 or 2008, and the number of words spoken in the debate. The unit of analysis is the candidate-debate pair, so each candidate is included once in the data for every debate she or he participated in, leaving us with 398 total observations over 2004 and 2008.

The results of the analysis are reported in Table 2.1. Although there was variation among candidates in both parties, candidates in Democratic debates

TABLE 2.1 *Mentions of War in Presidential Debates, 2004 and 2008.*

Independent Variable	(2.1) Positive Attitude toward War	(2.2) Negative Attitude toward War	(2.3) War	(2.4) Iraq	(2.5) Afghanistan	Descriptive Statistics Mean (Std. Dev.)
	Dependent Variable: *Count of Occurrences per Candidate per Debate*					
Democratic Debate = 1	-1.4358***	0.6670**	0.2728*	0.2950*	0.0797	0.6357
	(0.2845)	(0.2416)	(0.1237)	(0.1160)	(0.2424)	(0.4870)
General Election Debate = 1	0.1953	0.5715	1.3187***	0.7232*	1.5652**	0.0402
	(0.7781)	(0.7496)	(0.3793)	(0.3407)	(0.5963)	(0.1967)
Year Is 2008 = 1	-0.6296*	0.3236	0.2170	-0.0833	0.8603***	0.6407
	(0.2937)	(0.2327)	(0.1234)	(0.1143)	(0.2704)	(0.4856)
Words Spoken	0.0003**	0.0001	0.0001	0.0002***	0.0003***	0.6407
	(0.0001)	(0.0001)	(0.0000)	(0.0000)	(0.0001)	(0.4856)
Constant	0.0412	-1.3586***	0.6831***	0.5766***	-2.4618***	
	(0.3449)	(0.2927)	(0.1531)	(0.1410)	(0.3154)	
α	3.0073***	2.6052***	0.7867***	0.6246***	1.4047***	
	(0.5082)	(0.4378)	(0.0850)	(0.0718)	(0.3725)	
Sample Size (N)	398	398	398	398	398	
Mean of Dependent Variable	0.9196	0.6884	3.5578	3.8342	0.6407	
Log Likelihood	-409.1130***	-427.9805***	-927.4695***	-927.1978***	-328.6984***	
Likelihood Ratio χ^2, $df = 4$	75.1900	14.2400	53.9300	107.1500	107.9300	

Note: * $p \leq 0.050$, ** $p \leq 0.010$, *** $p \leq 0.001$. Standard errors in parentheses. Parameters were estimated by using panel negative binomial regression.

were significantly less likely to espouse positive attitudes toward war and significantly more likely to espouse negative attitudes toward war, than were candidates in Republican debates. These findings lend support to $H_{2.2}$, the partisan policy hypothesis. This finding suggests that partisan politics did not stop at the water's edge in the 2000s. Democratic candidates were also more likely to raise the issue of war, in general, and Iraq, in particular, than were candidates in Republican debates. There were no differences, however, between candidates in Democratic and Republican debates regarding their mentions of Afghanistan, which was largely ignored by both parties, receiving less than one mention per candidate per debate.

General election debates, on average, were no more positive or negative about war than were primary debates. However, war issues were raised significantly more often in general election debates than in primary debates. Candidates were significantly less likely to make positive statements about war in 2008 than in 2004. They were also more likely to mention Afghanistan in 2008. The number of words spoken by a candidate in a given debate provides an important statistical control, appearing as a significant factor in equations 2.1, 2.4, and 2.5.

While the war positions of Democrats and Republicans were not always completely clear, the evidence presented here indicates that, overall, the two parties diverged on war issues in 2004 and 2008. Candidates speaking in Democratic primary debates were more likely to raise issues of war, and to do so in a critical fashion, than were candidates in Republican primary or general election debates. These debates should have provided signals to antiwar voters that the Democratic Party favored an antiwar position more than the Republican Party did.

Given that Democrats and Republicans tended to take competing positions on issues of war in the 2000s, to what extent did voters reward or penalize candidates for these positions? A difference between the parties on a policy issue does not necessarily indicate that this difference is decisive in determining an individual's vote choice. Voters may, instead, base their choice, for example, on ideology, party membership, the leadership qualities of the candidates, or other issues (Bartle and Laycock 2012; Clarke et al. 2011). Still, when issues are highly salient – as is often the case with matters of war and peace – it is reasonable to expect that they may have a significant effect on vote choice (Gadarian 2010). For example, an analysis by David Karol and Edward Miguel (2007) demonstrates that casualties in the Iraq War likely cost President Bush approximately 2 percent of the national vote in the 2004 election (see also Myers and Hayes 2010). Other research reveals that war spending has direct negative effects on the incumbent's popularity (Geys 2010).

To answer this question, we assembled data from exit polls taken after congressional and/or presidential elections held in 2002, 2004, 2006, and 2008 (National Election Pool 2004; 2006; 2008; Voter News Service 2002). We tested the idea that individuals expressing attitudes critical of the Iraq War were more likely to vote for the Democratic Party's candidate in these elections than to vote for a candidate of the Republican Party (or, in a very small percentage of cases, a minor party). The exact version of the question to tap antiwar attitudes varied from election to election. For the 2002 general election exit poll, the question was "Do you support or oppose the U.S. taking increased military action against Iraq to remove Saddam Hussein from power?" [Options: Support/Oppose] (Voter News Service 2002). For the 2008 general election exit poll, the question was "How do you feel about the U.S. war in Iraq?" [Options: Strongly approve/Somewhat approve/Somewhat disapprove/ Strongly disapprove] (National Election Pool 2008). We controlled for other factors expected to affect individuals' vote choices, including the respondent's economic outlook, whether or not the respondent self-identifies as a Democrat, the respondent's self-described political ideology, sex/gender, race/ethnicity, age, and income.[2]

The results of our analysis of general election exit polls are reported in Table 2.2. The results show a consistent, positive effect of antiwar attitudes on voting for the Democratic candidate in general elections from 2002 through 2008. The effect was weakest in the 2002 elections, prior to the Iraq War. The coefficient on *Opposed to Iraq War* is positive and significant in the 2002 U.S. House election but is not significant in the 2002 U.S. Senate election. After the commencement of the Iraq War, the votes of individuals opposed to the war were significantly more likely to go to Democrats than to Republicans in each election we analyzed.[3]

It is important to recognize that the effects of antiwar attitudes hold up after controlling for whether the respondent self-identifies as a Democrat, whether s/he thinks of herself as a liberal, as well as her/his outlook on the economy, sex/gender, race/ethnicity, age, and income. The results demonstrate that it is not just that liberal Democrats were more likely to vote Democratic – as they were – but also that people opposed to the Iraq War were more likely to vote Democratic even if they were not liberal or self-identified Democrats. This effect held not only in the 2006 and 2008 elections, when Democrats won a majority of the votes cast, but also in the 2004 election (and, to a lesser extent, in the 2002 election), when the Republicans secured the majority. That is, the

---

[2] A complete list of variable definitions for all equations in this section appears in Appendix B. Descriptive statistics are reported in Appendix C.

[3] A critical reader may be concerned that some respondents may have become Democrats because they opposed the wars in Iraq and/or Afghanistan. Indeed, it is very likely that some small percentage of respondents switched parties for precisely this reason. However, this issue is not a serious threat to the validity of our statistical analysis. First, party switching in the mass electorate is relatively uncommon (Levendusky 2009), implying that only a small number of our observations would be affected. Second, the statistical consequence of this issue would be to create a downward bias in the coefficient on *Opposed to Iraq War*. Yet since this coefficient is positive and significant in seven of the eight reported equations, any effect of this nature appears to have little consequence for our conclusions.

TABLE 2.2. *Vote Choice in General Elections, 2002–2008*

Independent Variable	Dependent Variable: *Voted for Democratic Candidate*							
	2002 (2.6) House	(2.7) Senate	2004 (2.8) House	(2.9) President	2006 (2.10) House	(2.11) Senate	2008 (2.12) House	(2.13) President
	Coefficient (Standard Error)							
Opposed to Iraq War	0.2990*	0.3204	0.5113***	0.8315***	0.4338***	0.3906***	0.5048***	0.6900***
	(0.1142)	(0.1824)	(0.0208)	(0.0424)	(0.0337)	(0.0334)	(0.0329)	(0.0490)
Positive Economic Outlook	-0.4094***	-0.3309***	-0.1911***	-0.2846***	-0.3218***	-0.2505***	-0.1551***	-0.0320
	(0.0361)	(0.0495)	(0.0420)	(0.0596)	(0.0461)	(0.0455)	(0.0419)	(0.0539)
Democrat = 1	1.6949***	1.1177***	1.3078***	1.2660***	1.3480***	1.0916***	1.2689***	1.0930***
	(0.0763)	(0.1126)	(0.0815)	(0.1151)	(0.0662)	(0.0940)	(0.0828)	(0.1008)
Liberal Political Ideology	0.4850***	0.5124***	0.3551***	0.5420***	0.3970***	0.4182***	0.4308***	0.5151***
	(0.0537)	(0.0803)	(0.0439)	(0.0574)	(0.0340)	(0.0357)	(0.0426)	(0.0530)
Sex/Gender Is Female =1	-0.0701*	-0.0177	-0.1380*	-0.1342*	-0.1681**	-0.1535**	-0.1393*	-0.0833
	(0.0320)	(0.0393)	(0.0484)	(0.0644)	(0.0524)	(0.0473)	(0.0602)	(0.0795)
Race/Ethnicity Is African American/Black = 1	0.8507***	0.6799**	0.0681	-0.0648	0.7001***	0.5346***	0.8379***	1.4428***
	(0.1686)	(0.2206)	(0.0793)	(0.1204)	(0.1222)	(0.1220)	(0.1385)	(0.2396)
Age in Years	0.0001	-0.0001	-0.0044*	-0.0087**	-0.0006	0.0017	-0.0004	-0.0074**
	(0.0020)	(0.0020)	(0.0018)	(0.0028)	(0.0014)	(0.0012)	(0.0018)	(0.0025)
Income in Thousands of Dollars	-0.0023	-0.0010	0.0000	-0.0009	-0.0006	-0.0001	-0.0012	-0.0001
	(0.0013)	(0.0014)	(0.0009)	(0.0009)	(0.0004)	(0.0005)	(0.0007)	(0.0005)

Table 2.2. *(cont.)*

	Dependent Variable: *Voted for Democratic Candidate*							
	2002		2004		2006		2008	
	(2.6)	(2.7)	(2.8)	(2.9)	(2.10)	(2.11)	(2.12)	(2.13)
Independent Variable	*House*	*Senate*	*House*	*President*	*House*	*Senate*	*House*	*President*
Constant	-0.8676***	-0.9642**	-1.9049***	-2.4084***	-1.4322***	-1.5133***	-2.3093***	-2.9896***
	(0.2957)	(0.3843)	(0.1994)	(0.2571)	(0.2376)	(0.2222)	(0.1805)	(0.1893)
Mean of the Dependent Variable	0.4617	0.4703	0.4680	0.4789	0.5220	0.5422	0.5228	0.5356
Sample Size (N)	8,368	4,296	3,485	3,660	6,812	5,057	4,267	4,482
F statistic	90.23***	25.56***	113.37***	106.67***	132.12***	59.47***	177.54***	180.48***
F Degrees of Freedom	8,34	8,21	8,36	8,37	8,38	8,21	8,41	8,41

Note: * $p \leq 0.050$, ** $p \leq 0.010$, *** $p \leq 0.001$. Estimates are adjusted using sample weights. Standard errors in parentheses.

Democrats benefited significantly from the votes of war opponents even when they lost the overall election. These results provide strong support for the partisan policy hypothesis.

Opposition to the Iraq War was a part of what proved to be an overall winning electoral strategy for the Democrats in the late 2000s. After the 2006 congressional elections, the Democrats held majorities in both houses of Congress. After 2008, an antiwar Democrat occupied the Oval Office. With the opening gavel of Congress in 2009, the Democrats nearly held a filibuster-proof margin of control in the Senate (Koger 2010). So, did these antiwar voters get what they bargained for? Did a Democratically controlled Congress and Democratic president deliver an antiwar foreign policy? We address these questions in the following section.

CONTINUITY AND CHANGE IN WAR POLICY

In order to answer the question of whether the transition to Democratic political control in the United States led to a switch in policy in the antiwar direction, it is necessary to answer a counterfactual question: What would have happened to policy if the Republican Party had remained in control of the White House and Congress? Since this question is hypothetical, we cannot provide an unambiguous answer. It is impossible to know definitely what would have been the content of a Republican-defined foreign policy after 2008. However, by looking at policy trends and statements made by administration officials, we can reasonably speculate about where the differences would likely have been.

In comparing the similarities and differences between the Bush and Obama administrations on war policies in Iraq and Afghanistan, we find more continuity than change in policy. The large decline in forces in Iraq, as well as their ultimate withdrawal, were set in motion during the Bush administration. With respect to Iraq, the Obama administration largely carried out the Bush administration's policy without substantially changing direction. As we explain later, there may be some dispute about how differently the two administrations would have negotiated to extend the final Status of Forces Agreement (SOFA) in Iraq. It is possible to argue that the Obama administration was somewhat less prowar with respect to the SOFA than another Republican administration would have been, but it is also possible that the two administrations would have ultimately reached the same or similar agreements. It seems possible that a Republican administration would have called for an increase of troops in Afghanistan, as did the Obama administration, but it would be reasonable to argue that Obama's increase was greater than would have been undertaken by a Republican administration. Regardless of which argument the reader finds most plausible, the differences between the administrations are subtle. At best, the Obama administration was slightly more peaceful than another Republican administration likely would have been. At worst, the Obama administration was somewhat more bellicose.

This section proceeds in three parts. First, we provide an overview of U.S. policy in Iraq and how it changed from the Bush to Obama administrations. Second, we provide a similar analysis of U.S. policy in Afghanistan. Third, we offer a general assessment of the bellicosity of the two administrations in comparison to one another.

U.S. Policy Toward Iraq since 1990

Animosity between the United States and Iraq can be traced most directly to the Iraqi invasion of Kuwait, its neighboring oil-rich nation, in August 1990. In response, the United States led a United Nations–authorized war against Iraq in coalition with thirty-five other nations, beginning in January 1991 (Arabic Media 2013). The coalition quickly expelled Iraqi forces from Kuwait but elected not to topple the Iraqi government, headed by Saddam Hussein and his Ba'ath Party. Instead, the United Nations Security Council imposed sanctions on Iraq, including limitations on imports and exports; enforced "no-fly zones" over northern and southern Iraq; and required Iraq to undergo regular inspections to demonstrate that it had abandoned its program of maintaining and developing weapons of mass destruction. Iraq resisted the sanctions regime, leading to an ongoing conflict between the United States and Iraq from 1991 to 2001. Both Democratic and Republican presidential administrations in the United States regularly engaged in military conflict with Iraq after 1991.

In the immediate aftermath of 9/11, the Bush administration sought to establish a connection between Saddam Hussein's Ba'athist regime and the 9/11 attacks. Vice President Dick Cheney alleged in December 2001 that Iraq was sheltering terrorists wanted by the United States and that Iraqi officials had met with terrorists responsible for 9/11 before the attacks (White House 2001). Several administration officials, such as National Security Adviser Condoleezza Rice, claimed that the administration had evidence that Iraq attempted to acquire aluminum tubes for refining the uranium necessary for a nuclear weapon (CNN Politics 2002). The Bush administration argued that these facts justified an invasion of Iraq by the United States. The ultimate case for the invasion was made before the United Nations Security Council on February 6, 2003, by U.S. Secretary of State Colin Powell, who argued that Iraq had failed to meet its disarmament obligations resulting from the 1991 war (Powell 2003). Despite its failure to receive approval from the United Nations Security Council, the United States and a "Coalition of the Willing" (including the United Kingdom, Spain, Australia, and more than forty other nations) attacked Iraq on March 19, 2003 (Newnham 2008).

The United States and its allies quickly achieved victory over the Iraqi army, effectively removing Saddam Hussein from power. On May 1, 2003, President

Bush declared that major combat operations in Iraq had come to an end, thus commencing the coalition's postwar occupation of Iraq. At this time, the coalition set up and administered a provisional government, with an eye toward eventually establishing a new Iraqi-administered government that would assume responsibility for police and military functions. Early in the occupation, the focus of policy was to fill in the gaps left by the then-defunct Ba'athist state (Katzman and Elsea 2004).

The institution initially responsible for administering Iraq was the U.S.-controlled Coalition Provisional Authority (CPA), which governed from April 2003 through June 2004. The CPA was responsible for programs such as redeveloping/reforming government institutions (e.g., the courts), disbanding and retraining the Iraqi army, and privatizing the Iraqi economy, which had been mostly nationalized by Hussein's government (Halchin 2004). The CPA was followed by a series of other institutions that acted as the government of Iraq, including the Iraqi Interim Government (June 2004–May 2005, headed by U.S.-anointed Prime Minister Iyad Allawi), the Iraqi Transitional Government (May 2005–May 2006, headed by Prime Minister Ibrahim al-Jaafari), and the first permanent Government of Iraq (May 2006–2014, headed by Prime Minister Nouri al-Maliki).

The period from 2003 through 2006 was a time of escalating violence in Iraq. The violence stemmed from a variety of sources, including the long-standing tension between Sunni and Shia Muslims, clashes between coalition forces and Iraqi rebel groups, and the influx of non-Iraqis into Iraq who organized insurgent groups, such as Al-Qaeda in Iraq. Much of the violence was episodic and was often perpetuated using improvised explosive devices. However, there was also a considerable amount of organized conflict between Iraqi groups and U.S. armed forces, such as the Battles of Fallujah of 2004 (Malkasian 2006). The escalation of violence from 2003 through 2006, and the absence of a strong Iraqi state in the months following the end of the Hussein regime, led the Bush administration to plan for a long-term presence in Iraq. To this end, the administration articulated the desire to establish permanent bases in Iraq, in order to guarantee security in Iraq and to serve as a launching point for U.S. military operations in the region (Englehart 2006). During this time, the United States maintained an occupation of between 120,000 and 160,000 troops, working in coalition with approximately 20,000 troops from its coalition partners, as well as military contractors (O'Hanlon and Livingston 2012, p. 13).

During the early years of the occupation, the Bush administration resisted calls for a timetable for withdrawal from Iraq. Administration officials claimed that setting a timetable would help the enemy to coordinate its plans and that it was not appropriate to fit such a complex mission – fostering security in a postwar region – into a timetable (Associated Press 2003; MacAskill 2007). As a result, there were few official statements early in the occupation about how long the occupation would last. Instead, policy discussions revolved around overall troop levels and strategies of pursuing goals in the field, such as capturing former Iraqi leaders or securing chemical weapons stockpiles (Jehl and Filkins 2003).

January 2007 marked the beginning of a new stage in the Bush administration's policy in Iraq. Sectarian violence in Iraq had drastically increased. The new Government of Iraq was not effective in controlling violence, negotiating a political settlement, or protecting ethnic or religious minorities in Iraq. In response to these conditions, the administration presented *The New Way Forward* as a strategy to develop Iraq's capacity for self-government (United States Department of State 2007). The administration turned its focus to training leaders, providing short-term loans, undertaking construction projects, and directly supporting the management of local government functions, such as courts and schools. *The New Way Forward* recognized the long-term nature of the tasks necessary to build a secure state but did not specify a timeline. Consistent with this new vision, the White House emphasized that benchmarks of progress should be substituted for a timeline as an indicator of when the United States would be ready to withdraw from Iraq (White House 2007a).

In May 2007, Congress passed, and President Bush signed, the U.S. Troop Readiness, Veterans' Care, Katrina Recovery, and Iraq Accountability Appropriations Act of 2007 (Public Law 110–28 2007). This supplemental appropriations law guaranteed funding to continue the Iraq War but also included provisions to prevent the establishment of permanent U.S. military bases in Iraq or U.S. military control over oil resources in Iraq. Furthermore, the law required the United States Government Accountability Office (2007) to report on whether the government of Iraq met eighteen benchmarks established in the act, such as de-Ba'athification, equitable distribution of oil resources, protection of minority rights, and provision of trained military personal to improve security in Baghdad. The report detected only scant progress by Iraq's government toward these goals (United States Government Accountability Office 2007).

At the same time that the administration introduced benchmarks for progress in Iraq, they articulated a new policy, widely known as "the surge." More accurately, the policy could be described as "surge and substitute": first, raise the level of U.S. troops by approximately thirty thousand (i.e., surge) and then replace those troops over time with native forces (i.e., substitute) (Duffy and Kukis 2008). In September 2007, military commanders in Iraq claimed that the surge had worked and noted that U.S. casualties in Iraq markedly decreased (Patraeus 2007). Scholarly research corroborates these claims, in large part, noting that the surge, in combination with voluntary insurgent stand-downs, was responsible for the reduction in violence (Biddle, Friedman, and Shapiro 2012; for contrary views, see Cordesman 2008; Hagan et al. 2013).

The declining violence in Iraq, as well as the surge that presumably brought about the decline, provided the backdrop for new negotiations between the United States and the Government of Iraq. On November 26, 2007, Bush and

Prime Minister Maliki signed a *Declaration of Principles* that was the beginning of negotiations to disengage U.S. troops from Iraq (Mason 2009). They agreed that the objective of cooperation between the United States and the Government of Iraq was to train, equip, and arm the Iraqi government so that Iraq could take primary responsibility for its own security (White House 2007b). In a July 2008 interview, Maliki predicted that Iraq would shortly reach an agreement with the Bush administration on a timetable for withdrawal (Müller von Blumencron and Zand 2008).

In keeping with Maliki's prediction, and after months of negotiations, the United States and Iraq signed a Status of Forces Agreement (SOFA) on November 17, 2008. A SOFA is a legal agreement between the United States and the government of another nation that allows the U.S. military to operate within that nation. The SOFA stipulated that U.S. forces would legally operate within Iraq only until December 31, 2011. Thus, the Bush administration had laid the foundation for the withdrawal of the U.S. military from Iraq.

Barack Obama campaigned for president advocating a sixteen-month timetable for withdrawal of U.S. forces from Iraq (Bohan 2008). This time-table would have sent all U.S. troops home in April 2010, a full twenty months earlier than promised in the SOFA. However, once in office, the Obama administration largely followed the timetable set out in the SOFA signed by the Bush administration, although there were some delays in meeting the intermediate withdrawal targets (Whitlock 2010). Under the Obama administration, the United States accomplished a partial withdrawal by August 2010, and then a full withdrawal by the scheduled December 2011 departure date (Robinson 2011). Even though military forces left the country, the United States retained its embassy in Baghdad with approximately seventeen thousand personnel; its consulates in Basra, Mosul, and Kirkuk with one thousand staff each; and thousands of military contractors (Denselow 2011).

One wrinkle in the story that Obama essentially followed the Bush timeline for withdrawal is that the Obama administration commenced negotiations with the Maliki government to extend the presence of U.S. troops beyond what Bush had agreed to in the SOFA. As the deadline for withdrawal approached, U.S. officials worried that Iraq had not achieved sufficient stability to maintain security without the U.S. military presence. To address this problem, U.S. negotiators sought an extension of the SOFA (Katzman 2012, p. 38). Prime Minister Maliki indicated that he would be willing to support the request for an extension if the proposal could gain the support of 70 percent or more of Iraq's Council of Representatives (Davis 2011). When it appeared likely that Iraq's government would grant the necessary approval, officials in the Obama administration began discussing the parameters of the U.S. presence, which would have likely consisted of approximately fifteen thousand troops (Katzman 2012, p. 38). However, Iraq issued a statement on October 5, 2011, that it would permit U.S. troops to remain in Iraq, but they would not have the legal protections granted by the SOFA, making them subject to the jurisdiction of Iraqi courts (Katzman 2012, p. 39). As a result, President Obama announced that all U.S. troops would leave Iraq by the end of 2011, in accordance with the existing SOFA. U.S. troops left Iraq because of Iraq's unwillingness to extend the legal protections of the SOFA, not because of the preferences of the Obama administration (Dreazen 2011). Nevertheless, during his 2012 campaign for reelection, Obama cited the full withdrawal of all U.S. troops from Iraq as one of his administration's major accomplishments (Obama 2012).

Some conservative commentators and politicians criticized Obama's willingness to withdraw troops from Iraq (in accordance with the SOFA negotiated by the Bush administration) as a mistake. For example, U.S. Senator John McCain (R-AZ), who ran against Obama as the Republican nominee for president in 2008, stated that withdrawal was "a serious mistake. I believe we could have negotiated an agreement. And I'm very, very concerned about increased Iranian influence in Iraq" (Trinko 2011). Thus, McCain implied that if he had been elected president – in place of Obama – the U.S. troop presence would have continued, as he presumably would have been more successful in negotiating an extension of the SOFA with Iraq.

These observations leave us with three possible conclusions about how Obama's policy in Iraq compares with a hypothetical alternative Republican presidential administration's. The first possible conclusion is based on events as they actually happened. The Obama administration implemented the SOFA close to the way that it was negotiated by the Bush administration. Thus, the Democratic and Republican policies could be considered to be nearly identical. The second possible conclusion is that the Democrats were more prowar than the Republicans in their Iraq policy since they sought to negotiate a longer stay in Iraq than a Republican administration would have. The third possible conclusion is that the Republicans were more prowar than the Democrats because a McCain administration would have been more successful in negotiating an extension of the SOFA than the Democrats were.

Our purpose in conducting this exercise is not to claim that any one alternative is more or less plausible than another. We leave it to the reader to make that judgment. Rather, our point is that the difference between these alternatives is subtle. Perhaps Obama ordered the troops home a little earlier than a hypothetical President McCain would have. But perhaps they would have implemented exactly the same policy. Either way, the maximum difference between the policies of the parties is about 15,000 troops – a relatively small number after an occupation that was sustained by more than 100,000 troops for more than seven years. No matter which set of assumptions the reader accepts, U.S. policy in Iraq looks very similar, regardless of whether we imagine political control being wielded by Democrats or Republicans.

U.S. Policy toward Afghanistan since 2001

In his televised address from the Oval Office on the evening of September 11, 2001, President Bush declared that "we will make no distinction between the terrorists who committed these acts and those who harbor them" (Bush 2001, p. 58). At the time of the 9/11 attacks, Osama bin Laden – the mastermind of the attacks – was a guest of the Taliban government in Afghanistan, headed by Mullah Omar. In keeping with Bush's declaration, the U.S. government demanded that the Taliban government turn over bin Laden and all Afghanistan-based terrorists in the Al-Qaeda network, as well as close all terrorist training facilities in the country, subject to U.S. verification (CNN World 2001). When the Taliban rebuffed the U.S. demands, the United States and its allies invaded Afghanistan on October 7, 2001. By December 2001, initial military operations against the Taliban had been completed. Major Afghan groups signed an agreement in Bonn, Germany, to form an interim government (United Nations 2001). Hamid Karzai was anointed as head of the interim government. He remained as head of the permanent Afghan govern- ment after elections in 2004 and 2009, serving until 2014.

During the early years of the American occupation (from 2001 through mid-2003), the major goal of U.S. policy in Afghanistan was counterterrorism (Bergan 2011). The U.S. military focused on defeating the remnants of the Taliban and Al-Qaeda in the mountainous regions of the country. Given the limited scope of its mission, the United States kept the size of its military occupying force relatively small, with less than ten thousand U.S. troops. The United States gradually expanded its troop levels in 2004 and 2005, as it turned greater attention to security. As in Iraq, the U.S. government did not offer timetables for withdrawal from Afghanistan at that time; instead, the government insisted that "conditions on the ground" would be used to formulate policy (Stout 2006). However, the U.S. presence in Afghanistan was never as contentious as it was in Iraq, allowing the U.S. and Afghan governments to reach a mutually agreeable SOFA quickly (Mason 2011, pp. 7–10).

The U.S. policy in Afghanistan led to a gradual, modest escalation of forces. These forces sought to quell local leaders in many areas of the country who, while not formally part of the Taliban, continued to resist U.S. control. They worked to train the Afghan military so that the government of Afghanistan might assume greater responsibility for its own security (Department of Defense 2006). Further, the United States and its allies worked to reform Afghan institutions, for example, by banning poppy cultivation (Felbab-Brown 2005) and building secular schools (Wood 2009). However, for the most part, the U.S. government aspired to leave a "light footprint" in Afghanistan (Miller 2011, p. 61). In practice, this aspiration meant that the United States neglected Afghanistan from 2003 through 2008, as it was bogged down with its military adventure in Iraq (Miller 2011, p. 61).

Presidential candidate Barack Obama sought to return the war in Afghanistan to the public agenda in the United States. As Obama explained in his first general election debate against John McCain:

Yes, I think we need more troops [in Afghanistan]. I've been saying that for over a year now. And I think that we have to do it as quickly as possible, because it's been acknowledged by the commanders on the ground [that] the situation is getting worse, not better.... So I would send two to three additional brigades to Afghanistan. (Obama 2008c)

In response, Senator McCain was clear that he, too, favored increasing troop levels in Afghanistan:

So we've got a lot of work to do in Afghanistan. But I'm confident, now that General Petraeus is in the new position of command, that we will employ a strategy which not only means additional troops – and, by the way, there have been 20,000 additional troops, from 32,000 to 53,000, and there needs to be more. (McCain 2008; see also McCain 2007)

Obama's position on Afghanistan allowed him to claim during the election that he was simultaneously antiwar (regarding Iraq) and prowar (regarding Afghanistan), thus enabling him to appeal to a broad segment of the electorate. By splitting the difference between the wars, Obama may have hoped to appear flexible on foreign policy issues.

Once in office, Obama was in a position to put his vision into practice. While it would have been possible for him to walk away from his campaign pledge regarding Afghanistan, the president and his leading advisers (with the notable exception of Vice President Joe Biden) instead agreed to conduct a surge in Afghanistan analogous to the one that Bush authorized in Iraq. As presidential historian Andrew Polsky (2012, p. 332) recounts, they "envisioned a kind of Baghdad II, a troop surge of indefinite duration in which American forces and their NATO [North Atlantic Treaty Organization] allies would practice 'seize, hold, and build' tactics to bring population security and economic development to rural Afghanistan." This strategy led to an increase of troops in Afghanistan from roughly 35,000 when Obama took office to a peak of 100,000 between August 2010 and April 2011 (Livingston and O'Hanlon 2012, p. 4). This increase of 65,000 troops far exceeded the two to three brigades (a maximum of about 15,000 troops) proposed by Obama during the election campaign.

More than just increasing the number of troops present, Obama's surge brought about a change in policy. Rather than focusing only on counterterrorism, the surge aimed to degrade the capacity of the Taliban so that the Afghan central government might exert greater control of its territory (Polsky 2012, p. 336). Despite these efforts, insurgent-initiated violence spiked in Afghanistan during the surge. American troops were subject to more attacks by insurgents in 2010 than in any other year of the occupation, making 2010 the deadliest year on record for American troops in Afghanistan (Livingston and O'Hanlon 2012, pp. 10–11). In September 2014, the United States and Afghanistan signed a new Bilateral Security Agreement to maintain the presence of U.S. troops for another six years (Walsh and Ahmed 2014).

When looking at the record of the Obama administration, it is obvious that it cannot be characterized as "antiwar" with respect to its policy in Afghanistan. In the first four years of the administration, 1,530 U.S. service members died in Afghanistan, almost three times the number (630) who died in Afghanistan during all eight years of the Bush administration (Livingston and O'Hanlon 2012, p. 11). It is possible that a hypothetical President McCain would have reached exactly the same policy decision as did Obama. After all, McCain did promise to increase troops in Afghanistan. However, given that Obama increased troop levels far above what was discussed in the election, and the fact Obama used the Afghanistan issue as a way of distinguishing himself as a candidate, it also seems plausible that Obama's surge was uniquely his doing. Thus, on the issue of Afghanistan, the plausible arguments range from an equal position between Democrats and Republicans to a position in which the Democratic administration was notably more prowar than a Republican administration would have been.

Comparing Republicans and Democrats

When examined in comparison with one another, Republican and Democratic policies exhibit more continuity than change from the Bush to the Obama administrations. There are two likely areas of difference. One is that a Republican president after 2008 might have fought harder to extend the SOFA in Iraq, allowing the United States to keep a small residual force in the country, whereas the Obama administration did not. A second is that a Republican president might not have insisted on such a substantial surge in Afghanistan as President Obama did.

The policy comparison over time is clearest when examining a chart of U.S. troop levels, which we plot in Figure 2.1. The rise of Democratic majorities in Congress did not result in a policy turn in the antiwar direction, as many Democratic candidates elected in 2006 had sought. Rather, the Bush administration met the new Congress with a major surge in Iraq, as well as a gradual escalation of forces in Afghanistan. The deescalation of forces in Iraq began in late 2007, well before Barack Obama assumed the presidency. However, the chart suggests that Obama "owns" the surge in Afghanistan. The sharp upward climb in forces there did not begin until he entered the Oval Office. In fact, the surge in Afghanistan offset troop reductions in Iraq such that by July 2009, total U.S. troops deployed in Iraq and Afghanistan reached 192,800, only 3,000 shy of the peak during the Bush years (of 195,800 in October 2007). President Obama carried out his promise – and President Bush's agreement – to send U.S. troops home from Iraq. At the same time, he ordered an "Iraqification" of the U.S. presence in Afghanistan.

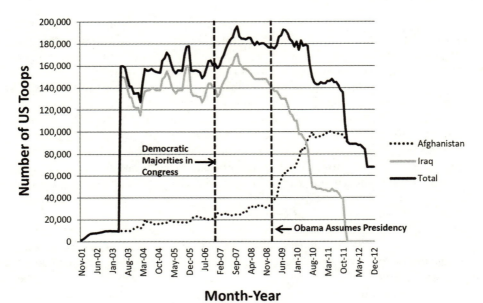

FIGURE 2.1. Monthly U.S. Troop Levels in Afghanistan and Iraq, 2001–2012
Note: Sources are Livingston and O'Hanlon (2012, p. 4) and O'Hanlon and Livingston (2012, p. 13).

It is tempting to extend our analysis to other aspects of military policy related to the Middle East. For example, President Obama dramatically expanded the use of remote-control drones as a way to fight terrorism in Afghanistan and other Middle Eastern nations without having to put U.S. troops in harm's way (Benjamin 2013). Further, Obama committed U.S. military support to regime change in Libya in 2011 without obtaining authorization required by the War Powers Act (Ackerman and Hathaway 2011). In 2013, the president proposed launching missile strikes against Syria in retaliation for its use of chemical weapons during its civil war; however, a peaceful settlement was reached before a strike was launched. One could attempt to argue about how these policies were similar to or different from those that might have been implemented under a Republican administration. However, such discussions would be pure speculation. Without evidence of how a Republican administration actually dealt with new drone technologies or the unexpected situations in Libya and Syria, it is impossible to offer an empirically grounded analysis. Some willingness to address counterfactuals is necessary, but we limit this analysis to the major contours of U.S. military involvement in Iraq and Afghanistan.

On balance, the evidence considered in this section supports the water's edge hypothesis, $H_{2.1}$. *Candidates* may have attempted to exploit the issues of Iraq and Afghanistan for partisan gain, but the *policies* themselves do not appear to have been driven by partisanship. The policy differences between the parties are subtle; the parties agree more on the substance of policy than their political rhetoric suggests.

In the next section, we turn to the reaction of the public to these policy changes. We pay close attention to the timing of changes in mobilization. How did levels of antiwar mobilization correspond to changes in U.S. troop levels? Did declines in antiwar protests precede or follow declines in troop levels? The precise timing of decline suggests a puzzle for the way that we understand the mobilization of social movements.

PARTISAN MOBILIZATIONS?

Given the relative continuity of policy from the Bush to the Obama administration, we should expect the level of antiwar activity in the United States to be unaffected by changing partisan majorities, as the water's edge hypothesis predicts. However, as we have already noted, activity in the antiwar movement declined as the Democratic Party became more successful in elections. In this section, we look closely at the scale of antiwar mobilizations and how they corresponded to changes in policy. We argue that understanding the inconsistency between the patterns of movement mobilization and policy change requires a new theoretical perspective on movement mobilization.

We look at the scale of antiwar demonstrations as our primary indicator of movement activity. First, the street demonstration has been the signature tactic of antiwar movements in the United States since at least the Vietnam War era. From the vantage point of many movement leaders, a large public demonstration seems to be the best way to challenge the state's position on a grand policy issue, such as war and peace. Second, even though street demonstrations are not the only tactic that antiwar movement activists utilize, most activists who engage in other tactics also participate in street demonstrations.[4] Consequently, looking at the scale of participation in street demonstrations yields a sense of the total number of people who are working toward the movement's goals. Third, the scale of demonstrations reveals the extent to which the movement has mobilized the "general public" for the cause of the movement, rather than only highly committed activists. As Ken Kollman (1998) explains, demonstrations are a credible way to signal the public's commitment to a cause to policy makers. Fourth, larger protests are more likely to affect the public's agenda than are smaller protests, making them an indicator of the movement's potential importance (Walgrave and Vliegenthart 2012).

Measuring the size of public demonstrations is a controversial matter (Lapidos 2009). Since scientific methods of measuring crowds are rarely employed, various actors interested in the demonstrations usually offer their own subjective impressions of the demonstrations. The demonstration organizers tend to claim a large number, after which police officials usually suggest a

---

[4] We establish this fact with empirical evidence presented in Chapter 4.

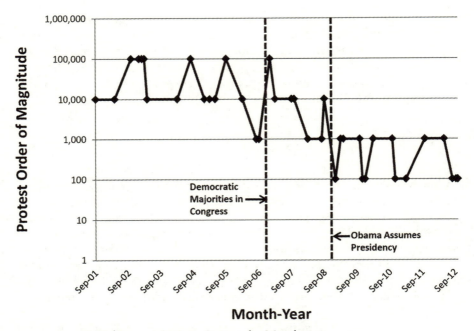

FIGURE 2.2. Size of Largest Antiwar Protests by Month, 2001–2012
Note: For sources, see Appendix D.

smaller number. The media may offer their own number, present a variety of estimates, or take sides in the dispute between the police and the organizers.

We note that while various sources almost always disagree on the exact number of persons in a crowd, they often agree on the order of magnitude of the crowd size. For example, immediately after the historic antiwar protest on February 15, 2003, in New York City, the organizers claimed a crowd size of 375,000, whereas the city's policy commissioner put the crowd size at around 100,000 (CNN 2003b). In this case, the organizers and the police commissioner disagreed on the exact number of demonstrators but agreed on the order of magnitude: The event numbered in the hundreds of thousands. Thus, rather than attempting to decide on an exact number of demonstrators, we examine how the order of magnitude of antiwar protests in the Unites States changed over time.

We construct a measure of protest size based on reports by protest organizers, newspaper accounts, and our own direct observation of events in the field. This measure combines protest of wars in both Iraq and Afghanistan because these protests were generally combined and were sponsored by same organizations. In Figure 2.2, we chart the order of magnitude of the largest protest held each month in which there were national or nationally coordinated protests. For example, in the month of March 2003, there were widespread protests in cities across the United States. Some of these protests were small, perhaps consisting of a dozen or so people. Yet, some of these protests reached the hundreds of thousands, so we report "hundreds of thousands" as the order of magnitude for March 2003. We document national or nationally coordinated antiwar protests in thirty-eight months between September 2001 and December 2012. In only six of these cases do we observe some disagreement among the sources regarding the order of magnitude of the demonstrations. In these instances, we resolve the conflict either by splitting the difference between the sources or by making a judgment based on our direct observation of the event. In cases when neither organizers nor media offered estimates (usually when rallies were small in scale), we report estimates based on our own direct assessment of the crowds.

It is important to note that plotting order of magnitude (as opposed to actual counts) of protests greatly compresses the variation in the vertical axis of Figure 2.2. If we had plotted actual protest size, then the decline of the movement would appear much more dramatic than it does in this figure.

Our first observation from Figure 2.2 is that between September 2001 and December 2006, the antiwar movement regularly organized demonstrations that drew crowds in the tens and hundreds of thousands of participants. There were at least six demonstrations during this period that drew upward of 100,000 participants, though crowds in the United States never reached the millions, as they did in some European nations (Walgrave and Rucht 2010). From 2001 to 2006, the antiwar movement was truly a mass movement.

The antiwar movement drew a crowd in the hundreds of thousands to Washington, D.C., immediately after the rise of Democratic majorities in Congress in the November 2006 elections. However, after this rally, we never again observed an antiwar protest in the hundreds of thousands.[5] The decline in the size of protest at this particular time is curious, as it coincides with the surge of the U.S. troop presence in Iraq. Given that the president increased troops – contrary to the expressed will of the voters in the November 2006 congressional elections – we would have expected protests to increase in size if involvement in them was based primarily on public reactions to policy. But *the movement declined at a time that policy moved in the opposite direction of the movement's aims and even though the White House was still under Republican control.*

The election of Barack Obama similarly marked a further decrease in the scale of the antiwar movement. The size of antiwar protests fell immediately after Obama's election. Only a few hundred people participated in the antiwar movement events outside Obama's inauguration. Thus, protests declined before Obama called any troops home from Iraq and at the same time that he ordered a surge in Afghanistan. It is worth noting that the decline during this period is very large, a fact that is somewhat obscured by using the order-of-magnitude scale.

---

[5] We estimated a regression with Newy-West standard errors (Newy and West 1987) that indicates that the order of magnitude of protests occurring after November 2006 was significantly smaller than that of those held before that date ($p \leq 0.001$).

After Obama's election, the antiwar movement never again organized a protest with tens or hundreds of thousands of participants. Some nationally coordinated protests with marquee speakers, such as Ralph Nader and Dennis Kucinich, drew only a few hundred participants.[6] As the scale of the movement shifted from large to small crowds, protests did not appear to become systematically more or less violent, or more or less mobile. The movement transitioned from a genuine mass political movement to a smaller movement of intensely committed supporters. A primary concern of movement activists became preserving the movement and its values while waiting for another policy window to open (Kingdon 1995).

We wish to be clear that we are not arguing that the antiwar movement died entirely after Obama's inauguration. There was still movement activity after this time, only on a smaller scale. Given this scale shift, many intensely dedicated activists changed their tactics from traditional demonstrations and marches to focus on higher-risk activities, such as those involving highly visible stunts that put participants at personal risk of arrest. For example, activists held "die ins" at the White House and unfurled a large banner outside the DNC (Tucker 2011; Wootson 2012).

A skeptical reader may wonder whether the switch to smaller-scale activity paid dividends for the movement in terms of greater attention by the media. In other words, is it possible that more creative smaller-scale activities were more effective in generating attention than were large public demonstrations? If this concern is valid, then our method of looking at the size of demonstrations would understate the impact of the movement. In order to check for the possibility that the movement adopted higher impact tactics as the size of protests declined, we examine media coverage of the movement over time.

Figure 2.3 charts the mention of the antiwar movement in North American newspapers from 2000 to 2012. We find that there was a baseline level of coverage for the movement of approximately five hundred articles per year, even in years when the antiwar movement was not highly active, such as 2000. In low-activity years, newspaper mentions of the antiwar movement were likely to occur in the context of the biographies of individuals or discussion of historical events. Similar to our analysis of the order of magnitude of antiwar demonstrations, we find that the peak years of the movement were 2003 through 2007, with the highest point in 2003, the year of the U.S. invasion of Iraq. Newspaper coverage of the antiwar movement was much lower from 2008 to 2012. After Obama's election, there was never a year in which more than one thousand articles mentioned the antiwar movement.

We recognize that newspaper articles are not a perfect reflection of social movement activity. For example, newspapers exhibit selection biases regarding

---

[6] A regression with Newy-West standard errors (Newy and West 1987) shows that the order of magnitude of protests occurring after November 2008 was significantly smaller than that of those held before that date ($p \leq 0.001$).

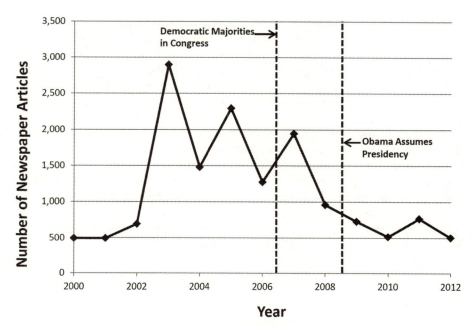

FIGURE 2.3. Mentions of the Antiwar Movement in U.S. Newspapers, 2000–2012
Note: Data are from NewsBank (2013). Searches were performed on U.S. newspapers for the terms "antiwar movement" or "anti-war movement."

what they consider to be newsworthy (Earl, Martin, McCarthy, and Soule 2004). Conflict and violence are more likely to be covered than routine movement activity. However, by looking at newspaper articles, we see that it is unlikely that our analysis of protest size mischaracterizes the antiwar movement as having declined after Obama's election. The smaller-scale activities of the movement did attract the attention of the media. However, the amount of attention that they received per year after Obama's election is only slightly higher than the number of mentions that the movement received in 2000, a year without any substantial antiwar movement activity. Our assessment of the rise and fall of the movement, based on protest size, is not contradicted by the newspaper record.

A skeptical reader may also wonder whether the movement did not decline as much as it shifted from contentious, outsider action to more cooperative, insider actions once the Democrats regained power. We show in Chapter 5, however, that insider actions – such as lobbying – mostly declined along with mass mobilization after January 2007.

In order to reconcile the patterns observed in this chapter, we require a theoretical perspective that accounts for why the mobilization of the antiwar movement appears to depend more on variations in partisan control than on variations in foreign policy. Why did the size of the antiwar movement not grow after the surge in Iraq in 2007? Why did the antiwar movement demobilize before President Obama ordered any troops home? Why did the antiwar movement fail to grow during the surge in Afghanistan? Perhaps it is to be expected that the statements of candidates on the campaign trail are mainly cheap talk; that elected officials in office are unlikely to exhibit as much partisan difference as they appear to have in preelection debates. But, if this is the case, then why do activists mobilize and demobilize *as if* there is a difference between the parties?

We argue that the identification of antiwar movement actors with the Democratic Party discouraged antiwar mobilization once the Democrats held majorities in Washington, D.C. Partisanship filtered the way these movement actors evaluated public policy. In the next chapter, we articulate a perspective on parties and movements that understands their relationship in terms of multiple identities held by interested political actors. In doing so, we provide a framework that allows us to understand the mobilization and demobilization of social movements as a deeply partisan process.

3

Multiple Identities and Party-Movement Interaction

I ... know that Saddam [Hussein] poses no imminent and direct threat to the United States or to his neighbors, that the Iraqi economy is in shambles, that the Iraqi military is a fraction of its former strength, and that in concert with the international community he can be contained until, in the way of all petty dictators, he falls away into the dustbin of history. I know that even a successful war against Iraq will require a U.S. occupation of undetermined length, at undetermined cost, with undetermined consequences. I know that an invasion of Iraq without a clear rationale and without strong international support will only fan the flames of the Middle East, and encourage the worst, rather than best, impulses of the Arab world, and strengthen the recruitment arm of al-Qaida. I am not opposed to all wars. I'm opposed to dumb wars.

Barack Obama, October 2, 2002 (National Public Radio 2009)

The peace rally at Chicago's Daley Plaza on October 2, 2002, was among the first of a new wave of antiwar demonstrations against the Bush administration's plans for Iraq. According to an article appearing in the *Chicago Tribune*, approximately one thousand people attended the rally, which was organized by a newly formed coalition, Chicagoans Against War in Iraq (Glauber 2002). The same *Tribune* article neglected to mention that among the speakers at the event was Barack Obama, an African-American state senator from the thirteenth district of Illinois, pictured in Figure 3.1.

Obama's speech rejected the invasion of Iraq, along with the rationale for invasion offered by the Bush administration, though it did not reject all wars. Obama criticized the Iraq War as a "dumb war" and a "rash war" that attempted "to distract us from a rise in the uninsured, a rise in the poverty rate, a drop in the median income – to distract us from corporate scandals and a stock market that has just gone through the worst month since the Great Depression" (National Public Radio 2009). At the same time, Obama noted

FIGURE 3.1. Illinois State Senator Barack Obama Speaks at an Antiwar Rally in Chicago
(© 2002 Marc PoKempner, used by permission)

the potential good that could result from war, such as the Civil War's role in
"driv[ing] the scourge of slavery from our soil" (National Public Radio 2009).
He concluded the speech by noting, "We may have occasion in our lifetime to
once again rise up in defense of our freedom, and pay the wages of war. But we
ought not—we will not—travel down that hellish path blindly" (National
Public Radio 2009). Former SDS leader Carl Davidson, who was a member
of the committee that invited Obama to speak, took note of the particular
framing that Obama adopted. He recalled that "my friend nudge[d] me [during
Obama's speech] and he said, 'Who is this speech for? It's not for this crowd.'
So now we know that he was really speaking to a much broader audience and
he had much bigger things in mind" (Davidson 2008).

Barack Obama had gained notice among leading antiwar activists for his
long-standing activism in the Chicago community. Obama's bona fides in
Chicago included work as a community organizer, service on foundation
boards, a civil rights law practice, and years in the Illinois state legislature
(Obama 2004). Carl Davidson recalled:

I was working with a group called ACORN [Association of Community Organizations
for Reform Now], and an organization called the New Party, and we were looking for
candidates who would cross-endorse our platform, which was mainly centered on equal
school funding and the fight for the living wage.... So this young kid from Project Vote
shows up, Barack Obama, and we interviewed him to see if his positions were in tune
with ours. It was me and about eight ACORN ladies. I remember thinking, boy, this kid

is very smart. He answers each question very carefully and he says just the right thing. I said he'll probably go far, he might even be *Alderman* someday [laughter]. (Davidson 2008, emphasis in original)

Obama impressed many activists whom he knew as being genuinely committed to progressive causes. We interviewed an activist who had contact with Obama through numerous actions in the fair housing movement in the late 1990s, while she was a student at the University of Chicago. In remembering these times, she remarked, "Now *that* guy was a real radical" (Anonymous 2011, emphasis in original). Obama's positive reputation in movement circles led directly to his invitation to speak at the Chicago peace rally in October 2002 (Davidson 2008).

Although Obama's 2002 speech was not a pure peace treatise, it facilitated his effort to court the antiwar faction within the Democratic Party during the 2008 Democratic primaries and caucuses by documenting his early stand against the war. During a Democratic candidates' debate at South Carolina State University in April 2007, Obama declared, "I am proud that I opposed this war from the start, because I thought that it would lead to the disastrous conditions that we've seen on the ground in Iraq" (Obama 2007). He used this history to buffer claims about his priorities as president. During a debate at the College of Southern Nevada in January 2008, Obama promised, "My first job as president of the United States is going to be to call in the Joint Chiefs of Staff and say, 'You've got a new mission,' and that is to responsibly, carefully, but deliberately start to phase out our involvement there" (Obama 2008b). From the lesson of Iraq, Obama offered better judgment on issues of war and peace. In a February 2008 debate jointly sponsored by MTV (Music Television) and MySpace, Obama told an Internet audience that "the Iraq War was not well thought through, it is not a war that had to be fought, and I will not make those same mistakes when I'm the president of the United States" (Obama 2008a).

Obama was not a hard-core peace candidate, as might be an apt description of Congressman Dennis Kucinich (D-OH), one of Obama's opponents in the 2008 Democratic presidential primary contest. Yet Obama relied heavily on a clearly articulated antiwar stance in his nomination battle against Hillary Clinton (Walker 2008, p. 1096). Indeed, it would have been reasonable for Democratic voters to walk away from the 2008 primaries with a strong impression that Obama had aligned himself with the antiwar faction within the Democratic Party, if not necessarily with the formally organized antiwar movement.

The political career of Barack Obama embodies the party in the street. Obama's identity is linked both to social movements and to a political party. He "grew up" in, and was cultivated by, social movements. He sought and achieved numerous elected offices as a Democrat. Obama's success was driven jointly by movements and parties. Movements provided training, resources, and legitimacy to his electoral efforts. The Democratic Party established organizational structures that enabled Obama to win elections. Just as it is hard to imagine how Obama could have won the presidency in 2008 without being a member of the Democratic Party, it is also hard to imagine how he would have framed his candidacy in the absence of strong movement ties. However, in January 2009, the question of how Obama would govern as president was an open one. Would he stay true to his social movement roots? Would he cater more to promoting the success of the Democratic Party, even if that meant moderating some of his issue positions? How would he balance these multiple identities?

Barack Obama's biography is distinctive in many ways. Yet, in some respects, his biography is typical of many people who become activists in social movements and political parties. People generally do not wake up one day and say, "I'm going to be a committed, long-term activist in the Democratic Party" or "I'm going to devote my life to working for the antiwar movement." Rather, they are drawn in to specific events by an interest in an issue or by the compelling nature of a candidate's campaign. The initial draw to activism may arise from no more than the desire to spend the afternoon helping a friend (Munson 2008). Over time, as opportunities present themselves, their biographies weave in and out of the spaces created by political parties and social movements. Like Obama, they develop identities that attach – in varying degrees – both to parties and to movements (McAdam and Paulsen 1993).

Previous scholars have documented the critical role that identity plays in the engagement and mobilization of activists into the work of political parties (Green, Palmquist, and Schickler 2002) and social movements (Gamson 1991). Ann Mische's (2008) book on the development of youth activism in Brazil makes the important point that the intersection of partisan and movement identities can play a vital role in movement politics. Our book builds upon these insights and extends them to reveal how intersecting partisan and movement identities can motivate both the mobilization and the demobilization of mass movements. This contribution is broadly important to the study of collective action. As Francesca Polletta and James Jasper (2001, p. 299) note in their review of the field, "We have little evidence about how individuals sort out and combine different sources of identity." The present volume provides such evidence by offering a theoretical and empirical basis for understanding when and how individuals and organizations combine and choose between partisan and movement identities.

In grounding our analysis of party-movement alliances in the attitudes and behaviors of individual actors, we explain how systematic shifts in individual identities have the potential to yield macrolevel consequences for parties and movements. Much of the scholarly literature on party-movement interaction concentrates on institutions and macrolevel processes but neglects to investigate the behavior of individual actors very closely (see, for example, Frymer 1999; Goldstone 2003; Kriesi, Koopmas, Duyvendak, and Giugni 1995; Schwartz 2006, 2010). However, once the behavior of individual actors is taken into account, macrolevel analyses of party-movement alliances are difficult to understand satisfactorily. Parties and movements may form alliances as organizations, but the fate of those agreements rests on the behavior of individual, autonomous actors that may not feel bound by these agreements. Theories of party-movement alliances that treat parties and movements as a whole as the units of analysis (cf. Schwartz 2006; 2010; Schlozman 2015) must be revised to take into account individual behavior in alliances that form from loose collaborations of decentralized actors.

In order to explain how intersecting partisan and movement identities can be consequential for political mobilization, this chapter explains how the presence of multiple, relevant social identities matters for actors' engagement in parties and movements by grassroots activists, political elites, and organizational actors. Drawing upon scholarship in the intersectionality tradition, we theorize why partisan identities tend to dominate movement identities in the United States. Finally, we situate our partisan theory alongside contemporary social movement theories to derive expectations for movement mobilization.

IDENTIFYING WITH PARTIES AND MOVEMENTS

Identity is a powerful social force. At its extremes, identity can motivate individuals to commit acts of violence or to exercise great compassion. On a daily basis, identity affects the food people eat, how organizations make political contributions, and who grieves for whom after tragedy strikes. Identities may be actively contested, as when transgendered persons challenge society's definition of gender. Or, identities may be easily accepted, as when a person of English ancestry is considered to be "white." Identities may change rapidly, as during periods of political transformation. For example, identification with the lower "99 percent" of the income distribution spread quickly in 2011 along with the popularity of the Occupy Wall Street movement. Or identities may remain stable for hundreds of years as an ethnic group maintains continual residence in a particular geographic region. But what exactly is identity? How does an actor acquire one? And what difference does this make for politics?

Identity is the recognition of membership by an actor in a social category (Abrams and Hogg 1990; Stets and Burke 2000). It may be held by either individuals or organizations (Albert and Whetten 1985; Heaney 2004b). Identities depend both upon how an actor understands itself, as well as on its reputation among relevant audiences (such as family, friends, the media, or competitors). They fluctuate with the boundaries of social categories, which change over time as understandings of the categories evolve. Importantly, identities need not be dichotomous. Actors may have tenuous or conditional attachments to an identity. For example, a person may identify somewhat with his/her Slavic ethnic background but not think about it very often and find that others rarely recognize it. Along these lines, identities vary in their *salience*, as some may be very important to actors, while others may be much less important (Burke and Stets 2009, p. 41). This salience may depend largely on how closely connected the actor is to the social groups associated with the identities. An individual may think more about his/her Slavic ethnic identity when s/he interacts more with family members from the Slavic side of the family, but think less about that identity when interacting with coworkers.

Acquisition of identities occurs through processes of socialization (Lalonde, Jones, and Stroink 2008). Socialization processes encourage actors to identify themselves closely with the symbols, practices, and hierarchies of the fields in which they participate. Guided by unarticulated "moods and dispositions," actors internalize what is valued by others in the field and pursue sanctioned goals using the resources within the field (Bourdieu 1977). Actors then adopt (or reject) identities as they learn what the identities mean and how they compare to their (changing) self-understandings. Observers of an actor, too, learn identity standards – models of what qualifies as possession of a particular identity – and reach judgments about whether the actor meets a particular standard. At times, an actor may attempt to forge new identities when the most prevalent identities fail to capture the way in which the actor imagines its relationship to other groups in society. These new identities emerge and become socially relevant through the process by which the actor and its audiences agree on – or come to dispute – the categories of which the actor should be considered a member.

In this section, we argue that political parties and social movements are common bases for identities among the individuals and organizations that have contact with them. Identities may also be based on an explicit rejection of partisan or movement affiliations. For example, an activist may not affirmatively identify with the Democratic Party, but she or he may unequivocally reject identification with the Republican Party. The possession of partisan or movement identities affects the behavior of political actors by shaping their loyalties, their knowledge, the frameworks through which they interpret political reality, and the kinds of political activities that they believe to be legitimate or illegitimate.

Political scientists have long noted the fundamental role that political parties play in shaping the political identities of individuals. V. O. Key (1948, p. 596) observes that "once established, party allegiance and loyalty seem to have a remarkable persistence." He attributes this persistence to the socialization that takes place primarily in the family and, secondarily, in the community at large. In their seminal study, *The American Voter*, Angus Campbell and his colleagues (Campbell, Converse, Miller, and Stokes 1960, p. 121) ground partisan identities firmly in social psychological theories, noting that identities "characterize the individual's affective orientation to an important group-object in his environment." More recent work by Donald Green, Bradley Palmquist, and Eric Schickler (2002) stresses that partisan identity is fruitfully understood as an individual's self-categorization as a member of a party, which is a social group. Individuals feel that belongingness as a matter of degree. Nancy

Rosenblum (2008, p. 323) clarifies that "party [identification] refers to an individual voter's avowed affiliation with a political party and has both cognitive and affective elements. It is a matter of personal identification, not legal status or membership." Individuals may feel a close attachment to the party or may have only weak feelings of membership. Of course, individuals may not identify as a member of any party. For some, consciously rejecting partisanship is an important feature of a person's identity.

According to the social group view of party identity, an individual's *identification* with a party is quite distinct from her or his *evaluation* of the party. Individuals may change their evaluations of parties regularly as they receive new information about the parties' performance in office. They change their party identification itself much less frequently, as it is their connection to a social group to which they feel they belong. Research by Matthew Levendusky (2009) finds that when individuals have a conflict between the policy stands taken by their party and their personal beliefs, they are substantially more likely to change their personal beliefs than to change their partisan identification. Occasionally, individuals change their partisan identities because, upon substantial reflection, they decide that their personal ideology is more compatible with membership in another party, or in no party at all. However, more often than not, party switching is presaged by switches by prominent others in the individual's self-perceived social group (Levendusky 2009). That is, individuals are most likely to switch their partisan identities when they perceive that doing so is necessary in order to retain another, more salient social identity. Similarly, Thomas Carsey and Geoffrey Layman (2006) find that at least some members of the mass electorate switch their issue preferences to align with their partisan identification, even when that issue is highly salient to them. They conclude that "the fact that partisanship leads to changes in attitudes on issues like abortion, government provision of services, and government help for blacks for many citizens clearly runs counter to the idea that party identification is largely a summary of other evaluations. Our results demonstrate that party identification indeed serves as a perceptual screen that shapes attitudes toward policy issues for many citizens" (Carsey and Layman 2006, p. 474).

Partisan identity has far-reaching implications for how individuals think about and participate in politics. Most obviously, partisan identity has long been recognized as a strong predictor of vote choice (Campbell, Converse, Miller, and Stokes 1960). People who identify with a party generally have warmer feelings toward the members of their party than toward members of other parties (Green, Palmquist, and Schickler 2002, p. 27). Further, people who identify as members of parties have stronger emotional reactions to political events and are more likely to participate in institutional politics (by voting, for example) than people who do not identify as members of parties (Green, Palmquist, and Schickler 2002, p. 49).

Partisan identities play an important role in shaping the way that people receive and process information about the world. People filter information about everyday events through the lens provided by their party membership. Research by Larry Bartels (2002) demonstrates that individuals who have competing partisan identities interpret "objective" political events quite differently. After analyzing data on citizens' perceptions of objective political conditions (such as the rate of unemployment) during presidential administrations from Jimmy Carter to George W. Bush, Bartels (2002, p. 117) concludes that "partisan bias in political perceptions plays a crucial role in perpetuating and reinforcing sharp differences in opinion between Democrats and Republicans." Partisanship not only filters reality for partisans, but has the potential to reinforce misperceptions about reality, even when individuals are subsequently presented with factually correct information. In an ingenious experiment by Brendan Nyhan and Jason Reifler (2010), subjects were exposed to mock news articles that reported misleading claims by a politician (about weapons of mass destruction in Iraq, the effect of tax cuts on federal revenue, and federal stem cell policy). When a correction was offered to the misleading information, partisans resisted accepting the correction if the misleading claim was consistent with their prior partisan worldview. In some cases, correcting the story backfired by strengthening the subject's belief in the misleading claims. The kind of biased reasoning uncovered in these studies results from a psychology of motivated skepticism in which individuals readily accept information that conforms to their prior beliefs but extensively question information that disconfirms those beliefs (Taber and Lodge 2006). Partisan identities help individuals to construct views of the world that lead them to continually reaffirm the perspectives advocated by their home party.

Party elites are molded by their party labels in much the same way that ordinary citizens are. The leaders of political parties regularly make decisions to change their party's position on issues that are controversial and salient. These changes may be inspired, in part, by the political intellectuals who craft and refine broad ideological statements for the parties to follow (Noel 2013). Changes almost always aim to broaden the party's appeal to constituencies that they believe will be electorally consequential. In *The Politics of Women's Rights*, Christina Wolbrecht (2000) provides an example of how a sequence of such incremental changes can eventually manifest as a major reversal of party positions. Specifically, she recounts how the Republican and Democratic Parties switched places on issues of women's rights during the 1960s and 1970s. Democrats transitioned from a position of neutrality or opposition to women's rights, to a much more supportive, liberal posture. In contrast, Republicans transitioned from a liberal or neutral stance to one of opposition. These kinds of changes generate dilemmas for elected politicians who won their offices through stands that they have taken on these and other issues.

What does a politician do when she or he is left behind by the party on a key issue? One option is to defect to the opposing party. It is rare that politicians do that, however. Rather, as David Karol (2009) shows, politicians are much more likely to delicately adjust their issue positions to the party's new stand. Some politicians refuse to conform and are swept out of office or retire. But Karol's examination of longitudinal data on legislators' policy positions reveals that adaptation is much more common than replacement. As was demonstrated for individual citizens, politicians also seek to retain membership in their parties, social groups to which they have firm social attachments. Politicians who elect to leave the group – especially those who hold prominent positions – are met with great scorn by their former colleagues. Partisan fidelity is among the most closely held of elite political values.

Like individuals, political organizations may develop identities that are closely related to a specific political party, or they may cultivate a reputation for political independence. In some cases, organizations explicitly brand themselves with a party label and devote themselves to the service of one party. For example, the National Federation of Republican Women, Log Cabin Republicans, Progressive Democrats of America, and College Democrats of America have all indelibly linked their identities to a particular party. A few organizations, such the Club for Growth and EMILY's List, are self-consciously founded with the intention of influencing the tenor of a particular party (Murakami 2008). Nonetheless, the overwhelming majority of political organizations do not broadcast their partisan ties so unambiguously. Instead, they tend to prefer to anchor their identities on the constituencies they represent and/or the issues on which they have their expertise (Browne 1990; Heaney 2004b, 2007).

Despite organizational efforts to maintain the pretense of nonpartisanship, many organizations become associated with a party. If most observers think of an organization as tied to a party, then it has a de facto partisan identity. Examples of such organizations include the National Rifle Association (for the Republicans) and the National Organization for Women (for the Democrats). As information about these partisan affiliations diffuses through social networks, individuals have a propensity to sort themselves into organizations that reflect their partisan outlook. For example, research on delegates attending the Democratic and Republican National Conventions in 2008 shows that there is relatively little overlap in organizational membership between the two parties. According to Michael Heaney and his colleagues (Heaney, Masket, Miller, and Strolovitch 2012), only 1.78 percent of organizational comemberships between delegates crossed party lines, while only 2.74 percent of the ties between organizations sharing common delegates were bipartisan in nature. Similarly, organizations betray their true natures through the behavior of their staff members. Research by Gregory Koger and Jennifer Nicoll Victor (2009) uncovers that more than 85 percent of organizational lobbyists gave 95 percent or more of their campaign contributions only to members of one party.

Once rumors surface about the true partisan identities of organizations, the ability of organizations to navigate the political process is affected, both positively and negatively. When joining lobbying coalitions, organizations carefully weigh the partisan reputations of their potential partners, lest they offend their core supporters (Heaney 2004a). In debates over Social Security and Medicare, for instance, suspicions about partisan bias by the AARP (formerly the American Association of Retired Persons) raised questions about its trustworthiness in negotiations (Lynch 2011, p. 173). In the short run, strong ties between an organization and a dominant party may enable the organization to boost its influence over public policy (Heaney 2006). In the longer run, however, having identities that are closely wedded to a single political party may have the reverse effect. In his investigation of Congress and the farm lobby from 1919 to 1981, John Mark Hansen (1991) demonstrates that the gradual evolution of farm groups from a position of bipartisanship to an alliance with the Republican Party undercut their reputations as reliable and neutral sources of information on agricultural policy. Consequently, their influence over the policy process declined. Partisan identities cut both ways for political organizations.

Identity is an integral component of movement politics, as it is of party politics. Analogous to parties, both individuals and organizations develop attachments and loyalties to movements. Within the parlance of social movement studies, these attachments and loyalties form *collective identities* that refer to "emergent shared belief[s] about membership, boundaries, and activities of [social movements] held by movement members" (Stryker, Owens, and White 1990, p. 6). However, identity operates quite differently in the movement context than it does in the partisan context.

Political parties are mass objects in the American political system. They spend billions of dollars each decade on political advertising. They are the subject of constant media attention. Virtually everyone who lives in the United States experiences substantial exposure to political parties over the course of her or his lifetime. In contrast, social movements often fly beneath the radar of public attention (McCarthy, McPhail, and Smith 1996). Occasionally, they receive coverage by the mass media, particularly when they are in some way creative, deviant, or violent. But regular media coverage is the exception rather than the rule. Movements rarely have extensive funds to spend on media campaigns or advertising. More often than not, citizens learn about movements directly by having personal contact with them. The upshot of these differences is that partisan identities are heavily mediated by elite institutions and penetrate the society deeply, while movement identities are formed more intimately by movement actors themselves and penetrate the society unevenly.

Work that aims to build, sustain, and extend movement identities is core to the everyday mission of movement actors. Actors often begin to identify with movements concurrently with the formation of collective identities by movements. Collective identity provides actors with something to connect with. William Gamson (1991) explains that these identities emerge through interaction of movement participants who negotiate a sense of the "we" through engaging in collective action (see also Armstrong 2002; Melucci 1989).

Individuals' movement identities are usually formed directly through personal interaction with the movement. Ziad Munson (2008) provides a vivid example of this process in his ethnography of the prolife movement. He finds that individuals are seldom prompted to join the movement because of preexisting prolife beliefs. Instead, they are attracted to the movement through their social ties (see also Blee 2002). Their friends, neighbors, fellow church members, and others invite them to participate in activities of the movement. Once they begin participation, they have the opportunity to develop a deeper understanding of the movement, its beliefs, arguments, and ideology. Through this active participation, individuals develop movement identities. This finding underscores the essential role of movement organizations in promoting individual identification with movements. While people certainly have direct contact with political parties – through volunteer opportunities or contact by a canvasser, for example – direct interaction with movement organizations is indispensable for the formation of movement identities in a way that is not the case for partisan identification.

The construction and possession of movement identities influence how individuals act in and toward social movements. Strong movement identities help to foster the solidarity and commitment that generate individual mobilization (Hunt and Benford 2004). Movements may be able to sustain participation by their adherents over long periods if they can reinforce activists' identities (Nepstad 2004). Movement identities are closely associated with activists' tastes for certain tactics and help to stimulate creative participation (Jasper 1997). At the same time, movement identities may contribute to movement demobilization as well. Francesca Polletta and James Jasper (2001, p. 292) observe that "one of the chief causes of movement decline is that collective identity stops lining up with the movement. We stop believing that the movement 'represents' us." When movement identities are fragile, movements may be unable to maintain critical mass.

Movement and political elites often establish strong movement identities, as do rank-and-file activists. This chapter begins with the case of Barack Obama, who was well known in movement circles before he was ever a candidate for public office. While Obama's route into public office is not the most common one, it is certainly not uncommon for political leaders to have long-standing movement identities decades before they enter public life (Botetzagias and Van Schuur 2012). For example, many elected officials in the United States have had prior backgrounds in movements for labor, women's rights, civil rights, peace, the right to life, the Tea Party, the flat tax, and other causes. As these backgrounds become known, they can have positive and/or negative consequences for individuals' lives, careers, and future political involvement (McAdam 1989; Taylor and Raeburn 1995). Individuals who have strong movement identities may make a career of activism. However, intensive involvement may also lead to burnout and steer individuals away from future activism (Fisher 2006).

The organizations that support social movements often identify closely with these movements. It is much less common for organizations to eschew movement identification deliberately than it is for them to avoid partisan identification. Indeed, the proliferation of supporting organizations is one of the principal ways that social movements manifest themselves (Zald and Ash 1966). As movements diffuse and evolve over time, it is not uncommon for hundreds of organizations to affiliate with a single movement (Minkoff 1995; Nownes 2004).

Organizations deploy movement identities in ways that are consequential for movements. The nature of organizational identities makes a difference for their ability to mobilize constituencies in support of their cause. For example, organizations whose identities link to more than one movement are often critical in the process of mobilizing constituencies across movement boundaries (Goss and Heaney 2010; Heaney and Rojas 2014; Meyer and Whittier 1994; Vasi 2006, 2011). Strategic use of organizational identities may help movements to frame arguments against their opponents. For example, Lisa Leitz (2014) shows how military peace movement organizations leverage their identities as part of groups that are expected to support war in order to frame counterhegemonic arguments for peace. Of course, organizational identities need not necessarily serve a positive function for movements. For example, links between the organization ACORN and cases of voter fraud in 2006 became an impediment to the mobilization of low-income constituencies during the 2008 presidential election in the United States (Dreier and Martin 2010). Whether or not they serve the goals of the movement, organizational identities are a linchpin for movement action.

This section explains that identity is a mechanism that links actors to political parties and social movements. Actors develop attachments to parties and movements because they represent social groups in which they have a sense of belonging. These attachments matter for how actors behave in the political world. Knowledge of identity allows us to formulate expectations about behavior in partisan and movement contexts. When actors possess strong partisan or movement identities they are more likely to contribute to the goals of these fields than when these identities are weak or conflicted. We argue that actors are more likely to develop strong partisan identities than strong movement identities, though organizations advertise their movement identities more readily than their partisan identities.

Like much of the scholarly literature on partisan and movement identities (see, for example, Bartels 2002; Gamson 1991; Green, Palmquist, and Schickler 2002; Hunt and Benford 2004; Levendusky 2009; Polletta and Jasper 2001), this section skirts the issue of what happens when actors have multiple identities, especially identities that overlap with one another. But the presence of multiple, overlapping identities is at the heart of this book. Actors that hold both partisan and movement identities make up the party in the street. In the following section, we consider how the presence of overlapping or intersectional identities affects the motivations of actors to participate in politics.

MULTIPLE IDENTITIES AND INTERSECTIONALITY

If actors have the possibility of identifying with either a party or a movement, then the question arises as to what happens when they identify with *both* a party and a movement. If the party and the movement both call them to do the same thing, then no conflict arises, and it seems likely that the actor will do what the party and the movement are advocating. In fact, the likelihood that the actor will conform to the call is increased by the fact that the request was made by two separate sources, rather than just from one. In this case, partisan and movement identities reinforce each other. But what happens if the party asks the actor to do one thing and the movement asks the exact opposite? How will the conflict likely be resolved in light of these cross-pressures?

Insight into this question is provided by the German sociologist Georg Simmel (1955). Simmel does not refer to "identity," per se, but his concept of "group-affiliations" is very similar (though not equivalent) to what we mean by identity. Simmel explains that the possibility for a single individual to have simultaneous memberships in a wide array of social groups is a marker of modernity. The social position of the individual, then, is determined by "the groups that 'intersect' in his person by virtue of his affiliation with them" (Simmel 1955, p. 150). He theorizes that intersecting group-affiliations present both risks and benefits for the individual:

It is true that external and internal conflicts arise through the multiplicity of group-affiliations, which threaten the individual with psychological tension or even a schizophrenic break. But it is also true that multiple group-affiliations can strengthen the individual and reinforce the integration of his personality. Conflicting and integrating tendencies are mutually reinforcing. (Simmel 1955, pp. 141–2)

From this point of view, an essential challenge for the individual living in society is to balance the cross-pressures created by identification with multiple social groups (Lazarsfeld, Berelson, and Gaudet 1948, pp. xxi–xxii). The individual wants to maintain each group affiliation, but the presence of conflict may make that difficult or impossible.

The tensions that Simmel identifies are an issue not only for the actor, but also for the social groups of which it is a member. For the political scientist David Truman (1971), overlapping group memberships pose a problem of cohesion for both groups. According to Truman (1971, p. 159), if one of the groups (**A**) finds that a large percentage of its members are also members of another group (**B**), then the cohesion of **A** is threatened any time an issue arises that is at odds with the interests of **B**, and vice versa. Intersecting loyalties raise the question of whether a group can really count on the support of all of its members. Since the loyalties of actors to groups **A** and **B** are evoked as a result of intermittent events, "the direction and intensity of overlapping and conflict are constantly changing.... Both individuals and groups, therefore, are constantly in the process of readjustment" (Truman 1971, pp. 161–2; see also Schattschneider 1935, p. 163). Intersecting memberships are sources of dynamism for both groups.

While a number of scholars turn to multiple identities in their accounts of social dynamics (see, for example, Gould 1995; Mische 2008; Padgett and McLean 2006), we argue that research on the intersectionality of disadvantaged identities offers special insight on how these identities interact with one another. According to Ange-Marie Hancock (2007, p. 63), the study of intersectionality is the investigation of the "simultaneous and interacting effects of gender, race, class, sexual orientation, and national origin as categories of difference." In some respects, this research tradition is a specialized extension of Simmel's (1955) analysis of the effects of overlapping group-affiliations (see also McAdam and Paulsen 1993). However, by choosing to focus on identities associated with disadvantage and difference, and by self-consciously adopting a critical perspective on the subject, research on intersectionality (see, for example, Chun, Lipsitz, and Shin 2013; Cohen 1999; Collins 2000; Combahee River Collective 1995; Crenshaw 1989; hooks 1984; McCall 2005; Strolovitch 2007, 2012; Weldon 2011) generates a number of general insights that inform our thinking on the intersection of parties and movements.

Scholars of intersectionality stress that there is a distinct effect of interaction between overlapping identities. A new identity has the potential to develop out of two intersecting identities to create a unique form of experience. Ange-Marie Hancock (2007) offers the example of "black women" as a category that is meaningfully different from African Americans as a group or women as a group. Specifically, black women may have distinctive experiences with respect to violence, unwanted pregnancy, and workplace discrimination in comparison to blacks in general or women in general. Thus, the effects of multiple identities are multiplicative, rather than additive. To reflect this possibility, Hancock (2007, p. 66) "argues for new conceptualizations of categories and their role in politics, rather than seeing an abolition of the categories themselves."

Social movements may be an especially good way to represent the marginalized social groups that are forged by the intersection of multiple identities (Chun, Lipsitz, and Shin 2013). In her analysis of public policy and the women's movement, Laurel Weldon (2011) argues that most democratic institutions do a poor job of representing marginalized intersectional identities because they tend to concentrate on identities that make up a plurality of the electorate. Electing a heterosexual white person to Congress is more likely, in most districts, than electing a homosexual Latino person, simply because heterosexual whites are more likely to constitute a plurality of the electorate than are homosexual Latinos. However, social movement organizations are one way in which these interests can gain representation. Since it is relatively easy to create organizations at the intersections of these categories, social movement organizations form a wide variety of hybrid organizations that fill this niche (Armstrong 2002; Goss and Heaney 2010; Heaney and Rojas 2014). Forming an organization to represent homosexual Latinos is more easily accomplished than is electing a member of this group to Congress.

Despite the constitution of new social categories, actors existing at the intersection of multiple identities may experience discrimination at the hands of actors who are part of one identity group but do not have intersectional identities. Actors who share a collective identity may also share a belief in a "linked fate" among those who possess the identity, which leads actors to assume that others who have the identity are homogeneous with respect to the defining characteristics of the identity (Dawson 1994). As a result, they may attack those actors who violate the homogeneity assumption by expressing an intersecting identity. In her study of AIDS in the African-American community, Cathy Cohen (1999) documents the ways that gay black men, in particular, experience discrimination within the black community because of their expressed deviation from the community's heterosexual norms. Informal sanctions by community members against subgroups often persist over long periods, even though the ways in which these sanctions are expressed change as institutions evolve (Strolovitch 2012).

Dara Strolovitch (2007) demonstrates that similar processes operate at the organizational level. In her study of advocacy groups that address issues of race, class, and gender, Strolovitch develops the concepts of *advantaged subgroups* and *disadvantaged subgroups*. She shows that even if an advocacy organization formed for the purpose of redressing disadvantage, distinctions emerge between advantaged and disadvantaged subgroups that guide organizational policies, behavior, and decision making. The interests of advantaged subgroups are more likely to be an organizational priority, while disadvantaged subgroups tend to be ignored or deprioritized. For example, in a group dedicated to representing African Americans generally, women's interests are likely to be subordinated to those of men. In an organization dedicated to women's rights, black women are neglected. In an organization founded to advance the goals of black women, low-income black women receive less attention, and so on.

Insights from the intersectionality research tradition can be extended to the party in the street. Since intersectionality research suggests that intersectional identities may become meaningful identities themselves, we expect the party in the street often to become a recognized social category. To this end, we expect self-identified partisans to emerge regularly in social movements and movement activists to become visible within political parties. Individuals who identify at these intersections are recognized as such by other actors in the movement and the party and are treated differently on this basis. For example, dual identifications may affect the likelihood that they are recognized to speak at meetings and whether their projects are allocated organizational resources. Movement activists stand out for their movement sympathies in partisan contests on the basis of their organizational affiliations, public statements, or displays of signs, T-shirts, or buttons. Likewise, partisans stand out for their party loyalties in movement contexts. If these expectations are fulfilled, then organizations are created to represent these intersections. Examples include organizations dedicated exclusively to the representation of lesbian and gay Republicans (such as Log Cabin Republicans) or prochoice Democrats (such as EMILY's List).

The concepts of advantaged/disadvantaged subgroups are also directly applicable to the party in the street. Given the enormous comparative advantage that the major parties have over movements (with regard to financial resources and media coverage, for example), we expect that partisans tend to be an advantaged subgroup and movement activists tend to be a disadvantaged subgroup during party-movement interaction. We expect that within political parties, movement interests tend to be overlooked and deprioritized when they conflict with broader party objectives. This marginalization occurs at multiple levels within the party, such as in the selection of candidates, development of platform planks, and allocation of financial resources. Likewise, within movements, we expect that partisan interests tend to be advantaged, and movement interests set aside, in cases of conflict. This priviledge extends throughout the work of movements, such as in the selection of issues, the appointment of partisans to boards and coalition leadership positions, and financial expenditures. Examples include the Democratic Party's neglecting to pursue women's interest's "for the good of the party" (Freeman 1987) and the labor movement's diverting attention from workplace organizing to campaign for Democratic candidates (Francia 2010).

In her analysis of the politics of partisan identification, Nancy Rosenblum similarly concludes that partisan identification tends to dominate movement identities. For Rosenblum (2008, pp. 347–8), parties gain power because they represent broader social groups than movements:

Partisans avow identification with others in a political group some of whose members also belong to narrower identity and interest groups – environmentalist and lesbian and gay groups, Christian conservatives and sectoral business associations. But partisanship alters these, often transcends them, and for many it has the character to and force of an original, self-standing political identity.... In the United States and other established democracies today, partisanship cannot be understood simply as a vehicle or expression of some other anterior social identities. Partisanship is not epiphenomenal. Once partisan identity is formed, it has independent life force.

While movements may articulate concerns around one issue (or set of issues) that concerns the individual, parties offer people a broader political identity. Because of this breadth, partisan identities are more generally applicable and, thus, more enduring than movement identities.

When the agendas of parties and movements conflict, movement partisans are likely to experience cognitive dissonance as a result (Festinger 1957). They may not explicitly or consciously reject their previous identities (although it is possible that they choose to do so), but they are likely to make decisions that lead them to attribute greater salience to one identity over the other. The discussion in this section suggests that political actors are more likely to resolve this dissonance in favor of their partisan identities than in favor of their movement identities. First, actors' longer-standing connections with parties – and the greater breadth of these ties – make it more likely that they will believe the party over the movement in a case of conflict. Actors are more likely to have a deeper sense of trust in the party than in the movement. Second, parties structure their activities around competition in elections, an orientation that appeals to people's innate sense of competition and their need to make social comparisons (Garcia, Tor, and Schiff 2013; Tajfel, Billig, Bundy, Flament 1971; Turner, Brown, and Tajfel 1979). That is, people are drawn more toward parties, in part, because of their way of addressing and managing conflict (Schattschneider 1960).

Some readers may wonder how our argument differs from claims about the effects of cross-pressures in politics. Intersectional identities have some similarities to cross-pressures, but there are some important differences as well. The term "cross-pressures" is typically used in the study of voting behavior to refer to cases in which voters have conflicting opinions on different issues such that their opinions on issue **A** suggest that they should choose candidate **X**, while their opinions on issue **B** suggest that they should vote for candidate **Y** (see, inter alia, Berelson, Lazarsfeld, and McPhee 1954; Hillygus and Shields 2008; Lazarsfeld, Berelson, and Gaudet 1948; Mutz 2006). People who have intersectional identities may indeed be subject to cross-pressures, but not necessarily. Sometimes intersectional identities generate cross-pressures, but sometimes they are mutually reinforcing. Moreover, cross-pressures are generally analyzed in terms of how they affect an individual's *inner* decision-making processes. Yet, because they are *social* identities, intersectional identities may also affect the way that *other* social actors treat the intersectional actor. This feedback means that intersectional identities affect not only the way an actor sees the world, but also the way the world sees the actor. Finally, the concept of identity generalizes to corporate actors, such as parties and social movement organizations, while the concept of cross-pressures does not.

Some readers may ask how our analysis compares to previous research on the intersectionality of race/ethnicity, sex/gender, sexuality, class, and other dimensions of disadvantage and difference. Perhaps the most substantial difference is that our claims are limited to political contexts, while the intersectional effects of race/ethnicity, sex/gender, and other personal identities often extend much more broadly. The reason for this difference is that actors usually display signs of movement and partisan identifications mostly within political contexts – or, at least, those are the contexts in which partisan/movement identities are considered most relevant. In contrast, race/ethnicity, sex/gender, and other personal identities are usually relevant across the domains of an individual's life. Being a black woman is likely to affect a person's education, career advancement, marriage opportunities, treatment by police, and so on; this identity is not something that she can walk away from. In contrast, a person's identity as a movement partisan is much less likely to matter to these broader aspects of life. Thus, we do not argue that party-movement intersectionality is "the same" as other types of intersectionality. Rather, we argue that the lessons and patterns of intersectionality theory apply to the politics of the party in the street. Similar to the work of Dara Strolovitch (2007), we examine the effects of intersecting identities within particular institutional and organizational settings.

While research to date on intersectionality provides significant guidance into the individual and organizational consequences of intersecting identities, the question remains as to what effect these forces have on the mobilization of social movements more broadly. In the following section, we situate partisan, movement, and movement-partisan identities within the frameworks developed in the extant literature on social movements. By combining these theoretical perspectives, we formulate expectations for the dynamics of social movement mobilization.

SOCIAL MOVEMENT MOBILIZATION

Mobilizing social support for social-movement goals requires varied ingredients. Social movement actors must extract resources from their environments to found organizations, communicate with supporters, advertise, compensate staff, and stage events (McCarthy and Zald 1977). Since no one actor is likely to be able to assemble all the needed resources, actors frequently rely on coalitions as a way to secure what they need (Gerhards and Rucht 1992; Levi and Murphy 2006; Staggenborg 1986). Timing is of the essence. Movement actors are more likely to be successful if they are skilled at recognizing and seizing opportunities in the political system when they are open, rather than delaying until after windows of opportunity close (Eisinger 1973; Meyer and Minkoff 2004; Tarrow 1989). Threats also play an important role in spurring movements to action. If potential supporters of a movement feel threatened by the status quo, they may be more easily convinced to mobilize than if they feel content with the status quo (Berejekian 1997; Hansen 1985; Kahneman, Slovic, and Tversky 1982).

The way that movement actors frame appeals to their potential supporters may be as important as the substance of the appeals themselves. Frames are most likely to promote mobilization when they align closely with the interpretive frameworks already accepted by potential supporters (Snow, Rochford, Worden, and Benford 1986; Taylor and Van Dyke 2004). Actors advance their causes by drawing upon tactics in their repertoires – the set of tools that they have learned how to use, such as demonstrations, lobbying, strikes, and petition drives (Tilly 1978, p. 151). Movement actors are wise to wield these tools with sensitivity to the cultural context of the institutions that enable and constrain their actions (Polletta 2004). Each of these components combines with the others to drive cycles of contention in which mobilization rises and falls over time (Tarrow 1993).

In order to integrate these diverse elements of social movements within a common theoretical framework, Doug McAdam, Sidney Tarrow, and Charles Tilly (2001) advance the *Dynamics of Contention* project (see also McAdam and Tarrow 2011; Tarrow 2011). They endeavor to identify the principal *mechanisms* and *processes* that account for episodes of contention. Mechanisms are "chains of aggregations of actors, problem situations, and habitual responses" that unfold over time to mediate between cause and effect, specifying in a general way how aggregate phenomena are driven by events at a lower order of complexity (Gross 2009, p. 369). For example, elections are a mechanism for allocating state authority to particular persons. Processes are sequences of mechanisms that combine to produce more complex configurations of actors, situations, and responses (McAdam, Tarrow, and Tilly 2001, p. 24). For example, mobilization and demobilization are processes.

Our focus in this study is on the mechanism of *identity shift*. According to McAdam, Tarrow, and Tilly (2001, p. 27), identity shift occurs when there is a change in how actors answer the question "Who am I?" during an episode of contention, either by adopting a new identity or by shifting emphasis from one identity to another. In our case, we observe changes over time in the relative salience of two identities, linked to movements and parties. We seek to understand the effect of these shifts on the process of social movement mobilization. Other scholarly research addresses the consequences of identity shifts within movements (see, for example, Della Porta 2005; Diani and Bison 2004; and Romano 2006) but neglects to examine the type of cross-category identity dynamics on which we concentrate. Thus, our work contributes to the dynamics-of-contention project by elaborating on the operation of the identity-shift mechanism with respect to two commonly intersecting identities. From this exercise, we advance the understanding of identity shift as a mechanism in contentious politics.

Drawing upon key concepts from this chapter – identity, intersectionality, and identity shift – we derive expectations for the dynamics of the party in the street. To start, we are interested in the process of mobilization. What accounts for movement growth? We expect that social movement mobilization is more vibrant when movement actors are able to attract supporters on the basis of partisan affiliation, in addition to their issue sympathies. If the aims of the movement are aligned with the interests of the party, we expect the projection of partisan frames by movement actors to be associated with movement growth. Partisan frames are likely to be especially effective if potential supporters feel threatened by the status quo. In this case, the growth of the movement is coupled with expansion in the size of the party in the street. If the aims of the movement are not aligned with the interests of the party, then the movement may be stymied in its efforts to grow. In this case, movement identifications would have to dominate partisan identifications in order to attract large numbers of supporters; that would be relatively unlikely given the way that parties and movements have coevolved vis-à-vis one another (Oliver and Myers 2003).

When movements use partisan appeals effectively, they may be able to attract supporters who are only marginally concerned with the issue, but who wish to see the party succeed. Supporting the movement, then, becomes one more way to aid the party; movement identities are subordinate to partisan identities. Copartisanship among activists thus becomes a resource for mobilization, much as coethnicity among neighbors in a community is often a resource in promoting the provision of public goods (Chandra 2004; Habyarimarn, Humphreys, Posner, and Weinstein 2009). Movement growth is likely to imply not only larger street demonstrations, but also the formation of coalitions that are broader and more resourceful. Many of the organizations that tend to support the party may wish to join movement coalitions. As these organizations are accustomed to operating in the high-stakes, high-cost environment of party politics, they are more likely than movement-only actors to have disposable financial resources to expend on the movement's work. With movement and partisan actors working together, the movement is likely to employ a wider diversity of tactics, including those preferred by actors primarily in the movement (such as sit-ins and protests) and those preferred by actors primarily in the party (such as lobbying and election canvassing).

The accumulating presence of partisan actors during mobilization is likely a source of tension in the movement. While the originators of the movement are sure to appreciate the greater public support for their cause, they are also likely to notice that the movement becomes populated with more moderate supporters as it grows. These moderates may be less committed to the cause than are the movement's originators; their identities are less closely linked to the movement than they are to the party. Early participants in the movement, whose identities are more closely linked to the movement than the party, may fear that the new crowd of party loyalists would settle for less than complete victory. Worse yet, the new partisan activists might attempt to co-opt the movement's energy to the party's goals, rather than the movement's. These risks may be especially pronounced during periods of high partisan polarization (Abramowitz 2010). In response, primarily movement-identified activists may attempt to exclude primarily party-identified activists from the movement. Separate coalitions that have different perspectives on the movement's relationship with the party may arise. If these coalitions are able to coexist, then the movement is strengthened. But if the coalitions clash, then infighting may impede the movement's pursuit of its objectives.

Demobilization of the movement may begin for any number of reasons. The movement's political opportunities may evaporate. Activists may burn out or become frustrated by lack of success. Alternatively, activists may quit as a *result* of success, or at least *perceived* success (Bernstein 2005; Chong 1991; Jenkins and Eckert 1986; McAdam 1982; Meyer 2008; Rupp and Taylor 1990;

Tarrow 1993). We are particularly interested in evaluating the extent to which identity shift may be a cause of demobilization. If there is dealignment between the goals of the party and the goals of the movement, then we expect demobilization to follow. One cause of dealignment may be a removal of a sense of threat that previously amplified partisan frames. Without this threat, the size of the party in the street is almost certain to shrink.

Dealignment forces actors to choose between their loyalties to the party and the movement and, thus, prompts identity shifts. Actors who may have identified closely with both the party and the movement start to identify more closely with one or the other. For example, an organization may choose between allocating scarce resources to a get-out-the-vote campaign for a party and a protest campaign sponsored by the movement. Or an activist may choose between remaining focused on leading an advocacy organization or seeking office as part of the party's ticket. Drawing on the insights of intersectionality research, we expect partisan identities to be advantaged relative to movement identities. Since the majority of actors favor their partisan identities over their movement identities, the aggregate result of their choices is to leave the party in a much stronger place than the movement. After partisans leave the movement, the movement is likely to be left with only its hard-core supporters.

Once the movement's support drops below critical mass (Oliver 1989; Oliver, Marwell, and Teixeira 1985), movement actors begin the process of transitioning the movement to abeyance. They shift focus from achieving the goals of the movement to preserving the movement's resources and values until another opportunity arises to fight for the cause. Peak movement organizations at the national and international levels are likely to continue to receive financial support, but local and regional organizations are likely to suffer fiscal deficits. Organizations at all levels may need to cut their paid staff. With less capacity, the movement may no longer be able to stage large-scale protests or other highly visible movement gatherings.

Demobilization may spur the unraveling of coalitions that formed when the movement was on the rise (see Ainsworth 2002, pp. 79–82 on "unraveling"). With fewer moderates in the movement, it is more difficult for coalitions to sustain brokerage across different movement constituencies. With less capacity to broker across constituencies, coalitions become more specialized and radical (Della Porta and Tarrow 1986). As coalitions become more radical, they are less likely to adopt institutional tactics, such as lobbying and participation in elections. Collectively, coalitions become more polarized from one another and unable to work together, much as is the case for political parties in an electoral system with partisan polarization. These developments mean that coalitions are less effective in promoting the movements' goals.

Our theory of social movement mobilization based on partisan identification adds to other theories of mobilization that do not explicitly consider the effects of partisanship. For example, Anthony Downs (1972) claims that all issues go through an "issue-attention cycle," in which the public discovers a problem, becomes engaged with it, and then loses interest. Downs points out that attention to a problem tends to decline gradually as the public realizes how difficult and costly it would be to solve it. Albert Hirschman (1982) adapts and extends these ideas to a social movement milieu by arguing that mobilization dynamics depend on subjectively perceived costs and benefits. From this perspective, movements may demobilize when they face disappointments and activists become burned out. But, then, movements may rebound when time has elapsed and activists miss engagement with the movement's cause.

David Meyer (1990) and other scholars stress the emergence and disappearance of political opportunities as key to the mobilization and demobilization of movements (see, inter alia, Bernstein 2005; Jenkins and Eckert 1986; McAdam 1982; Meyer 2008; Meyer and Minkoff 2004; Rupp and Taylor 1990; Tarrow 1993). From the political opportunity perspective, movements grow and shrink as larger political forces become more or less conducive to their organizing. For instance, the election of a sympathetic presidential administration might be conceptualized as an opportunity for a movement. Still other scholars emphasize the mass psychology of responding to gains and losses. Dennis Chong (1991) points to opportunities for policy success as a determinant of mobilization. From this perspective, movements are most likely to mobilize when their members believe that they are on the verge of achieving a policy success and to demobilize once they believe that they have attained that success. This model presumes that movement actors are driven by actual changes in policy.

Our partisan mobilization theory does not disregard the insights of these previous theories but offers an important corrective to their arguments. We acknowledge that issues vacillate through an attention cycle, yet we document conditions under which declines of attention can be sharp, rather than gradual, and how they may be caused by political perceptions, rather than the substance of the problem. We do not deny that subjective perceptions of costs and benefits play a role in mobilization. But we argue that partisanship may play a critical role in shaping these perceptions. In contrast to political opportunity theory, we point out how the rise of governing actors sympathetic to a movement's cause may actually hurt that cause. In contrast to Chong's model of policy success, our model of partisan identification suggests that the dynamics of mobilization may be driven by partisan success. According to this model, movement actors see policy through the lens of their partisan identification. As a result, they often mobilize to address a policy issue when the opposition party is in power and then demobilize once their party attains electoral success.[1] Thus, mobilization is often driven by *partisan* success and failure, rather than *policy* success and failure.

---

[1] Along these lines, research based on cross-national comparisons of protests demonstrates that social movements are most likely to mobilize when their most closely aligned party is out of power and fail to mobilize when their most closely aligned party is in power (Anderson and Mendes 2005; Foweraker 1995; Kriesi, Koopmans, Duyvendak, and Giugni 1995).

The remainder of this book is devoted to the empirical evaluation of the expectations generated from our theoretical framework. In the next chapter, we examine the mobilization of individual grassroots activists against the wars in Iraq and Afghanistan. We argue that actors in the Democratic Party and the antiwar movement relied heavily on partisan identification as a lens to interpret an ambiguous reality. Many of the actors in the antiwar movement viewed *partisan* change as synonymous with *policy* change. As a result, the antiwar movement demobilized in response to Democratic victories, even though war policy changed relatively little.

4

Identities and Grassroots Participation

On the morning of Monday, January 21, 2013, a few hundred thousand people gathered on the National Mall to witness the second inauguration of President Barack Obama. At the same time, about 150 activists assembled three miles away at the south entrance to Meridian Hill Park in Washington, D.C. (Hatic 2013). The rally was spearheaded by the longtime Washington, D.C. activists Joan Stallard and Malachy Kilbride and organized under the banner of the newly formed Arc of Justice Coalition. Seizing upon the coincidence of Inauguration Day and Martin Luther King Jr. Day, the coalition borrowed its name from a well-known statement of King's (1965) that "the arc of the moral universe is long, but it bends toward justice." The coalition was formally endorsed by eighteen organizations of the antiwar movement of the past decade, such as Code Pink, MoveOn, Veterans for Peace, Peace Action, United for Peace and Justice, World Can't Wait, and the Backbone Campaign.

The Arc of Justice contingent marched down 16th Street, toward the inaugural ceremonies (pictured in Figure 4.1). Participants carried banners that stressed antiwar themes, such as "Obama: Earn Your Nobel Peace Prize," "Drones Kill Thousands of Non-Combatants," "End War Now!" and "Crimes Are Crimes No Matter Who Does Them" (with accompanying photos of Presidents Bush and Obama). Activists from World Can't Wait had a series of giant model drones to emphasize their opposition to the Obama administration's increased use of remote control drones as weapons in the War on Terror. The march proceeded with the supervision of three uniformed police officers, one marked police car, and a few unmarked police cars with plainclothes officers.

We recognized many of the participants in the rally from a decade of antiwar activism. These activists had remained loyal to the antiwar cause through thick and thin, protesting even on a day of celebration for a president who will likely be remembered as a liberal icon. Their persistent resistance is impressive. Yet, as

FIGURE 4.1. Arc of Justice Coalition March, Washington, D.C., January 21, 2013 (Photo by Michael T. Heaney)

organizer Malachy Kilbride (2013) noted as he marched, it is hard to forget "the 10,000-some people that gathered in this very spot, eight years ago, to protest Bush's second Inauguration." We wondered how many of those onetime protesters had, this time, traveled instead to the Mall to celebrate the inauguration. What could account for the divergent points of view on the president between those supporting the Arc of Justice Coalition and those witnessing Obama's second swearing-in?

We maintain that an answer to this question can be provided by the partisan identification theory presented in the previous chapter. This theory has implications for the mobilization of the antiwar movement among individual grassroots activists, political elites, and political organizations. In this chapter, we test the implications of our theory by focusing on the attitudes and behavior of individual grassroots activists. We show how the identification of many antiwar activists with the Democratic Party helps to explain both the rise of a grassroots movement and its decline.

We begin with a qualitative sketch of the identity shifts that contributed to the rise and fall of the antiwar movement and then state a series of empirically testable hypotheses that coincide with the contours of this account. Next, we explain our methods for testing these hypotheses using surveys of activists in the antiwar movement and the Democratic Party. We then present the results of our empirical analysis in three parts. First, we test hypotheses related to the idea that partisanship motivates antiwar mobilization; second, that partisan and movement identities trade off against one another; and third, that partisanship shapes activists' worldviews. Each of these hypotheses is consistent with the partisan identification theory discussed in Chapter 3. Overall, the findings offer strong support for the partisan identification theory as a way of understanding the mobilization of grassroots activists. Partisan identification fueled the growth of the antiwar movement during the Bush years but then trimmed the grass roots in the Obama era.

A SKETCH OF SHIFTING IDENTITIES AFTER 9/11

Identities matter during the mobilization of social movements, in part because actors in movements and parties invoke those identities when attempting to stimulate grassroots participation. In the case of the antiwar movement, antiwar leaders crafted partisan frames to help get people into the streets. UFPJ's use of the slogan "The World Says No to the Bush Agenda," for the protest outside the 2004 Republican National Convention is a classic example of this strategy in operation. Partisan frames were a readily available way to develop opposition to war among the general public. Candidates in the Democratic Party, too – most notably Howard Dean and Barack Obama – sought to tap antiwar identities in generating support for their candidacies (Kreiss 2012, pp. 35–6). Antiwar sentiments, then, helped to shape the choice of a new party leader in Barack Obama.

The broadcast of partisan or movement frames by strategic actors does not automatically generate mobilization. Grassroots activists may choose to respond to these calls or not. Frames are most likely to resonate with activists and, thus, successfully spur mobilization, when the identity in question is salient and threatened. For Democrats with antiwar sympathies, the combination of salience and threat likely registered most acutely from 2003 to 2006. At this time, a Republican president governed with majority support in both houses of Congress. Little could be done to quell the president's will in prosecuting the wars in Iraq and Afghanistan. These were dark days to be an antiwar Democrat. For these activists, participating in antiwar mobilizations was one way to respond to the threat that they perceived from the Bush administration. Partisan and movement identities reinforced one another.

The electoral fortunes of the Democrats improved in 2006 when they reclaimed majorities in both houses of Congress. Although Bush continued his war policies – and even expanded U.S. military involvement in Iraq with the surge – antiwar Democrats may have felt less threatened because of their party's congressional majorities. These Democratically identified activists may have expected that Congress would now hold the president in check. Thus, the motivation subsided for activists to work with the antiwar movement, even in the face of government policies that moved in the opposite direction of their preferences.

When Barack Obama was elected president in 2008, the antiwar movement may or may not have gained an ally in the White House. However, it definitely lost its prime enemy: President Bush. The antiwar movement had relied on Bush as a mobilizing meme for almost eight years. For example, the radical antiwar organization World Can't Wait had adopted "Drive Out the Bush Regime!" as its slogan (Sweet 2008), though it never adopted the slogan "Drive Out the *Obama* Regime!" With Bush leaving the White House, some activists may have felt that their goal had been achieved. The threat that initially mobilized them had been removed. Even before Obama made any policy changes, his election was an immediate removal of a partisan (i.e., Republican) threat. Demobilization of the antiwar movement was, in part, a consequence of this leadership change.

Activists in the antiwar movement cared about the substance of foreign policy. They wanted more than just a change of party. However, for many of them, partisanship served as a lens through which to see policy. On the most basic level, Obama had promised a withdrawal from Iraq. Perhaps it would require substantial grassroots pressure to compel him to keep this promise. But for self-identified Democrats, it might also make sense to trust Obama to keep his word without actively applying pressure. These activists might not necessarily look closely at the details of the administration's policies. Yet, even if they did, they would find considerable ambiguity, leaving room for interpretation. While it was possible to consider Obama's policies to be mostly prowar, it was also possible to see them as antiwar. Self-identified Democrats might have been more likely to see Obama's policies in an antiwar light than non-Democrats would have. They might also be more likely than non-Democrats to make excuses for the president's policies, seeing them as the only practical option under the circumstances.

The period from 2001 to 2012 was a time of shifting identities for Democrats and antiwar activists. The initial shift occurred from 2001 through 2003, as Democratic identities began to be coupled with antiwar identities. Democratic identities raised the salience of antiwar identities, and vice versa. From 2003 to 2006, antiwar and Democratic identities were (mostly) self-reinforcing.[1] However, starting in 2007, antiwar and Democratic identities began to conflict with one another. For some activists, the emergence of Democratic majorities in Congress was enough to satisfy their demand for change. Others, however, were troubled when Congress not only failed to use its power of the purse to end the war in Iraq, but also voted for supplemental appropriations to fund Bush's surge in Iraq. Likewise, once

---

[1] The selection of John Kerry as the Democratic presidential nominee in 2004 caused cognitive dissonance for many activists. Kerry was undoubtedly less prowar than Bush, but his occasionally bellicose rhetoric was troubling to many avowed peace activists.

Obama became president, his promises of withdrawal from Iraq were good enough for some. Others were troubled by the prolonged timetable in Iraq, negotiations to extend the SOFA, the escalation in Afghanistan, the administration's liberal use of drones, the U.S. intervention in Libya, and the president's unsuccessful efforts to close the controversial U.S. prison at Guantanamo Bay, Cuba. Activists were increasingly compelled to choose between their identities. "Am I a Democrat? Or am I an antiwar activist?" It became difficult to be both.

The bad news for the antiwar movement was that activists were more likely to favor their Democratic identities over their antiwar identities. Especially once Obama became president, there were too many good reasons to be a Democrat. The country had its first African American in the Oval Office, an important symbolic outcome after centuries of struggle for racial equality. The Democratic majority in Washington – which was nearly a supermajority – meant that comprehensive health care reform would stand a real chance for the first time in fifteen years. Thus, many former antiwar activists shifted their attention to other issues on the progressive agenda.

Not all party members saw Obama's presidency as a positive development. Some Democrats were so disgusted by Obama's militaristic foreign policies that they dropped their Democratic Party affiliations. They continued to protest the administration's foreign policies. But these peace Democrats were vastly outnumbered by Obama Democrats. Antiwar and Democratic identities had become mostly decoupled. As a result, the party in the street was much smaller by 2009 than it had been in 2003.

TESTABLE HYPOTHESES

The qualitative sketch offered in the preceding section draws upon the theory of partisan identification to interpret the grassroots mobilization dynamics of the antiwar movement. This sketch helps to connect the theoretical argument of the book with the case at hand. It is also possible to state each of the major elements of this account as a formal hypothesis that can be tested empirically using data from our surveys of grassroots activists. In this section, we explain these hypotheses in order to lay the groundwork for the empirical analysis in the remainder of the chapter.

The first testable element of our account is the idea that partisanship motivated people to participate in the antiwar movement. In particular, partisan frames were a way to motivate self-identified Democrats to join the movement. They also are an explanation for why self-identified Democrats left the movement. Thus, we state the following hypotheses:

H$_{4.1}$. *Partisan frames were more effective in drawing participants to the antiwar movement the greater the unity of Republican control in Washington, D.C. Partisan frames were less effective in drawing participants to the antiwar movement the greater the unity of Democratic control in Washington, D.C.*

H$_{4.2}$. *The participation of self-identified Democrats in the antiwar movement was more likely to be motivated by partisan frames than was participation of non-Democrats in the antiwar movement.*

H$_{4.3}$. *Self-identified Democrats were more likely to reduce their participation in the antiwar movement over time than were non-Democrats.*

The second testable element of our account is the idea that partisan and movement identities sometimes trade off against one another. In particular, once the goals of the party and the movement start to diverge, then attachment to one of these is likely to reduce participation in the activities of the other. This trade-off favors partisan identities over movement identities. Thus, we state the following hypotheses:

H$_{4.4}$. *The more salient an individual's identification with social movements, the more likely that she or he maintained participation in the antiwar movement over time.*

H$_{4.5}$. *The more salient an individual's identification with the Democratic Party, the less likely she or he was to participate in the antiwar movement at all.*

H$_{4.6}$ *In cases of conflict, individuals participating in the antiwar movement were more likely to maintain their party loyalties than their movement loyalties.*

The third testable element of our account is the idea that partisan identities shape an individual's worldview, especially on matters related to politics. Once the Democratic Party "owned" the wars in Iraq and Afghanistan, then self-identified Democrats started to see these policies in a more positive light. Strong identifications with the Democratic Party led former antiwar activists to direct their attention to other issues that were in line with the emerging Democratic agenda. Thus, we state the following hypotheses:

H$_{4.7}$. *Self-identified Democratic activists were more likely than non-Democrats to view wars in Iraq and Afghanistan as being managed well by the Obama administration.*

H$_{4.8}$. *After the election of President Obama, self-identified Democrats were more likely to shift their attention to nonwar issues than were non-Democrats.*

The hypotheses stated in this section reflect the major implications of our partisan identification theory for the dynamics of grassroots activism. It is also important to consider how these hypotheses compare to the implicit alternative hypotheses. These alternatives are, first, that mobilization is motivated by factors other than partisanship. Thus, people's partisan identifications make no difference for whether or not they turn out at a protest, the kind of frames that catch their attention, or the timing of their involvement. Second, partisan and movement identities fluctuate independently of one another. Thus, the strength of movement and partisan identities did not affect the persistence of their movement participation. In cases of conflict, they did not systematically favor one identity over the other. Third, individuals develop their worldviews for nonpartisan reasons. Thus, partisan identification did not affect how they evaluated the management of wars by the president or how they shifted their attention among policy issues. While each of these alternatives likely contains an element of truth, the question that we must address is whether these alternatives undercut our focal hypotheses. Does the presence of alternatives mean that our focal hypotheses cannot be supported?

While we argue that partisanship motivates mobilization, we do not deny that nonpartisan motivations also likely contributed to the rise and decline of mobilization. We only claim that the presence of these nonpartisan motivations does not erase the relevance of our partisanship claims. For example, some readers may be inclined to wonder whether the mobilization arc of the antiwar movement was due to the personal enmity that activists held toward President Bush, in contrast to a more likable persona of President Obama. From this point of view, people may have mobilized against war because they did not trust President Bush as a *person*, not as a *Republican*, per se. We obviously cannot rule out that some people were motivated by personal animosity. Yet, if mobilization was based purely on nonpartisan personal animosity, then we would not observe a difference in the mobilization patterns and attitudes of Democrats and non-Democrats. That is, if mobilization against the war were purely personal, then we would expect that Democrats, Republicans, members of minor parties, and nonaligned persons would mobilize at roughly the same rates. If, instead, self-identified Democrats follow a distinctive pattern, then it is reasonable to conclude that the pattern is in large part due to partisanship.

We argue that our claims about partisanship hold even after taking into account alternative explanations for the decline of participation in the antiwar movement. Activists may be less likely to participate in the movement because they become burned out after years of involvement. They may no longer have the encouragement from their friends or financial resources necessary to spur them to action. They may believe that the movement's cause is not as pressing as other causes, that it does not afford them genuine opportunities for participation, or that the movement is ineffective and, as a result, no longer worthy of their volunteer effort. We recognize that these factors likely contributed to the movement's decline. As a result, we ask whether these explanations replace partisanship, or operate in conjunction with it, in explaining the variations that we observe.

In the following section, we describe a series of surveys that enable us to test our hypotheses against their implicit alternatives.

ACTIVIST SURVEYS

We wish to understand the participation of a broad cross section of antiwar activists over time. Ideally, we would like to have a random sample of all people who participated in the antiwar movement in the United States from 2001 to 2012. Unfortunately, there is no centralized directory of antiwar activists from which to draw a sample. Were we to take a random sample of the entire population in the United States, we would likely find that only a small percentage of our respondents were participants in the antiwar movement.[2] Population-level surveys are not a reliable way to study a specific movement.

Rather than attempt to sample from the entire population, social movement scholars typically survey individuals whom they identify through direct participation in social movement events. This approach has both advantages and disadvantages. One advantage is that it allows a high degree of confidence that people participating in the events under investigation are actually involved in the social movement in question. Thus, event surveys eliminate the need to speak to a large number of nonparticipants in order to identify a few bona fide participants. A second advantage is that surveying participants at movement events tends to yield a very high response rate, usually 70 percent or greater. Participants are willing to participate in surveys administered at movement events because they have gone to the event to express their opinion, and the survey affords one more opportunity for them to do so. Moreover, they are a somewhat captive audience, as much of the time at movement events is often spent waiting for action to occur; taking a survey helps participants to pass the time. In contrast, other methods of administering surveys – via telephone, mail, or the Internet – generally yield substantially lower response rates, typically between 20 percent and 40 percent (Kaplowitz, Hadlock, and Levine 2004). A third advantage is that recent research shows that if movement event surveys are conducted systematically – that is, if an effort is made to canvass the crowd comprehensively and if nonresponses are taken into account – then the results of movement event surveys reasonably approximate those of a random sample (Walgrave and Verhulst 2011).

One disadvantage of relying on movement event surveys is that doing so only captures the attitudes of people who have reached a certain threshold of participation – those who cared enough about the movement's goals to actually attend an event. This method misses people who may participate in the movement with lower levels of involvement. A second disadvantage is that it is not possible for surveyors to attend all events across the United States. Therefore, not all participants in the movement have an equal probability of being selected into the sample.

In light of these advantages and disadvantages, we crafted an approach to sampling participants in the antiwar movement, adapted from standard exit poll methodology (Levy 1983, p. 59), that captures a broad cross section of those who participated in the movement over time. We attended national and nationally coordinated antiwar protests. At each protest, we fielded a team of four to ten surveyors, depending on the expected size of the protest. We gave each surveyor an initial starting point such that the team as a whole spanned

---

[2] Previous studies, such as Corrigall-Brown (2012) and Caren, Ghoshal, and Ribas (2011), have attempted to quantify the incidence of protest participation in the general public. However, these studies have examined the participation of individuals in any protest, rather than protests pertaining to a specific movement. Population-level data on antiwar protest participation do not exist.

across the crowd. Surveyors were instructed to begin by identifying an arbitrarily selected anchor person from the crowd. The anchor person was not invited to take the survey. The surveyor then counted five persons in a line from the anchor and invited the fifth person to take the survey. The surveyor was instructed to repeat the counting process – inviting every fifth person to take the survey – until three surveys were accepted by event participants. After obtaining three surveys, the surveyors selected a new anchor and repeated the process. We recorded our best estimates of the race/ethnicity and sex/gender of all nonrespondents in order to assess the possibility of nonresponse bias.

We conducted two waves of surveys. During the first wave, we administered surveys at all of the national or nationally coordinated antiwar protests in the United States between August 2004 and September 2005. There were four national events in this period held in New York, New York, and Washington, D.C., as well as nationally coordinated demonstrations around the nation for the second anniversary of the start of the Iraq War (March 19–20, 2005). For the second anniversary protests, we undertook coordinated field surveys in Washington, D.C.; New York, New York; Fayetteville, North Carolina; Indianapolis, Indiana; Chicago, Illinois; San Diego, California; and San Francisco, California.[3] In total, we conducted 2,349 surveys with a response rate of 87.49 percent for 2004–2005, giving us a broad sample of activists who participated during a peak time for the antiwar movement. One-page surveys administered in this first wave gathered information on participants' demographic information, partisan identification, voting behavior, organizational membership and contacts, sources of information about the event, and reasons for participation.

During the second wave, we administered surveys at all of the national or nationally coordinated antiwar protests in the United States between January 2007 and December 2010. In 2007, there were three national events in New York, New York, and Washington, D.C., as well as nationally coordinated protests in multiple cities on October 27. In 2008, there were national events in Denver, Colorado, for the DNC and St. Paul, Minnesota, for the RNC, as well as nationally coordinated protests from March 15 to 22 for the fifth anniversary of the U.S. invasion of Iraq. In 2009, there were five national events in New York, New York, and Washington, D.C., as well as two rounds of nationally coordinated protests – one for the anniversary of the war in Afghanistan in October and one in opposition to the escalation of the war in Afghanistan in December. In 2010, there was one national event in Washington, D.C., as well as two rounds of nationally coordinated

---

[3] When nationally coordinated protests were held in multiple cities, we selected cities where major rallies were expected to occur, while seeking to achieve a regional balance among the survey sites. We attended fewer protests in the South than in other regions because of the infrequent occurrence of large antiwar demonstrations in southern cities. The antiwar movement was more prevalent in other regions. A list of all protest events at which we conducted surveys is provided in Appendix E.

protests: one for the anniversary of the war in Iraq in March and one for the anniversary of the war in Afghanistan in October. In total, we conducted 6,334 surveys with a 79.46 percent response rate for 2007–2010, giving us a four-year sample of activists who participated during a time of decline for the antiwar movement. Two-page surveys in this second wave collected the same information obtained in the first wave but also included questions on political ideology, past social movement involvement, arrests, education, income, and opinions on policy and candidates.

We decided to stop conducting protest surveys at the end of 2010. Antiwar demonstrations did continue in 2011 and beyond. However, as we discuss in Chapter 2, antiwar protests reached a stable equilibrium of a few hundred or a few thousand participants. Our judgment was that the movement had unambiguously shifted to a state of abeyance and was unlikely to rebound in the short term. We believed that the sample that we had collected was sufficient for testing our hypotheses and had adequately documented the transition from a Republican administration to a Democratic administration. In fact, our research produced the largest survey of participants in a single social movement ever conducted in the United States.

Because we collected surveys at events over time, our research design allows us to observe how the composition of the antiwar movement changed over time. One drawback of this approach is that while it allows us to gather opinions of people who continued participating in antiwar demonstrations, it fails to provide information about the opinions of people who stopped attending demonstrations. We would like to answer questions such as, Why did they stop attending? Did their policy views change? Did they alter their partisan identifications?

Given that our theory is as much about nonparticipation in the antiwar movement as it is about participation, the next move in our research design was to gather information that would allow us to compare current participants and past participants. We did so by identifying events attended by a broad cross section of activists that were likely to include both current participants and past participants in the antiwar movement. We identified two such events. The first was the United States Social Forum, held in Detroit, Michigan, from June 22 to 26, 2010. The Social Forum was attended by a wide variety of dedicated social movement activists, many of whom had participated in the antiwar movement at one point. Although the forum did address peace themes among other issues, the event was not advertised as promoting any particular issue or cause, but rather as a process for exploring questions of social justice writ large. The second event was the 2008 DNC, held in Denver from August 25 to 28. This event was attended by most of the leading grassroots activists in the Democratic Party, some of whom had been involved in the antiwar movement, and many of whom had not.

At the Social Forum, we fielded a ten-page survey among participants using the same sampling methodology as the protest surveys. The survey took the average respondent approximately fifteen minutes to complete. The survey was completed by 691 respondents with a response rate of 66.06 percent.[4] For the DNC, we conducted a mail-return survey in 2011 of 1,000 randomly selected pledged delegates to the convention, using addresses generously provided to us by the Democratic National Committee. We estimate that this nine-page survey similarly took the average respondent approximately fifteen minutes to complete. After one remailing and two postcard reminders, we received responses from 371 pledged delegates, giving us a response rate of 37.10 percent.[5] In addition to asking the same questions included on the protest surveys, both surveys had questions on changes in participants' involvement over time. Had the respondent ever participated in the antiwar movement? If so, how had her or his participation changed over time, and why? To what extent did she or he identify with the Democratic Party? These surveys allowed us to take a more in-depth look at the dynamic participation of two dedicated groups of activists, one with greater commitment to social movements (i.e., Social Forum participants) and one with greater commitment to party politics (i.e., pledged delegates at the DNC).

We use the survey data to test hypotheses related to our partisan identification theory. In the remainder of this chapter, we examine hypotheses related to partisan motivations for mobilization, the trade-off between partisan and movement identities, and the effects of partisanship on political worldviews.

PARTISANSHIP MOTIVATES MOBILIZATION

Partisanship played a major role in attracting support for the antiwar movement after 9/11. This partisanship manifested itself largely in terms of opposition to President Bush and was stoked by movement frames that attacked Bush and the Republicans. As we state in $H_{4.1}$, we expect that the effectiveness of these frames was conditional on the unity of Republican control in Washington, D.C. If partisanship were not a significant motivation behind opposition to the Republican Party, then we would expect that this opposition would not correlate with variation in Republican control.

While our account emphasizes the partisan motivations for protest participation, we recognize that people have multiple and varied reasons for participating in protests. People may participate because they oppose war. Alternatively, an antiwar protest may be an opportunity to gain attention for another issue, such as Israel's policies toward Palestine. Or individuals may attend because of personal reasons, such as the desire to see friends or to enjoy a beautiful day.

In order to understand why individuals participated in antiwar demonstrations, we asked respondents an open-ended question, "What are the most important reasons you came to this event?" The open-ended format has the advantage of

---

[4] The response rate to the Social Forum survey was somewhat lower than the response rate to the protest surveys because of the greater length of the Social Forum survey.

[5] This response rate is typical for mail surveys with postcard reminders (Kaplowitz, Hadlock, and Levine 2004).

TABLE 4.1. *Framework for Content Analysis*

Reason	Example: I am here …
Emotional	because I am angry.
General Politics	to hold the House of Representatives accountable.
Morality	to make our country do the right thing.
Movement Related	to help grow my movement organization.
Nonwar Domestic Policy	for jobs and education.
Nonwar Foreign Policy	to bring justice to Palestine.
Opposition to the Republican Party	to impeach Bush.
Opposition to the Democratic Party	because John Kerry is not what we need.
Personal	to spend time with my friends.
Religious	because my Catholic faith calls me to be here.
Self-Expression or Participation	to make my voice heard.
Support of the Democratic Party	to help John Kerry get elected President.
War Related	to end the war.
Other	because I was passing by.

allowing us to explore broadly the motivations behind movement participation (Haddock and Zanna 1998). At the same time, we recognize that respondents may not have recalled all of the possible reasons they attended the event, but only those reasons that had easy cognitive accessibility. Thus, the reasons that people gave in response to this question reflect the frames that were most salient to them – at the "top of the head" – rather than a comprehensive summary of all their reasons (Nisbett and Wilson 1977; Zaller 1992). Indeed, we recognize that respondents may have had motivations other than the ones that they stated explicitly.

We developed a framework for content coding respondent's reasons for participating in protests into thirteen categories, as well as a catch-all residual category of "other." This framework is laid out in Table 4.1. For example, an answer stating, "I am here because I want to see an end to the Iraq War" was coded as "War Related." An answer stating, "I am here to speak my mind" was coded as "Self-Expression or Participation." We coded answers into as many categories as appropriate, so an answer stating, "I am here to speak my mind about the need to end the Iraq War" would be coded as both "Self-Expression or Participation" and "War Related."[6]

In Table 4.2, we summarize respondents' answers to this question in three periods characterized by unified Republican control (2004–2005), divided government (2007–2008), and unified Democratic control (2009–2010).

---

[6] Coding was performed by a team of research assistants at the University of Michigan. Multiple team members evaluated each statement in order to achieve maximum consensus among team members.

TABLE 4.2. *Reasons for Attending Antiwar Protests*

2004–2005 Unified Republican Control			2007–2008 Divided Government			2009–2010 Unified Democratic Control		
Rank	Reason	Percent	Rank	Reason	Percent	Rank	Reason	Percent
1	War Related	58.30%	1	War Related	70.07%	1	War Related	65.71%
2	Self-Expression or Participation	27.15%	2	Self-Expression or Participation	19.09%	2	Self-Expression or Participation	18.42%
3	Opposition to the Republican Party	23.05%	3	Personal	16.37%	3	Personal	17.14%
4	Movement Related	20.74%	4	Movement Related	15.33%	4	Movement Related	16.95%
5	Nonwar Domestic Policy	16.51%	5	Opposition to the Republican Party	12.29%	5	Nonwar Domestic Policy	15.24%
6	Personal	16.49%	6	Morality	8.24%	6	Nonwar Foreign Policy	10.79%
7	Nonwar Foreign Policy	12.54%	7	Nonwar Domestic Policy	8.00%	7	Morality	7.02%
8	Morality	9.42%	8	General Politics	7.15%	8	General Politics	6.06%
9	Emotional	7.18%	9	Nonwar Foreign Policy	5.40%	9	Emotional	4.61%
10	General Politics	5.94%	10	Emotional	5.19%	10	Opposition to the Democratic Party	2.97%
11	Religious	0.82%	11	Opposition to the Democratic Party	0.56%	11	Opposition to the Republican Party	1.13%
12	Opposition to the Democratic Party	0.30%	12	Support of the Democratic Party	0.56%	12	Support of the Democratic Party	1.09%
13	Support of the Democratic Party	0.30%	13	Religious	0.39%	13	Religious	0.61%
NA	Other	2.04%	NA	Other	1.54%	NA	Other	2.41%
N=2,319			N=3,892			N=2,656		

Note: Respondents' reasons were coded into multiple categories, if appropriate. As a result, column percentages total to more than 100 percent. Percentages were adjusted using survey weights.

We ranked each category on the basis of its popularity in each period under investigation. This table allows us to see how the reasons for participating in antiwar demonstrations changed over time from 2004 to 2010.[7] Our purpose in presenting these data is not to make a claim about the specific percentages of people who attended protests for each type of reason, but rather to discover the trends in the reasons that were offered voluntarily.

For all three periods, the overwhelming majority of antiwar demonstrators explicitly stated that they attended protests because they are opposed to war. Similarly, the second most common reason that people gave in all three periods is that they attended protests in order to express their views or to participate in the political process. Variation over time appears with the percentage of people who report that they attended demonstrations because of their opposition to Republicans, in general, or President Bush, specifically. From 2004 to 2005, during the peak of the antiwar movement and unified Republican control, roughly a quarter of respondents (23 percent) stated – unprompted by us – that they participated in antiwar demonstrations because of partisan antipathy. This was the third most common reason offered by respondents. Examples of such sentiments are expressed in the photo in Figure 4.2, where demonstrators at a September 24, 2005, rally in Washington, D.C., carried anti-Republican signs with messages such as "BUSH LIES, WHO DIES? BRING THE TROOPS HOME NOW!" and "SUPPORT OUR TROOPS. IMPEACH BUSH."

In 2007 and 2008, however, the frequency with which respondents volunteered anti-Republican reasons was cut in half to merely 12 percent (significant change at $p \leq 0.001$), making it only the fifth most common reason for participation. The decline in partisan antipathy in 2007–2008 is counterintuitive because President Bush launched the surge during this period. Finally, the percentage of respondents offering anti-Republican motivations fell again in 2009–2010 as the Democrats claimed unified control of Congress and the White House (significant change at $p \leq 0.001$). Still, a few respondents (1 percent) mentioned anti-Republican motivations for participation in 2009–2010, such as the desire to see former President Bush, former Vice President Dick Cheney, or former Defense Secretary Donald Rumsfeld brought to justice for war crimes. By 2009, most of the partisan motivation for protest was gone.

Our results reveal a steady, significant decrease in the percentage of antiwar demonstrators who articulated their motivations for protest participation in partisan terms. If partisanship had not been a factor fueling the antiwar movement, then we would have expected partisan motivations to be invariant with time. Instead, partisan motivations declined along with the unity of Republican control, thus providing support for $H_{4.1}$. Partisanship manifested

---

[7] The percentages in the survey are weighted on the basis of response-rate differences corresponding with sex/gender and race/ethnicity. The survey weights for the protest surveys are reported in Appendix F.

FIGURE 4.2. UFPJ-ANSWER Joint Demonstration in Washington, D.C., September 24, 2005 (Photo by Michael T. Heaney)

as opposition to the Republican Party, rather than support of the Democratic Party. Less than 1 percent of respondents explained their participation as being part of an effort to propel the Democratic Party to victory. Once Obama assumed the presidency, Republican antipathy was not replaced by Democratic antipathy. Only 3 percent of respondents discussed opposition to the Democrats as a motivation for participating in protest in 2009–2010.

We posit that the existence or absence of partisan motivations affects the composition of the antiwar movement. If opposition to war is understood in partisan terms, then self-identified partisans may be likely to participate in the movement. If the antiwar movement is explicitly opposed to President Bush and the Republicans, then Democrats are likely to want to join. However, independents and members of minor parties are less likely to be motivated by the same anti-Republican frames that send Democrats out into the streets. As we state in $H_{4.2}$, we expect that participation in the antiwar movement by Democrats was more likely to be driven by partisanship than was the participation of non-Democrats.

In order to measure the changing partisan composition of the antiwar movement, we included a question on the protest survey that asked, "Do you consider yourself to be a member of a political party? (circle one) [YES/NO]

If 'YES,' which political party are you a member of?" This question deliberately uses a high standard for attachment to a party. Specifically, we asked whether the respondent considered himself or herself to be a "member" of that party. We asked the question in this way because we seek to establish whether respondents *identify* with the party, not merely whether they agree with the party. We expected antiwar demonstrations to include a larger number of people who embraced minor parties, or who rejected the party system entirely, than would be found in a survey of the general population. For this reason, we decided not to force respondents to rate themselves on a continuum from strong Democrat to strong Republican, but to allow an open-ended response. The open-ended format is more agreeable to respondents who identify themselves with the radical fringes of politics (e.g., Socialists, Communists) or who identify in a way that crosscuts the dominant party affiliations in the United States (e.g., Libertarians). Our approach likely yields a larger number of persons with no partisan attachment than would be the case if we used a traditional continuum measure.[8] Thus, individuals who indicate party membership on our survey should be viewed as relatively strong partisans, as they are willing to embrace the notion of "membership" in the party.

We estimated multinomial probit regressions on the partisan identifications of individuals attending demonstrations. We coded responses into four mutually exclusive categories: Democratic, minor party, Republican, or no party affiliation (the base category).[9] We included the variable *Opposition to the Republican Party* to test hypothesis $H_{4.2}$ that the participation of self-identified Democrats was more likely to be motivated by partisanship than was the case

---

[8] We included a continuum measure of party agreement on a survey fielded in Washington, D.C., on September 24, 2005. Specifically, we asked, "We are interested in knowing whether you tend to agree more with the Democratic Party or with the Republican Party." We received valid responses on party membership and party agreement from 429 respondents. Of these, 50.98 percent considered themselves to be members of the Democratic Party. Of the remaining respondents, 70.94 percent said that they tended to agree with the Democratic Party usually or sometimes, while only 5.26 percent of non-Democrats claimed that they usually or sometimes agree with the Republican Party. Only 23.80 percent of non-Democrats reported that they "rarely agree with either party."

[9] Because we allowed open-ended responses, it was possible for respondents to answer that they were members of more than one party. A very small percentage of respondents availed themselves of this opportunity, as 1.51 percent of respondents gave answers that placed them in more than one category. The overwhelming majority of these cases (97.69 percent) are persons identifying with the Democratic Party and at least one minor party (such as the Green Party). Of a total of 8,618 respondents, two individuals reported comembership in the Republican Party and a minor party (such as the Libertarian Party) and only person claimed membership in both the Democratic and Republican Parties. In cases when respondents indicated membership in multiple parties, we dealt with this conflict by estimating the regression in two different ways. First, we coded all conflicts between a major party and a minor party as belonging to the major party; these are the results that we report in Table 4.3. Second, we coded all conflicts between a major party and a minor party as belonging to the minor party. Differences in these results do not lead to different conclusions about the hypotheses tested in this chapter.

for non-Democrats. To account for alternative motivations for participation in demonstrations, we entered additional variables in the regression including political attitudes, organizational membership, sex/gender, race/ethnicity, age, education, income, and the month that the individual took the survey (cf. Corrigall-Brown 2012; Han 2009; Schlozman, Verba, and Brady 2012; Rosenstone and Hansen 1993).[10] We divide the survey data into three periods, corresponding to unified Republican control (2004–2005), divided government (2007–2008), and unified Democratic control (2009–2010). We report the results of the multinomial probit regressions in Table 4.3.[11]

The results of our analysis show, consistent with hypothesis $H_{4.2}$, that Democrats were more likely to be motivated by partisan antipathy than were non-Democrats. However, the strength of this motivation varied over time in conjunction with the degree of unified Republican control in Washington, D.C. During 2004–2005 (equation 4.1), a period of unified Republican control and a peak period for the antiwar movement, opposition to the Republican Party was a distinct predictor of turnout by Democrats, but not by members of minor parties or Republicans. Thus, at the peak of the movement, partisan antipathy was an important explanation for Democratic turnout. Partisanship helped to build the antiwar movement.

During 2007–2008 (equation 4.2), a period of divided government and decline for the antiwar movement, opposition to the Republican Party predicts turnout by Democrats, as well as turnout by members of minor parties, but not turnout by Republicans. This finding is consistent with $H_{4.2}$ with respect to Democrats and Republicans, but contradicts $H_{4.2}$ with respect to minor party members.

Finally, during 2009–2010 (equation 4.3), a period of unified Democratic control and a period of abeyance for the antiwar movement, opposition to the Republican Party does not predict turnout by members of any party. By 2009–2010, partisan antipathy was no longer a significant factor that motivated turnout by Democrats or members of any other political party. The fuel of partisan antipathy was no longer available to the movement.

The inclusion of control variables allows us to rule out the possibility that our results are simply an artifact of common alternative motivations for turnout at a demonstration. For example, women are disproportionately more likely to self-identify as Democrats than are men. By including sex/gender as a variable in the regression analysis, we are able to rule out the possibility that the findings on Republican antipathy hold only because of women's proclivity to identify as Democrats. Controlling for variation in political attitudes is especially important because doing so allows us to examine the effects of our focus variables after accounting for the fact that some activists may be toward the

[10] We report the exact wording of our survey questions for control variables in Appendix G.
[11] Descriptive statistics are reported in Appendix H. Note that not all variables are available for 2004–2005 because we fielded a shorter survey than we did beginning in 2007.

TABLE 4.3. *Explanations for Partisan Identification at Demonstrations*

Independent Variable	2004–2005 (4.1) Unified Republican Control			2007–2008 (4.2) Divided Government			2009–2010 (4.3) Unified Democratic Control		
	Democrat	Minor Party	Republican	Democrat	Minor Party	Republican	Democrat	Minor Party	Republican
Opposition to the Republican Party = 1	0.5545*** (0.0962)	-0.0944 (0.1231)	0.2480 (0.2325)	0.2390** (0.0973)	0.2991** (0.1226)	-0.3107 (0.4141)	0.1089 (0.3699)	0.1369 (0.3755)	1.2482 (0.6898)
Political Attitudes (1 = Extremely Conservative to 7 = Extremely Liberal)				-0.0217 (0.0456)	-0.1710** (0.0825)	0.4011*** (0.0735)	0.0859* (0.0383)	-0.1554** (0.0554)	0.4875*** (0.0623)
Organizational Member = 1	0.0612 (0.0804)	0.4963*** (0.0974)	-0.2081 (0.1805)	0.0287 (0.0661)	0.5389*** (0.0896)	0.4672* (0.2022)	0.1299 (0.0840)	0.5581*** (0.0900)	0.1941 (0.2310)
Sex/Gender Is Female = 1	0.5830*** (0.0796)	0.0577 (0.0927)	0.0659 (0.1921)	0.5706*** (0.0629)	-0.0946 (0.0808)	-0.2901 (0.2031)	0.5092*** (0.0773)	-0.1951* (0.0795)	-0.1386 (0.2315)
Race/Ethnicity Is White = 1	0.4349*** (0.1007)	0.0669 (0.1121)	0.4980 (0.2750)	0.3809*** (0.0861)	0.0472 (0.1063)	0.2284 (0.2559)	0.1595 (0.0977)	-0.0916 (0.0974)	0.9073** (0.3286)
Age in Years	0.0250*** (0.0025)	0.0156*** (0.0029)	0.0182*** (0.0055)	0.0160*** (0.0023)	0.0085** (0.0030)	0.0066 (0.0062)	0.0167*** (0.0025)	0.0123*** (0.0026)	-0.0030 (0.0072)
Level of Education (1 = Less than High School to 7 = Graduate Degree)				-0.0214 (0.0216)	-0.0418 (0.0276)	0.0243 (0.0563)	-0.0532* (0.0257)	-0.0084 (0.0269)	-0.0856 (0.0575)
Annual Income in Thousands of Dollars				0.1871*** (0.0221)	0.0281 (0.0283)	0.1129* (0.0517)	0.0871*** (0.0272)	-0.0178 (0.0292)	0.2290*** (0.0617)

Table 4.3. (cont.)

Independent Variable	2004–2005 (4.1) Unified Republican Control			2007–2008 (4.2) Divided Government			2009–2010 (4.3) Unified Democratic Control		
	Democrat	Minor Party	Republican	Democrat	Minor Party	Republican	Democrat	Minor Party	Republican
Months since September 2001	0.0168	-0.0123	0.0726*	-0.0180***	-0.0065	0.0063	-0.0252***	-0.0117	0.0133
	(0.0119)	(0.0135)	(0.0342)	(0.0052)	(0.0064)	(0.0178)	(0.0073)	(0.0071)	(0.0154)
Constant	-2.6156***	-1.2699*	-6.5326***	-0.4012	-0.8483	-4.8062***	0.6479	0.0714	-5.9262***
	(0.5208)	(0.5946)	(1.4467)	(0.4197)	(0.5467)	(1.4462)	(0.7421)	(0.7233)	(1.5427)
Fraction of Observations in Category	0.3993	0.1430	0.0111	0.4458	0.0997	0.0076	0.2582	0.2147	0.0105
N	2,349			3,670			2,664		
F Statistic	16.3800***			21.1400***			11.8700***		
F Degrees of Freedom	18, 2,331			27, 3,643			27, 2,637		

Note: * $p \leq 0.050$, ** $p \leq 0.010$, *** $p \leq 0.001$. Base category is no party affiliation. Multinomial probit estimates are adjusted with sample weights. Standard errors in parentheses.

radical end of the ideological spectrum, while others are more moderate. Likewise, opposition to the Republican Party is a significant factor in encouraging turnout by Democrats after considering organizational membership, race/ethnicity, age, education, income, and month when the survey was taken.

Our predictions under our first and second hypotheses can be combined to generate our third hypothesis. $H_{4.1}$ holds that the effectiveness of partisan frames in motivating participation in the antiwar movement declined with the rise of Democratic power in Washington, D.C. $H_{4.2}$ holds that partisan frames are more likely to motivate Democrats than non-Democrats to participate. When these two hypotheses are combined, we are led to expect a greater decline of participation by Democrats than non-Democrats, which is our hypothesis $H_{4.3}$.

Hypothesis $H_{4.3}$ can be tested using the results reported in Table 4.3 by looking at the coefficients on the variable *Months since September 2001*. The coefficients on this variable indicate whether members of a given party are more or less likely to turn out as time passes. Results from August 2004 to September 2005 (equation 4.1) reveal no time trend in the participation of Democrats or members of minor parties. This absence of a trend is consistent with $H_{4.3}$, as we would not expect any substantial realignment during the peak of the movement. We do find a significant uptick in Republican participation during this period. Participation of self-identified Republicans rose from roughly 1 percent of respondents in August 2004 to approximately 3 percent of respondents in September 2005.

We observe the significant time trend in Democratic participation, predicted by $H_{4.3}$, beginning in 2007. Starting in 2007, we observe a decline in participation by Democrats. The decline is significant during both the 2007–2008 period and the 2009–2010 period. Participation by members of minor parties did not change significantly *within* those periods, but participation by members of minor parties did increase significantly *between* periods (from 10 percent to 21 percent).

The declining participation by Democrats substantially altered the partisan composition of the antiwar movement. This change is best illustrated graphically. We plot the time trend of the partisan affiliations of antiwar demonstrators in Figure 4.3. From August 2004 to September 2008, the percentage of self-identified Democrats participating in antiwar demonstrations vacillated between 36 and 54 percent. However, after Obama assumed the presidency in January 2009, the percentage of Democrats at demonstrations fell sharply to the 20 percent range. At the same time, the percentage of minor party members increased from the 10 percent range to the 20 percent range.

The results reported in Figure 4.3 reflect profound changes in the composition of the antiwar movement after Obama's election. Prior to 2009, self-identified Democrats had been the backbone of antiwar demonstrations. Democrats were an enormous potential constituency for the antiwar movement, given that approximately 33.20 percent of the adult population in United States identified as members the Democratic Party between 2001 and

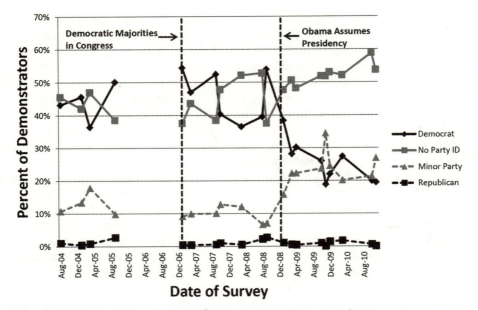

FIGURE 4.3. Partisan Composition of Antiwar Street Demonstrations

2010 (General Social Survey 2013). Once the movement's message no longer resonated with this group, the overall effectiveness of its appeals was considerably diminished. When Democrats stopped turning out, the movement could no longer achieve critical mass.

IDENTITY TRADE-OFFS

A key feature of our argument is that partisan and movement identities trade off against one another under certain conditions. As long as the Republicans held power in Washington, D.C., Democratic and antiwar identities could be viewed, to some extent, as being mutually reinforcing. If an activist viewed the Republicans as responsible for unjust wars, then supporting the Democratic Party could be considered a way to express that identity: Supporting the Democrats meant supporting an end to war. Once the Democrats seized control of Congress and the White House, it was harder to see antiwar identities as consonant with Democratic identities. If the Democrats were genuinely antiwar, then why were U.S. troops still fighting overseas? When were the troops going to come home?

We are not claiming that it was *impossible* to sustain both antiwar and Democratic identities after 2009. Rather, we argue that there was an increased tension between them. It *was* possible to articulate a rationale for being an antiwar Democrat after 2009. For example, one could argue that President

Obama was not responsible for launching the wars in Iraq and Afghanistan, but he was obligated to guide them to smooth conclusions. From this perspective, Obama's surge in Afghanistan might even be viewed as part of ultimately ending the war. Or activists may maintain that they are not against *all* wars, but only against the war in Iraq. Nonetheless, the need to make such arguments – to actively reconcile support for the party and the movement – is an indicator of identities in conflict with one another. Individuals put in this position would be likely to experience cognitive dissonance. Many individuals resolved this conflict and maintained both identities. Yet, for others, the conflict led them to shift greater emphasis to one identity rather than the other.

The likelihood that an individual retains an identity under conditions of conflict depends on the salience of the identity in question. We begin by testing hypothesis $H_{4.4}$ that the more salient an individual's identification with social movements, the more likely she or he was to remain in the antiwar movement over time. To test this hypothesis, we draw upon data collected in surveys of participants at the 2010 United States Social Forum. This sample is composed of a self-selected group of activists with greater-than-average commitments to social movements. Participants in the Social Forum were attracted to the event as a result of their involvement in a wide variety of left-leaning social movements, such as movements for peace, the environment, labor rights, civil rights, fairness for immigrants, and justice for native peoples. Thus, these individuals may or may not have been intensely involved in the antiwar movement, per se, thus generating a sample with variations in levels of commitment to the cause of peace.

We asked respondents, "Have you ever been involved in the movement to prevent or end the U.S. wars in Iraq and/or Afghanistan?" Most Social Forum participants had some history of involvement in the antiwar movement; 77.82 percent of respondents answered yes to this question.[12] We also asked respondents who had participated in the antiwar movement, "What kinds of actions have you taken while participating in the antiwar movement?" Almost all of these respondents (92.00 percent) indicated that that they had participated in protests against wars in Iraq and Afghanistan. Thus, the forum yielded a sample of respondents who had, at one time, been involved in the antiwar movement in a way similar to those individuals analyzed from the previous section.

Hypothesis $H_{4.4}$ calls for us to examine the relationship between the changing involvement of individual antiwar demonstrators over time and the salience of their identification with social movements. To measure changing involvement, we asked respondents who had indicated prior involvement in the antiwar movement at some point, "Since Barack Obama

---

[12] All estimates reported in this section are adjusted with survey weights to account for nonresponse effects.

has been President of the United States, how has your level of involvement in the antiwar movement changed?"[13] We found that the antiwar involvement of Social Forum participants decreased after Obama's election, as was the case for the antiwar movement as a whole. Almost twice as many respondents indicated a decrease in involvement (39.37 percent) as reported an increase in involvement (21.05 percent).

To measure the salience of respondents' identifications with social movements, we asked, "Some people closely identify with the term 'activist,' while other people do not think of themselves in this way. How important is the idea of being an 'activist' to your personal identity?"[14] Within the context of the movement-building activities of the Social Forum, the meaning of being an "activist" was likely to be interpreted as someone who is involved in social movement activities. To test $H_{4.4}$, we estimated an ordered probit model on the change of respondents' involvement as a function of the salience of her or his movement identification. We estimated this model controlling for partisan identification, political attitudes, membership in political organizations, sex/gender, race/ethnicity, age, education, and income.

The results of our analysis, reported in Table 4.4, provide evidence of the trade-off proposed in $H_{4.4}$. Individuals with a stronger movement identity – those who leaned toward stating that activism is "core" to their personal identities – were more likely to report increased or maintained antiwar movement involvement than were individuals who leaned toward stating that activism is not part of their personal identities. At the same time, identification with the Democratic Party predicted that individuals decreased their involvement in the antiwar movement (as indicated by the significant, negative coefficient on the Democratic identity variable). Thus, our estimates support $H_{4.4}$ and demonstrate that partisan and movement identities pulled activists in different directions after Obama's election. Other factors equal, salient movement identities were associated with individuals who increased or maintained their movement involvement, while Democratic identities were associated with individuals who eventually withdrew from antiwar activism.

The presence of control variables allows us to conclude that these results are not merely an artifact of other common explanations for decreasing movement involvement. For example, the inclusion of a measure of political attitudes demonstrates that the result is not merely a product of the fact that self-identified Democrats may be more conservative than other Social Forum activists, who may lean toward the radical edges of politics. Being a self-identified

---

[13] Options: My involvement in the antiwar movement has INCREASED SUBSTANTIALLY; INCREASED SOMEWHAT; STAYED THE SAME; DECREASED SOMEWHAT; DECREASED SUBSTANTIALLY.

[14] Options: Being an "activist" is CORE to my personal identity; SOMEWHAT IMPORTANT to my personal identity; NOT THAT IMPORTANT to my personal identity; NOT PART of my personal identity; an idea that I REJECT; Don't know.

TABLE 4.4. *Explanations for Change in Antiwar Involvement*

Independent Variable	(4.4)	(4.5)
	Social Forum Participants	
Salience of Movement Identity	0.1083*	0.1069*
(5 = Activism core to identity, 1 = reject activism)	(0.0531)	(0.0535)
Self-Identified Democrat = 1	-0.2827*	-0.2550*
	(0.1250)	(0.1260)
Dropped Democratic Party Identification = 1		0.3180
		(0.1888)
Political Attitudes	-0.0346	-0.0350
(9 = Radical Left, 1 = Radical Right)	(0.0616)	(0.0614)
Organizational Member = 1	0.2612	0.2703
	(0.1482)	(0.1491)
Sex/gender Is Female = 1	-0.3062**	-0.2997**
	(0.1060)	(0.1059)
Race/Ethnicity Is White = 1	-0.3267**	-0.3321**
	(0.1201)	(0.1213)
Age in Years	0.0079*	0.0083**
	(0.0035)	(0.0036)
Level of Education (1 = Less than High School	-0.1224***	-0.1262***
to 7 = Graduate Degree)	(0.0339)	(0.0337)
Annual Income in Thousands of Dollars	0.0000	0.0003
	(0.0026)	(0.0026)
First Cut Point	-1.6797**	-1.6483**
	(0.5478)	(0.5481)
Second Cut Point	-0.7236	-0.6889
	(0.5433)	(0.5435)
Third Cut Point	0.4207	0.4617
	(0.5407)	(0.5410)
Fourth Cut Point	0.9302	0.9727
	(0.5386)	(0.5390)
Mean of Dependent Variable	2.8060	2.8060
N	467	467
F Statistic	5.59***	5.14***
F Degrees of Freedom	9, 458	10, 457

Note: $* \ p \leq 0.050$, $** \ p \leq 0.010$, $*** \ p \leq 0.001$. Ordered probit regression. Estimates are adjusted using sample weights. Standard errors in parentheses.

Democrat has a negative effect on participation, holding constant political attitudes. Similarly, our conclusions cannot be explained away because of variations in organizational membership, sex/gender, race/ethnicity, age, education, or income, all of which have been accounted for within the model.

A skeptical reader may be concerned that our results are partly a product of the fact that some self-identified Democrats dropped their party identities after President Obama's election. This reader may suspect that party withdrawals create the appearance of a party-movement trade-off when none actually exists. To account for this possibility, we asked respondents, "Have you ever considered yourself to be a member of a political party OTHER THAN the one that you listed in question 21 above? (CIRCLE ONE) [YES/NO] If YES, which OTHER PARTY were you most recently a member of? What YEAR did you leave that other party?" We found that 9.41 percent of Social Forum participants dropped their Democratic Party identifications between 2008 and 2010. Using this information, we estimate a new version of our model – reported in equation 4.5 in Table 4.4 – including a dummy variable for dropped Democratic Party identification. We find that the pattern of statistically significant results is unaffected by the inclusion of this variable. Thus, it is reasonable to conclude that the trade-off between partisan and movement identities holds even in the presence of party switching by some activists.

Among individuals closely allied with the Democratic Party, strong identification with the party may be a barrier to social movement involvement. Some individuals who identify closely with parties may be inclined to see party politics as *the* route to policy change, leading them to eschew other forms of activism. Using surveys of delegates at the 2008 DNC, we test $H_{4.5}$ that the salience of an individual's identification with the Democratic Party affects the likelihood that she or he engaged with the antiwar movement at some point. We measure participation in the movement using the same question that we asked of Social Forum participants, the responses to which indicated that 31.61 percent of DNC delegates had some involvement in the antiwar movement. Given that all delegates at the DNC have a strong identification with the party – demonstrated by their willingness to devote a week of their time to attend the convention – we established variations in identification by asking them about the stages of their lives at which they came to identify with the party. Specifically, we asked, "Some people identify with one political party for most of their lives. However, some people come to identify with a political party later in life. Please check ONE of the following which best describes your identification with the Democratic Party," with options including age ranges for when they first identified as a Democrat.[15] We consider identifications developed earlier in

---

[15] Options: I first began to identify with the Democratic Party in my childhood (before age 18); during early adulthood (ages 18–24); in my mid-to-late 20s (ages 25–29); in my 30s (ages 30–39); in my 40s (ages 40–49); in my 50s or later (ages 50 on); I have never identified with the Democratic Party.

TABLE 4.5. *Explanations for Participation in the Antiwar Movement*

Independent Variable	(4.6)
	DNC Delegates
Democratic Identification in Youth (by Age 24) = 1	-0.5457*
	(0.2501)
Participation in Nonwar Social Movement Activism	0.0699*
(Number of Nonwar Social Movements, 0 to 9)	(0.0279)
Political Attitudes	0.3664***
(9 = Radical Left, 1 = Radical Right)	(0.0824)
Organizational Member = 1	-0.0143
	(0.2170)
Sex/Gender Is Female = 1	-0.0701
	(0.1491)
Race/Ethnicity Is White = 1	0.6207***
	(0.1839)
Age in Years	-0.0111*
	(0.0056)
Level of Education (1 = Less than High School	-0.0643
to 7 = Graduate Degree)	(0.0473)
Annual Income in Thousands of Dollars	0.0022
	(0.0034)
Constant	-2.2423*
	(0.7758)
Mean of Dependent Variable	0.3161
N	367
F Statistic	5.60***
F Degrees of Freedom	9, 358

Note: * $p \leq 0.050$, ** $p \leq 0.010$, *** $p \leq 0.001$. Base category is no party affiliation. Probit regression estimates are adjusted with sample weights. Standard errors in parentheses.

the life course to reflect stronger attachments than those acquired at later times, as they are more likely to reflect an ingrained part of a person's life (Converse 1969; Erikson and Stoker 2011, p. 235; Dinas 2013; Jennings, Stoker, and Bowers 2009).

We estimate a probit regression model on whether an individual participated in the antiwar movement after 9/11 as a function of whether she or he identified with the party in her or his youth. We control for identification with social movements by counting involvement in nine nonwar issues (criminal justice, education, the environment, health care, immigration, labor, gay rights, racial justice, and women's). Other variables include measures of political attitudes, organizational membership, sex/gender, race/ethnicity, age, education, and income.

The results of our analysis, reported in Table 4.5, confirm a relationship between the salience of Democratic identities and participation in the antiwar movement. Convention delegates who began to identify with the antiwar movement in their youth (in college years or earlier) were less likely to have participated in the antiwar movement than were delegates who realized their Democratic Party identities later in life, thus supporting $H_{4.5}$. We find that delegates with a history of involvement in nonwar issues were more likely to participate in the antiwar movement, thus providing additional evidence of the trade-off between Democratic Party identification and movement identification. The inclusion of a control variable for political attitudes ensures that our results are not an artifact of heavily left-leaning delegates' being more likely to participate in the antiwar movement. We have accounted for these ideological differences. Similarly, greater participation in the antiwar movement by whites and youth is captured in the model.

A skeptical reader may be concerned that the withdrawal of some delegates from the Democratic Party in the period between the convention (in 2008) and the survey (in 2011) may affect the conclusions of our analysis. To check for this possibility, we asked delegates, "Since the 2008 Democratic National Convention, have you remained a member of the Democratic Party or have you dropped out of it?" We found that only 4 of the 371 delegates who returned the survey reported leaving the Democratic Party between 2008 and 2011: slightly more than 1 percent of the sample (1.08 percent). All of these respondents were also participants in the antiwar movement. Because of this perfect correspondence, it is statistically impossible to reestimate the probit regression with a parameter for dropped Democratic Party identification. Nonetheless, it does seem likely that there was some nonrandom relationship between antiwar movement participation and withdrawal from the Democratic Party. However, given the small percentage of cases to which this applies, it also seems unlikely that party switching occurred with sufficient frequency to undercut the statistical relationships identified in the data.

Having established the trade-off between partisan and movement identities, it is possible to ascertain which of these identities has the more favorable position in the trade-off. Thus, we are able to test hypothesis $H_{4.6}$ that party loyalties were more likely to be maintained than were movement loyalties. We make use of informative biases in the data to approximate the relative retention of partisan and movement identities. We expect that participants in the Social Forum were more highly committed to social movements than were typical antiwar movement participants; thus we expect this sample to be on the high side of Democratic abandonment and on the low side of movement abandonment. In contrast, we expect that delegates to the DNC were more highly committed to the Democratic

Party than were typical antiwar movement participants; thus we expect this sample to be on the high side of movement abandonment and on the low side of Democratic abandonment. Using this information, we can place bounds on the frequency of identity shifts among activists who identified at the intersection of the antiwar movement and the Democratic Party.

First, looking at the results of the Social Forum survey, we are able to assess the participation dynamics of a sample of activists highly committed to movements. Slightly more than one-fifth (21.82 percent) of Social Forum participants reported that they identified at the intersection of the Democratic Party and the antiwar movement as of 2008. How did these activists change their involvement with the movement and the party after Obama's election? More than a third (39.56 percent) of these activists reported that they decreased their involvement in the antiwar movement after 2008. In contrast, only 27.33 percent of intersectionally identified activists reported leaving the Democratic Party during the same period. Thus, in this movement-leaning sample, we estimate that activists were 1.45 times more likely to reduce their involvement in the antiwar movement than they were to renounce their membership in the Democratic Party. Somewhat surprisingly, partisan identities were held more strongly than were antiwar identities in the movement-leaning sample.

Second, looking at the results of the DNC survey, we are able to assess the participation dynamics of a sample of activists highly committed to parties. Slightly less than one-third (31.56 percent) of DNC delegates reported that they identified at the intersection of the Democratic Party and the antiwar movement as of 2008. How did these activists change their involvement with the movement and the party after Obama's election? Almost half (43.77 percent) of these activists reported that they decreased their involvement in the antiwar movement after 2008. In contrast, only 1.11 percent of intersectionally identified activists reported leaving the Democratic Party during the same period. Thus, in this party-leaning sample, we estimated that activists were 39.43 times more likely to reduce their involvement in the antiwar movement than they were to renounce their membership in the Democratic Party. As we would expect, partisan identities were held more strongly than were antiwar identities in the party-leaning sample.

Our examination of two biased samples is informative of the nature of the trade-off between partisan and movement identities. We show that the trade-off *slightly* favors partisan identities in a sample biased toward respondents with strong movement identities. When the sample is biased toward respondents with strong partisan identities, the trade-off *greatly* favors partisan identities. Thus, it is reasonable to conclude that the range of possibilities runs from a small advantage for partisan identities to a large advantage for partisan identities. Either way, the weight of the data strongly supports $H_{4.6}$, which indicates that parties have an advantage over movements. This finding offers a critical piece of evidence supporting our intersectionality argument. Partisan identities hold a relative advantage, and movement identities have a relative disadvantage, in contexts where they intersect.

The analysis of this section also speaks to the declining participation of Democrats in the antiwar movement that we observe in Figure 4.3. It is probably the case that some of the decline that we witnessed can be attributed to individuals' growing frustrated with the party and then switching their identification from the Democratic Party to no party or a minor party. However, our analysis of the trade-off strongly indicates that the majority – if not the overwhelming majority – of this decline is produced by Democrats leaving the antiwar movement, not antiwar activists leaving the Democratic Party. Our evidence robustly supports the view that self-identified Democrats became proportionately less active participants in the antiwar movement after Obama's election. Democratic identities trumped antiwar identities.

PARTISAN WORLDVIEWS

Partisan identification affects the way that individuals see and understand the world. It has the potential to help them to interpret an ambiguous reality and make judgments about what problems are most important. One reason why some Democrats disengaged from the antiwar movement was the perception that the wars in Iraq and Afghanistan were being handled well by their fellow Democrat in the White House. With the wars being adequately addressed by Obama, activists were free to redirect their energies to other causes.

In order to assess the relationship between Democratic Party membership and activists' judgments about war, we asked Social Forum participants, "Since BARACK OBAMA has become President of the United States, how do you think that he has done in managing the situation in IRAQ?"[16] We followed up with a parallel question on Afghanistan. Using only the responses of individuals who indicated that they had a history of involvement in the antiwar movement, we estimated ordered probit regression models using the same independent variables as equation 4.4 in the previous section.

Before discussing the multivariate results, we consider the descriptive statistics resulting from the questions on Obama's management of Iraq and Afghanistan. From the mean values of the dependent variables, reported in Table 4.6, it is apparent that President Obama did not impress antiwar activists at the Social Forum in the way that he dealt with these wars. Antiwar activists rated Obama's management of Iraq at slightly better than 3 on a 5-point scale, indicating that, on average, they saw him as having made no difference in Iraq. Interestingly, this rating precisely matches our policy analysis in Chapter 3. Regarding Afghanistan, antiwar activists were substantially less satisfied, rating

---

[16] Options: 1 = SIGNIFICANTLY WORSENED the situation in Iraq; 2 = SLIGHTLY WORSENED; 3 = MADE NO DIFFERENCE; 4 = SLIGHTLY IMPROVED; and 5 = SIGNIFICANTLY IMPROVED.

TABLE 4.6. *Activists' Attitudes about Obama's Management of Iraq and Afghanistan*

Independent Variable	(4.7)	(4.8)
	Iraq	Afghanistan
Self-Identified Democrat = 1	0.5055***	0.5860***
	(0.1318)	(0.1331)
Salience of Movement Identity	0.0531	-0.0306
(5 = Activism Core to Identity, 1 = Reject Activism)	(0.0511)	(0.0551)
Political Attitudes	-0.0778	-0.2282***
(9 = Radical Left, 1 = Radical Right)	(0.0572)	(0.0706)
Organizational Member = 1	-0.2104	-0.3568**
	(0.1431)	(0.1376)
Sex/Gender Is Female = 1	0.0805	0.2561*
	(0.1129)	(0.1158)
Race/Ethnicity Is White = 1	-0.0855	0.1105
	(0.1292)	(0.1244)
Age in Years	0.0093*	-0.0069
	(0.0041)	(0.0040)
Level of Education (1 = Less than High School	-0.0065	0.0010
to 7 = Graduate Degree)	(0.0343)	(0.0353)
Annual Income in Thousands of Dollars	-0.0027	-0.0024
	(0.0029)	(0.0028)
First Cut Point	-1.7331***	-2.6743***
	(0.4964)	(0.6054)
Second Cut Point	-1.2371***	-2.0343***
	(0.4985)	(0.6009)
Third Cut Point	0.2874	-0.9263
	(0.5014)	(0.5964)
Fourth Cut Point	1.7542	0.3901
	(0.5112)	(0.6163)
Mean of Dependent Variable	3.0726	2.1464
N	442	439
F Statistic	4.19***	8.25***
F Degrees of Freedom	9, 433	9, 430

Note: * $p \leq 0.050$, ** $p \leq 0.010$, *** $p \leq 0.001$. Ordered probit regression estimates are adjusted using sample weights. Standard errors in parentheses.

Obama's conduct of policy at a little better than 2 on a 5-point scale. This score implies that, on average, antiwar activists at the Social Forum believed that Obama had made the situation in Afghanistan slightly worse. Clearly, the antiwar movement did not slow during Obama's presidency because activists supported the war policies in Afghanistan; we find that the reverse is true. Nonetheless, there was considerable variation among antiwar respondents in how they answered these questions based on their partisan identification. With respect to Iraq, Democratic antiwar respondents rated Obama's performance at 3.42, on average, while non-Democratic antiwar respondents rated Obama's performance at 2.96, on average. With respect to Afghanistan, Democratic antiwar respondents rated Obama's performance at 2.62, on average, while non-Democratic antiwar respondents rated Obama's performance at 2.01, on average. In the case of both wars, partisan identification accounted for approximately a half a point in rating Obama's performance.

The multivariate results reported in Table 4.6 demonstrate that the differences between Democratic and non-Democratic antiwar activists are statistically significant, even after alternative explanations for war attitudes are taken into account. For example, the difference between Democrats and non-Democrats is not simply due to political ideology; self-identified Democrats are more likely to view Obama's policies in a favorable light, even after allowing for the fact that more left-leaning activists were more opposed to Obama's policies than were ideologically moderate activists. Faced with the same reality of continued war in Iraq and Afghanistan, self-identified Democrats in the antiwar movement viewed Obama's performance in a more favorable light than did non-Democrats in the antiwar movement, which is our claim in hypothesis $H_{4.7}$. Importantly, these findings hold for attitudes on both Iraq and Afghanistan, thus demonstrating that differences in attitudes toward these conflicts do not erase the effects of Democratic Party identification.

The analysis in Table 4.6 considers responses from Social Forum activists who indicated that they had been involved in the antiwar movement after 9/11. We wondered what we might learn specifically from those activists who reduced their participation in the antiwar movement after Obama's election. Did partisan differences in their evaluation of Obama's policy account for their disengagement with the movement, consistent with our expectation in $H_{4.7}$? To address this question, we asked these respondents, "If you answered [that your involvement in the antiwar movement] DECREASED SUBSTANTIALLY or DECREASED SOMEWHAT, then please check all of the reasons that you decreased your involvement in the anti-war movement." This question allows us to compare our argument with alternative explanations for declining participation. The responses to this question are reported in terms of partisan affiliation in Table 4.7.

Democrats and non-Democrats alike offered similar reasons for their disengagement from the antiwar movement. Common answers included that their energies had been drawn into different issues, that they had few opportunities

TABLE 4.7. *Reasons for Reduced Antiwar Involvement by Social Forum Participants*

Reason	Democrats	Non-Democrats
Because of changes in my life, I have LESS TIME for activism.	37.51%	41.50%
I have fewer FINANCIAL RESOURCES available to me for activism.	11.77%	16.71%
I have received LESS ENCOURAGEMENT to participate from my friends.	13.97%	16.80%
Barack Obama is DEALING WITH THE PROBLEMS in Iraq and Afghanistan.	18.93%*	6.76%*
Antiwar issues now seem LESS PRESSING THAN OTHER ISSUES.	51.31%	46.71%
There have been FEWER OPPORTUNITIES for my involvement.	35.17%	38.04%
Other (Selected): The antiwar movement is INEFFECTIVE.	3.87%	7.29%
$N = 189$	51	138

Note: $* p \leq 0.050$, $** p \leq 0.010$, $*** p \leq 0.001$. Significance tests are based on difference of means tests between Democrats and non-Democrats.

to be involved in the antiwar movement, and that they had less time for activism. The only answer for which responses differed on the basis of partisan identifications was that "Barack Obama IS DEALING WITH THE PROBLEMS in Iraq and Afghanistan." Democratic respondents were almost three times more likely than non-Democrats to say that they disengaged with the antiwar movement because of positive views of Obama's stewardship. This finding further supports hypothesis $H_{4.7}$ that self-identified Democrats tended to view foreign policy through a partisan lens. If Obama were dealing with problems of war in an objectively better way, then we would expect Democrats and non-Democrats alike to say so. But the fact that self-identified Democrats differed from non-Democrats suggests that respondents' realities have a partisan tint to them. Moreover, their analysis reveals that among those departing from the antiwar movement, the major difference between Democrats and non-Democrats was their attitudes. Differences in demobilization between Democrats and non-Democrats cannot be accounted for with common alternative explanations such as burnout and lack of resources. Instead, Democrats and non-Democrats differed principally in how they interpreted Obama's foreign policy.

Partisan identification may have the power to redirect the agendas of activists. The rise of the Obama administration opened up the possibility of progressive policy change in the form of comprehensive health insurance reform (Jacobs and Skocpol 2010), a subject on which Democrats had been hungering for change since the defeat of President Bill Clinton's proposed Health Security Act in 1994 (Skocpol 1997). As grassroots organizations mobilized to advance this Democratic agenda, we suspect that many self-identified Democrats in the antiwar movement were siphoned away to this new calling.

To evaluate hypothesis $H_{4.8}$ – that after the election of President Obama, self-identified Democrats were more likely to shift their attention to nonwar issues than were non-Democrats – we focus on the issue of health care. We recognize that there may well be other issues that steered peace advocates away from the antiwar cause, but we focus on health care because of its high salience and agenda status. We asked respondents to rate their involvement on health care issues separately during the presidential administrations of George W. Bush and Barack Obama.[17] We calculated the difference between the respondent's activity level on health care during the Obama administration and her or his activity level on health care during the Bush administration. We then estimated an ordinary least squares regression model on these changes as a function of the same independent variables included in equations 4.4, 4.7, and 4.8. Our analysis included only Social Forum participants who indicated past involvement in the antiwar movement.

The results of our regression analysis, reported in Table 4.8, support hypothesis $H_{4.8}$ with respect to health care issues. Democratic antiwar activists were more likely to increase their attention to health care issues once Obama entered office than were non-Democratic antiwar activists. This finding holds while including the standard battery of control variables. Self-identified Democrats were more likely than others to take the cue from the administration that health care was an important issue for them to work on *now*, even if it meant neglecting other issues that they cared about, such as peace. If the high agenda status of the health care issue alone had been enough to impede the antiwar movement, then we would have seen Democrats and non-Democrats redirect their attention in equal measure. But our results show that this effect pertained to self-identified Democrats more than others, thus signaling the importance of partisanship in the switch.

Some observers may be inclined to criticize antiwar Democrats as "hypocrites" because they marched against war when President Bush was in office, but then

---

[17] The exact questions were "Thinking only of the PAST TWO calendar years since Barack Obama has been President (2009–2010), HOW ACTIVE have you been in the following issues?" and, "Thinking only of the years when George W. Bush was President (2001–2008), HOW ACTIVE were you in the following issues?" Respondents were shown a list of 42 policy issues, which included health care. They were asked to rate their involvement as Not Active (1), Somewhat Active (2), Moderately Active (3), or Highly Active (4). We scored these answers according to the values in parentheses.

TABLE 4.8. *Explanations for Changing Involvement in Health Care Issues by Antiwar Activists*

Independent Variable	(4.9)
	Social Forum Participants
Self-Identified Democrat = 1	0.2469*
	(0.1202)
Salience of Movement Identity	0.1222***
(5 = Activism Core to Identity, 1 = Reject Activism)	(0.0396)
Political Attitudes	-0.0116
(9 = Radical Left, 1 = Radical Right)	(0.0414)
Organizational Member = 1	-0.0627
	(0.1127)
Sex/Gender Is Female = 1	0.0102
	(0.0948)
Race/Ethnicity Is White = 1	0.2426**
	(0.0930)
Age in Years	-0.0125***
	(0.0032)
Level of Education (1 = Less than High School	0.0409
to 7 = Graduate Degree)	(0.0288)
Annual Income in Thousands of Dollars	-0.0004
	(0.0021)
Constant	0.1033
	(0.3685)
Mean of Dependent Variable	0.4141
N	443
F Statistic	3.65***
F Degrees of Freedom	9, 434

Note: * $p \leq 0.050$, ** $p \leq 0.010$, *** $p \leq 0.001$. Ordinary least squares regression estimates are adjusted using sample weights. Standard errors in parentheses.

condoned the same wars during Obama's presidency (Ford 2011). Our findings, however, suggest an alternative explanation for the behavior of these Democrats. They did not necessarily start believing in war as soon as Obama became president. Instead, they saw the war and its foreign policy context in a new light once it was managed by one of their own. Although they may not have been avowed pacifists, they continued to dislike the war and trusted Obama to do what was right to remedy the situation. Similarly, they took direction from party elites to turn their attention to another vital issue: health care. They believed that their energies could be applied in that area to seize the opening of a policy window, which eventually enabled the passage of the Affordable Care Act in 2010.

DEMOCRATS AND THE ANTIWAR GRASS ROOTS

The evidence presented in this chapter demonstrates that identification with the Democratic Party was an important factor that contributed to the demobilization of the antiwar movement from 2007 through 2010. Democrats had originally turned out at antiwar demonstrations, in part, because of their loathing of President Bush and the Republican Party. As the threat from Republicans receded, so did participation by Democrats in the antiwar movement. We demonstrate this pattern using the results of surveys collected on the streets at antiwar demonstrations, as well as in retrospective surveys of activists involved in left-leaning causes (at the Social Forum) and of delegates to the 2008 DNC.

We establish that the conflicting imperatives of Democratic and antiwar identifications contributed to Democratic disengagement from the movement. The more that Democrats exerted control in Washington, D.C., the more that Democratic antiwar activists were pulled in two directions. As activists' identities shifted, they were more likely to shift in favor of partisan identities over movement identities. The result created substantial mobilization challenges for the antiwar movement.

Finally, we document that Democratic partisans in the antiwar movement understood the reality of foreign policy differently than did non-Democrats in the antiwar movement. Being a Democrat is associated with seeing the actions of Democratic leaders in a more favorable light. Self-identified Democrats were also more likely to follow the party's lead in shifting efforts away from the issue of war and toward other highly salient agenda items, such as health care.

All of our findings hold while accounting for the effects of a battery of control variables. These controls are important because they allow us to isolate the effects of partisanship apart from other related factors that may be significantly correlated with it, such as sex/gender. Our inclusion of a variable for political attitudes is especially critical because it measures where respondents stand on the ideological spectrum from the Far Left to the center to the Far Right. Respondents on the Far Left may be inclined to oppose war under all circumstances, while respondents to the center and the Far Right – even if they are inclined to oppose war – may be likely to see military action as justified under some circumstances. By including a variable for political attitudes in our models, we show that partisan attachments matter even after taking into account these ideological differences. The behavior of activists is affected not only by the ideological lens through which they see the world, but whether or not they identify with the Democratic Party.

We do not claim that partisanship entirely explains the decline of the antiwar movement. There is no doubt that a long list of factors played a role. Activists were frustrated by a lack of policy success, meager resources, intramovement conflicts, and more. Many activists burned out from too many years of traveling to protests. Yet our analysis validates a very important role for partisanship in the decline. If partisan identities were not a contributing factor to the movement's decline, then we would not have observed differences between Democrats and non-Democrats in their behavior vis-à-vis the movement. For example, if the decline of the movement is explained entirely by activist burnout, then why did Democratic and non-Democratic activists burn out at similar rates? Partisanship helps to explain the pattern of demobilization in terms of *who* withdrew from the movement and *when*.

What was the overall effect of the dynamics discussed in this chapter on the position of the antiwar grass roots within the Democratic Party? Were elites within the Democratic Party heavily pressured by their grass roots to move the wars in Iraq and Afghanistan to a quick end? To gauge these pressures, we asked delegates to the 2008 DNC to rate the level of involvement over the past ten years (roughly 2001–2011) in ten major issues of concern to liberals and progressives.[18] We found that peace/antiwar issues were a relatively low priority among this prominent group of Democratic activists ($N = 362$). Education was the highest priority, which was an area that received at least "moderate" involvement from 66.00 percent of delegates, followed by health care (62.54 percent), women's issues (54.20 percent), the environment (50.15 percent), labor (48.89 percent), and racial justice (43.56 percent). Peace/antiwar issues ranked seventh on our list, receiving moderate involvement from 33.01 percent of delegates, which was merely half the level of activity in the education domain. The only issues that received less attention than peace/antiwar were criminal justice (30.34 percent), immigration (27.40 percent), and lesbian/gay/bisexual/transgender issues (27.10), all of which pertain to the interests of relatively marginalized constituencies. Tests of statistical significance show that peace issues ranked significantly lower than each of the six issues above them ($p \leq 0.001$) and were in a statistical tie with criminal justice ($p \leq 0.413$) and immigration ($p \leq 0.055$). Lesbian/gay/bisexual/transgender issues was the only issue category with a significantly lower level of involvement than peace/antiwar issues ($p \leq 0.037$). On the whole, participation in efforts on behalf of other liberal-leaning social movements edged out antiwar involvement among leading Democratic activists.

---

[18] Specifically, we asked, "While some people devote most of their political involvement to working with candidates and/or political parties, other people choose to work directly on political issues. For example, they may work to have a law passed or repealed, or to have the government change its policies in some way. Thinking of the past 10 years, how active have you been in working on each of the following political issues. For EACH ISSUE, please CHECK THE BOX that best describes your level of political involvement." The issues listed included Criminal Justice, Education, Environmental, Health Care, Immigration, Labor, LGBT, Peace/Anti-War, Racial Justice, Women's, and Other Issues (open-ended response).

Given the comparatively low level of involvement by DNC delegates in peace/antiwar issues, it is unlikely that the Obama administration felt much pressure from its grassroots base to act swiftly in this area. Considering the limited supply of attention in the political system (Baumgartner and Jones 1993; Kingdon 1995), the administration would have to be selective about where it assigned its priorities. To the extent that it felt worried about discontent from the grass roots, education and health care appear to be issues on which it would be more beneficial to be responsive. If the Obama administration was likely to act on issues of war, it seems unlikely that it would do so simply to bow to grassroots pressure.

In the next chapter, we consider the effects of partisan identification on the behavior of social movement organizations active in the antiwar movement. We find that organizational commitments of resources, networks, and coalition maintenance are similarly responsive to changes in partisan context.

5

Identities and Organizational Action

> Americans of all ages, all stations of life, and all types of disposition are forever forming associations. There are not only commercial and industrial associations in which all take part, but others of a thousand different types – religious, moral, serious, futile, very general and very limited, immensely large and very minute.... [If Americans] want to proclaim a truth or propagate some feeling by the encouragement of a great example, they form an association.
>
> Alexis de Tocqueville, *Democracy in America* (1988 [1840], p. 513)

Alexis de Tocqueville observed long ago that Americans have a strong propensity to turn to associations for remedies to their social, political, and moral problems. These associations take a variety of forms, including formal organizations, informal networks, and temporary coalitions. Without such associations, American politics would be scarcely recognizable to the contemporary observer. Associations provide leadership, frame issues, mobilize resources, and undertake innumerable tasks that shape events and influence political processes.

On issues as weighty as war and peace, activists rely heavily on participation in associations. As we discuss in Chapter 1, the peace field has evolved and institutionalized over the past century such that there are a number of longstanding peace organizations – the War Resisters League, Peace Action, and the Women's International League for Peace and Freedom, to name a few – that provide stability and leadership as antiwar movements rise and fall over time. The post-9/11 period saw important new organizations added to this set, such as UFPJ, ANSWER, and Code Pink. Still, by naming these leading organizations, we have only scratched the surface of organizations that mobilize against war. It is impossible to know exactly how many organizations had at least some involvement in the antiwar movement after 9/11. As a lower bound for this number, we counted more than two thousand unique organizations that formally associated with at least one national antiwar coalition between 2001 and 2012.[1] Some of the most well-known political organizations in the United States belong to this set, such as the NAACP, Sierra Club, Greenpeace, Service Employees International Union, and National Organization for Women. At the same time, the field was also populated with more ephemeral groups, such as Cabbies Against Bush, An Absurd Response to an Absurd War, and Sarasota for Dean.

The organizations active in the antiwar movement after 9/11 varied widely in their ideological and partisan orientations, though they were mostly on the left side of the political spectrum. They ranged from avowedly pro-Democratic groups (e.g., Progressive Democrats of America) or pro-Socialist groups (e.g., Freedom Road Socialist Organization) to ostensibly nonpartisan issue-oriented groups (e.g., American Civil Liberties Union). Many social movement organizations try to avoid explicit identification with political parties, as we discuss in Chapter 3. Nonetheless, these "nonpartisan" groups often have informal partisan connections through the identifications of their constituents or the group's participation in the electoral process. The question of the present chapter is whether and how partisan identifications at the organizational level mattered to the mobilization of the antiwar movement.

We expect that partisan identifications affect the choices that groups make about how to allocate their attention and resources, their abilities to attract supporters, and the ways that they cooperate in coalitional contexts. We evaluate these expectations in this chapter. First, we provide a sketch of our account in order to clarify how our examination of organizations relates to the overall argument of the book. Second, we state a series of testable hypotheses that are derived from this argument and the theory presented in Chapter 3. Third, we analyze the role of organizations, networks, and coalitions in the antiwar movement writ large in order to test these hypotheses. We draw data from the protest surveys described in Chapter 4 to examine grassroots networks among the leading organizations in the antiwar movement. This information reveals how the positions of organizations in the movement varied with changes in the partisan context. Further, we look at the activities of eleven national antiwar coalitions by drawing upon archival materials, interviews, and ethnography. We consider how their activity levels and tactics depended on the nature of ties between their members and the Democratic Party. Fourth, we discuss three case studies of major organizations in the antiwar movement that illustrate the principal contours of our account. Specifically, we look at United for Peace and Justice (UFPJ), MoveOn, and the Black Is Back Coalition for Social

---

[1] We list the major national antiwar coalitions and their organizational membership counts in Table 5.3. There were likely many other organizations that opposed war after 9/11 but were not included in our list because they did not join a national antiwar coalition.

Justice, Peace and Reparations. Examination of these cases extends our understanding of the organization of the party in the street.

A SKETCH OF ORGANIZATIONAL INVOLVEMENT

As we discuss in Chapter 1, organizations such as UFPJ, ANSWER, and MoveOn were instrumental to the rise of the antiwar movement in the aftermath of 9/11 and during the run-up to the war in Iraq. In Chapter 5, we address the issue of variations in organizational involvement over the life of the movement and through its descent into abeyance. We argue that the differences in the degrees to which organizations identified with the Democratic Party help to account for these variations in involvement. The degree of Democratic identification varies across organizations, as well as within individual organizations over time. Only a few organizations identify explicitly as "Democratic" organizations – such as Progressive Democrats of America – yet the degree of an organization's identification with a party may be indicated by factors such as whether it or its members give campaign contributions to the party or the percentage of its members who identify with the party.

As we discuss in Chapter 2, the number of antiwar protesters declined by several orders of magnitude between 2003 and 2009. While the decline was ostensibly due to decisions by fewer individuals to attend demonstrations, it was also due to the decisions by organizations to reduce or end their assistance with antiwar mobilizations. Thus, the mix of organizations assisting with antiwar mobilizations changed over the course of the movement. As we demonstrate in Chapter 4, partisan threat was a declining motivation for individual activists after the 2006 congressional midterm elections. However, in Chapter 5 we argue that Democratically identified organizations were more likely to see the rise of Democratic majorities after 2006 as an opportunity to be seized. As a result, these organizations were more likely to move to the center of the antiwar network in 2007 and 2008 as they sought to synergize the movement and the party. The movement of Democratic-leaning organizations to the center of the network meant that they had greater opportunities for brokerage, which facilitated their efforts to draw progressive-liberal organizations – which were not necessarily focused on antiwar issues – into the movement. With the possibility that the Democrats would recapture the presidency in 2008, the leaders of some of these organizations may have seen participation in antiwar activism, in part, as a way to promote Democratic electoral success. When Obama assumed the presidency in 2008, these organizations backed away from the center of the movement; doing so reduced their capacity for brokerage. The consequence of these developments is that the partisan dynamic for *organizations* looks somewhat different than it does for *individuals*. Partisan motivations for involvement peaked in 2007–2008 for organizations, rather than in 2004–2005, as they did for individuals.

Variations in organizational involvement in a movement are reflected not only in the level of organizational effort and organizational positions vis-à-vis the network as a whole, but also in the types of tactics that organizations introduce to the movement. Organizations closely aligned with the Democratic Party were more likely to make use of lobbying and other institutional approaches to advocacy. Greater participation by Democratically identified organizations in 2007–2008 spurred some coalitions to use lobbying and electoral mobilization more extensively. For example, efforts to mount lobbying campaigns were brokered by coalitions such as Americans Against Escalation in Iraq and Win Without War. These coalitions reduced their efforts after Obama's election, which drained the capacity of the movement to undertake lobbying. Indeed, lobbying efforts were contingent on leadership from strongly Democratically identified groups.

The demobilization of Democratically identified organizations after Obama's election affected the structure of the antiwar movement's leading coalitions. The most significant change was the 2010 collapse of UFPJ, which was the broadest coalition in the antiwar movement during the presidency of George W. Bush. UFPJ had been a fragile coalition since its inception, as it worked to broker differences between strongly progressive-radical elements on the Left with more moderate progressive-liberal elements from the center-Left. Mutual animosity among movement factions toward President Bush kept the coalition together. But many of UFPJ's members no longer wanted to focus on antiwar opposition once a Democrat was in the White House. Member organizations clashed on whether the Obama administration represented a real change in U.S. foreign policy or was simply another incarnation of more of the same. As a result, the coalition that had been the backbone of the grassroots antiwar movement for more than six years reconstituted itself as a "network" that no longer possessed the budget, membership, or political structure to lead the movement.

Changes in the structure of the post-Bush antiwar movement were not the result of decisions by any single organization. Rather, we observe subtle transitions within many organizations that had occupied niches within the party in the street. Organizations with intersectional identities – which identified with both the antiwar movement and the Democratic Party – tended to shift their identities away from the movement. MoveOn, which was founded in 1998 to oppose the impeachment of President Bill Clinton, epitomized this type of shift. The organization became a more central player in progressive and Democratic politics as a result of its leadership of the antiwar movement. Among other things, MoveOn helped to found, lead, and sustain the Win Without War coalition, which was a prominent coalition for Democratically aligned interests in the movement. While MoveOn formally continued to hold antiwar positions after Obama's election, it threw its weight behind health care organizing, rather than antiwar mobilizations. With MoveOn's new emphasis, the antiwar movement was no longer able to draw upon the membership e-mail list of one of its principal Democratic-leaning allies.

The collapse of UFPJ – along with the end of Americans Against Escalation in Iraq and the reduced activity of Win Without War – created space for narrower and more radical coalitions to rise up as leaders in the antiwar movement.[2] New coalitions such as End US Wars, the Black Is Back Coalition for Social Justice, Peace and Reparations, and the National Assembly to End the Iraq and Afghanistan Wars and Occupations (which later became the United National Peace Coalition) stepped to the fore. Speakers at events organized by these coalitions tended to frame antiwar concerns in a narrow way that was not likely to resonate outside the community of hard-core peace activists. These coalitions, along with the ANSWER Coalition, pushed the antiwar movement in multiple directions, with organizations split over questions such as whether a U.S. presence in Afghanistan could yield any benefit to the region and whether the Obama administration could be trusted as long as the United States maintained even a minimal military presence in Iraq. The exit or collapse of relatively moderate antiwar organizations afforded radical organizations greater flexibility to define the public identity of the movement, a trend that likely hastened the exit of more moderate actors, thus creating both negative and positive bandwagon effects. As a result, the movement never again regained the unity it had achieved between 2003 and 2005. By 2012, organizations such as ANSWER, Code Pink, and Iraq Veterans Against the War were still vocal opponents of war, but they no longer were able to broker broad antiwar alliances that reached across the liberal-progressive spectrum.

TESTABLE HYPOTHESES

Our analysis in Chapter 4 examines the participation of individuals in antiwar demonstrations. Individuals' decisions to participate are critical if a movement seeks to gain broad public attention through mass mobilizations. Not to be overlooked, however, is the involvement of social movement organizations in encouraging that participation. First, organizations decide whether or not to use their mailing lists for the purpose of movement mobilization. They recognize that there are limits to the frequency with which they can make requests of their supporters. Organizations have to prioritize which issues or causes are worth their attention at a particular point in time. Multiissue groups may need to be especially careful when weighing competing requests for causes such as immigration reform, universal health care, and peace. Second, organizations decide whether or not to subsidize participation by their supporters. They may be able to provide buses for transportation or otherwise assist individuals in joining a collective action. Third, organizations may shape the kinds of experiences that their supporters have at a movement event. They may help to supply

---

[2] Donatella Della Porta and Sidney Tarrow (1986) observed a similar dynamic in the Italian protest cycle of the late 1960s and early 1970s. In that case, the defection of more moderate organizations also left radical groups with a greater role in the movement.

food, T-shirts, banners, amplification systems, or other materials that promote subgroup solidarity at the event. Participating in a movement event is a very different experience when it means joining with one's friends in a cohesive small group than when it means marching alone as an anonymous person in a crowd of thousands of people.[3] In short, organizations may aid mobilization by offering information, resources, and solidarity to prospective movement participants. They have the potential to make a real difference.

We test three sets of hypotheses about organizational participation in the antiwar movement that are derived from our partisan identification theory in Chapter 3. The first set addresses the effect of partisan identification on the participation of organizations in antiwar networks. The second set probes the effect of partisan identification on involvement of organizations in antiwar coalitions. The third set considers how intersectionally identified organizations react to partisan shifts in the overall movement environment.

In developing our first set of hypotheses, we note that when organizations attempt to activate their supporters on behalf of the movement, they participate in a network of organizations that is working toward the same end. Each organization in the network has a specific niche. That is, it has a constituency that it is able to reach. Some of these constituencies overlap with one another such that multiple organizations are able to make contact with some of the same people. Other organizations have niches that are largely disconnected from other groups in the network. The overall pattern of overlapping and nonoverlapping ties yields a distinct position for each group in the network (Diani 2009; Heaney and Rojas 2008).

An organization may be able to leverage its position in a network of overlapping and nonoverlapping constituencies if it is situated between difficult-to-connect groups (Ansell, Reckhow, and Kelly 2009; Grossmann and Dominguez 2009; Heaney 2006). Positions of high centrality may allow a group to act as a broker among competing interests (Freeman 1979). McAdam, Tarrow, and Tilly (2001) emphasize that this brokerage is a vital ingredient in collective action during contentious political periods. As a result, organizations that are able to achieve high levels of centrality in mobilization networks may be able to influence the direction of a movement's work to their advantage. Of course, the fact that an organization may be able to *leverage* its position does not mean that it is able to *determine* its position, per se. The ability of an organization to achieve high centrality is determined not only by its own relationships forged in the network, but also by the presence or absence of relationships among its allies and competitors.

Consonant with our partisan identification theory, we posit that the partisan identities of organizations affect their abilities to achieve central positions in

---

[3] See Salisbury (1969) for a more extensive discussion on how organizations affect mobilization by supplying solidarity benefits to their members.

movement networks. We anticipate that organizations that are closely identified with a party are likely to step up their involvement in networks when there
is an alignment between partisan and movement goals, and to step back from
the networks when the party and the movement are dealigned. Organizations
that are not closely identified with a party maintain their involvement irrespective of partisan fluctuations. Nonetheless, the positions of nonpartisan organizations are affected as partisan-leaning organizations step up and step back from
the network. These considerations allow us to state the following hypotheses:

H$_{5.1}$. *The greater an organization's identification with the Democratic Party, the more*
likely it was to improve its centrality in movement networks when the Demo-
cratic Party and the antiwar movement aligned.

H$_{5.2}$. *The greater an organization's identification with the Democratic Party, the more*
likely it was to lose centrality in movement networks when the Democratic
Party and the antiwar movement dealigned.

In developing our second set of hypotheses, we note that coalitions are
essential in defining the factional structure of social movements. As we discuss
in Chapter 1, social movements are not unified, coherent political actors. Among
the many organizations in a movement, there may be wide disagreement on
goals, tactics, and styles of advocacy. Organizations may disagree considerably
on goals, with some movement supporters calling for only a modest adjustment
in the status quo and others calling for a radical restructuring of American
society. Some organizations in the movement may prefer institutional tactics,
such as lobbying and electoral mobilization, while others prefer more confrontational tactics, such as mass demonstrations and sit-ins. Some may rely on
inflammatory rhetoric, while others stick close to facts and figures. Coalitions –
which exist any time two or more organizations elect to work together for the
purpose of engaging in collective advocacy – are a principal mechanism for
sorting movement organizations into groups that share goals, tactics, and styles.
Organizations that want to lobby deliberatively for modest changes in the status
quo may join one coalition, while organizations that desire to stage sit-ins
demanding the end to capitalism may join another.

Memberships in coalitions are not mutually exclusive. Organizations may
create portfolios of memberships in multiple coalitions in order to mix and
match their preferences regarding which activities they wish to back (Heaney
and Lorenz 2013). Likewise, organizations vary their degrees of involvement in
a coalition – sometimes working as a leader of a coalition, sometimes specializ-
ing in a few tasks of the coalition, and other times participating in name only
(Hula 1999). Alternatively, organizations may choose not to participate in
coalitions at all and to work entirely on their own. Whatever their objectives
may be, organizations may be able to turn to collaboration in coalitions as a
way of realizing these objectives.

We argue that partisan identities influence the ways that organizations work
together in movement coalitions. Since coalitions are tools that organizations

use to pursue their objectives, we expect that organizations change the way that they use coalitions, depending on variations in partisan imperatives across coalitions and over time. Specifically, we hypothesize:

H$_{5.3}$. *Coalitions were more likely to use institutional tactics, such as lobbying or electoral mobilization, when more of their members were closely identified with the Democratic Party than when fewer of their members were closely identified with the Democratic Party.*

H$_{5.4}$. *Alignment between the antiwar movement and the Democratic Party promoted broader coalitions, while dealignment between the antiwar movement and the Democratic Party promoted narrower coalitions.*

Our third set of hypotheses pertains to the effects of intersectionality on an organization's participation in movements. As we discuss in Chapter 3, organizations often find that they have identities linked both to movements and to parties. Movement identities are often articulated more explicitly through the organization's mission statement, web page, and other documents than are partisan identities. Partisan identities are more likely to surface in subtle ways, since they are held largely through the political commitments of the organization's members. Partisan identities tend to be longer standing and more firmly held than are movement identities. As a result, organizations are more likely to shift away from their movement identities and toward their partisan identities when these identities are in conflict. We do not expect the advantage of partisan identities to hold in all cases – as some organizations may hold movement identities more strongly – but to hold in the majority of cases. Morever, intersectionality need not favor major parties if organizations intersect identities that are antipartisan in nature. Specifically, we hypothesize:

H$_{5.5}$. *Organizations that identified at the intersection of the Democratic Party and the antiwar movement were more likely to shift their energy toward the goals of the party than toward the goals of the movement when the two identities came into conflict.*

H$_{5.6}$. *Organizations that identified at the intersection of movement and antipartisan identities were more likely to play a greater role in the antiwar movement the greater the conflict between Democratic and antiwar identities.*

The hypotheses stated in this section reflect the major implications of our partisan identification theory for organizational action in the antiwar movement. It is also important to consider how these hypotheses compare to the implicit alternative hypotheses. These alternatives are, first, that the degree to which an organization is identified with the Democratic Party does not affect changes in the organization's network centrality. That is, Democratically identified organizations are neither advantaged nor disadvantaged in the network, with change in favorable positioning determined by nonpartisan factors. Second, the tactics and breadth of movement coalitions are unaffected by the degree to which their member organizations identify with the Democratic Party. Instead, Democratically identified coalitions are no different from other coalitions in the types of tactics they use, and the breadth of movement coalitions does not vary with the party-movement alignment. Third, organizations with intersectional identities are no more likely to shift their identities toward the Democratic Party than they are to shift their identities toward the movement. If this is true, then there should be at least a few notable cases of antiwar Democratic organizations' openly opposing the publicly stated positions of the Democratic Party. From these alternative perspectives, partisan identities at the organizational level do not matter to the mobilization and demobilization of the antiwar movement.

The following two sections take a macroview of organizations in the antiwar movement by focusing on the changing structure of antiwar networks and formally constituted, national coalitions. This analysis enables us to evaluate hypotheses $H_{5.1}$, $H_{5.2}$, $H_{5.3}$, and $H_{5.4}$. The third section examines three cases that provide a qualitative view of the implications of these hypotheses and enable us to consider $H_{5.5}$ and $H_{5.6}$.

THE EVOLVING ANTIWAR NETWORK

In order to investigate changes in the antiwar network, we draw upon the protest survey data detailed in Chapter 4. Specifically, we use responses to the question, "Were you contacted to attend today by any particular organization? (circle one) [YES NO] If 'YES,' which organizations?" Answers to this question inform us as to which organizations had direct contact with which respondents regarding an event. Of course, some of the effects of an organization's contacts may be indirect. For example, organization A contacts person 1 about an event; person 1 then forwards the information to organization B, which then contacts person 2, and so on. By examining direct contacts, we are able to approximate the place of the organization in this information flow.

We gain some sense of the dynamics of the network by reporting the leading grassroots organizations in the network in Table 5.1. As we did in Chapter 4, we divide the data into three periods: 2004–2005, 2007–2008, and 2009–2010. For each period, we draw upon data from 2,349 surveys, which enable us to track the relative positions of organizations in the network over time.[4] Within each period, we rank the top ten grassroots organizations according to the number of respondents who indicated that they were contacted by the organization (*Mobilization Count*). These organizations were the most commonly cited of the hundreds of organizations mentioned by our

---

[4] Our original sample contained 2,349 observations for 2004–2005, 3,670 observations for 2007–2008, and 2,665 for 2009–2010. In order to ensure that the samples are comparable to one another, we selected a random sample of 2,349 from the data collected in 2007–2008 and 2009–2010, thus making the samples in these periods equal to the sample for 2004–2005. We use the reduced sample for illustration purposes but revert to the entire sample for the regression analyses reported later in the section.

TABLE 5.1. *Leading Grassroots Organizations in the Antiwar Movement, 2004–2010*

Rank	Organization	Mobilization Count	Percentage Democrats
2004–2005			
1	United for Peace and Justice (UFPJ)	118	45.30%
2	ANSWER Coalition	75	38.66%
3	MoveOn	57	71.93%
4	Code Pink: Women for Peace	27	62.96%
5	International Action Center	20	30.00%
5	International Socialist Organization	20	10.00%
7	Not in Our Name	18	38.89%
8	Troops Out Now	14	23.08%
8	Peace Action	14	42.86%
10	Military Families Speak Out	12	66.67%
2007–2008			
1	ANSWER Coalition	114	39.29%
2	United for Peace and Justice (UFPJ)	106	46.15%
3	MoveOn	74	62.16%
4	Code Pink: Women for Peace	53	67.92%
5	World Can't Wait	40	37.50%
6	Students for a Democratic Society	27	19.23%
7	Peace Action	23	43.48%
8	Veterans for Peace	21	38.10%
9	Democratic Party	16	87.50%
10	Impeach Bush	14	61.54%
2009–2010			
1	ANSWER Coalition	186	24.73%
2	United for Peace and Justice (UFPJ)	87	37.21%
3	Code Pink: Women for Peace	80	44.30%
4	World Can't Wait	49	27.08%
5	Peace Action	38	44.73%
6	International Socialist Organization	33	6.06%

Table 5.1. *(cont.)*

Rank	Organization	Mobilization Count	Percentage Democrats
7	Students for a Democratic Society	32	21.88%
8	War Resisters League	26	7.69%
9	Green Party	25	8.00%
10	Washington Peace Center	21	31.81%

Note: Table is based on 2,349 observations for each period.

respondents. The counts reported here reveal the *relative rankings* of organizations within the movement, so they do not indicate the absolute number of supporters mobilized. We also report the percentage of respondents contacted by that organization who claimed membership in the Democratic Party. This statistic is an indication of the extent to which an organization had a mobilized constituency linked with the Democratic Party.

The mobilization counts in Table 5.1 reflect the shifting leadership of the movement. UFPJ was the leading mobilizer in 2004–2005, followed by the ANSWER Coalition. By 2007–2008, UFPJ and ANSWER were virtually tied as the leading mobilizers. However, ANSWER had clearly overtaken UFPJ by 2009–2010, as UFPJ disengaged from much of its mobilization activity. Over the course of the study, ANSWER more than doubled its relative mobilization, increasing its contacts from 75 respondents in 2004–2005 to 186 respondents in 2009–2010. Note that this increase demonstrates that ANSWER became a *relatively* more active mobilizer in comparison to other organizations in the antiwar movement, not that it mobilized more activists in total. As we document in Chapter 2, the size of antiwar demonstrations fell by roughly two orders of magnitude from 2004 to 2010. In terms of absolute numbers of people, ANSWER mobilized fewer supporters in 2009–2010 than it had in 2004–2005, but it suffered significantly less of a decline than did its peer organizations.

MoveOn was the third-ranked organization in the movement during the first two periods. Its mobilization count increased from fifty-seven respondents in 2004–2005 to seventy-four respondents in 2007–2008. By 2009–2010, however, MoveOn fell completely out of the top ten. In fact, in 2009–2010, only three of our survey respondents claimed that they had been contacted by MoveOn, landing it in a multiway tie for fifty-second place of 282 unique organizations. While MoveOn was an undisputed leader during the peak years of the antiwar movement, it essentially stood on the sidelines of the movement during the Obama era. Code Pink, which had been the fourth-ranked organization in 2004–2005 and 2007–2008, replaced MoveOn for the third spot, as it almost tripled its relative mobilization from twenty-seven respondents in 2004–2005 to eighty respondents in 2009–2010. Similarly, World Can't Wait and Peace Action rose in the relative rankings from 2007–2008 to 2009–2010, as the movement transitioned to abeyance.

Variations in the percentage of Democrats mobilized by each leading organization provide further insight into dynamics of the movement. UFPJ and ANSWER differed marginally in the extent to which they attracted self-identified Democrats through their contacts. From 2004 to 2008, UFPJ's Democratically identified constituency was roughly 7 percent larger than was ANSWER's, with that margin climbing to 12 percent in 2009–2010. The rising prominence of ANSWER coincided with a decrease in the standing of Democrats within the movement. Democratic-leaning groups, in general, appear to have experienced a high point in 2007–2008 when four majority-Democratic groups ranked in the top ten (MoveOn, Code Pink, the Democratic Party itself,[5] and Impeach Bush). This result is consistent with the expectation that these organizations were attempting to capitalize on the rise of a Democratically controlled Congress in the 2006 midterm election. The evidence suggests that Democratic-leaning groups were able to turn out supporters in response to their postelection mobilization efforts.

While Table 5.1 is informative with respect to changes in the leading organizations in the antiwar movement, it lacks information on the changing structure of the network. How did the positions of organizations evolve vis-à-vis one another over time? We illustrate this variation in two network diagrams, contained in Figures 5.1 and 5.2. In Figure 5.1, we map the connections between individuals (depicted as circles) and organizations (depicted as squares) for the middle period (2007–2008). A line from a circle to a square means that the organization in question contacted the individual in question. Circles are colored gray if the respondent identified with the Democratic Party, white otherwise. The networks are drawn using an algorithm that places nodes closer together when they are connected with similar partners and farther apart when they are connected with dissimilar partners (Borgatti, Everett, and Freeman 2011; Kamada and Kawai 1989). We insert labels for the eighteen organizations that are listed in Table 5.1 in order to visualize how they are positioned in the network.[6] Our diagram includes only the main component of the network, which means that organizations that are not connected to leading organizations are not part of the visualization.[7]

The network depicted in Figure 5.1 represents grassroots connections among leading antiwar organizations in 2007–2008. It reveals that some of the most

---

[5] We included both local and national party organizations under the label "Democratic Party."
[6] We limit the labels to these leading organizations because of concerns about the readability of the diagram.
[7] This limitation is for ease of visualization only and does not affect in any way the regression analysis.

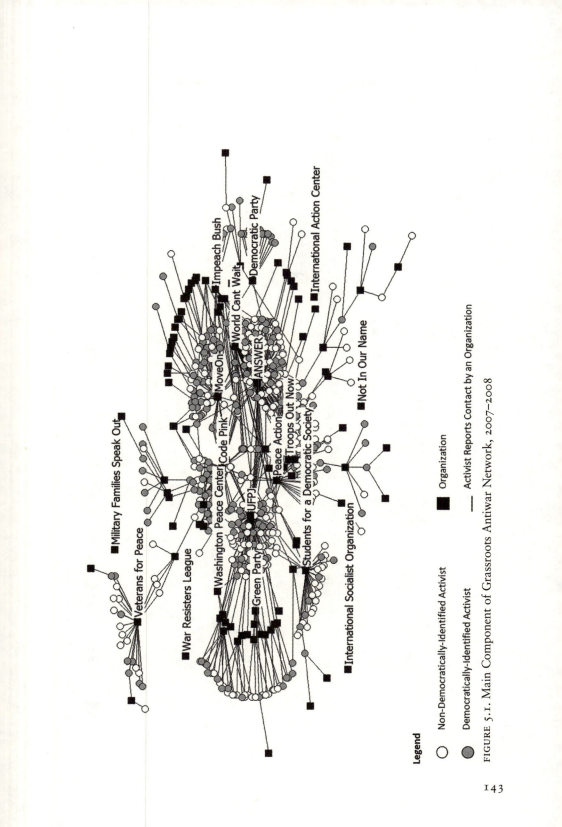

Military Families Speak Out

Impeach Bush

Democratic Party

International Action Center

Veterans for Peace

World Cant Wait

ANSWER

Not In Our Name

MoveOn

Code Pink

Washington Peace Center

Peace Action

War Resisters League

UFPJ

Troops Out Now

Students for a Democratic Society

Green Party

International Socialist Organization

Legend

○ Non-Democratically-Identified Activist

● Democratically-Identified Activist

■ Organization

— Activist Reports Contact by an Organization

FIGURE 5.1. Main Component of Grassroots Antiwar Network, 2007–2008

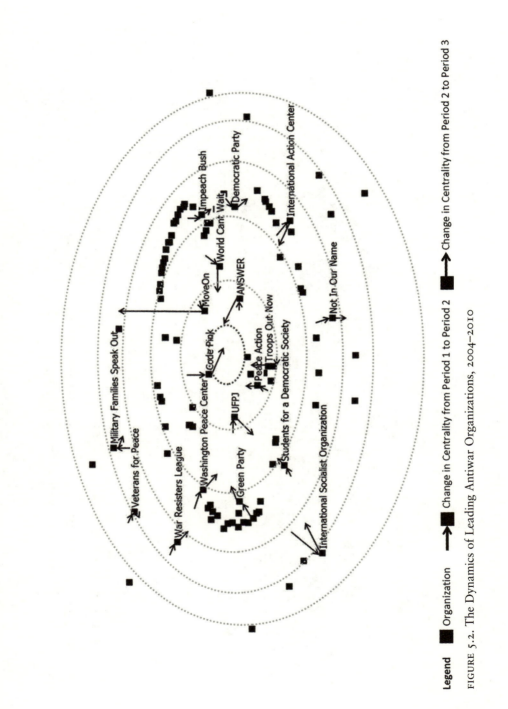

Legend   ■ Organization   ──→ Change in Centrality from Period 1 to Period 2   ■ Change in Centrality from Period 2 to Period 3   ──▶ Change in Centrality from Period 2 to Period 3

FIGURE 5.2. The Dynamics of Leading Antiwar Organizations, 2004–2010

central positions in the network were held by UFPJ, ANSWER, Peace Action, Code Pink, and MoveOn. These organizations played a critical role in broadly contacting participants to attend antiwar demonstrations. Behind this central core were organizations that had somewhat more specialized niches within the movement, such as the Washington Peace Center, the Green Party, Troops Out Now, World Can't Wait, and the Democratic Party. Beyond this group were organizations that opposed war, though they were not "antiwar organizations," per se, such as labor unions or civic associations. Also, there were groups, such as Veterans for Peace, whose niches had little overlap with peer organizations; their supporters tended to be contacted only by one organization.

We illustrate the dynamics of the antiwar network in Figure 5.2. In this network, we plot the organizations in the network for 2007–2008, while omitting network ties to individuals. This omission allows us to see the positions of organizations more clearly. For each of the eighteen leading organizations in Table 5.1, we add two vectors to the diagram, meant to convey the dynamics of the organization's position. The vector pointing toward the square indicates the approximate change in the organization's position from 2004–2005 to 2007–2008. The vector pointing away from the square indicates the approximate change in the organization's position from 2007–2008 to 2009–2010. The vectors are drawn to scale. A larger vector indicates more of a change and a smaller vector indicates less of a change. Coupled with concentric circles that denote proximity to the network's center, this information allows us to ascertain whether an organization moved toward or away from the center of the networks.

Figure 5.2 reveals that some organizations experienced substantial changes in network centrality over time, while other organizations secured relatively stable positions.[8] In the figure, change in centrality depends not only on an organization's activity level, but also on which other organizations it links to and how they are positioned relative to the overall network. Organizations with longer vectors experienced substantial change in their network position, while organizations with shorter vectors maintained relative stasis in their network positions. UFPJ increased its centrality slightly from 2004–2005 to 2007–2008, but then lost more than what it had gained from 2007–2008 to 2009–2010. ANSWER lost some centrality as highly Democratic-identified organizations pushed to the center of the network from 2004–2005 to 2007–2008, but then

---

[8] We measure centrality using the concept of "betweenness," which is an indicator of an actor's brokerage potential within a network. Betweenness is a descriptive statistic used in the analysis of social networks, first popularized for one-mode networks by Freeman (1979) and elaborated for two-mode networks in Borgatti and Everett (1997). It relies on the concept of a geodesic path: A path between two actors is a geodesic path if it is the shortest path, requiring the fewest number of intermediaries, between those actors. An actor's betweenness is the proportion of geodesics between each pair of actors in the network that pass through that actor.

more than made up for this loss as the movement declined from 2007–2008 to 2009–2010. MoveOn improved its position slightly from 2004–2005 to 2007–2008, but then swiftly moved to the periphery of the network by 2009–2010. Code Pink, World Can't Wait, the Washington Peace Center, the Green Party, and the War Resisters League continuously improved their positions from 2004 to 2010. Other organizations, such as Veterans for Peace, maintained relative stasis within the network.

The anecdotal evidence on leading grassroots organizations presented in Table 5.1, Figure 5.1, and Figure 5.2 suggests that Democratic-identified interests experienced a surge within the grassroots antiwar network during the 2007–2008 period. After this time, however, Democratically identified organizations – notably MoveOn and the Democratic Party itself – moved to the sidelines as a Democratic president assumed office. The question arises as to whether these conclusions are supported when a more systematic analysis of the network data is conducted. To this end, we conducted regression analyses in which the dependent variable is the change in an organization's network centrality from one period to the next. The focal independent variable is the fraction of an organization's contacts that identified as Democrats at the beginning of the period. Thus, equation 5.1 examines how the change in an organization's network centrality from 2004–2005 to 2007–2008 was affected by the fraction of its supporters that were self-identified Democrats in 2004–2005. Likewise, equation 5.2 examines how the change in an organization's network centrality from 2007–2008 to 2009–2010 was affected by the fraction of its supporters who were self-identified Democrats in 2007–2008. The estimates of equation 5.1 allow us to test $H_{5.1}$ and the estimates of equation 5.2 allow us to test $H_{5.2}$.[9] We estimate these equations using the full set of 8,684 protest surveys discussed in Chapter 4, rather than the more limited set of 6,947 surveys used for Table 5.1, Figure 5.1, and Figure 5.2.

Although we are primarily interested in the relationship between change in centrality and the fraction of an organization's supporters self-identified with the Democratic Party, it is also important to control for several organizational characteristics that may influence an organization's betweenness in a network. Organizational ideology (i.e., whether or not the organization is radical) may shape an organization's ability to relate to others in a network, affecting changes in its network position (Haines 1988; Heaney and Rojas 2008;

---

[9] We estimate the equations using Tobit regression models (Tobin 1958). The Tobit model allows us to account for censoring in the network, which is caused by the entry and exit of organizations from our data. An organization that was not in the data in 2004–2005 but entered the data in 2007–2008 would be right censored, since it experienced an infinite increase in its centrality score. Similarly, an organization that was in the data in 2007–2008 but was not in the data in 2009–2010 would be left censored, since it experienced an infinite decrease in its centrality score. The Tobit model permits consistent estimation of the independent variable coefficients in light of this censoring.

Woehrle, Coy, and Maney 2008).[10] Controlling for ideology is important because more radical organizations may be more likely to oppose war under any circumstances and less likely to bargain over or justify military occupations. As a result, more radical organizations may have a harder time connecting with mainline movement organizations than less radical organizations. Organizations structured as coalitions may be more likely than noncoalitions to take the lead in mobilizing participants in protest events because their organizational purpose is more likely to be focused on collective action, thus increasing the centrality of their network positions (Heaney and Rojas 2008; Meyer and Corrigall-Brown 2005; Gerhards and Rucht 1992; Levi and Murphy 2006; Murphy 2005; Tarrow 2005).[11] Organizations that hold open meetings may have a greater degree of democratization in their organizational styles, which may open access to a wider group of movement participants than do organizations without such meetings, thus expanding their network centrality (Fung 2003; Polleta 2002). Older organizations may be better adapted to their environments than are younger organizations and, therefore, more likely to achieve central positions in contact networks (Hannan and Freeman 1989). Organizations that are national or international in scope organize on a wider geographic basis than those organized at the local, state, or regional level, likely improving their relative network centrality (McCarthy and Wolfson 1996). Finally, the lack of a Web site indicates that an organization is not willing, or able, to maintain a point of contact for the public, likely affecting its ability to contact activists. Thus, organizations with functioning web pages may be more likely to reach broad audiences than are organizations without web pages, thus boosting their relative network centrality (Nah, Veenstra, and Shah 2006).

We report the results of the regression analysis in Table 5.2. In equation 5.1, we find the expected positive, statistically significant relationship between a change in an organization's network centrality from 2004–2005 to 2007–2008 and the fraction of its contacts who identified with the Democratic Party in 2004–2005. The more an organization drew its supporters from the ranks of

---

[10] We coded an organization as "radical" if information contained on its web page indicated that the organization promotes views that aspire to overturn the basic structure of American society and/or government. For example, an organization that explicitly advocated communism or socialism was coded as radical.

[11] We coded an organization as a coalition if it is an organization composed of other autonomous organizations (Wilson 1995, p. 267). An organization that has local chapters that are subordinate to a national or state organization (e.g., Code Pink: Women for Peace, Iraq Veterans Against the War) was not coded as a coalition. However, an organization formed to serve the interests of other freestanding organizations (e.g., United for Peace and Justice, ANSWER Coalition) was coded as a coalition. Having the word "coalition" in its title was neither a necessary nor a sufficient condition for an organization to be coded as a coalition. Some organizations may describe themselves as coalitions but not satisfy Wilson's definition, while others may not have "coalition" in the organization's name but satisfy the definition.

TABLE 5.2. Models of Change in Network Centrality

Independent Variable	Dependent Variable: Change in Network Centrality		Descriptive Statistics	Percentage Imputed
	(5.1) Change from 2004–2005 to 2007–2008	(5.2) Change from 2007–2008 to 2009–2010	Mean	
	Coefficient (Std. Err.)		(Std. Dev.)	
Fraction of Contacts Identified with the Democratic Party at Beginning of Period	2.3983*** (0.6952)	-1.6510** (0.5312)	0.400[a]/0.3915[b] (0.449)[a]/(0.450)[b]	1.73%[a]/1.73%[b]
Radical Organization = 1	1.7135 (0.9671)	0.8948 (0.7076)	0.1186 (0.3236)	10.16%
Coalition = 1	-0.6374 (1.1403)	0.7486 (0.8241)	0.0837 (0.2772)	17.10%
Holds Open Meetings = 1	0.4717 (0.6704)	0.4104 (0.5049)	0.6224 (0.4852)	16.98%
Year Founded	-0.0046 (0.0036)	-0.0007 (0.0024)	1976 (103)	28.87%
National or International Scope = 1	-0.6038 (0.6690)	0.0165 (0.5021)	0.4653 (0.4992)	12.39%
Has Web Page = 1	-0.7694 (0.7194)	1.0247 (0.5736)	0.7617 (0.4263)	4.83%

Constant	5.8700	-2.4655
	(7.1567)	(4.8864)
σ	6.4787	4.9012
	(0.6584)	(0.4496)
Mean of the Dependent Variable	0.0000	-0.0008
Number of Observations (N)	785	807
Left-Censored Observations	469	541
Uncensored Observations	87	104
Right-Censored Observations	229	162
Wald χ^2 (df = 7)	18.45**	20.67**
Log Likelihood	-765.8735	-750.9008

Note: * $p \leq 0.050$, ** $p \leq 0.010$, *** $p \leq 0.001$. [a] Estimate for 2004–2005. [b] Estimate for 2007–2008. Regression parameters were estimated using Tobit regression. Standard errors in parentheses.

the Democratic Party, the more likely it was to move to a position of higher centrality in the network. This result affirms hypothesis $H_{5.1}$ by showing that Democratically identified organizations gained ground in the network after the 2006 midterm elections. In equation 5.2, we find the expected negative, statistically significant relationship between a change in an organization's network betweenness from 2007–2008 to 2009–2010 and the fraction of its contacts who identified with the Democratic Party in 2007–2008. The more an organization drew its supporters from the ranks of the Democratic Party, the more likely it was to move to a position of lower centrality in the network. This result affirms hypothesis $H_{5.2}$ by showing that Democratically identified organizations lost ground in the network after Obama's election as president. None of the control variables was statistically significant, indicating that the relationship between change in centrality and Democratic contacts holds up irrespective of whether or not an organization was a coalition, held open meetings, was founded recently or a long time ago, had a national/international scope, or hosted a web page. Further, we ran the analysis both with and without the control variables in order to ensure that these results were not an artifact of the presence of the control variables in the models. The effects of Democratic contacts are robust to variations in the specification of the models.[12]

Some readers may be concerned that the effect of Democratic contacts is brought about only by a few influential points in the data. For example, MoveOn – an organization with a solidly Democratic constituency – exhibited a dramatic drop in centrality from 2007–2008 to 2009–2010. Are the regression results in Table 5.2 driven entirely by MoveOn, or just a handful of other highly active Democratic groups? To check for this possibility, we reestimated our models without the observations for MoveOn, Impeach Bush, and the Democratic Party itself. We found that the coefficients on Democratic contacts remained unchanged in their significance and direction, thus indicating that the hypothesized relationship holds beyond the leading Democratic-leaning organizations. Similarly, some readers may be concerned that the results were caused by large changes in the overall structure of the network. Yet, we observe that the mean of the dependent variable is close to 0 in equations 5.1 and 5.2. The fact that the average change in centrality is neither substantially positive nor negative implies that the antiwar network did not experience a substantial structural change. Some organizations became more central, while others became less central – and the specifics of these changes

---

[12] Because the centrality scores of individual organizations in a network are not independent of one another, we conducted permutation tests to determine whether the nonindependence of observations affected the conclusions of our analysis (Chochran and Cox 1957; Kirkland 2013). The models estimated using permutation tests yielded identical conclusions to those conducted using the standard Tobit methodology, which indicates that nonindependence is not a problem in our analysis. Special thanks go to Lorien Jasny for her assistance in conducting these tests.

were important – but the overall pattern of relations among organizations remained relatively stable during the period of the study.

The results of our network analysis add to the understanding of the relationship between the antiwar movement and the Democratic Party. While our analysis in Chapter 4 examined all participants in the antiwar movement on an equal footing, our analysis in Chapter 5 documents the relevance of divisions among antiwar activists according to their associations. Although the order of magnitude of antiwar demonstrations clearly declined starting in January 2007, organizations with Democratically identified constituents pushed toward the center of the antiwar network at that time, consistent with the desire to seize political opportunities created by the Democrats' antiwar-based electoral victories in 2006. This push offered increased opportunities for brokerage, as organizations with Democratically identified constituents were likely to increase their positions among organizations in the network. However, consistent with the pattern exhibited in public demonstrations, organizations with Democratically identified constituents backed away from the center of the antiwar network once Obama entered the White House. Much of their potential for brokerage was lost in this transition.

NATIONAL ANTIWAR COALITIONS

Beyond documenting the movement of organizations with Democratically identified constituencies toward and away from the center of the antiwar network, it is also important to grapple with the root cause of these changes. Did these Democratic-leaning organizations move to and away from the center of the network because of decisions made by the leaders of these organizations? Or were Democratic-leaning organizations more successful in their recruitment of supporters in 2007–2008, allowing them a more central perch within the movement? The equations reported in Table 5.2 are consistent with either possibility. Closer examination of the work of movement coalitions is necessary to reach a firmer conclusion on this point. To make progress in this direction, we take a closer look at the membership of coalitions, the tactics that they choose, and how coalitional efforts changed over time.

We gathered information on coalitions active in the antiwar movement from 2001 to 2012. To do so, we turned to several sources of information to identify these coalitions. First, we looked at the web pages of the organizations named by the respondents to our surveys to determine which of these organizations were organized as coalitions. Second, we subscribed to antiwar listservs, attended antiwar events, and spoke with antiwar activists to learn about which coalitions were active. Third, we reviewed articles on the antiwar movement appearing in major newspapers (e.g., *New York Times, Washington Post, Chicago Tribune, Los Angeles Times*). Finally, we reviewed scholarly books and journal articles that examined coalitions in the antiwar movement after 9/11 (such as Cortright 2004; Gillan, Pickerill, and Webster 2008; Meyer and

Corrigall-Brown 2005; and Woehrle, Coy, and Maney 2008). Using these diverse sources, we compiled a list of antiwar coalitions active during the period of the study.

We narrowed the list of coalitions in order to identify those that were most significant to the antiwar movement. First, we limited the list to antiwar coalitions organized at the national level in the United States, excluding coalitions organized around smaller geographic areas (such as cities, states, or regions, e.g., The Northeast Ohio Anti-War Coalition). Second, we limited the list to coalitions organized for the purpose of addressing substantive policy issues over time, not merely for staging a single protest event. Single-event coalitions are certainly a vital part of movement politics (Heaney and Rojas 2008; Levi and Murphy 2006; Tarrow 2005), but here we are more concerned with how organizations attempt to work together for a longer period. Third, we limited the list to coalitions that publicized the names of their organizational members or supporters. Most coalitions publish a list of their members, since a public expression of unity is usually at the heart of the coalition's goals. Organizations sometimes prefer to obscure the nature of their alliances, especially when an issue or the coalition's tactics may be controversial. We exclude these coalitions because it would not be possible for us to evaluate the nature of their members' links to the Democratic Party.[13]

Our criteria yield eleven national antiwar coalitions, which are reported in Table 5.3. This list includes most, if not all, of the major national antiwar coalitions active between 2001 and 2012. The coalitions are ordered in the table by their founding dates. We summarize the activities of these coalitions by noting their years in operation, the number of organizational members that they had during their membership peak (or at the end of 2012 if they did not disband and had not yet experienced a decline in membership), the number and percentage of their organizational members who contributed money to the Democratic Party at any time during the study period (Center for Responsive Politics 2013), the principal tactics that they adopted, and any other relevant facts.

We rely on the number and percentage of coalition members who contributed to the Democratic Party as indicators of partisan identification among coalition members. We counted an organization as a Democratic contributor if it – or an organization with which it was affiliated – made a contribution to a Democratic candidate for federal office at any time between 2001 and 2012.[14] For example, since the national office of the Service Employees International Union made contributions to the Democratic Party, we counted the union's

---

[13] Our criteria leave us with a mix of coalitions that Sidney Tarrow (2005, p. 167) refers to as "instrumental coalitions" and "campaign coalitions." The only coalition that we exclude because it did not publish a member list is the Anti-War Anti-Racism Effort (AWARE), which claimed to have organizational members but did not name them.

[14] We counted contributions by organizations only, not contributions by individuals.

TABLE 5.3. *U.S. National Coalitions against War in Iraq and/or Afghanistan, 2001–2012*

Coalition	Years in Operation	Number of Organizational Members at Peak	Democratic Contributors		Principal Tactics	Notes
			Number	Percentage		
ANSWER Coalition (Act Now to Stop War and End Racism)	2001–Present	52	0	0.00%	Public demonstrations; petitions; media outreach	Held Capitol Hill "Days of Action" in 2007
National Youth and Student Peace Coalition	2001–2008	20	1	5.00%	Public demonstrations; campus actions; conferences; get-out-the-vote drives	
United for Peace and Justice (UFPJ)	2002–Present	1,624	141	8.68%	Public demonstrations; lobbying; media outreach; conferences; electoral mobilization; advertising	Changed from a "coalition" to a "network," decreasing its activity level, in 2010
Win Without War	2002–Present	42	14	33.33%	Strategic advising to coalition members; media outreach; petitions; lobbying	
United States Labor Against the War	2003–Present	197	144	73.10%	Public demonstrations; international delegations; media outreach; electoral mobilization; conferences	

Table 5.3. (cont.)

Coalition	Years in Operation	Number of Organizational Members at Peak	Democratic Contributors		Principal Tactics	Notes
			Number	Percentage		
Troops Out Now	2004–2011	178	7	3.93%	Public demonstrations; petitions; sit-ins; conferences	
After Downing Street	2005–Present	261	14	5.36%	Sponsoring speakers; media outreach; petitions.	Changed name in 2010 to War Is a Crime
Americans Against Escalation in Iraq	2007–2008	12	6	50.00%	Paid advertising; lobbying; media outreach	
National Assembly to End the Iraq and Afghanistan Wars and Occupations	2008–Present	31	3	9.68%	Conferences; statements of policy and solidarity	Changed name in 2010 to United National Peace Coalition
Black Is Back Coalition for Social Justice, Peace and Reparations	2009–Present	33	0	0.00%	Public demonstrations; conferences	
End US Wars	2009–Present	76	2	2.63%	Public demonstrations; publishing information.	Organized only one protest, held in 2009.

Sources: Americans Against Escalation in Iraq (2008a, 2008b), Black Is Back (2011), End US Wars (2012), International ANSWER (2002), National Assembly (2008, 2010), National Youth and Student Peace Coalition (2007, 2008), National Peace Conference (2010), Troops Out Now (2011), United for Peace and Justice (2008a), USLAW (2012), War Is a Crime (2012), and Win Without War (2003).

local affiliates as Democratic contributors as well. This approach to measuring Democratic identification uses a high bar to determine whether an organization is Democratic-leaning or not, since many organizations have sympathies with the Democratic Party but do not make contributions. Our measure requires that the organization not only have Democratic sympathies, but formally support the party financially. Some readers may be concerned that certain organizations may be barred from making campaign contributions as a result of their charitable, nonprofit tax status. However, if an organization were interested in supporting political candidates, it would be straightforward to set up an allied political committee (such as a 527 or Political Action Committee) that was legally distinct from the charitable organization but still linked to it in a meaningful political sense (Berry 2003). Thus, the percentage of organizations in a coalition that are affiliated with organizations that make political contributions to the Democratic Party is a relevant indication of the extent to which a coalition's supporters also support the Democratic Party.

Coalitions active in the antiwar movement relied on a spectrum of tactics to express their opposition to war. The majority of coalitions – seven of the eleven that we examined – incorporated public demonstrations as part of their repertoire. Institutional tactics were less common, with only four of the eleven coalitions sponsoring sustained lobbying efforts or electoral mobilization. Other tactics included petitions, media outreach, paid advertising, conferences, international delegations, and publishing information.

The use of lobbying and electoral mobilization corresponded with member identification in almost all cases. Win Without War, Americans Against Escalation in Iraq, and United States Labor against the War – each of which had a substantial number of Democratic contributors among its members – relied on lobbying or electoral mobilization as one of their most important tactics. In contrast, coalitions such as ANSWER, the National Youth and Student Peace Coalition, Troops Out Now, After Downing Street, the National Assembly to End the Iraq and Afghanistan Wars and Occupations, Black Is Back, and End US Wars – all of which had a lower percentage of Democratic contributors among their members – all avoided lobbying and electoral mobilization. Each of these ten cases is consistent with our expectation in $H_{5.3}$. UFPJ is the one case that is anomalous with respect to $H_{5.3}$, since it engaged in both lobbying and electoral mobilization even though it had a relatively low percentage of members (8.7 percent) who were contributors to the Democratic Party. In the following section, we reconcile the case of UFPJ with hypothesis $H_{5.3}$ by considering divisions within the coalition on the tactics of lobbying and electoral involvement. Nonetheless, we find that $H_{5.3}$ is supported by the evidence presented in this section in 90.91 percent of cases (ten of eleven). Strong identification of a coalition's members with the Democratic Party usually corresponds with the use of institutional advocacy practices.

The coalitions that were active in the antiwar movement varied in the breadth of the interests that they represented over the 2001–2012 period; this variation can be understood by considering the membership and activities of coalitions listed in Table 5.3. As we explain in Chapter 1, ANSWER was the first national coalition that formed within the movement in 2001. ANSWER attracted its member organizations narrowly, drawing its core from organizations committed to the antiglobalization movement, anti-imperialism, and diasporadic concerns (such as the Haiti Support Network and the Mexico Solidarity Network). Similarly, the second coalition to form – the National Youth and Student Peace Coalition – was constituted on a relatively parochial basis, with its base consisting entirely of organizations catering to youth interests (such as United Students against Sweatshops, the Student Peace Action Network, and the Black Radical Congress-Youth Division). As long as U.S. military ambitions were focused on Afghanistan, the antiwar movement attracted most of its support from highly committed activists and received little sponsorship from Democratic or mainstream constituencies.

The prospect of war with Iraq led activists to begin to construct broader coalitions in 2002. The formation of UFP (and then UFPJ) was the first step in this broadening process, as the coalition sought to raise voices across the left side of the political spectrum. UFPJ succeeded in its effort to be broadly representative by forming a coalition that, at its peak, included 1,624 local, state, regional, national, and international organizations. A substantial number of these (141) had ties to the Democratic Party through the campaign finance system. Although these Democratically identified organizations made up only 8.68 percent of the coalition, they were a resourceful and vocal minority.

Win Without War was formed as an offshoot of UFPJ by some UFPJ members – such as the American Friends Service Committee, NETWORK: A National Catholic Social Justice Lobby, and Veterans for Peace – that preferred a quicker decision-making process than the larger coalition could manage (Cortright 2004). This more agile form allowed Win Without War to turn to paid advertising in the media and lobbying on Capitol Hill, which were anathema to many groups in UFPJ. Win Without War thus extended the reach of the antiwar movement to organizations connected to traditional Democratic constituencies. Indeed, one-third of its member organizations gave money to the Democratic Party at some point between 2001 and 2012, a much higher percentage than that of the coalitions formed prior to it. Similarly, United States Labor against the War attracted an overwhelmingly Democratic membership by organizing the labor movement for the antiwar cause.

Leaders in the antiwar movement took steps in 2004 and 2005 to use coalitions as a way to extend the reach of the movement. Troops Out Now was formed with the imprimatur of the International Action Center as part of an effort to expand its grassroots impact. After Downing Street was founded by David Swanson and others in an effort to penetrate the mainstream media on the issue of the 2002 Downing Street Memo, in which British intelligence recognized the Bush administration's desire to topple Saddam Hussein, regardless of whether or not the facts of the situation justified such a policy (Rycroft 2002).

A final step toward broadening the antiwar movement was the formation in 2007 of Americans Against Escalation in Iraq. This coalition was established by leading Democratic/progressive organizations – such as the Service Employees International Union, MoveOn, and the Center for American Progress – in an effort to oppose President Bush's proposed surge in Iraq. The coalition relied entirely on paid advertising in the media and congressional lobbying in an effort to leverage the nascent Democratic majority in Congress.

From an organizational perspective, 2007–2008 was the peak for the antiwar movement. UFPJ staged its last major antiwar events in 2008, notably by helping to coordinate the Five Years Too Many events surrounding the fifth anniversary of the U.S. invasion of Iraq, protests at the Democratic and Republican National Conventions in August/September, and the Million Doors for Peace campaign (which involved door-to-door canvassing) in the fall. Yet, by the end of 2008, signs of the movement's unraveling had begun to surface. The National Youth and Student Peace Coalition dissolved at the end of 2008 because of its inability to overcome collective action problems during (and immediately after) the presidential election season (Duhalde 2013; Rosenberg 2008). Americans Against Escalation in Iraq disbanded after claiming victory with the election of Barack Obama.

At the sixth anniversary of the U.S. invasion of Iraq in March 2009, it was clear that many of the coalitional activities of the movement had ground to a halt. UFPJ was in the midst of a leadership transition with the retirement of its longtime national coordinator, Leslie Cagan. By early 2010, UFPJ devolved from a representative national coalition structure to a more informal network (United for Peace and Justice 2010). Win Without War dramatically scaled back its activities in 2008 in deference to the new antiwar president (Cortright 2013).

Despite the overall decline in antiwar coalitions, some coalitions remained resolute into 2009 and beyond. ANSWER and Troops Out Now continued to call for and support public demonstrations (with Troops Out Now dissolving in 2011). United States Labor against the War and After Downing Street (renamed as War Is a Crime in 2010) persisted in much of their work within the movement, including sponsoring international delegations and disseminating information about U.S. military policies.

Even though some coalitions persisted after 2009, the collapse of UFPJ was a critical event that created space for a reconfiguration of the antiwar movement. Several new coalitions vied to fill the void left by UFPJ. The prominent new coalitions in the movement included National Assembly to End the Iraq and Afghanistan Wars and Occupations; the Black Is Back Coalition for Social Justice, Peace and Reparations; and End US Wars. Of these new coalitions, the National Assembly was the most deliberate effort to resurrect the antiwar movement on a grand scale.

The National Assembly attempted to imitate important features of UFPJ. Like UFPJ, it sought to create a representative structure in which any antiwar organization could join the assembly and then vote on resolutions and actions in meetings that followed parliamentary procedure. It emphasized the need for "unity in action, massive mobilizations, inclusion of the broadest popular sectors of society, democratic functioning, and the construction of a mass movement that operates independently of all political parties while seeking to influence their rank and file" (National Assembly 2010, p. 1). In practice, however, the assembly was successful in attracting support from the committed-Left segment of the antiwar movement without drawing moderate/Democratic elements to its side. When we attended the assembly's 2010 United National Peace Conference in Albany, New York, we found that the overwhelming majority of speakers couched their arguments in terms that would be appealing to committed peace activists but would be unlikely to resonate among the mass public. For example, Theresa Gutierrez (2010) of the International Action Center referred to "our beloved Cuban revolution" in her remarks to the assembly. In our opinion, only Kevin Martin of Peace Action and Medea Benjamin of Code Pink offered rhetoric at the conference that could be palatable to the general public. As a result, the mass mobilizations proposed by the assembly never took place. Instead, the assembly's main accomplishment was to issue a series of statements condemning aspects of U.S. foreign policy (United National Antiwar Conference 2013).

Other coalitions were no more successful than the National Assembly in revitalizing the antiwar movement. The End US Wars Coalition was organized by Laurie Dobson, a longtime activist with Peace Action and the Democratic Party, as well as a onetime independent candidate for U.S. senator from Maine (Dobson 2009). She was motivated by her disenchantment with President Obama and her desire to stop the escalation of war in Afghanistan. A wide range of peace organizations embraced the effort. Well-known independent and Democratic Party leaders, such as Dennis Kucinich, Cynthia McKinney, Ralph Nader, and Mike Gravel (pictured in Figure 5.3), agreed to speak at its events. Yet, the coalition's Anti-Escalation Rally held in Washington, D.C., on December 12, 2009, was attended by only a few hundred supporters. Although the coalition continues to publish a web page and support rallies held by other organizations, it never again mustered the resources to sponsor its own rally.[15] Instead, these coalitions amplified the radical image of the movement as one that was opposed to even reasonable and necessary military force during the occupations. This image heightened the political risks to moderate organizations should they remain involved with the cause. Some coalitions envisioned more limited niches for their efforts. As a case in point, the Black Is Back

---

[15] We include End US Wars in the study, even though it only staged one rally, because it was originally envisioned as being broader than a single event coalition.

FIGURE 5.3. Speakers at Anti-Escalation Rally Sponsored by End U.S. Wars on December 12, 2009 (Photo by Michael T. Heaney)

Coalition made no pretense of reaching out beyond the black-nationalist community in its rallies denouncing President Obama and racist-imperialistic policies in the United States and around the world. A few years earlier, national movement leaders may have tried to persuade coalitions like End US Wars and Black Is Back to integrate within an umbrella coalition framework, but movement leaders lacked the capacity to do so in 2009.

Beyond the reconstitution of coalitions in the antiwar movement, we observed organizations that had been key leaders in the movement redirect their mobilizing energies to coalitions formed around domestic policy issues. An exemplary case of this redirection was the One Nation Working Together Rally held on the steps of the Lincoln Memorial and around the Reflecting Pool on October 2, 2010 (pictured in Figure 5.4). The impetus for this rally arose principally from labor organizations with an eye toward the upcoming congressional midterm elections in November (in which the Democrats would lose control of the U.S. House of Representatives). It was endorsed by hundreds of progressive organizations – such as Democracy for America, NAACP, AFL-CIO, UFPJ, Sojourners, and American Federation of Teachers – which called for greater funding for education, criminal justice reform, immigration reform, embracing of diversity, and other liberal causes (One Nation Working Together 2010). This event led to the formation of the New Priorities Network, which drew antiwar organizations together with other advocacy groups to push for greater attention to domestic priorities, rather than military spending (Fithian 2013; LeBlanc 2013; New Priorities Network 2013).

The overarching trend for antiwar coalitions after 2008 was the dissolution, disengagement, or redirection of broad coalitions, followed by their

FIGURE 5.4. One Nation Working Together Demonstration, Washington, D.C.,
October 2, 2010 (Photo by Michael T. Heaney)

replacement with narrower coalitions or nonantiwar coalitions. The coalition
structure of the antiwar movement rapidly unraveled in 2009–2010, before
stabilizing in 2010–2011. This trend supports hypothesis $H_{5.4}$. Participation by
Democratic organizations in the antiwar movement corresponded with efforts
for antiwar coalitions to extend their boundaries beyond traditional antiwar
constituencies. Leaders worked for unity in the movement and achieved it to
some limited degree. The withdrawal of more moderate organizations created a
vacuum in the movement that was filled with smaller, narrower coalitions.

The analysis in this section speaks to the root causes of decline in antiwar
mobilization. Did the movement decline because individual antiwar activists
stopped showing up at public demonstrations? Or was the absence of organizational leadership the culprit? Our evidence suggests that the declining
magnitude of antiwar protests during the 2007–2008 period was in large
part, if not entirely, due to decreased interest among individual activists. If
anything, the major organizations and coalitions intensified their mobilization
efforts in 2007–2008, reflecting their access to financial and human resources
accumulated over the past few years. The institutionalized movement persisted in its opposition in 2007–2008, even in the face of declining interest
among its mass constituency. Still, decisions by organizational leaders had a
greater hand in the movement's decline in 2009–2010 than they had in the
earlier period. Leading coalitions disbanded or disengaged from the movement in 2009–2010, especially those containing influential actors connected
with the Democratic Party. More moderate and, perhaps, politically ambi-
tious people may have been discouraged by some of the more radical elements
of the movement. For instance, they may have sought to protect their organizations from the risks of opposing a popular new president. They were

replaced by leaders with less of an interest – or capacity – for connecting people across ideological and issue boundaries.

Our analysis in this chapter thus far takes a macroview of the transformations of the antiwar movement over time. We think that something important is missed if the movement is analyzed only from such a distant perspective. In the following section, we offer a closer inspection of groups that epitomize the organizational challenges faced by the antiwar movement after 9/11.

THREE CASE STUDIES

We tested the first four hypotheses of the chapter through comparative analyses of organizations and coalitions active in the antiwar movement. The final two hypotheses – which deal with the implications of intersectionality for organizations – require that we look inside the activities of organizations to understand how they shift their behavior in response to the changing alignments of the party and the movement. We examine three of the most significant cases in the movement to illustrate the dynamics under investigation. First, we consider UFPJ, which was the broadest and most prominent antiwar coalition after 9/11. Second, we discuss MoveOn, which was the largest organization to pursue a synthesis of the Democratic Party and the antiwar movement. Third, we analyze the Black Is Back Coalition, which was one of the more explicit cases of fusion between movement and nonpartisan identities within a single coalition.

United for Peace and Justice (UFPJ)

The formation of UFPJ was a bold attempt at unity in the antiwar movement after 9/11. The coalition's leaders endeavored to craft a genuinely national body that would extend to most sympathetic antiwar constituencies within the United States, while deploying all the potential advocacy tactics available to it. Thus, understanding UFPJ's capacity for – and failures of – organizational action is critical to interpreting the vicissitudes of the antiwar movement. In this section, we ask three questions about UFPJ. First, what was the partisan orientation of UFPJ? Was it Democratic, independent, or something else? Second, how did UFPJ's partisan orientation affect its choice of tactics? Third, to what extent did partisanship affect UFPJ's demise as a coalition in 2010? In answering these questions, we offer qualitative insight on the stated hypotheses, as well as on the processes through which intersectionality induces shifts in organizational identity.

We begin with the seemingly straightforward question of UFPJ's partisan orientation. In fact, the nature and depth of UFPJ's connections to the Democratic Party were disputed within the antiwar movement. We encountered numerous activists who referred to UFPJ pejoratively as a "Democratic coalition," especially when they derided it as a barrier to progress in ending war.

We were initially perplexed by such characterizations. It seemed to us that UFPJ's focus was unambiguously on opposing war and that its membership was open to all, regardless of party affiliation. As we document in Table 5.3, fewer than 10 percent of its member organizations made contributions to the Democrats, a substantially lower percentage than in several other coalitions. Key leaders in UFPJ were openly affiliated with the Communist Party USA – notably Leslie Cagan and Judith LeBlanc. Given these facts, we wondered why well-informed activists would see UFPJ as beholden to the Democrats.

We obtained some insight into movement perceptions of UFPJ in an interview with Brian Becker, national coordinator of the ANSWER Coalition – UFPJ's chief competitor in mobilizing grassroots activists in the movement. Becker's perspective should be considered with the caveat that ANSWER has a history of clashing with UFPJ (Heaney and Rojas 2008). He explains:

I think the fundamental difference between the ANSWER Coalition and other organizations, like UFPJ, is that we have no faith or confidence that the Democratic Party can be an answer to the problems of militarism, war, colonialism, racism, sexism, [and] class oppression. We do not believe that the Democratic Party represents any kind of authentic alternative, that the Democratic Party establishment leadership – I'm not talking about the rank-and-file, but the leadership, the ones that determine policy – are incurably connected to the same disease that afflicts the Republican Party. (Becker 2008)

From Becker's vantage point, the problem with UFPJ was not that it was avowedly Democratic or that its leaders carried membership cards in the Democratic Party, per se. The problem was that it acted as if the Democratic Party were marginally better than the Republican Party. Essentially, Becker's perspective is a contemporary restatement of George Wallace's 1968 presidential campaign adage "There's not a dime's worth of the difference between the Democrat and Republican Parties" (Pearson 1998).

We do not see UFPJ as a coalition as having had "faith or confidence" in the Democratic Party, as Becker claims. Rather, we recognize that there were influential actors within UFPJ's coalition who held such views. For example, Judith LeBlanc – vice chair of the Communist Party USA and a onetime paid staff member at UFPJ and Peace Action – explains that while the Communist Party disagrees with the Democratic Party on many issues, the Democrats are clearly preferable to the Republicans: "We see defeating Republicans as a critical step for a progressive agenda, even though some Democrats are right wing. We are in a better position when we struggle against Democrats in power than when we have to struggle against right-wing Republican government" (LeBlanc 2007). The dispute within UFPJ was not about whether the Democratic Party advocates the ideal policies – clearly it does not, according to UFPJ's members – but whether the Democrats are any better than the Republicans. Lisa Fithian (2013), a national convener of UFPJ who was a leader in the coalition since its founding, recounts that "UFPJ got pummeled from every direction over the years. It is so interesting. Some of the forces said we were too aligned with the Democrats. Some of the forces said we weren't aligned enough."

We believe that the best way to understand UFPJ is neither as a Democratically identified coalition nor as a nonpartisan coalition, but as a coalition that was deeply divided on issues of partisanship. While many organizations and coalitions disagree internally about how to relate to the Democrats, this matter was openly contentious in UFPJ in a way that it was not, for example, in Win Without War, Americans Against Escalation in Iraq, MoveOn, ANSWER Coalition, World Can't Wait, or Progressive Democrats of America.

Appreciating the divided partisanship of UFPJ helps us to resolve the anomaly of its use of lobbying and electoral tactics. Why did UFPJ engage in lobbying and electoral mobilization when so few of its members were Democratically identified, counter to $H_{5.3}$? The answer rests within UFPJ's bylaws, which allowed subgroups within the coalition to form "working groups" to advance projects in which all the members of the coalition need not be engaged. This rule enabled UFPJ to support a spectrum of tactics – from nonviolent direct action to get-out-the-vote drives – if there were at least some members of the coalition prepared to devote their energies to them. Peace organizations willing to engage with formal political institutions, such as Peace Action and Code Pink, led the way in drawing UFPJ into these activities. As Lisa Fithian (2013) explains, "Throughout the history of UFPJ, there has been a dynamic tension between those that wanted to do lobbying and those that wanted to do direct action." As a result, UFPJ only turned to institutional tactics when its Democratic-leaning faction was willing to devote time and resources to the effort.

UFPJ organized grassroots lobby days on Capitol Hill (see Figure 5.5) in September 2005, May 2006, and January 2007, but not after Obama's ascension to the presidency. That is, lobby days came to a useful partisan end. We are not suggesting that lobby days were planned by coalition leaders – such as UFPJ Lobbying Coordinator Sue Udry – with partisan purposes in mind. Rather, we are suggesting that the financial resources for institutional tactics became unavailable as a result of partisan considerations by member organizations. Thus, although UFPJ remains an exception to $H_{5.3}$, we find that variations in its use of institutional tactics corresponded with partisan rhythms, consistent with the principal argument of this book.

The case of UFPJ adds insight on the relationship between party-movement alignment and coalition breadth, as stated in $H_{5.4}$. Specifically, what explains the timing of UFPJ's transition in 2010 from a formal coalition aligned with the Democratic Party's agenda to an informal network? Judith LeBlanc, who was charged with closing down UFPJ's main New York office in 2009, recalls that

after the 2008 elections, it was abundantly clear that there were big shifts going on in the movement. Those activists who were committed to working on the Iraq War – once in

FIGURE 5.5. UFPJ Lobby Day on Capitol Hill, January 29, 2007 (Photo by Michael T. Heaney)

2009 President Obama made good on his promise to set a date certain for the end of the war – turned their attention to the most immediate, most drastic problems we were facing, which were economic. And, so many people who had been active, and had been doing lots of work on the local level, shifted their focus to the health care struggle and other issues. So, it became clear that we needed to rethink whether or not UFPJ was a vehicle that was needed to go forward. (LeBlanc 2013)

According to LeBlanc, the election of Obama, his promise of withdrawal from Iraq, and a financial crisis at UFPJ (which was linked to the global financial crisis) put pressure on UFPJ to reduce its financial commitments. Creating an informal network was one way to do that. Many members of UFPJ were concerned that continuing to protest after Obama's election would only "add fuel to the fire of the right wing" (Fithian 2013). All the members of the coalition did not agree that Obama's election reduced the need for antiwar mobilization. In fact, the coalition was unable to agree on a statement applauding the U.S. withdrawal from Iraq, since many members of the coalition believed this policy to be unchanged from that of the Bush presidency (LeBlanc 2013). Consistent with $H_{5.4}$, we observed insufficient political will to sustain UFPJ as a broadly representative coalition with a Democrat in the White House.

The collapse of UFPJ further indicates the consequences of party-movement intersectionality for the movement. Not all of the members of UFPJ viewed Obama's election as a victory. But, as we hypothesize in $H_{5.5}$, organizations that identified with both the Democratic Party and the antiwar movement were more likely to redirect their energies to other causes than to continue to devote effort to maintaining UFPJ. When they had to choose between partisan and movement priorities, they chose the party. Crucially, these Democratically identified organizations were more likely to leave with financial resources needed to keep the coalition afloat than were organizations that were not Democratically identified. Without this partisan-leaning financial base, UFPJ could no longer service its debt or pay a permanent staff. While UFPJ would eventually repay its debts and start to reestablish an annual budget, the coalition was compelled to switch to an all-volunteer team to lead the network in 2010. In the case of UFPJ, at least, intersectionality meant that money followed the party.

The Case of MoveOn

During the presidency of George W. Bush, MoveOn operated at the intersection of the antiwar movement and the Democratic Party, though it was never fully wedded to either. In this sense, MoveOn was emblematic of the party in the street. Its model of linking online and offline activism – and its penchant for raising and spending huge sums of money – enabled it to become a powerful player in American politics. In this section, we discuss how MoveOn illustrates the nature of party-movement intersectionality, consistent with $H_{5.5}$. Like that of the party in the street more generally, MoveOn's engagement was critical to the antiwar movement's rise between 2003 and 2008, but its disengagement was one catalyst for the movement's collapse in 2009.

MoveOn was founded in 1998 by Internet entrepreneurs Joan Blades and Wes Boyd when – during the debate over the impeachment of President Bill Clinton, a Democrat – they launched a one-sentence petition on the Internet that "the Congress must immediately censure President Clinton and *move on* to pressing issues facing the country" (Carr 1999, p. A9; emphasis added). The admonition to "move on" was an effort to push the country past the lurid details of the Clinton-Lewinsky sex scandal while retaining Clinton as president. The significance of MoveOn, however, was not only that it launched a petition that garnered a half-million signatures. As David Karpf (2012) forcefully argues in *The MoveOn Effect*, MoveOn's importance resulted from the way it introduced a new model of advocacy that combined online and offline political activities. MoveOn not only attracted outraged citizens to sign a petition, but also coaxed them into giving money, lobbying their elected representatives, and meeting locally with other like-minded people in small action groups. In important respects, MoveOn unlocked the secret of how to harness the vast connectivity of the Internet for political action.

At the beginning of the Bush presidency in 2001, MoveOn was still a small organization that had no formal or informal links to peace or antiwar activism. It became a force within the antiwar movement through a clever merger with another Web site. Karpf (2012, p. 28) explains that:

Elis Pariser, then a college student at Simon's Rock College, built a similarly large list [as had MoveOn] around his website, 9–11peace.org. Blades and Boyd recruited Pariser to join MoveOn's staff, merged the two large e-mail lists, and the three of them quickly brought the organization to the forefront of the burgeoning antiwar movement.

Pariser went on to become executive director of MoveOn in 2004. At that time, MoveOn attracted other tech-savvy staff from the antiwar movement, such as Anna Galland, who had been an antiwar organizer for the American Friends Service Committee (and who would become executive director of MoveOn in 2013; Hopkins 2013). This series of steps enabled MoveOn to integrate the highly Democratically identified constituency that spoke out against Clinton's impeachment with the antiwar-identified constituency recruited by Pariser. In doing so, MoveOn became an organizational embodiment of the intersection of the party and the movement.

MoveOn combined its e-mail list, financial resources, and advocacy-oriented staff to shape the direction of the antiwar movement. It helped to provide financial and mobilization support for antiwar rallies coordinated by UFPJ, though it never became a member of UFPJ. It added to the visibility of the antiwar movement by running antiwar advertisements in mainstream media sources, such as a full-page ad in the *New York Times* that referred to General David Petraeus – the commanding general of all U.S. forces in Iraq – as "General Betray Us" for allegedly "cooking the books for the White House" in representing U.S. progress in Iraq (Tapper 2007). It strengthened the coalitional structure of the movement by becoming the fiscal sponsor for Win Without War (Miles 2013), a coalition that split off from (and worked in tandem with) UFPJ in order to promote the use of more institutionally based tactics in the antiwar movement. David Cortright, co-chair of the Win Without War Coalition, explains that MoveOn was able to use its work through Win Without War to build its e-mail list without yielding that list to other antiwar organizations (Cortright 2013). As a result, MoveOn commanded capacity and resources that far outstripped anything that other antiwar organizations could garner on their own.

At the same time that MoveOn was fueling the antiwar movement, it was becoming a force within the Democratic Party. It channeled almost $100 million in campaign contributions and one million volunteers to the Obama campaign in 2008 (Karpf 2012, p. 29). This organizing enabled MoveOn to become one of the top-five most central organizations among Democratic Party convention delegates in 2008 (Heaney, Masket, Miller, and Strolovitch 2012, p. 1667). During the campaign, MoveOn grew its own member list by approximately 1.5 million people (Anonymous Former MoveOn Staff Member 2010). With its strong ties both to the antiwar movement and to the Democratic Party throughout the Bush presidency, MoveOn was a critical player in expanding the size of the party in the street.

While the work of MoveOn demonstrated the power of party-movement intersectionality, it also revealed intersectionality's downside to movements. MoveOn's internal decision-making processes did not favor continued largesse to the antiwar cause after 2009. An Anonymous Former MoveOn Staff Member (2010) explained that MoveOn bases its issue priorities on a survey of its members. After the 2008 election, a survey of MoveOn's members showed that the wars in Iraq and Afghanistan had become fourth-tier issues. The wars ranked behind (1) the economy and jobs, (2) health care, and (3) clean energy and climate as the issues where MoveOn's members wanted the organization to focus its attention.

In response to the changing priorities of its members, MoveOn significantly curtailed its antiwar organizing. It dropped its fiscal sponsorship of Win Without War (Miles 2013) and reduced its participation in coalitional activities to an intermittent level (Cortright 2013). MoveOn no longer used its list to promote antiwar demonstrations or paid for antiwar advertisements. By mid-2009, peace in the Middle East was no longer advertised on its web page as one of MoveOn's current campaigns (MoveOn 2009).

Neither MoveOn nor its members suddenly became "prowar" in 2009. Instead, their issue priorities shifted with the rise of a new administration. With so many of its members identified with the Democratic Party, it was unlikely that MoveOn would maintain an agenda that was counter to the party's trajectory. Democratic identities outweighed antiwar identities within MoveOn, so, one of the leading players of the antiwar movement from 2003 to 2008 moved on to a different agenda. Thus, the case of MoveOn is consistent with $H_{5.5}$, that intersectionally indentified organizations shift their energies toward party concerns once the party and the movement are no longer aligned.

The Case of Black Is Back

Our analysis of $H_{5.5}$ points to the consequences of intersectionality during the peak of the mobilization process. We argue that organizations with party-movement intersections pour their energy into the movement when partisan and movement identities are aligned, but then partisan identities take prominence during dealignment. However, it may also be possible for intersectional identities to suppress mobilization during periods of party-movement alignment. If an organization aligns with movement and nonpartisan identities, it may be more likely to mobilize when the movement and the party are dealigned, as we hypothesize in $H_{5.6}$. We note such an instance in the organizational mobilization of African Americans in the antiwar movement with the case of the Black Is Back Coalition for Social Justice, Peace and Reparations.

The relatively low participation of African Americans in the antiwar movement after 9/11 is a puzzle to be explained. In public opinion surveys, African Americans registered substantially higher rates of disapproval of President Bush's war ventures than did the public at large. For example, the 2003 Pre-War Racial Differences Study fielded by Michael Dawson of Harvard University (Knowledge Networks 2003) indicated that 52.09 percent of non-Hispanic black/African American respondents disapproved of the U.S. invasion of Iraq, in contrast to only 26.39 percent of non-Hispanic white respondents ($N = 1,102$, $p \leq 0.001$). Given this relatively high disapproval rate among African Americans, we would expect that African Americans would be core participants in the antiwar movement. However, our protest surveys showed that African Americans made up 7.66 percent of antiwar demonstrators in 2004–2005 ($N = 2,306$), 6.41 percent in 2007–2008 ($N = 3,645$), and 9.92 percent in 2009–2010.[16] These rates are well below the proportion of African Americans in the general population, which was estimated at 12.85 percent in 2008 (U.S. Census Bureau 2011). These below-average rates of participation are even more surprising when we consider that our surveys were mostly conducted in cities with larger-than-average African American populations (i.e., New York, Chicago, San Francisco, and Washington, D.C.).

Some readers may be inclined to attribute lower participation rates by African Americans to socioeconomic factors, such as income and education (Schlozman, Verba, and Brady 2012; Rosenstone and Hansen 1993). We certainly cannot deny the importance of these factors. Yet, we are also inclined to see organizational and cultural differences as a key explanation for the disparity. For example, we observed grassroots mobilizations of African Americans on nonantiwar issues parallel to antiwar mobilizations. Most strikingly, we stumbled upon a rally to "Free the Jena '6'" on September 20, 2007, on the north side of the U.S. capitol building. The crowd at this rally consisted of several thousand people who were almost entirely of African American backgrounds. They sought justice for the Jena Six, a group of African American teenagers in Jena, Louisiana, who received harsh penalties when they were convicted for assaulting a white student. The Jena Six mobilization took place only a few hundred feet from an antiwar rally – attended by an almost uniformly nonblack crowd – taking place on the western steps of the Capitol, at the end of a week of antiwar mobilizations in Washington, D.C. The racial polarization of these two rallies cannot be explained by levels of income or education. We believe that it is more useful to understand the differences between the rallies as instances of mobilization by different organizations from disconnected networks of activists concerned with unrelated issues and preferring alternative styles of organizing.

The occurrence of the Jena Six rally on September 20, 2007, proves that it is possible to mobilize thousands of African Americans at the same time and in the same place as an antiwar rally. The reasons why a proportionate share of African Americans did not protest war in Washington, D.C., on September 20, 2007, thus seem to be largely cultural and organizational, rather than linked to the willingness or ability of individuals to attend a protest. So, why did the antiwar organizations fall short in attracting African Americans to their ranks?

---

[16] These percentages are weighted to account for survey nonresponse.

Leading organizations within the antiwar movement made an effort to incorporate minority constituencies. UFPJ, for example, intentionally overrepresented persons of color on its steering committee and elected/appointed such persons to high positions within the coalition. Nevertheless, the movement lacked organizations that had credentials both within the antiwar movement and within the black community. Black Voices for Peace was an organization that aspired to accomplish exactly this goal, but it ceased operations in 2004 (Black Voices for Peace 2004) and never surfaced as a mobilizing organization in any of our surveys. From 2005 through 2008, there was no national organization dedicated primarily to the purpose of building a bridge between the cause of peace and the concerns of African Americans.

When African American organizations mobilize on antiwar issues, they often do so within racially segregated mobilization settings (Westheider 2008). Segregation may occur for a variety of reasons, such as differences between blacks and nonblacks in styles of organizing (Lichterman 1995), disconnected social networks, or divergent issue concerns. If these mobilizations are couched within black-nationalist frames, then they may also be imbued with a strong nonpartisan or antipartisan perspective (Dawson 2001). Such black-nationalist mobilizations may not integrate comfortably with mobilizations dominated by strongly Democratically identified protest events. Consequently, they may be more likely to surface at a time when the party and the movement are dealigned.

The Black Is Back Coalition for Social Justice, Peace and Reparations was founded in 2009 by Omali Yeshitela of the Uhuru Movement, which advocates Pan-Africanism. The coalition consists of organizations such as the African People's Solidarity Committee, Philly Against the War, and Hip Hop Party for the People. Its initial mobilizing event in Washington, D.C., on November 7, 2009, was billed as an antiwar rally, using the slogan "Resist U.S. Wars and Occupations in the U.S. and Abroad! Reparations Now!" The coalition sought to counter the perception that the election of Barack Obama had ended the suffering of black peoples around the world. To the contrary, Black Is Back activist Chioma Oruh (2009) explains the group's view of President Obama as a person who

adds insult upon injury because now we are doing imperialism with a black face.... Barack Obama has silenced the antiwar movement almost single-handedly by his actions, on the one hand, saying that he opposed war and promoting to pull all troops from Iraq and, on the other hand, throwing the antiwar movement under the bus by sending 30,000 more troops to Afghanistan. Keep in mind that the war budget is larger under Obama than it was under Bush. Obama has the same Defense Department Secretary as under Bush. Where is the change?

According to Oruh, Black Is Back has a special role in critiquing Obama because such scathing criticism of the president might come across as racist if it were by white organizations.

Black Is Back held a series of events starting in 2009, which were attended by small crowds of approximately one hundred or fewer people. Our surveys at two of these rallies, one in November 2009 and one in November 2010, found that the majority of the participants were of African descent (54.44 percent in 2009 and 70.00 percent in 2010). The rhetoric at these rallies is not likely to be palatable to a broad audience, with a heavy emphasis on conspiracy theories and alleged crimes by the U.S. Central Intelligence Agency (see, for example, Yeshitela 2009). With a strong stance against Barack Obama and the Democratic Party, Black Is Back ensures that it will not draw many activists from the party in the street.

Two aspects of Black Is Back are especially relevant to our analysis of identities and organizational action in the antiwar movement: the timing of its emergence and its relationship to the antiwar movement as a whole. First, Black Is Back did not emerge until after the peak of the antiwar movement had passed and after the election of a Democratic president of African descent (referred to by some in Black Is Back as "the son of a white woman"). Second, Black Is Back did not link itself to the broader antiwar movement by joining a wider coalition, such as UFPJ or ANSWER. Instead, the coalition's statements indicted that its leaders believed that they had been abandoned by the "white left." For example, the coalition reports that

by the time of the November 2010 march on the White House, much of the traditional white left had come to understand the nature of the [Black Is Back] Coalition and had begun to stay away. Other than the whites who function within the Uhuru Solidarity Movement, there was little or no participation from the white left on November 13, and only one other identified representative of the traditional peace movement attended the National Conference on the Other Wars. However, participation by the white left in BIB [Black Is Back] actions has only secondary significance at best. (Black Is Back 2011)

Thus, the only national organization that explicitly attempted to represent African Americans on the question of peace after 2004 did so when the antiwar movement had already receded into abeyance and in a way that was isolated from other elements of the movement that were still mobilized.

The case of Black Is Back suggests how intersectionality can prevent an organization from mobilizing in conjunction with a movement, as we state in $H_{5.6}$. The black/African-American identification of Black Is Back intersected with concerns about U.S. global imperialism and a strong antipartisan stance in a way that inhibited the coalition's compatibility with the rest of the antiwar movement. The absence of a black-identity organization with standing in the antiwar movement after 2004 is one (but certainly not the only) explanation for the low participation of African Americans in the movement.

In each of these cases, the internal politics of these organizations creates advantages for partisan identities over movement identities. Similar to the work of Dara Strolovitch (2007), we find that organizational processes systematically stack against disadvantaged identities. More often than not, movement interests were set aside by actors who ostensibly advocated for both the movement and the party.

THE INTERPLAY OF IDENTITY AND ORGANIZATIONAL ACTION

This chapter presents a variety of evidence that partisan organizational identities mattered to the mobilization and demobilization of the antiwar movement after 9/11. These organizations helped to throw the party in the street. They sent the invitations, paid for the party favors, and cleaned up afterward. Of course, the party in the street was not entirely driven by organizations. There were some party crashers, that is, people who participated without receiving prompting from an organization. The nature of the party was shaped by the partygoers, who made demands on the sponsoring organizations for what the party would be like and when it would take place. Still, the partisan identities of mobilizing organizations left an indelible imprint on the movement.

Part of the challenge of our analysis is to understand the extent to which the party in the street is driven by individual participation decisions (the theme of Chapter 4) versus the actions of organizations (the theme of Chapter 5). We see individual and organizational participation as being so deeply integrated that separating them cleanly is impossible. Nonetheless, this chapter introduces evidence that points to effects at both the individual and organizational levels.

Antiwar organizations and coalitions accelerated their involvement in 2007–2008 at the same time that individuals' participation in the movement was in decline. These results suggest that the decline of the antiwar movement in this period owed more to the decisions of individuals than to the actions of organizations. Nonetheless, organizations with a greater degree of identification with the Democratic Party moved to the center of the antiwar network during 2007–2008. This shift was likely due to a sense of partisan opportunity from the Democratic victory in the 2006 midterm congressional elections and the chance to elect a Democratic president in 2008. Organizations identifying with both the party and the movement – especially MoveOn – stepped up their involvement during the time between these potentially realigning elections. Americans Against Escalation in Iraq – a coalition closely identified with the Democratic Party – entered the fray with a barrage of advertising and lobbying for the antiwar cause. These organizations added to the partisan tint of the movement during these years.

If there was any ambivalence among grassroots activists as to whether or not the antiwar movement should continue into the Obama years, many organizational leaders made it clear that they did not want the antiwar movement to amplify right-wing opposition to Obama's presidency. Leaders within prominent antiwar organizations – notably UFPJ, MoveOn, Win Without War, and Americans Against Escalation in Iraq – made decisions to pull back their antiwar involvement. Organizations identified at the intersection of the antiwar movement and the Democratic Party tended to shift their attention to issues that served the party's interests better than did the war issue. Few on the political Left seemed to want to throw a party in the street in 2009 (though, as we discuss in Chapter 7, the political Right was another story in that year). As we observe in Table 4.7 of Chapter 4, more than a third of activists who reduced their antiwar involvement after Obama's election said that they did so, in part, because they had fewer opportunities for involvement. This evidence suggests that organizational resource allocation decisions made a difference. At the same time, it is important not to forget that these decisions were made in a context of dwindling organizational membership rolls and contributions, brought about jointly by decreased interest in the antiwar cause and the financial strictures of the global financial crisis of 2008–2009.

The organized antiwar movement greatly declined after Obama's election, but it did not dissipate entirely. Organizations such as ANSWER, Code Pink, Iraq Veterans Against the War, World Can't Wait, Black Is Back, Peace Action, and UFPJ (in a reduced role) continued to press the Obama administration on issues of war and national security. The institutionalized elements of the antiwar movement persisted. They attacked the administration's positions on military intervention in Libya, Syria, and Iran; the use of military drone technology inside and outside the United States; as well as the application of the USA PATRIOT Act and other laws to impinge upon the civil liberties of American citizens. But this abeyant movement was more fragmented, less resourceful, and greatly diminished in its political relevance. The associational energies of American politics had shifted to other causes.

6

Identities and Legislative Agendas

> Iraq is like many issues that progressives work on in the sense that you have a lot of organizations outside of Congress that are trying to change US policy. So, part of the challenge, frankly, is to connect like-minded members in Congress with the growing opposition around the country.... It requires, first of all, getting the progressives inside Congress better organized to advance their agenda and, equally important, that has to be organically connected to the movement outside of Congress.... We follow what we call the "inside-outside strategy," which guides us in efficiently organizing against Bush's policy inside Congress. Then, we link up with whatever coalitions exist outside of Congress.
>
> Bill Goold, executive director of the Congressional Progressive Caucus (Goold 2008)

A fundamental question for the party in the street is how to connect with other parts of the party, especially the party in government. One strategy that its adherents use – as Bill Goold explains in the opening quote – is to simultaneously work inside and outside political institutions, such as Congress.[1] Their objective is to use the power of those institutions to accomplish some of the goals of the movement (Weldon 2011). These efforts are facilitated by a handful of leaders who are both a part of the party in the street and the party in government. Members of Congress who regularly speak at movement rallies and conferences – such as Representative John Conyers Jr., pictured in

---

[1] Beyond Congress, the antiwar movement after 9/11 worked in a number of institutional arenas. The Cities for Peace initiative, for example, led to the passage of anti–Iraq War resolutions by 287 city governments by April 2008 (Cities for Peace 2008). In other cases, officials in government agencies used their positions to subvert U.S. war aims, such as when U.S. Army Private Bradley Manning passed on classified information to a whistleblowing Web site, WikiLeaks (Savage 2013).

FIGURE 6.1. Representative John Conyers Jr. Speaks to Progressive Democrats of America, Charlotte, North Carolina, September 4, 2012 (Photo by Michael T. Heaney)

Figure 6.1 in front of a banner reading "Healthcare Not Warfare" – might be counted as belonging to this group. For the antiwar movement after 9/11, we also think of Representatives Dennis Kucinich, Barbara Lee, Jim McGovern, Maxine Waters, and Lynn Woolsey as having filled this niche. Other members of Congress may straddle the fuzzy boundary (which we describe in Chapter 1) between the party in the street and the mainstream political party. Yet the vast majority of members of Congress do not fully embrace the sentiments of the party in the street, even if they do sympathize with some of its goals. A significant challenge for the movement is to recruit these potential supporters to promote the movement's agenda.

Efforts to organize antiwar voices inside Congress take place through informal and semiformal channels. From 2001 through early 2005, war opponents were an informally organized faction within Congress. Early antiwar resolutions were introduced by members such as Representative Barbara Lee (D-CA), Representative Alcee Hastings (D-FL), and Senator Diane Feinstein (D-CA). Each resolution received a small, cautious following. Congressional opposition began to grow in 2005 with the deterioration of the military situation on the ground in Iraq. Antiwar advocates turned to congressional caucuses as a mechanism to advance their agenda inside and outside Congress.

Caucuses are semiformal organizations within Congress that have no legal status in the legislative process. Still, they facilitate the ability of members to work on hundreds of issues that are important to them, such as diabetes, animal protection, and maintaining the army. These caucuses are usually supported by well-organized constituencies outside Congress, which rely on representation by interest groups and social movement organizations to press their legislative agendas (Hammond 1998). This approach to legislative politics is trendy. The number of caucuses in Congress has grown steadily in recent years, rising from 89 caucuses in the 103rd Congress (1993–1995) to 419 caucuses in the 111th Congress (2009–2011) (Ringe, Victor, and Carman 2013, p. 207).

The Congressional Progressive Caucus – which drew all of its members from the Democratic Party – had a strong hand in promoting antiwar legislation and generating congressional cosponsors for it. In 2005, Representative Maxine Waters (D-CA) and forty other members of the Progressive Caucus formed a separate caucus devoted entirely to ending the occupation of Iraq, called the "Out of Iraq Caucus" (Progressive Democrats of America 2005). The Out of Iraq Caucus would eventually attract seventy-three members by 2007, all of whom were also members of the Democratic Party (Center for Media and Democracy 2007). As attention to the issue of Iraq subsided, Representative John Conyers Jr. (D-MI) joined with twenty-eight other Democratic members of Congress to form the Out of Afghanistan Caucus in 2010 (Conyers 2010). Since each of these groups was composed entirely of Democrats, they worked closely with the party in the street in attempting to end the U.S. occupations of Iraq and Afghanistan.

By working through the caucus system, antiwar Democrats introduced a series of legislative measures to curtail the president's war-making powers. However, not all Democrats opposed the wars; in fact, many Democrats strongly supported the U.S. missions in Iraq and Afghanistan. Some Democrats wavered over time in what position they supported. Some Republicans, such as Representatives Ron Paul of Texas and Walter Jones of North Carolina, were outspoken war critics. Moreover, the tenor of antiwar advocacy in Congress changed when President George W. Bush, a Republican, was replaced by Barack Obama, a Democrat. These examples indicate that there was greater variation in the organization of war opponents in Congress than can be explained by variations in the caucus system alone. Instead, we argue that partisan identification played a role in stoking and curbing antiwar sentiment in Congress, as it did among street demonstrators. Partisan identification interacts with other identities and strategic considerations to shape legislative agendas. It matters to who supports antiwar legislation, as well as to the timing, progress, networks, and content of the legislation.

This chapter begins by presenting a sketch of our argument regarding support for antiwar agendas in Congress and outlines the hypotheses that we test. We then explain our procedures for compiling data on legislative sponsorship/cosponsorship to assess the progress of antiwar agendas in

Congress. Next, we examine why individual members of Congress sponsor or cosponsor antiwar legislation and how these decisions depend on partisanship. We look at the timing, progress, and networks of antiwar legislation over time. Finally, we consider how the content of antiwar legislation depended on partisan politics.

A SKETCH OF ANTIWAR AGENDAS IN CONGRESS

The wars in Iraq and Afghanistan enjoyed considerable formal support from Congress (Howell and Rogowski 2013), which created challenges in following the progress of antiwar agendas in Congress. The war in Afghanistan was authorized by a vote of 420–1 in the U.S. House of Representatives and 98–0 in the U.S. Senate (Library of Congress 2001). The war in Iraq was authorized by a vote of 297–133 in the House and 77–23 in the Senate. After authorizing the wars, Congress passed annual appropriations bills, as well as several supplemental appropriations bills, to fund the military occupations. Efforts to add antiwar provisions to these bills through appropriations riders and other tactics proved to be largely futile (Tiefer 2006). Republican control of Congress for most of the 2001–2006 period meant that few antiwar bills came to a vote and, thus, Congress put few obstacles in the way of how President Bush conducted war. Similarly, Democrats in Congress did not allow many votes on antiwar legislation after the inauguration of President Obama.

Given the paucity of antiwar bills that came to a vote, examining roll call votes in Congress – which Paul Burstein and William Freudenburg (1978) used to study changing support in Congress for the Vietnam War – would be a poor way to understand the dynamics of congressional opposition to war after 9/11. Instead, we look for evidence of congressional position-taking in the sponsors, cosponsors, timing, networks, and content of all antiwar legislation introduced from January 2001 to January 2013. Introducing or cosponsoring legislation is a way for members of Congress to communicate to attentive audiences their positions on matters of war and peace. This approach facilitates the investigation of the sources and causes of opposition to war in Congress, even if the vehicles of this opposition do not advance very far in the legislative process.

Each bill presented for consideration in the U.S. Congress has one unique sponsor. Since the mid-1930s in the Senate and 1967 in the House, members of Congress have been permitted to cosponsor legislation by adding their names to indicate support (Campbell 1982). Cosponsorship is a common practice; more than half of all bills have at least one cosponsor (Wilson and Young 1997). However, cosponsorship is neither a necessary nor a sufficient condition for members ultimately to support legislation on the floor. Noncosponsors may vote in favor of a bill, while cosponsors may withdraw their support at the last minute. A cosponsored bill might never come up for a vote. Rather than indicating solid commitments, cosponsorship is better understood as a low-cost method for members to signal policy positions to their constituents or other members (Kessler and Krehbiel 1996; Mayhew 1974, p. 61, n. 105). Cosponsorship may also be a way for members to attempt to manipulate Congress's agenda in favor of their preferences (Koger 2003; Talbert and Potoski 2002). Thus, examining sponsorship and cosponsorship is a particularly effective way to assess support for legislation that is unlikely to be voted on by the entire chamber, as was the case for much antiwar legislation between 2001 and 2013.

Our research reveals that the overall patterns of introduction, sponsorship, cosponsorship, timing, progress, networks, and content of antiwar legislation were highly responsive to partisan considerations. Sponsorship/cosponsorship of antiwar legislation grew slowly early in the Bush presidency, as Democrats in Congress calculated that the public was likely to side with the president on Iraq and Afghanistan. As the insurgency in Iraq became more deadly in 2005, sponsorship/cosponsorship of antiwar legislation began to gain steam. The antiwar movement in Congress reached its apex during the 110th Congress (2007–2009), as members of Congress sought to leverage public dissatisfaction with the president and the war. The U.S. House of Representatives was able to pass four antiwar bills in the 110th Congress, but, because the Senate did not do so, none of them became law. The push for antiwar legislation subsided during the 111th Congress (2009–2011) with the election of President Obama, even though his foreign policies bore a strong similarity to those of President Bush. Opposition to war resumed somewhat during the 112th Congress (2011–2013). This resurgence was driven chiefly by Republicans' outrage over President Obama's failure to seek congressional authorization for the use of force in Libya, as was legally required by the War Powers Resolution of 1973.

Throughout the 2011–2013 period, sponsorship/cosponsorship of antiwar legislation was primarily by Democratic members of Congress, though Republican opposition to war spiked during the 110th (2007–2009) and 112th congresses (2011–2013). To the extent that Republican members of Congress opposed war, they did so in a looser and less organized way than did Democrats. For example, Republicans never formed an "Out of Libya Caucus"; nor did they join any of the antiwar caucuses organized by Democrats.

The partisan identity of the president was a factor in mobilizing support for antiwar causes. Other factors equal, Democrats in Congress were more likely to oppose war when it was prosecuted by President Bush and less likely to oppose it when it was prosecuted by President Obama. Conversely, Republicans in Congress were less likely to oppose war when it was prosecuted by President Bush and more likely to oppose war when it was prosecuted by President Obama. Antiwar legislation was more likely to progress in Congress once the Democrats captured the congressional majority in 2006, as long as President Bush was in office. Democratic leaders did not allow antiwar legislation to progress far during the Obama presidency. Similarly, the rise of a Republican majority in the House during the 112th Congress facilitated the progress of antiwar legislation in that chamber.

The content of antiwar legislation, too, was sensitive to partisan fluctuations. Democrats in Congress proceeded cautiously with their proposals when they were at a partisan disadvantage but amped up their efforts when the partisan winds blew in their favor. Likewise, Republicans in Congress took a bolder course when President Bush was a lame duck in his final two years and when President Obama seemed potentially vulnerable on his handling of the situation in Libya.

The analysis of this chapter reveals both similarities and differences between the mobilization of the antiwar movement through grassroots demonstrations and its mobilization in Congress. War opponents in Congress proceeded more slowly and cautiously than did protesters. Members of Congress were loath to criticize Bush's policies in the early days of the wars. In contrast, street demonstrations drew their largest crowds before the U.S. invasion of Iraq. Instead, members of Congress followed the path of antiwar organizations – especially those with Democratic leanings – by staging their most aggressive battle against the war in the immediate aftermath of the 2006 congressional elections. Antiwar organizations and members of Congress sensed vulnerability of the Bush administration during these years.

Yet, as was the case for grassroots demonstrations and organizational actions, congressional opposition to war dissipated once Obama entered the White House. The abandonment of congressional opposition at this time is puzzling because Democratic members of the 111th Congress were in a stronger position to compel the new president to sign antiwar legislation than they had been during the 110th Congress. For example, legislation requiring the redeployment of forces from Iraq ought to have had a more favorable reception in the Obama White House than it had received in the Bush White House. Instead, the partisan loyalty of Democrats to a president of their own party appears to have trumped their concern with antiwar issues. They did not want to be in a position of tying the hands of their copartisan in the Oval Office. When new opposition to war did spring up during the 112th Congress, it was mostly among Republican members of Congress concerned with the president's misuse of war powers in another conflict.

TESTABLE HYPOTHESES

Members of Congress may identify with social movements and/or political parties. As a result, they may have both policy and partisan reasons to take positions on questions of war and peace. Members have beliefs about how the United States should or should not use force in the international arena. These beliefs may be influenced by ideology, the desire to represent constituents, personal characteristics (e.g., veteran status, gender), or other factors that shape members' understandings of the issues. At the same time, there may be strategic reasons for members of Congress to support or oppose going to war.

The beliefs of members of Congress about war may correlate with political party membership. This correlation may exist, in part, because of commonalities among the members of the party in their ideologies, the composition of their constituencies, and their personal characteristics. At the same time, antiwar identities have a long-standing connection with Democratic partisanship. In the post–World War II era, liberal Democrats arose as a voice for peace in a world dominated by a cold war with the Soviet Union and a developing nuclear arms race (DeBenedetti 1990). The connection between the Democrats and peace continued during the Vietnam War era with the emergence of peace candidates, such as U.S. Senators George McGovern and Robert Kennedy. Nevertheless, the Democratic Party has included strong advocates for war, particularly from among its members in southern states (Feldman 2009). The existence of this prowar faction means that the Democratic Party is often split on questions of war and peace. Analogously, the Republican Party contains a libertarian-isolationist wing, embodied by members such as former Representative Ron Paul of Texas (Edwards 2011). However, to the extent that antiwar voices are raised within Congress, they usually (but not always) are within the Democratic Party. Thus, we expect that

H$_{6.1}$. *Democratic members of Congress were more likely to support antiwar legislation than were Republican members of Congress, other things equal.*

Strategic incentives for members of Congress to take positions on matters of war and peace may arise from leaders of their party. Presidents, in particular, have been much more partisan actors since the Reagan era than they had been during the middle of the twentieth century (Skinner 2009). In the present era, presidents work actively to support their copartisans in Congress during elections, craft notably partisan agendas, and, in turn, find that their public support is largely among citizens identifying with their own party (Jacobson 2006). As Frances Lee (2009, p. 22) argues, "Members of Congress know that how they handle a president's priorities affects the party's collective reputation." As a result, members of the opposite party have little incentive to cooperate with the president in the legislative arena. The president comes to rely almost exclusively on the members of his own party to advance legislation and becomes intimately involved in the workings of his party's congressional caucus. The pressures of the strong partisan presidency, along with leader-enforced party discipline in Congress (Cox and McCubbins 1993), make it likely that if a member is of the same party as that of the president, then she or he may have political incentives to support the president's war initiatives (Kriner 2010; Howell and Pevehouse 2006). Conversely, if a member is of the opposite party from that of the president, then she or he may have political incentives to oppose the president's use of force. Thus, we expect that

H$_{6.2}$. *Members of Congress were more likely to support war when it was prosecuted by a president of their own party and more likely to oppose war when it was prosecuted by a president of the opposite party.*

The willingness of members of Congress to support antiwar legislation or not may depend not only on their partisan identities, but also on the overall balance of power in Congress as a whole. Members may be more likely to introduce legislation when they anticipate that it has a greater likelihood of gaining broad support. As a result, members may be more likely to introduce antiwar legislation when it is in line with the interests of the party leaders of the chamber. Likewise, antiwar legislation may be more likely to advance in Congress when it aligns with the agenda of the majority caucus in the chamber. Thus, we expect that

$H_{6.3}$. *Members of Congress were more likely to introduce antiwar legislation when the leaders of the majority party in the chamber opposed the president's war agenda and less likely to do so when they supported the president's war agenda.*

$H_{6.4}$. *Antiwar legislation was more likely to make progress on the floor when the leaders of the majority party in the chamber opposed the president's war agenda and less likely to make progress when they supported the president's war agenda.*

Partisan identity plays a key role not only in whether or not members of Congress oppose war, but also in how they organize their opposition to war. Social networks among members of Congress augment the formation of alliances around legislation (DeGregorio 1997). Given the strong tendency in social networks toward homophily – the propensity of actors to form social ties with others who are like them in important respects (McPherson, Smith-Lovin, and Cook 2001) – we anticipate that Democrats are likely to work with other Democrats on antiwar legislation and Republicans are likely to work with other Republicans on antiwar legislation. The likelihood for copartisans to work together on legislation is reinforced by trends toward partisan polarization in Congress (Theriault 2008). Thus, we expect that

$H_{6.5}$. *When members of Congress sponsored/cosponsored antiwar legislation, they were more likely to do so in conjunction with members of their own party than to do so with members of the opposite party.*

Partisan considerations are also a factor in determining the content of legislation that is introduced. If the partisan balance of power suggests that members may be unable to have much of an effect on policy through legislation, then legislation may be introduced largely for the purpose of scoring symbolic partisan victories. However, as the prospect of victory through legislation increases, then legislation becomes more substantive and focused on offering a governing challenge. Thus, we expect that

$H_{6.6}$. *Members of Congress were more likely to introduce symbolic antiwar legislation when the partisan balance of power was unfavorable to their cause. Members of Congress were more likely to introduce substantive antiwar legislation when the partisan balance of power was favorable to their cause.*

The hypotheses stated in this section reflect the major implications of our partisan identification theory for the dynamics of legislative agendas.

In proposing these hypotheses, we are casting them against three alternative hypotheses. First, we expect members of Congress to guard their institutional prerogatives vis-à-vis the chief executive. Indeed, we recognize that the desire of members of Congress to protect their constitutionally endowed war-making powers ought to explain some of members' behavior in this domain. However, to the extent that members seek to protect these powers for constitutional/institutional reasons, they ought to do so without regard to their own party or the party of the president. Evidence that opposition to war corresponds significantly to partisan variations suggests that partisan identification matters in addition to institutional prerogatives. Second, we expect that members' personal backgrounds, beliefs, and constituencies influence their willingness to take up the antiwar cause. Thus, in order to be supported, our hypotheses must hold when these factors are held constant. Finally, we expect that members of Congress modify their degree of support for/ opposition to war as the factual situation of the war changes. In order to receive support, our hypotheses must be substantiated after taking into account this possibility.

In the following section, we explain how we compiled data on legislative agendas in Congress to test the hypotheses stated in this chapter.

DATA ON ANTIWAR AGENDAS

We gathered data on antiwar legislation by searching the Thomas.gov Web site hosted by the Library of Congress (2011–2013). We searched the database for legislation containing any of sixteen key terms related to war and peace.[2] Four research assistants read each piece of legislation identified by this search to determine whether it was antiwar in nature. Legislation was labeled as antiwar if it appeared to have the intent to impede the ability of the president to carry out military actions or if it was intended to express disapproval of those actions, or war in general. If any reader marked the legislation as potentially antiwar, then the legislation was placed on a list for further discussion. All the legislation on this list was then discussed among all readers and one of the authors to reach consensus on the final list.

For each of the 150 pieces of legislation reaching the final list (which is provided in Appendix I), the sponsors and cosponsors of the legislation were recorded. The sponsorship/cosponsorship data were compiled on a member-by-member basis. We noted whether a bill was sponsored by a Democratic or Republican member. Using these data, the determinants of sponsorship/

---

[2] The terms were *armed forces and national security, Afghanistan, civil liberties, Department of Defense, detention of persons, Iraq, Libya, military agreements, military bases, military intervention, military operations, military personnel, military policy, military withdrawal, National Guard and Reserves,* and *war crimes.*

cosponsorship can be assessed. By listing the members who sponsored or cosponsored each piece of legislation, we have the basic data necessary to graph networks of sponsors/cosponsors within each chamber.

We were interested not only in which legislation was introduced, but also in how far it progressed in the legislative process. In particular, we noted whether a bill was discussed in committee, whether a vote was taken on it, and whether it passed the House or the Senate. None of the legislation in this study was signed into law by the president.

We read each piece of legislation and coded the content of its provisions. We placed each bill into one or more of fourteen substantive categories: immediate withdrawal; set withdrawal in motion; no escalation of troops; no permanent bases; redeployment of troops away from war zone; condemn doctrine of preemption; alter institutional powers for peace; require Iraqi or Afghan approval for U.S. actions; adopt policies to stabilize Iraq or Afghanistan; focus on diplomatic relations; censure of American leadership; no war on Iran, Libya, or Syria; no war without congressional authorization; and other antiwar provisions. These categories were intended to encompass the major issues of contention over war during the period of the study.

In the following four sections, we use the data described here to test the hypotheses outlined in the previous section.

PARTISANSHIP, SPONSORSHIP, AND COSPONSORSHIP

Most members of Congress did not sponsor or cosponsor any antiwar legislation in the 107th Congress (2001–2003). In those years, 40 members each sponsored or cosponsored one piece of antiwar legislation, 24 members each supported two pieces, and 3 members each got behind three pieces. An overwhelming majority of 475 members (88 percent) supported no antiwar legislation at all. Support for the antiwar cause grew in the ensuing years, reaching a peak of support in the 110th Congress (2007–2009). During that Congress, 81 members each sponsored or cosponsored one piece of antiwar legislation, 56 members each supported two pieces, and 149 members each signed on to three or more pieces of antiwar legislation. Slightly less than a majority of 263 members (48 percent) did not back any antiwar legislation. Thus, the antiwar movement fluctuated from being a tiny, minority faction to constituting a slight (albeit inchoate) majority. What accounts for this variation?

This section reports the results of three regression models for the sponsorship or cosponsorship of antiwar legislation by members of Congress. The dependent variable in these models is the count of the number of times, per Congress, that a member sponsored or cosponsored antiwar legislation. This measure provides a useful (though imperfect) indication of the strength of a member's public opposition to war. Members sponsoring/cosponsoring more antiwar bills/resolutions are assumed to take a stronger public antiwar stance than are members sponsoring/cosponsoring fewer bills/resolutions.[3]

The regressions are estimated using negative binomial regression models. This approach is appropriate when the dependent variable is an overdispersed count of a phenomenon that has zero value occurring frequently (Hilbe 2007, pp. 4–6). Equation 6.1 examines the count of all antiwar sponsorships and cosponsorships by all members of the 107th through 112th Congresses (2001 to 2013). Equations 6.2 and 6.3 break the results down by party; equation 6.2 includes only Democrats and equation 6.3 includes only Republicans. All three models were estimated using random effects negative binomial models with bootstrap standard errors, because of the panel nature of the data (Hilbe 2007, p. 478). The data are "panel data" because there are repeated observations of individual members of Congress, with some members appearing in all six congresses.

Each model contains four sets of independent variables: (1) partisanship and ideology, (2) Iraq and Afghanistan, (3) position in Congress, and (4) personal characteristics. The partisanship and ideology variables include whether a member is a Democrat or not (scored 1 or 0), whether or not the member is of the same party as the president, and the degree to which the member has a liberal ideology (scored from −1.315, extremely conservative, to 0.779, extremely liberal) (Carroll, Lewis, Lo, McCarty, Poole, and Rosenthal 2013).[4] The Iraq and Afghanistan variables include total U.S. deaths in Iraq and Afghanistan (per Congress), and whether or not the member voted in favor of the Iraq War (H.J.Res.114) (United States Department of Defense 2013; Gallup 2013a, 2013b; Clerk of the United States House of Representatives 2002). The position-in-Congress variables include whether a member is in the House of Representatives (=1) or the Senate (=0), whether or not the member is part of her/his party's leadership (scored 1 or 0), whether or not a member served on the Armed Services Committee or the Veterans' Affairs Committee (scored 1 for membership, 0 otherwise), and seniority as indicated by the number of congresses of which she or he has been a member. The personal characteristics variables include sex/gender (female = 1, male = 0), race (black/African American = 1, nonblack = 0),

---

[3] This measure is imperfect because members may choose to express their opposition to war, for example, by making strong speeches against war instead of cosponsoring legislation. Or they may express only tepid opposition to war by choosing to cosponsor weak antiwar bills/resolutions. However, the underlying assumption behind using this measure is that these indicators of opposition to war are likely to correlate highly with sponsorship/cosponsorship of legislation.

[4] For an explanation of this method, see Carroll, Lewis, Lo, Poole, and Rosenthal (2009). For ease of interpretation, we have multiplied the first dimension of DW-NOMINATE scores by -1 in order to reverse the interpretation of the variable from "conservative" ideology to "liberal" ideology.

ethnicity (Latino/Hispanic = 1, non-Latino = 0), and military veteran status (veteran = 1, nonveteran = 0).[5]

The estimates of the three models are reported in Table 6.1. The estimates of equation 6.1 provide evidence in favor of $H_{6.1}$ that Democrats were more supportive of antiwar legislation than were Republicans. The coefficient on this variable is positive and statistically significant. This result implies that being a Democrat increased the expected number of antiwar bills/resolutions that a member sponsored/cosponsored. Republicans sponsored/cosponsored legislation against war, but they did so less often than did Democrats, other factors equal.

We test $H_{6.2}$, that members of Congress were less likely to sponsor/cosponsor antiwar legislation when they were of the same party as the president, in equations 6.1, 6.2, and 6.3. This hypothesis is supported in all three equations. In each case, the coefficient on *Same Party as President* is negative and significant, supporting $H_{6.2}$. This effect holds when we analyze all members of Congress (equation 6.1), Democrats only (equation 6.2), and Republicans only (equation 6.3).

In addition to testing $H_{6.1}$ and $H_{6.2}$, we included several variables in our models for the purpose of statistical control. These variables ensure that tests of our hypotheses are valid even after taking into account alternative explanations for the results. First, we included a variable for political ideology. Because of the nearly perfect correlation (0.9380, $p \leq 0.001$) between ideology and party membership in an era of political polarization, it is not possible to estimate separate coefficients for party and ideology in equation 6.1. The effects of party and ideology on sponsorship/cosponsorship were essentially indistinguishable when all members of Congress were included in the equation. Nevertheless, we detected a distinct effect of ideology when the data were split by party. Within the Democratic Party, we found that members were more likely to sponsor/cosponsor antiwar legislation the more liberal that they were. In contrast, within the Republican Party, we found that members were more likely to sponsor/cosponsor antiwar legislation the more conservative that they were. This conclusion is indicated by the positive and significant coefficient in equation 6.2 (Democrats) and the negative and significant coefficient in equation 6.3 (Republicans). Thus, in both parties, vocal opponents of war were more likely to be from the ideological extremes of the party than from the moderate center. This result may emerge because ideologically extreme legislators may be less likely to defer to the executive's use of military force under a wide range of circumstances.

The second set of control variables accounts for the situation in Iraq and Afghanistan, public reactions to the situation, and past positions that members took on the Iraq War. Members of Congress are likely to be sensitive to battle

---

[5] These data were drawn from various sources, including official and unofficial congressional biographies, members' official web pages, and Wikipedia entries.

TABLE 6.1. *Determinants of Antiwar Legislative Sponsorship/Cosponsorship in Congress, 2001–2013*

	Dependent Variable: Sponsorship/Cosponsorship of Antiwar Legislation			Descriptive Statistics		
Independent Variable	(6.1) All Members	(6.2) Democrats	(6.3) Republicans	All Members	Democrats	Republicans
	Coefficient (Bootstrap Standard Error)			Mean (Standard Deviation)		
Partisanship and Ideology						
Democrat = 1	1.6843***			0.5000	1.0000	0.0000
	(0.1430)			(0.5001)	(0.0000)	(0.0000)
Same Party as President = 1	−1.0302***	−1.4941***	−1.0702***	0.5153	0.3525	0.6817
	(0.0761)	(0.1070)	(0.1721)	(0.4998)	(0.4779)	(0.4660)
Liberal Ideology		6.6516***	−1.7135*	−0.0833	0.3803	−0.5526
		(0.4274)	(0.7887)	(0.4943)	(0.1428)	(0.1803)
Iraq and Afghanistan						
Thousands of U.S. Deaths in Iraq and Afghanistan (per Congress)	0.3481***	0.1025	0.4904***	1.0965	1.0952	1.0984
	(0.0493)	(0.0695)	(0.0860)	(0.5854)	(0.5727)	(0.5974)
Percentage of Public against War in Iraq (per Congress)	0.0641***	0.0536***		49.7339	50.0538	49.4320
	(0.0054)	(0.0049)		(7.8689)	(7.8595)	(7.8615)
Percentage of Public against War in Afghanistan (per Congress)	0.0124**	0.0500***		27.3677	27.6717	27.0895
	(0.0047)	(0.0057)		(10.5959)	(10.5147)	(10.6621)
Voted in Favor of Iraq War (H.J.Res.114) = 1	−1.0331***	−0.3048		0.4865	0.2980	0.6786
	(0.1638)	(0.1787)		(0.4999)	(0.4575)	(0.4672)

Table 6.1. (cont.)

Independent Variable	Dependent Variable: Sponsorship/Cosponsorship of Antiwar Legislation			Descriptive Statistics		
	(6.1)	(6.2)	(6.3)			
	All Members	Democrats	Republicans	All Members	Democrats	Republicans
Position in Congress						
Member of House of Representatives = 1	0.7971***	0.9723***	−0.0619	0.8127	0.8118	0.8162
	(0.1564)	(0.1690)	(0.3486)	(0.3902)	(0.3910)	(0.3875)
Member of Party Leadership = 1	−0.0146	0.0011	−0.6348*	0.2097	0.2183	0.2011
	(0.1032)	(0.0914)	(0.3095)	(0.4071)	(0.4132)	(0.4010_)
Member of Armed Services Committee = 1	−0.0112	0.1832	0.2152	0.1511	0.1478	0.1555
	(0.1427)	(0.1379)	(0.2557)	(0.3582)	(0.3550)	(0.3625)
Member of Veterans' Affairs Committee = 1	−0.0453	0.0566	−0.9202	0.0776	0.0754	0.0771
	(0.1984)	(0.1391)	(2.7691)	(0.2675)	(0.2641)	(0.2669)
Seniority in Number of Congresses Served	0.0682***	−0.0064	0.0683**	6.1199	6.6070	5.6342
	(0.0139)	(0.0127)	(0.0250)	(4.5378)	(4.8985)	(4.0967)
Personal Characteristics						
Sex/Gender Is Female = 1	0.4150***	0.2437*	0.0547	0.1551	0.2152	0.0956
	(0.1239)	(0.1240)	(0.2886)	(0.3621)	(0.4111)	(0.2942)
Race Is Black/African American = 1	0.7498***	0.2203*	2.0347	0.0717	0.1410	0.0025
	(0.1339)	(0.0873)	(4.4601)	(0.2581)	(0.3481)	(0.0496)
Ethnicity Is Latino/Hispanic = 1	−0.1364	−0.2099	0.5616	0.0558	0.1018	0.0099
	(0.1583)	(0.1283)	(6.8976)	(0.3771)	(0.5202)	(0.0989)

Military Veteran = 1	0.2491	0.0986	0.6253***	0.2403	0.1919	0.2881
	(0.1669)	(0.1396)	(0.1877)	(0.4274)	(0.3939)	(0.4530)
Constant	-4.5272***	-5.6976***	-2.8975***			
	(0.4456)	(0.5107)	(0.6891)			
ρ	6.0318***	15.8608***	3.8715			
	(1.0330)	(3.8067)	(7.6338)			
σ	0.9712***	3.3393***	1.9745			
	(0.1111)	(0.6438)	(4.1925)			
Sample Size (N)	3,262	1,631	1,621	3,262	1,631	1,621
Mean of the Dependent Variable	0.9700	1.7560	0.1690	0.9700	1.7560	0.1690
Log Likelihood	-2,822.3805	-2,061.7596	-617.9666			
χ^2	3,3952.97***	1,619.14***	160.76***			

Note: * $p \leq$ 0.050, ** $p \leq$ 0.010, *** $p \leq$ 0.001. Parameters estimated using panel negative binominal regression. Standard errors in parentheses.

deaths in lending their support to war (Burstein and Freudenburg 1978; Kriner 2010, p. 243). Consistent with this concern, we find positive and significant coefficients on *Total Deaths* (per Congress) in equations 6.1 and 6.3, implying that members were more likely to back antiwar legislation when the casualties rose among U.S. service members. The corresponding coefficient in equation 6.2 falls short of the threshold for statistical significance. Politicians are similarly sensitive to public opinion about war (Berinsky 2009). The estimates of equations 6.1 and 6.2 show that members of Congress were more likely to endorse antiwar legislation when a higher percentage of the public opposed the wars in Iraq and Afghanistan.[6] Furthermore, we included a control variable for whether or not a member of Congress voted in favor of the resolution that authorized the Iraq War. It was possible to vote in favor of this resolution only if the member was serving in Congress on October 16, 2002. As a result, any person joining Congress after this date is scored as a zero on this variable. We anticipated that having voted in favor of the Iraq War would serve as a constraint on members' willingness to support antiwar legislation, as opposing war at a later date may make them appear inconsistent, even if the factual situation changed over time. Consistent with this expectation, the results of estimating equation 6.1 show the expected negative, significant relationship when all members of Congress are analyzed. However, the coefficient falls short of statistical significance when Democrats alone are analyzed.[7]

The third set of control variables examines the effects of members' positions in Congress on sponsorship/cosponsorship. The results of equations 6.1 and 6.2 suggest that members of the House of Representatives were more likely to turn to sponsorship/cosponsorship as a political tool than were members of the Senate. This result may be attributable, in part, to the different sizes of the chambers: 100 members in the Senate and 435 members in the House. Sponsorship/cosponsorship may be more politically valuable in the larger, more anonymous chamber than in the smaller, more intimate chamber. This finding does not hold in equation 6.3, which examines Republicans only. The estimates of equation 6.3 indicate that Republican Party leaders were significantly less likely to sponsor/cosponsor antiwar legislation than were rank-and-file members of the party, though this finding does not obtain in equations 6.1 and 6.2. We find no statistically significant differences between members of Congress who served on committees holding jurisdiction over armed services or veterans' affairs and members of Congress who did not serve on these committees. Seniority is a positive, significant predictor of sponsorship/cosponsorship for Congress as a whole, and for

---

[6] We did not include these variables in equation 6.3 because problems with multicollinearity prevented the statistical model from converging when these variables were included in the equation.

[7] We did not include this variable in equation 6.3 because problems with multicollinearity prevented the statistical model from converging when this variable was included in the equation.

members of the Republican caucus specifically, but not for members of the Democratic caucus when considered separately.

The final set of control variables takes into account the potential effect of personal characteristics on sponsorship/cosponsorship behavior. Women appear to be significantly more likely to sponsor/cosponsor legislation when examining Congress as a whole, and when examining Democrats in particular, but not with respect to the Republican caucus, where women are underrepresented. Members of Congress who are black/African American were more likely to sponsor/cosponsor antiwar legislation than were those not identified in this way. This effect holds for Congress as a whole and for the Democratic caucus, but not for the Republican caucus, which had few individuals identified as black/African American. It is notable that we find a positive, significant effect of African American mobilization within Congress, even though we found this constituency to be underrepresented in grassroots antiwar mobilizations (see Chapters 4 and 5). African American members of Congress are more likely than their nonblack counterparts to work on antiwar issues, in keeping with the strongly held views of their constituents on these issues. In fact, many of the leading antiwar voices in Congress were African American representatives. Members of Latino/Hispanic ethnicity were not statistically different from other members in any of our models. Finally, Republicans who were military veterans were more likely to sponsor/cosponsor antiwar legislation, though this factor did not make a statistically significant difference for Congress as a whole or for the Democratic caucus specifically.

Overall, the regression analysis presented in this section highlights the importance of partisan identity in affecting congressional resistance to war. Consistent with $H_{6.1}$, we find that Democrats were much more likely to support antiwar legislation than were Republicans. While the antiwar cause sometimes received backing from Republicans, and not all Democrats were doves, the core constituency for peace was on the Democratic side of the aisle. Consistent with $H_{6.2}$, we find that this propensity reversed, in part, if the members were of the same party as that of the president. Democrats become somewhat less concerned with military intervention during a Democratic presidency and Republicans worry more about projecting American military power abroad when it is done by a Democratic president. Thus, the transition from President Bush to President Obama reduced Democratic concerns about war – as was the case for grassroots activists – and heightened the concerns of Republicans. Not all partisans are created equal, however. Within the Democratic caucus, the strongest opposition to war was by its most liberal members. Yet, Republicans were more likely to speak out against war if they were more conservative, other factors equal. Thus, when members found themselves on the ideological extremes of the chamber, they were more likely to raise their voices against war. In contrast, moderates of either a liberal or conservative persuasion were less likely to join the antiwar cause. These conclusions hold after taking into account alternative explanations for sponsorship/cosponsorship of antiwar legislation, such as the

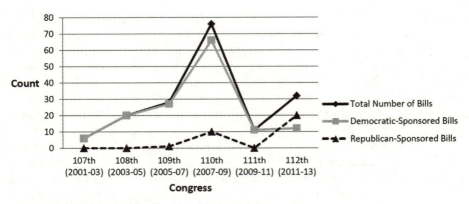

FIGURE 6.2. Volume of Antiwar Legislation in Congress, 2001–2013

situation in, and opinions about, Iraq and Afghanistan; members' positions in Congress; and members' personal characteristics. As a result, we conclude that partisan identification has a robust effect on congressional opposition to war.

THE TIMING AND PROGRESS OF ANTIWAR LEGISLATION

Members of Congress may introduce antiwar legislation because they sincerely oppose war or because they want to convey an antiwar stance to their constituents and other political actors. Legislation that is introduced, but not enacted into law, may influence public policy if it receives a great deal of support within Congress. The expression of support signals the salience of the issue to political actors, such as the president, who may wish to preempt future congressional action by resolving the issue administratively (Howell 2003; Howell and Kriner 2008; Mayer 2001). Nevertheless, the likelihood of success of the legislation may be a factor when determining whether or not to introduce it. Since parties take strong stands on the issue, it may be advisable for members to look at the partisan composition of Congress and the party of the president in deciding whether or not to introduce a bill. The data reported in Figure 6.2, which tracks the volume of antiwar legislation in Congress over time, strongly suggest that members do, indeed, pay close attention to the partisan balance in Congress when making these decisions.

Republican control of the presidency and both chambers of Congress for most of the 107th through 109th congresses made it highly unlikely that antiwar bills would progress much during this period. Figure 6.1 reveals that, in keeping with this expectation, members of Congress introduced fewer than thirty antiwar bills per year during that period. All but one of these bills were sponsored by Democrats. The Democrats' capture of both houses of Congress in the 2006 midterm elections changed this calculus. Democrats had ridden a wave of antiwar sentiment in the public to achieve a governing majority (Gartner and Segura 2008). Thus, there was reason to believe that antiwar legislation stood a chance in the 110th Congress, even though Blue Dog

Democrats in the House and the filibuster rule in the Senate would have obstructed its success. Democrats introduced sixty-six pieces of legislation with antiwar content. Seeking to have a voice on this emerging issue, Republicans also introduced ten bills with antiwar content in the 110th Congress.

After the election of a Democrat as president in 2008, the amount of antiwar legislation plummeted to its lowest level since the period immediately following 9/11. As we discuss in Chapter 2, there was no substantial change in policy or the military situation in the field that would be sufficient to explain this large shift. Democrats introduced only eleven antiwar bills in the 111th Congress, while Republicans introduced none. Even though the Democrats still controlled both chambers of the 111th Congress, changing war policy through legislation was a smaller part of the Democrats' political strategy with Barack Obama in the White House. The Republicans' recapture of majority control in the House after the 2010 midterm elections revived the possibility for Republicans to achieve success with antiwar legislation. In the 112th Congress, Democrats maintained roughly the same level of antiwar activity as they had in the 111th Congress, introducing twelve antiwar resolutions. Republicans, on the other hand, surpassed this level by introducing twenty antiwar resolutions.

The overall pattern depicted in Figure 6.2 is consistent with $H_{6.3}$. Democrats were most likely to seize the opportunity to advance an antiwar agenda when they controlled the majorities in Congress and when a Republican president was in office. Likewise, Republicans were most likely to propose antiwar resolutions when they held the majority in the House and a Democratic president was in office.

Introducing legislation allows members of Congress to express their positions on issues that might not come up for a vote and to signal to their constituents that they are "doing something" about matters that concern the public. Be that as it may, legislation generally has a greater policy impact if it actually becomes law than if it is merely logged into the *Congressional Record*. To measure how close war opponents came to this goal, the progress of antiwar legislation is documented in Figure 6.3.

Antiwar legislation did not make much progress from the 107th through 109th Congresses. As indicated in Figure 6.3, the Republican leadership did not allow committee meetings or floor votes on antiwar legislation, except in a few cases. Not a single antiwar bill was passed by either house of Congress. The situation changed noticeably in the 110th Congress with the resurgence of Democratic control. Sixteen antiwar bills were discussed in committee meetings, five were voted on in the House, and four passed the House.[8] None of these bills

---

[8] The bills that passed the House were H.Con.Res.63, a resolution disapproving of the decision of the president announced on January 10, 2007, to deploy more than twenty thousand additional U.S. combat troops to Iraq; H.R.2929, a bill to limit the use of funds to establish a military installation or base for the purpose of providing for the permanent stationing of U.S. Armed Forces in Iraq; H.R.2956, the Responsible Redeployment from Iraq Act; and H.R.4156, the Orderly and Responsible Iraq Redeployment Appropriations Act.

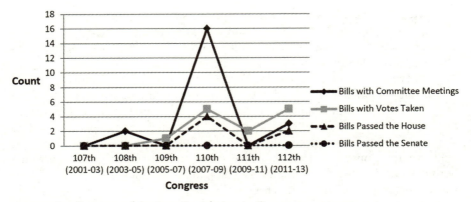

FIGURE 6.3. Progress of Antiwar Legislation in Congress, 2001–2013

passed the Senate on its own, preventing them from becoming freestanding legislation. But it is important to mention that an antiwar provision prohibiting the establishment of permanent military bases in Iraq was included in H.R. 1591, which passed the Senate and was signed into law (Public Law 110–28). Overall, this legislation was not "antiwar," per se – as it funded the continuation of the war – but it did enact an important goal of the movement.

With Obama's ascension to the presidency, the Democratic leadership lost its interest in advancing antiwar legislation during the 111th Congress. Indeed, rates of consideration and passage of antiwar legislation returned to the levels during the period of Republican control. Democrats in Congress had no plans to tie President Obama's hands in dealing with Iraq or Afghanistan. Yet, Republicans in the House drove a resurgence of antiwar legislation in the 112th Congress, second only to the 110th Congress. The House held hearings on three bills and allowed votes on five of them. Two related resolutions passed in the House, which addressed President Obama's use of military force in Libya.[9] Without agreement from the Democratically controlled Senate, Republican opposition to Obama's Libya policy failed to pass Congress.

The overall pattern depicted in Figure 6.3 is consistent with $H_{6.4}$. Antiwar legislation made the most progress when Democratic majorities in Congress faced a Republican president and when a Republican majority in the House faced a Democratic president. Without the assent of party leaders, antiwar legislation received little formal consideration.

---

[9] The resolutions that passed the House were H.Res.292, Declaring that the President shall not deploy, establish, or maintain the presence of units and members of the United States Armed Forces on the ground in Libya, and for other purposes; and H.Res.294, Providing for consideration of the resolution (H.Res.292) declaring that the President shall not deploy, establish, or maintain the presence of units and members of the United States Armed Forces on the ground in Libya, and for other purposes, and providing for consideration of the concurrent resolution (H.Con.Res. 51) directing the President, pursuant to section 5(c) of the War Powers Resolution, to remove the United States Armed Forces from Libya (Library of Congress 2011–2013).

LEGISLATIVE NETWORKS

The evolution of partisan support for antiwar legislation can be understood more clearly by mapping the alliance networks for legislation over time. Network analysis is a method of assessing the patterns of support for cosponsored legislation (Cho and Fowler 2010; Fowler 2006a; Fowler 2006b). In the six figures that follow, the connection between members of Congress and antiwar legislation are mapped for each of the six congresses in this study. In these figures, black squares represent bills, white circles represent Democratic members of Congress who joined antiwar legislation, and gray circles represent Republican members of Congress who joined antiwar legislation. The presence of a line between a circle and a square represents a member of Congress (circle) who sponsored/cosponsored a piece of legislation (square). The graphs are drawn using an algorithm that places circles closer to one another if they are connected with the same squares and places squares closer to one another if they are connected with the same circles (Borgatti, Everett, and Freeman 2011; Kamada and Kawai 1989). The most central pieces of legislation (using betweenness centrality) are identified in each graph with the labels for their bill numbers (Freeman 1979; Borgatti and Everett 1997).

The alliance network of antiwar legislation from the 107th Congress is represented in Figure 6.4. This network includes six bills – five from the House and one from the Senate – a relatively small amount of legislative activity. The most popular bills/resolutions were H.R.2459, H.Con.Res.473, H.J.-Res.110, and S.Con.Res.133. H.R.249 was a resolution introduced by Representative Dennis Kucinich (D-OH) to create a Department of Peace, a long-standing cause of the congressman. H.Con.Res.473 was a resolution introduced by Representative Barbara Lee (D-CA), which was perhaps the first comprehensive statement by antiwar voices within Congress. It "express[ed] the sense of Congress with respect to the United States working through the United Nations to assure Iraq's compliance with United Nations Security Council resolutions and advance peace and security in the Persian Gulf Region" (Library of Congress 2011–2013). H.J.Res.110 was a resolution introduced by Representative Alcee Hastings (D-FL) that would have required the United States to obtain sanction from the United Nations Security Council before attacking Iraq. S.Con.Res.133 was a resolution introduced by Senator Diane Feinstein (D-CA) expressing the sense of Congress that the United States should not attack Iraq without explicit authorization from a vote of the U.S. Congress.

In the House, H.J.Res.110 drew on a different coalition of support than did H.R.2459 and H.Con.Res.473. H.J.Res.110 used more bellicose language than did the other two bills as, in principle, it would have authorized war if certain (highly unlikely) conditions were met by the president. This language appealed to more hawkish members of the Democratic caucus but was unpalatable to the relatively liberal Democrats who signed on to H.R.2459 and H.Con.Res.473, helping to explain its comparative isolation from the rest of the network. On

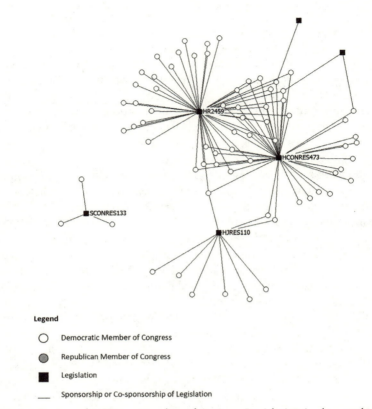

FIGURE 6.4. Sponsorship/Cosponsorship of Antiwar Legislation in the 107th Congress (2001–2003)

the whole, the network displays a fledgling opposition to war that had only begun to gather strength.

The network of legislation from the 108th Congress is represented in Figure 6.5. This network is notably larger than the network of the 107th Congress because antiwar voices in Congress grew louder. A series of additional proposals were put forward, creating a core in the center of the network. The network was still overwhelmingly Democratic in orientation, as indicated by the dominance of white circles in the figure. The lone gray circle in this figure indicates that Republican Representative Ron Paul of Texas joined the network by cosponsoring H.J.Res.20, as a resolution to repeal the authorization for the use of military force against Iraq. At the core of this network were a series of proposals that challenged President Bush's approach to Iraq, Afghanistan, and terrorism. The emergence of this core reflected the coalescence of war opposition within Congress.

The most central antiwar proposal in the 108th Congress was H.Con.Res.392, which called for a multilateral response to terrorism. Other key pieces of legislation were H.R.1673, which would have established a Department of Peace, and H.Res.640, which addressed torture at Abu Ghraib. In the Senate, S.Res.28, which

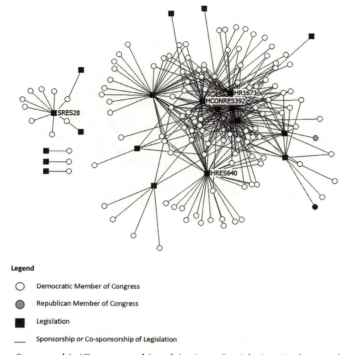

Legend

○   Democratic Member of Congress

◉   Republican Member of Congress

■   Legislation

──   Sponsorship or Co-sponsorship of Legislation

FIGURE 6.5. Sponsorship/Cosponsorship of Antiwar Legislation in the 108th Congress (2003–2005)

sought to allow United Nations weapons inspectors more time to do their work, gained the support of nine senators. These bills/resolutions sprouted from a mix of long-standing proposals (such as for a Department of Peace) as well as efforts to respond to emerging problems (such as the torture of prisoners at Abu Ghraib).

The network of antiwar legislation from the 109th Congress is represented in Figure 6.6. This graph reflects the increased density of the network resulting from a 40 percent increase in proposed legislation. Members of Congress were likely emboldened by a number of visible missteps by the Bush administration and decreasing public support for war. This network is no longer homogeneously Democratic, as eight Republicans joined Democrats in the antiwar cause. However, Republicans largely confined their involvement to the periphery of the Democrats' antiwar efforts, rather than coalescing around proposals of their own. The most central proposals in the House were H.R.3760, to establish a Department of Peace; H.J.Res.73, to redeploy U.S. forces from Iraq; and H.Con.Res.197, opposing the formation of permanent U.S. military bases in Iraq. Although several bills were introduced by war opponents in the Senate, none managed to attract a significant following during this Congress.

The network of antiwar legislation from the 110th Congress is represented in Figure 6.7. The contrast between this network and the network from the 107th Congress (in Figure 6.4) is quite striking. In response to the Democrats'

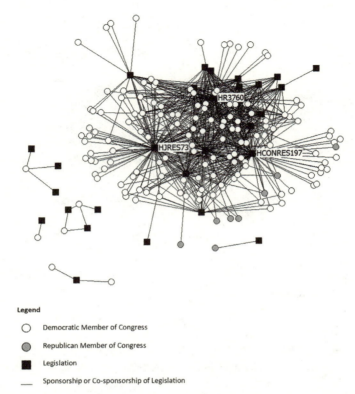

FIGURE 6.6. Sponsorship/Cosponsorship of Antiwar Legislation in the 109th Congress (2005–2007)

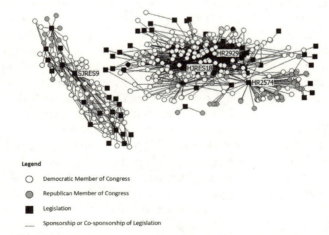

FIGURE 6.7. Sponsorship/Cosponsorship of Antiwar Legislation in the 110th Congress (2007–2009)

reclaiming of the House and Senate, the network expanded dramatically, encompassing slightly more than half the Congress. While the network still had an overwhelmingly Democratic lean, more than fifty Republicans also cosponsored antiwar legislation.

Rather than work only at the margins of Democratic efforts, some Republicans also forged their own proposals in the 110th Congress. For example, H.RES.1123 was introduced by Representative Dana Rohrabacher (R-CA) and aimed to prevent the United States from entering into a SOFA with the government of Iraq unless Iraq agreed to reimburse the United States for the costs of a continued military presence. Nevertheless, most antiwar Republicans signed on to H.R.2574, sponsored by Mark Udall (D-CO), which sought to implement the Iraq Study Group's recommendations (Baker, Hamilton, and the Iraq Study Group 2006). These measures included shoring up diplomatic relations in Iraq and redeploying U.S. combat brigades by early 2008. As is clear from the lower-right corner of Figure 6.7, H.R.2574 not only attracted many Republican cosponsors, it also attracted Democratic cosponsors who did not support most of the other antiwar legislation that was introduced in the 110th Congress. As such, H.R.2574 was an effort to find a middle ground in the debate over the Iraq War.

The core of Democratic opposition to war in the House during the 110th Congress was represented by H.R.2929 and H.J.Res.18. H.R.2929 sought to prevent the United States from establishing permanent military bases in Iraq, while H.J.Res.18 called for the redeployment of U.S. forces from Iraq. Democratic opposition in the Senate gelled around S.J.Res.9, which also called for redeployment of U.S. forces out of Iraq. Limited Republican opposition in the Senate emerged on the periphery of the antiwar network.

The network of antiwar legislation from the 111th Congress is represented in Figure 6.8. This figure depicts the collapse of antiwar efforts in Congress following the election of Barack Obama as president. As the number of bills fell from seventy-six to eleven, the participation of many members of Congress evaporated as well. The structure of this network more closely resembles that of the 108th Congress (presented in Figure 6.5) than its immediate predecessor in the 110th Congress (presented in Figure 6.7), underscoring the profound changes in the network with the onset of the Obama era. During the 111th Congress, antiwar efforts in the Senate were reduced to only one bill (S.3197), supported by two Democrats and one Republican, calling for the redeployment of U.S. forces out of Afghanistan. In the House, Democrats constituted the largest number of antiwar cosponsors, though Republican allies scattered their support across a variety of bills. The most central bills in the House were H.R.1052, which attempted to limit the deployment of troops to combat zones; H.R.5015, which proposed to redeploy forces out of Afghanistan; and H.R.2404, which called for the Secretary of Defense to submit a report outlining an exit strategy from Afghanistan.

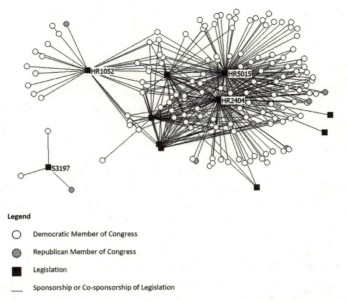

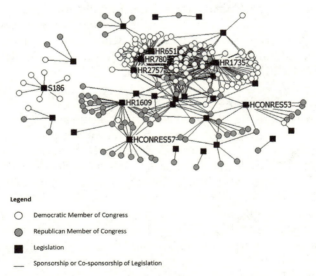

FIGURE 6.8. Sponsorship/Cosponsorship of Antiwar Legislation in the 111th Congress (2009–2011)

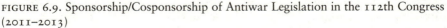

FIGURE 6.9. Sponsorship/Cosponsorship of Antiwar Legislation in the 112th Congress (2011–2013)

The antiwar network for the 112th Congress, reported in Figure 6.9, reflects both stasis and change in antiwar politics. The dense cluster of bills and representatives in the top center of the network more or less maintained the core of the liberal-Democratic antiwar coalition that existed in the 111th

Congress and earlier. The most central bills in this cluster include efforts to withdraw from Iraq (H.R.2757), modify the SOFA in Afghanistan (H.R.651), and end the war in Afghanistan (H.R.780, H.R.1735). The more scattered clusters of bills and representatives in the lower center emerged from Republican concerns about the War Powers Act and its application to the military conflict in Libya (H.R.1609, H.Con.Res.53, and H.Con.Res.57). Senate bills similarly included a mix of Democratic initiatives to speed the U.S. exit from Afghanistan (S.186) and Republicans' condemnation of President Obama's use of force in Libya (S.J.Res.14, S.J.Res.16, S.J.Res.18, S.Res.146).

The evidence reviewed in this section demonstrates the power of partisan identification in organizing opposition to war through legislative networks. Members with Democratic identities composed the core of antiwar networks throughout the entire period of the study (2001–2013). When Republicans elected to press antiwar causes, they did so on the periphery of Democratic efforts (especially in the 109th and 111th Congresses) or as part of separate, partisan clusters (especially in the 110th and 112th Congresses). These observations support $H_{6.5}$, that the sponsorship/cosponsorship of antiwar legislation tends to coincide with partisan identification. We likely detect this pattern because of pressures for partisan homophily and partisan polarization in Congress. The reliance on parties – whether induced by judicious trust in copartisans, blind loyalty, or some other reason – not only influenced whether members of Congress raised their voices against war, but also how they organized that opposition through legislative networks.

THE CONTENT OF LEGISLATION

The nature of the conflicts in Iraq and Afghanistan changed dramatically from 2001 to 2011. U.S. policy evolved from planning invasions, to prosecuting active wars, to managing occupations, to seeking viable exit strategies, with some nonlinear back and forth among these conditions. As a result, the substance of congressional opposition to war varied with changing conditions and U.S. policy. Examination of the content of congressional proposals to oppose war highlights the limits of Congress's capacity to challenge the commander in chief of the armed forces. Congress is constrained by the mandate given by the Constitution to the president, the informational advantages of the executive, and public opinion. At the same time, the substance of antiwar proposals varied with the alignment between the party of the president and control of congressional majorities in Congress.

This section considers the variation of antiwar proposals over time. Legislation was introduced for a mix of symbolic and substantive purposes. Tracking changes in this mix reveals much about the contours of the debate on the issues in Congress. Legislative agendas evolved from a greater symbolic focus in the 107th and 108th Congresses, to a more substantive tinge in the 109th and 110th Congresses, and then reversion to a more symbolic emphasis in the 111th and 112th Congresses. To this end, Table 6.2 reports the evolution of antiwar legislative provisions from 2001 to 2013.

In the immediate aftermath of 9/11, members of 107th Congress chose to tread lightly in the introduction of antiwar proposals. The wars in Iraq and Afghanistan both enjoyed high levels of public support at that time (Berkinsky 2009, pp. 28, 32). Members of Congress limited their opposition to the symbolic issue of condemning the doctrine of preemption – which holds (in theory) that the United States has the right to attack nations that are preparing to attack it before they do so – and calls for greater institutional powers for peace, diplomacy, and stabilization in Iraq. These mild proposals might be expected from a "loyal opposition" during wartime.

Antiwar proposals became more common during the 108th Congress. They followed a similar symbolic focus to those of the 107th Congress, though the new proposals placed a greater emphasis on condemning the doctrine of preemption. With public opinion turning against the war and the situation on the ground in Iraq beginning to deteriorate, members of Congress were more willing to take a stronger stand against the war than they had been immediately after 9/11.

The U.S. military occupation of Iraq faced troubled times in 2005 and 2006 (Allawi 2007). With a rising insurgency and increasing U.S. battle deaths, public opinion turned more solidly against the war. In an effort to respond to a shifting public mood, war opponents offered a wider range of proposals in the 109th Congress, including both symbolic and substantive elements. Three resolutions called for an "immediate" withdrawal, while six resolutions sought to set withdrawal in motion by setting a specific date or a timetable prescribed by Congress. However, the most frequently advanced proposal in the 109th Congress adopted more cautious language. Seeking to avoid the potential negative connotation associated with the word "withdrawal," eight bills proposed to "redeploy" troops away from war zones. The term "redeployment" signals that the resolution still supports military power, but that this power may be better used in another battlefield. Using "redeployment" makes it less likely that the advocate will seem weak or in favor of "surrender," than using the term "withdrawal."[10]

Members of Congress began to introduce legislation to block the establishment of permanent U.S. military bases in Iraq during the 109th Congress. Various other new provisions emerged in these years, such as resolutions to stop plans for a war on Iran, censure American leadership, and require Iraqi approval for a continued American military presence in Iraq. Thus, while the 109th Congress reflected only a marginal increase in the *volume* of legislation over the 108th Congress, the *content* of antiwar legislation underwent a qualitative shift that reflected a more aggressive and substantive antiwar agenda.

---

[10] For a discussion of how peace advocates moderate their language in order to preclude questions about their patriotism, see Woehrle, Coy, and Maney (2008).

TABLE 6.2. *Provisions in Antiwar Legislation by Congress, 2001–2013*

Provision Type	**Number of Bills per Congress**					
	107th Congress (2001–2003)	108th Congress (2003–2005)	109th Congress (2005–2007)	110th Congress (2007–2009)	111th Congress (2009–2011)	112th Congress (2011–2013)
Immediate Withdrawal	0	0	3	2	1	2
Set Withdrawal in Motion	0	0	6	26	6	9
No Escalation of Troops	0	0	0	24	2	0
No Permanent Bases	0	0	3	8	0	2
Redeployment of Troops away from War Zone	0	0	8	32	2	2
Condemn Doctrine of Preemption	1	8	2	6	1	0
Alter Institutional Powers for Peace	4	12	5	5	3	1
Require Iraqi or Afghan Approval for U.S. Actions	0	0	2	7	0	0
Adopt Policies to Stabilize Iraq or Afghanistan	1	3	4	25	1	0
Focus on Diplomatic Relations	4	6	6	21	1	1
Censure of American Leadership	0	1	4	6	0	8
No War on Iran, Libya, or Syria	0	0	1	4	0	14
No War without Congressional Authorization	0	0	0	0	0	7
Other Antiwar Provisions	0	2	2	1	0	3
Total Bills	6	20	28	76	11	32

Note: Bills were coded in as many provision types as relevant, so the sum of each column exceeds the total number of bills. Authors' tabulations from Library of Congress, *Thomas.*

The substance of antiwar proposals underwent another qualitative shift after the Democrats assumed control of the 110th Congress. The Democrats offered a governing challenge to the Bush administration's management of Iraq. Proportionately less attention went to purely symbolic legislation – such as condemning the doctrine of preemption or censuring American leaders – and proportionately more attention was devoted to management issues. Commonly offered resolutions called for a greater focus on diplomatic relations with neighboring countries and stabilization policies in Iraq. The language of "redeployment" was used in thirty-two bills, more than any other category identified in the content analysis. In twenty-four bills, Congress directly challenged President Bush's proposed "surge" of troops in 2007 (Feaver 2011). The overall trends in legislative provisions signal an increasing seriousness in Congress about taking control of the situation in Iraq.

Once Barack Obama moved into the White House, the volume of proposals attempting to manage the Iraq War from Congress declined sharply. Afghanistan became the focus of the small number of antiwar proposals that were introduced, including resolutions to withdraw from Afghanistan or stop President Obama's planned surge there. The 111th Congress was less insistent about its institutional prerogatives in the war-making arena than its predecessor had been, even though public opposition to the wars remained high (Gallup 2013a, 2013b). The partisan alignment between the president and Congress was decisive in curtailing Democrats' push for peace legislation. Republicans in Congress abated their efforts as well.

Hard-core antiwar Democrats continued to press their long-held concerns during the 112th Congress. They especially fought to withdraw U.S. troops from Afghanistan and prevent the establishment of permanent U.S. military bases there. The most notable change in the 112th was the concern by Republicans with U.S. military intervention in Libya. They introduced legislation to condemn U.S. military action and to withdraw forces as quickly as possible. There was a heavy emphasis in Republican-introduced legislation on censuring American leadership (i.e., President Obama) during this Congress. In fact, eight of the thirty-two bills introduced (25 percent) contained symbolic language focused on censorship, which is a higher absolute number (and a higher percentage) of bills of this nature introduced during any Congress in the study. There was more formal attention to censuring President Obama's involvement in Libya – which resulted in no American deaths – than there ever was in condemning President Bush for the revelations of the Downing Street Memo, faulty intelligence about weapons of mass destruction, torture at Abu Ghraib, or the deaths of thousands of American service members in Iraq and Afghanistan.

The evidence introduced in this section illustrates how partisan identification shapes the content of antiwar legislation. Our findings are consistent with $H_{6.6}$, that members are more likely to introduce legislation with symbolic content when the partisan balance of power leaves them at a disadvantage and to introduce legislation with greater substantive content when the partisan balance of power is in their favor. Democrats in Congress placed greater emphasis on symbolic legislation during the 107th through 109th Congresses when Republicans controlled both houses of Congress. Somewhat counter to $H_{6.6}$, Democrats began to place greater emphasis on substantive legislation during the 109th Congress than they had in the 108th Congress, even though the Republicans remained firmly at the helm of both chambers. Yet, as we posit in $H_{6.6}$, the greatest shift to substantive antiwar resolutions occurred in the 110th Congress when the Democrats controlled majorities in the House and Senate. Proposals at that time offered concrete plans to redeploy troops, to stabilize Iraq and Afghanistan, to refocus on diplomacy, and to prevent the establishment of permanent bases. Democrats retracted their efforts to control the substance of policy in Iraq and Afghanistan at the outset of the Obama presidency. Finally, Republicans sought to score symbolic points by attacking President Obama and his Libya policy during the 112th Congress. Partisan alignments determine not only whether members of Congress critique presidential war making, but the nature of their critiques as well.

AGENDAS INSIDE AND OUTSIDE CONGRESS

The barriers to success for antiwar legislation were enormous during the six congresses examined in this chapter. Any legislation must pass by a majority in the House, pass by a supermajority in the Senate (i.e., it must overcome a potential filibuster), and either obtain the signature of the president or override a president's veto with two-thirds support in both chambers. Surmounting these obstacles is challenging for *any* piece of legislation, but a herculean feat when it also involves questioning the prerogatives of the commander in chief of the armed forces. Looking at laws enacted alone might leave the impression that antiwar agendas had little momentum in Congress after 9/11. The analysis of this chapter, however, demonstrates how antiwar agendas advanced and retreated during this period.

Partisan identification is a critical element that links the movement and the party as they pursue antiwar agendas in Congress. Democratic partisanship spurred members to support the antiwar movement, especially when a Republican president was in office. They introduced antiwar proposals on a time frame that aligned mostly with partisan leadership and found that their degrees of success correlated with partisan control. Partisanship helped to define the networks surrounding legislation, as well as its symbolic and substantive content.

Antiwar organizing inside Congress did not grow as quickly as did grassroots antiwar demonstrations. Members of Congress are mindful that their opposition to a president during wartime might be interpreted critically by many of their constituents, whom they are careful not to offend. Yet, opposition to war grew when political opportunities appeared ripe during the 110th Congress. Like many grassroots organizations with Democratic leanings, Democratic members of Congress saw their control of the chamber as an opportunity to strike blows against President Bush. The election of a Democratic president in 2008, however, led to the simultaneous collapse of war opposition in Congress, by organizations, and among the grassroots.

7

Beyond the Antiwar Movement and the Democratic Party

Our empirical analysis to this point in the book focuses on interaction between the antiwar movement and the Democratic Party. Nonetheless, we argue that the concept of the party in the street applies beyond this party-movement pair. Social movements and political parties vary from pair to pair in the extent to which they overlap with one another; as a result, the party in the street may constitute anywhere from a relatively large share of party-movement activity to a relatively small fraction of that activity. The size of the party in the street may vary across time, as well as across party-movement pairs. What difference, if any, do these fluctuations make?

The size of the party in the street reflects the balance of power within both the party and the movement. When the party in the street is small, neither the party nor the movement has many incentives to accede to its demands. In this case, party leaders receive little electoral benefit from addressing movement issues, while movement leaders only lose grassroots support by compromising with the party. When the party in the street is large, however, the incentives are reversed because the balance of power in its favor. Party leaders may worry that failing to address the concerns of the movement may have negative electoral consequences, especially in primary elections (Boatright 2013). Movement leaders know that their grassroots supporters identify strongly with the party, so they are more likely to keep these supporters happy by coordinating their efforts with the party's agenda.

In this chapter, we consider two hypotheses for how variations of the size of the party in the street affect the dynamics of parties and movements. First, we consider the effect on the protest cycle. When there is a high degree of party-movement overlap, we expect that movement activists are threatened by the opposing party's success. As a result, the movement mobilizes when the opposing party achieves victories and demobilizes when the opposing party experiences defeats. That is, there is a high degree of correspondence between the electoral cycle and the protest cycle. Conversely, when there is a low degree of party-movement overlap, we expect that movement activists are inattentive to party success. As a result, there is a low degree of correspondence between the electoral cycle and the protest cycle. Thus we state:

H$_{7.1}$. *The greater the size of the party in the street, the greater the correspondence is between the electoral cycle and the protest cycle. The smaller the size of the party in the street, the lesser the correspondence is between the electoral cycle and the protest cycle.*

Second, we consider the choice of tactics by the movement. When there is a high degree of party-movement overlap, activists in a social movement are accustomed to relying on political institutions in devising their tactics. They are likely to be comfortable with electoral involvement and lobbying, for example. As a result, movements tend to evolve toward a greater engagement with political institutions when the party in the street is relatively large. In contrast, when there is a low degree of party-movement overlap, activists in a social movement are accustomed to working outside political institutions in devising their tactics. Political institutions are likely to be anathema to them. As a result, movements tend to evolve away from engagement with political institutions when the party in the street is relatively small. Thus we state:

H$_{7.2}$. *The greater the size of the party in the street, the more likely a movement is to evolve toward using institutionally based political tactics. The smaller the size of the party in the street, the less likely a movement is to evolve toward using institutionally based political tactics.*

To test these hypotheses, we gather and analyze evidence on two additional party-movement pairs: (1) the Tea Party movement and the Republican Party and (2) the Occupy Wall Street movement (also referred to as the "Occupy movement") and the Democratic Party. The Tea Party movement (2009–present) and the Occupy movement (2011–present) both originated during the Obama administration to voice concerns about a spectrum of policies put forward by the president's administration and the general political-economic situation in the United States. The Tea Party registered grave concerns about high taxes, growing deficits, mounting debt, fiscal stimulus policies, and prospects for health care reform. The notion of a "Tea Party" is both a reference to colonial American resistance to taxes at the Boston Tea Party and an acronym (TEA) for "Taxed Enough Already." The Occupy movement criticized inadequate regulation of financial institutions, nonresponsive political institutions, and deepening inequality in the United States. It pioneered the slogan "We are the 99 percent" in response to the growing share of national wealth held by the top 1 percent of Americans. These movements attracted support from mostly distinct constituencies. The Tea Party mobilized activists, ideas, and resources largely from the conservative/right side of the political spectrum, while the Occupy movement mobilized forces predominantly from the liberal/progressive/left side of the political spectrum.

In the space of one chapter, we cannot examine the Tea Party-Republican and Occupy-Democratic relationships with the same level of thoroughness and rigor as we investigated the antiwar-Democratic relationship. Our goals are more modest. We seek to demonstrate the relevance of the party in the street outside the context of our focal case. We acknowledge that more research is required before all the hypotheses tested on the antiwar-Democratic relationship can be rigorously evaluated for the Tea Party, Occupy, or other movements in relation to their most closely allied political parties.

The chapter begins by assessing the relative size of the party in the street for our two party-movement pairs. We investigated activist identities by conducting in-depth, semistructured interviews with activists from a quasi-random sample of organizations affiliated with the Tea Party and Occupy movements. We interviewed thirty-four activists in the Tea Party and forty activists in the Occupy movement between March and August 2013. These interviews informed us about the ways in which partisan and movement identities intersect in these two movements. Second, we test $H_{7.1}$ by examining variation in the level of grassroots mobilizations over time by looking at public events advertised by Tea Party Patriots and Occupy Together (through its Meetup Web sites). These data are revealing of the nature of the protest cycles in the two movements and the degree to which they correspond with political events. Third, we test $H_{7.2}$ by looking at the (near) universe of newspaper articles published in the United States about the Tea Party and Occupy movements in the three to four years after their founding. Using computer-aided content analysis, we identify changes over time in the degree of overlap between these movements and their corresponding political parties. We conclude by comparing how the antiwar, Tea Party, and Occupy movements related to political parties.

ACTIVIST IDENTITIES AND ATTITUDES IN COMPARATIVE PERSPECTIVE

The way in which social movement activists relate to political parties is a critical variable in shaping the mobilization dynamics of social movements. In this section, we assess the degree to which movement activists identify with parties, their attitudes toward parties, and their view of the two-party system in the United States. In order to understand how these factors varied between our party-movement pairs, we obtained a sample of activists in the Tea Party and Occupy movements through the organizations that mobilized them.

For the Tea Party, we turned to the Web site of the Tea Party Patriots (TPP), which is a federation of state and local organizations active in the Tea Party movement (Tea Party Patriots 2013). TPP is only one of several national organizations active in the Tea Party movement; others of which include Americans for Prosperity, Freedom Works, Tea Party Nation, and Tea Party Express. Yet, there are several practical advantages of focusing on TPP. First, TPP allows local organizations to join its Web site freely without exercising centralized control or implementing onerous litmus tests. If an organization genuinely antithetical to the movement were to join the Web site – for example, a parody organization created by liberal activists – it would likely be removed. But TPP does not otherwise police its organizational membership rolls, making its Web site a useful resource to almost any organization involved in the movement. Moreover, the Web site allowed us to identify all the organizations registered with it and to contact individuals representing each of these organizations directly. Thus, we were able to select a random sample of one hundred organizations listed on the TPP web page. Individuals from thirty-four of these organizations agreed to be interviewed, giving us a response rate of 34 percent. As a practical matter, we could not have drawn an organizational sample of Tea Party activists using the Web site of any national Tea Party organization other than TPP. The other organizations exert more centralized control over who can access and use the data generated by their Web sites.

For the Occupy movement, we turned to a variety of sources to identify organizations active in the movement: Twitter, YouTube, Facebook, Meetup, and individual organizational web pages. From these sources, we compiled a list of 580 organizations in the United States that identified themselves as affiliated with the Occupy movement. We selected a random sample of 60 of these organizations. Individuals from 40 of these organizations agreed to be interviewed, giving us a response rate of 67 percent.[1]

---

[1] The significantly higher response rate by Occupy activists over Tea Party activists has two plausible explanations. First, we suspect that our method of contacting Occupy activists was more effective at actually reaching the activists than was our method of contacting Tea Party activists. We contacted most Occupy activists through Facebook, since almost all Occupy groups had a Facebook page up and/or a Meetup page (with links to organizers' Facebook pages). As a result, we are confident that most Occupy activists received our invitations, even if they declined to respond. In contrast, we contacted almost all Tea Party activists directly through the TPP e-mail service. While many activists may have their TPP e-mail forwarded to their personal e-mail accounts, we suspect that many activists may not do so. As a result, our messages may not have been received by some activists if they did not log on to their TPP account, thus giving us a lower response rate for the Tea Party. Second, we imagine that Tea Party activists were more suspicious of us than were Occupy activists. It is not that Occupy activists were unsuspicious. Some of them questioned whether we worked for a government agency such as the National Security Agency. However, many Tea Party activists are openly critical of higher education and academics, which many of them believe to be dominated by liberal professors intent on indoctrinating students with leftist ideologies. Thus, even if Tea Party activists accepted at face value that we were who we claimed to be, they had reason to believe that we were up to no good, thus decreasing their willingness to participate in the study. In recognizing that these factors would likely affect our response rates, we drew a somewhat larger sample of one hundred TPP organizations, in comparison to only sixty Occupy organizations.

Neither our sample of Tea Party activists nor our sample of Occupy activists should be understood to be a genuine random sample of their respective movements. Both samples almost certainly overrepresent heavy users of Internet technology, making it likely that they also overrepresent highly educated and professional individuals. Given that the Tea Party is organized in a comparatively hierarchical fashion, the TPP Web site directed us to individuals at the top of local hierarchies. The Occupy movement is organized in a comparatively decentralized fashion, which enabled us to obtain contact information from people with greater variation in their levels of involvement in the movement. At the same time, there are important merits to our sampling approach. Our samples include representatives from movement organizations across the United States. They comprise activists from relatively small, moderate-sized, and large organizations. The samples are unlikely to be biased toward any one philosophy or approach to activism within the movements. All Occupy organizations had an equal probability of being selected. And, while our Tea Party sample draws exclusively from TPP, our impression is that this federation is open enough that it is not slanted toward any one faction within the movement. Our samples may not be perfect, but we have confidence that they provide a workable basis for comparison to the antiwar movement.

We observed considerable demographic and cultural differences between the two samples of activists. Although respondents in both samples overwhelmingly identified as white/Caucasian, Occupy respondents (28 percent) were significantly more likely to identify (at least in part) as a racial/ethnic minority (African American, Latino, Asian, Native American) than were Tea Party respondents (9 percent, $p \leq 0.050$). The mean age of Tea Party respondents was fifty-seven years old, which was significantly older than Occupy respondents, who had an average age of thirty-nine years old ($p \leq 0.001$). Tea Party respondents (77 percent) were almost twice as likely to be married as were Occupy respondents (40 percent, $p \leq 0.010$). Tea Party respondents (76 percent) were more than three times more likely than were Occupy respondents (23 percent) to indicate that they were members of a formally organized religious community ($p \leq 0.010$). We did not observe statistically significant differences in the sex/gender or formal education levels of the respondents in the two samples. Both samples were somewhat more male than female (Tea Party: 53 percent male, 47 percent female; Occupy 57 percent male, 43 percent female). Half or more of respondents in both samples held college degrees at the bachelor's level or higher (Tea Party: 65 percent; Occupy: 50 percent). Thus, as a starting point for our analysis, we see that the Tea Party and Occupy consist of two reasonably different groups of people.

Beyond demographics, activists in the Tea Party and the Occupy movement differ substantially in the ways that they identify with their closest major-party ally. Tea Party respondents, on average, expressed a significantly greater connection with the Republican Party than did Occupy respondents, on average, with the Democratic Party. Of the Tea Party activists we interviewed, 58 percent identified as members of the Republican Party, 15 percent leaned toward the Republican Party, 12 percent identified as members of a minor party (such as the Conservative Party or the Libertarian Party), 3 percent leaned toward a minor party, and 12 percent claimed to have no party lean of any kind.

The Occupy activists had a less favorable view of the Democratic Party than Tea Party activists had of the Republican Party. Occupy activists had a more favorable view of minor parties than did the Tea Party activists. Of the Occupy activists whom we interviewed, 30 percent identified as members of the Democratic Party, 20 percent leaned toward the Democratic Party, 15 percent identified as members of a minor party (such as the Green Party or the Socialist Party), 20 percent leaned toward a minor party, and 15 percent claimed to have no party lean.

Looking only at respondents who considered themselves "members" of the Democratic or Republican Party (which is a high threshold for identification), our results show that the Tea Party had almost twice as many major-party identifiers in its ranks as did the Occupy movement. This difference is statistically significant ($p \leq 0.050$). If we combine party members and party leaners, the difference changes to 73 percent (of Tea Party activists identifying with the Republican Party) to 50 percent (of Occupy activists identifying with the Democratic Party), which remains statistically different ($p \leq 0.050$). This result strongly suggests that the Tea Party had a considerably greater overlap with the Republican Party than the Occupy movement did with the Democratic Party.

Field survey research on the Tea Party and Occupy movements corroborates our interview results on the relative proportion of Republican and Democratic Party identifiers in these movements. We conducted surveys at Tea Party rallies outside the U.S. Capitol Building in Washington, D.C., on March 20 and 21, 2010. These rallies (one of which is pictured in Figure 7.1) were a response to congressional votes on the Affordable Care Act of 2010 (aka "Obamacare") and part of the Tea Party's attempt to "Kill the Bill." We administered a survey at these rallies analogous to the protest survey described in Chapter 4 and followed the same field procedures. We collected ninety-two surveys, with 53 percent of respondents reporting membership in the Republican Party, 35 percent reporting membership in no party, 12 percent reporting membership in a minor party, and 1 percent reporting membership in the Democratic Party.[2] A field survey by Costas Panagopoulos (2011) conducted October 14–18, 2011, with 301 participants at the original Occupy Wall Street encampment in Zuccotti Park found that 25 percent of respondents identified as members of the Democratic Party, 39 percent did not identify with any party, 36 percent identified with a minor party, and 2 percent identified as Republicans.[3] The party memberships reported in both of these surveys – conducted on the

---

[2] Percentages add to 101 percent because of rounding error. The survey had a response rate of 89 percent.

[3] The survey had a response rate of 78 percent.

FIGURE 7.1. Tea Party Rally to Kill the Bill, Washington, D.C., March 20, 2010 (Photo by Michael T. Heaney)

street at prominent events sponsored by the movements – are within a few percentage points of our interview results. These findings validate the representativeness of our interviews of activists in these movements.

The fact that many of the activists we interviewed identified with one of the major political parties does not mean that they were uncritical of the parties. Indeed, every single Tea Party activist whom we interviewed expressed discontent with the Republican Party and every single Occupy activist whom we interviewed voiced disapproval of the Democratic Party. Nevertheless, we found a strong connection between movement identification and party politics in these interviews. It is telling that no activist whom we interviewed in the Tea Party currently identified as a Democrat and no activist whom we interviewed in the Occupy movement currently identified as a Republican.[4] Tea Partyers may not all love the Republicans, but they know for certain that

---

[4] Some activists reported that they had identified with one of the major political parties in the past but no longer did. Among Tea Party respondents, 15 percent revealed that they had identified as members of the Democratic Party in the past and 6 percent indicated that they had identified as Republicans in the past. Among Occupy respondents, 25 percent revealed that they had identified as Republicans in the past and 41 percent indicated that they had identified as Democrats in the past. At the time of the interview, however, respondents rejected these identities.

they are not Democrats. Conversely, Occupiers may not love the Democrats, but they know for certain that they are not Republicans.

The orientation of movement activists toward the party system is exposed not only by their willingness to identify as party members, but also in the sentiments that they expressed in talking about the parties. We asked each respondent to describe what the Democratic and Republican Parties stand for and what it means to be a member of the Democratic and Republican Parties. While activists frequently had a tendency to describe their closer major party as having "lost its way" and being "in need of reform," they were much more likely to describe the more distant of the two parties using pejorative language, often attributing the party's actions to the evil motives or derelict character of the party's leaders and/or members. When asked what it means to be a member of the Democratic Party, one Tea Partyer from Louisville, Kentucky, responded that "it means that you are confused about life in general." When asked what it means to be a member of the Republican Party, one Occupier from Brooklyn, New York, responded that "I assume that you are selfish and that your only concern is yourself." Not every respondent engaged in character assassination, but the expression of strong antipathy toward members of the more ideologically distant party was not uncommon.

To be more precise about activists' assessments of the parties, we conducted a content analysis of respondents' answers to our series of questions about party descriptions and membership. We coded answers as "evenhanded" (i.e., they described each party in neutral terms or equally positive/negative ways), "favoring the Democrats," or "favoring the Republicans" (i.e., they described one party in either more positive or less negative terms). We found that 79 percent of activists in the Tea Party described the Republicans in more positive/less negative terms, while 21 percent of these activists described both parties in an evenhanded way. On the other hand, we found that 52 percent of activists in the Occupy movement described the Democrats in more positive/less negative terms, while 48 percent of these activists described both parties in an evenhanded way. Thus, activists in the Occupy movement were more than twice as likely to discuss the two parties evenhandedly as were activists in the Tea Party (which was significantly different at $p \leq 0.050$). No activists in the Tea Party described the Democrats in more positive/less negative terms than they described the Republican Party. Similarly, no activists in the Occupy movement described the Republicans in more positive/less negative terms than they described the Democratic Party. These results reinforce our conclusion that the Tea Party is more closely connected with the Republican Party than the Occupy movement is with the Democratic Party. They also bolster the notion that the Tea Party is unequivocally opposed to the Democratic Party, while the Occupy movement is unequivocally opposed to the Republican Party.

The partisan attitudes of Tea Party and Occupy activists can be understood by examining not only their views of specific parties, but also their attitudes toward the two-party system in general. Activists in both movements universally spoke of the need to reform the political system in the United States. However, Occupy activists were somewhat more likely to view the system as irreparably broken, while Tea Party activists were somewhat more likely to be willing to work within – and attempt to reform – the Republican Party. For Occupiers, American government needs to become radically more decentralized and people focused (as opposed to corporate focused) in order to be improved. Such a shift would require entirely new political institutions. For Tea Partyers, on the other hand, the current governmental system could be saved if only it would return to the principles of constitutional government, fiscal restraint, and individual freedom.

We assessed activists' attitudes toward the two-party system by asking, "Do you think that there is a need for a new political party to address the concerns of the [Tea Party or Occupy] movement?" Occupy respondents were exactly twice as likely as Tea Party respondents to say that they favored the creation of a new political party (which was significantly different at $p \leq 0.010$). Among Occupiers, 70 percent favored the creation of a new party, 22 percent opposed its creation, and 8 percent were unsure.[5] Among Tea Partyers, 35 percent favored the creation of a new political party, 59 percent opposed its creation, and 6 percent were unsure.

Beyond the willingness of activists to endorse the formation of a new political party, we found notable differences between the movements in the ways that activists explained their opposition to a new party. Many of the Occupiers who opposed creating a new party held this position because *any* political party – even one intended to represent Occupy – would be unlikely to serve the interests of the people. For example, an Occupy activist from Marlborough, Massachusetts, typified this perspective when he stated that "parties in the United States are designed to keep hegemonic interests safe. With any party, you're going to have that happen." Thus, many Occupy activists who preferred not to see a new party emerge held this view, not because they supported the two-party system, but because they opposed parties of any kind. Along these lines, Figure 7.2 reprints an Occupy postcard depicting the view of the two-party system of some in the movement. In contrast, many of the Tea Partyers who opposed creation of a new party held this position because of the potential negative consequences of minor parties to the two-party system. For example, a Tea Party activist from Evansville, Indiana, told us, "I don't believe in third parties because they enabled Bill Clinton to win the presidency with only 39 percent [*sic*] of the vote.[6] So it doesn't do any good. It just takes

---

[5] Some respondents answered that they would like to see the creation of more political parties, in general, not just a party to represent the concerns of the Tea Party or Occupy movements. If the respondent answered in this way, we coded it as a response in favor of creating a new political party.

[6] In fact, Bill Clinton won the presidency in 1992 with 43 percent of the popular vote and in 1996 with 49 percent of the popular vote (U.S. Election Atlas 2013a, 2013b).

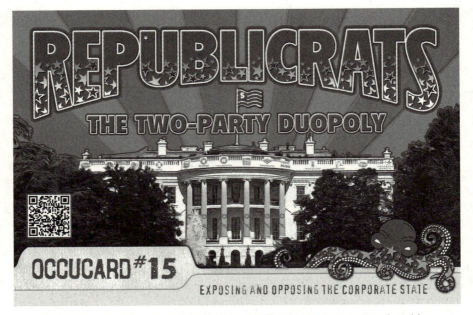

FIGURE 7.2. Occupy Movement Postcard on the Two-Party System (Produced by Occucards 2013. Used by permission.)

votes away from the Republican Party." These perspectives reveal the depth of the contrast between the way Occupiers and Tea Partiers approached American political institutions. Participants in the Occupy movement, for the most part, preferred to work outside the party system, while participants in the Tea Party movement sought to leverage the existing party system to promote their vision of American society.

Divergence between the movements in their activists' attitudes toward political parties and the party system has major consequences for their participation in, and influence on, American politics. The philosophy of Tea Party activists, in general, drives them toward greater engagement with elections and parties. As one Tea Party activist from Greenfield, Indiana, surmised, "The best thing to do is what the Socialists have done. They have infiltrated the Democratic Party. The Tea Party needs to infiltrate the Republican Party with Tea Party values. Get them elected at all levels and then hold them to the values of the Tea Party." Occupiers, on the other hand, are more likely to believe that sustainable social change is driven by introducing new analyses of the political and economic system, which will change people's consciousness. To this end, continued work in local organizations, such as community gardens, and collaborative service efforts, such as directly providing hurricane relief, are preferred tactics. According to an Occupy activist from Grand Terrace, California, "The way that Occupy can make an impact is not through political parties, but through grassroots. Parties are too top-down and are begging to be corrupted.

Instead, we should dissect the issues and focus on local concerns.... Instead of 'trickle down', we should 'trickle up', using approaches such as the public banking model."

The antipartisanship of Occupy extended beyond individual activists' self-identification and attitudes. Participants in Occupy forcefully rejected attempts by partisan-affiliated organizations to support the Occupy movement. For example, attempts by MoveOn – a Democratic-leaning organization – to "stand in solidarity with Occupy Wall Street" (MoveOn 2011) were viewed by many in the Occupy movement as ploys to co-opt Occupy (Horn 2011). Occupy-related electronic media (such as Web sites, Facebook, and Twitter) circulated a profanity-laced attack ad against MoveOn, which stated:

> Dear MoveOn.org,
> While we at #OWS [Occupy Wall Street] do really appreciate your attempts to spread the word about our 'American Autumn', we would like to take this moment to say: F**k off. We are not a movement preaching the DNC [Democratic National Committee] message. We are not the 'Liberal Tea Party.' We are not conservative, liberal, communist, libertarian, fascist, technocratic, republican, monarchist, gynocratic, or andocratic. We are pragmatic. We are egalitarian. We are isocratic. In short, we're free. Neither you, nor anyone else, will own us.
>
> Sincerely,
>
> The Occupation (Oak 2011; this text has been edited to remove profanity, add punctuation, and eliminate the use of all caps)

This message makes clear the antipartisan stand of Occupy and its rejection of MoveOn as an agent of the institutionalized Democratic Party. Given the immediate and negative message from Occupy activists, a MoveOn-Occupy alliance never materialized.

While not necessarily representative of the views of all (or even most) of the activists in the Occupy movement, the rejection of MoveOn was not atypical of how the Occupy movement engaged partisan actors in movement settings. For example, we directly observed the on-the-ground implications of antipartisanship by Occupy activists during a visit to the Occupy encampment outside the DNC in Charlotte, North Carolina, on September 12, 2012. Green Party presidential candidate Jill Stein and the Poor People's Economic Human Rights Campaign had called a joint press conference to highlight their issues of mutual concern. They chose to locate the conference at Marshall Park – the same location as the week's Occupy encampment – on the morning of Friday, September 12. We observed Occupy activists aggressively and loudly disrupt (and end) the press conference in what bordered on a violent confrontation. The disrupters made clear that Occupy would not tolerate any organized political party in their midst, even one as sympathetic to the cause as the liberal/progressive Green Party.

Just as the antipartisanship of Occupy manifested as concrete collective actions with political consequences, the propartisanship of the Tea Party also manifested itself through collective actions with electoral and legislative consequences. Tea Party activists were especially engaged in the 2010 congressional elections, during both the Republican primaries and the general election. The Tea Party movement created pressures inside the Republican Party for more contested Republican primaries by endorsing candidates and criticizing incumbents (Berry and Sobieraj 2014). The effects of primary involvement spilled over into the general election by helping to nationalize issues around common themes (Aldrich, Bishop, Hatch, Hillygus, and Rhode 2012). These factors assisted in mobilizing an electorate favorable to Republicans, who would gain sixty-three seats (and the majority) in the U.S. House and six seats in the U.S. Senate (Jacobson 2011). Once these new members arrived in office, Tea Party pressure swung votes on highly salient issues, such as the budget and the debt ceiling (Bailey, Mummolo, and Noel 2012). Sympathetic members of Congress moved to institutionalize the Tea Party influence by forming a Tea Party Caucus in the House (Gervais and Morris 2012). The strong partisan leaning of Tea Party activists meant that their politics could be incorporated within the framework of the institutionalized Republican Party (Schnabel 2014).

The Tea Party and Occupy are both heterogeneous movements. Within each of them there are strong partisans, as well as people who reject identification with political parties. Each movement has activists who see the two major parties in neutral, dispassionate terms, as well as activists who see one party as much better or worse for America than the other. Each has activists who embrace minor parties and those that prefer to hedge their bets with the two-party system. Nonetheless, each movement has a strong lean. These leanings manifest not only in the attitudes of individual activists, but also in their collective actions in group settings. In the following sections, we test the implications of these differences for the dynamics of social movement mobilization.

THE PROTEST CYCLE

Given the relatively high degree of overlap between the Tea Party and the Republican Party, as opposed to the lower degree of overlap between the Occupy movement and the Democratic Party, $H_{7.1}$ predicts a strong correspondence between the protest cycle and electoral politics in the Tea Party case, but not in the case of the Occupy movement. This section compares the grassroots mobilization of the Tea Party and Occupy movements to evaluate this prediction.

The Tea Party movement arose in response to a partisan threat. It was precipitated by a call for a "Chicago tea party" by the television financial reporter Rick Santelli, who complained on February 19, 2009, that the government was "promoting bad behavior" by developing a plan to refinance homeowners' mortgages in the wake of the financial crisis of 2008–2009 (Santelli 2009). He issued this call shortly after the election of a Democratic president, and the reelection of a Democratic Congress, in November 2008. With an almost filibuster-proof majority in the Senate, prospects were strong that Democrats could enact a wide-ranging agenda, from fiscal stimulus and financial regulation to health care and immigration reform. From the perspective of a conservative Republican, it may have seemed as if America was on the brink of (or past) a socialist turn (Parker and Barreto 2013). The identity of the president as someone who was unlike the typical conservative Republican – a black man, the son of a foreigner, a law professor, and a community organizer – also likely contributed to a sense of threat (Maxwell and Parent 2012). Given this background, we expect the protest cycle of the Tea Party to correspond to the ebb and flow of this partisan threat. If the rise of a partisan threat prompted the Tea Party, then an abatement of that partisan threat should correspond with the Tea Party's demobilization.

The Occupy movement arose in response to events that were ostensibly nonpartisan in nature. The idea for the first Occupy protests originated with *Adbusters*, a Canadian anticonsumerist publication. Labeling Wall Street as "THE FINANCIAL GOMORRAH OF AMERICA," it called for twenty thousand people to go to Wall Street on September 17, 2011, "to set up tents, kitchens, peaceful barricades and occupy Wall Street for a few months. Once there, we shall incessantly repeat one simple demand in a plurality of voices.... It's time for DEMOCRACY NOT CORPORATOCRACY, we're doomed without it" (Adbusters 2011, emphasis in original). A key question is what made this protest on Wall Street stand out from any of the thousands of other protests in the United States every year.[7] The answer is likely linked to the dissemination of videos through the Internet and the mainstream media of police mistreatment of protesters, which galvanized public sympathy and support for the movement, helping it to grow (Gillham, Edwards, and Noakes 2013; Roberts 2012; Rodriguez 2012; Vasi and Suh 2013). As a result, we expect the dynamics of Occupy mobilization to be driven more by police-protester interaction than by partisan politics.

We documented the vicissitudes of the protest cycles in the Tea Party and Occupy movements by counting the number of events sponsored on a monthly basis by TPP and by the Occupy movement through the Meetup Web site.[8] For the purpose of this study, an "event" is any meeting or gathering that is public and open to any supporter of the movement. An event need not be a protest or demonstration – it could be a chapter meeting or an informational session – but our definition excludes events that are only open to leaders or movement elites. Counting the number of events is not a perfect measure

---

[7] For example, we attended (and conducted surveys at) an antiwar/anti–Wall Street protest in New York City on April 4, 2009. But this protest received little attention in the media or elsewhere.

[8] For a study using a similar approach, see Cho, Gimpel, and Shaw (2012).

of mobilization, since it does not account for variations in the size of events, which may be very important. Moreover, organizational event calendars may not post all of the events sponsored by the organization. Yet, the count of events is a good indication of the breadth of grassroots support for a social movement and how it changes over time. Even if a calendar does not list all events, changes in the aggregate number of posted events should correlate strongly with the actual number of events.

The TPP Web site provides an excellent resource for groups in the Tea Party that are planning events. Anyone who registers with the Web site can post information on its calendar about a public meeting, including the location, time, and how to contact the organizers. The TPP calendar did not include all events sponsored by the Tea Party movement. Yet, given that the calendar is free and easy to access, and that we have no reason to believe that the events are biased toward any particular ideological perspective within the Tea Party, it provides a good indicator of grassroots mobilization within the movement. Using the TPP calendar function, we extracted data on 5,207 Tea Party events held in the United States between January 2009 and December 2012.[9] Figure 7.3 reports the frequency of Tea Party events, by month, during the period of the study.

Mass mobilization of the Tea Party began in April 2009, shortly after Obama's inauguration. In conjunction with Tax Day (April 15), TPP reported that it held events at more than eight hundred locations around the United States "to protest government spending, bailouts, deficits and high taxes" (Meckler 2009). This count may be somewhat inflated, since it is based on TPP's press releases, rather than on archival records of individual events, as are the other events reported in Figure 7.3. Grassroots Tea Party mobilizations sputtered for most of the next year but then surged again around April 15, 2010. The movement grew in subsequent months as conservatives expressed severe frustration surrounding the push for the Affordable Care Act. The movement's surge culminated with more than three hundred events held in the month immediately prior to the November 2010 congressional midterm elections.

The gains of the Republican Party in the 2010 elections appeared to pacify the Tea Party. The Republicans seized control of the House of Representatives and made gains in the Senate but failed to reclaim the upper chamber of Congress. This change gave Republicans a veto over Democratic proposals and substantially reduced the likelihood that major new liberal laws would be on the horizon. With this decreased partisan threat, TPP events declined considerably. There was a modest spike of activity around April 15, 2011, but the

---

[9] We searched the Web site using archive.org to ensure that our count of events includes events that were removed during redesigns of the Web site. In examining more than five thousand events, we removed only one event from the data, which appeared to have been posted fallaciously by opponents of the Tea Party.

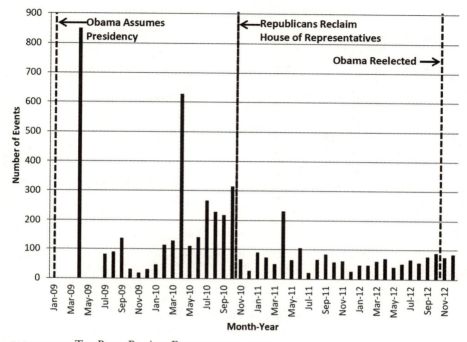

FIGURE 7.3. Tea Party Patriots Events, 2009–2012

Tea Party otherwise staged fewer events during the 2012 election cycle. For example, Tea Party events did not spike for Tax Day 2012 or in the months prior to the 2012 presidential election. This pattern is consistent with our expectation in $H_{7.1}$ for cases of high party-movement overlap.

We examined the mobilization of Occupy movement events by turning to the Occupy Together pages of Meetup.com. Not all groups used the Meetup platform. Nonetheless, it was adopted widely and without any clear bias toward certain regions or political perspectives within the movement. For each Occupy group, we were able to access the date and location for each event. We selected a random sample of one hundred Occupy groups, which yielded 1,121 events between September 2011 and December 2012. Figure 7.4 reports the frequency of Occupy events, by month, during the period of the study.

The results reported in Figure 7.4 demonstrate that the Occupy movement proliferated quickly in the fall of 2011 after the confrontational events of September, October, and November in New York City and elsewhere. The movement gained international media attention after the arrest of more than seven hundred activists on the Brooklyn Bridge and the crackdowns on occupants at Zuccotti Park and other places (CBS News 2011). In solidarity with the original Zuccotti protesters, activists set up encampments throughout the United States (and the world) that mimicked the spirit and rules of Occupy Wall Street (Piven 2013). Participants sought out parks and other public places

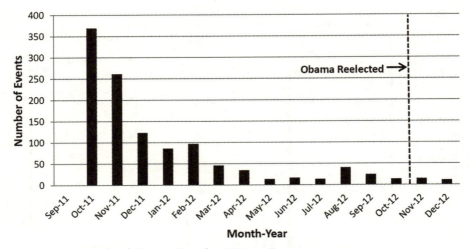

FIGURE 7.4. Sample of Occupy Together Meetup Events, 2011–2012

for twenty-four-hour encampments. By the end of November 2011, nearly every major city in the United States had been occupied.

The movement's incursions on public spaces were met with resistance by local authorities that pointed to violations of city ordinances, such as prohibitions on camping in public parks, as well as concerns about sanitation and safety. Police in many of these cities would eventually shut down the occupations (Gillham, Edwards, and Noakes 2013). Beyond the force exerted by authorities, the arrival of winter weather made the principal tactic of Occupy – an outdoor activity without the comfort of reliable heat and electricity – less tenable than it had been in the early fall. Adding to these external pressures were internal organizational difficulties posed by the consensus decision-making rules that accompanied the Occupy model (Leach 2013; Smith and Glidden 2012). By the end of February 2012, Occupy had lost most of its momentum, less than six months after its initiation. Occupy continued to meet and protest in the years and months that followed. Occupy-affiliated groups continued to hold national meetings and meet in some communities for years after fall 2011. Still, the Occupy movement never regained the energy, the attention, or the mass involvement that it had in the fall of 2011.

Much more could be said about the multiple conjunctive causes of the fall of Occupy, such as the intrusion of the police, the presence of agents provocateurs, the dysfunctions of consensus decision making, strategic mistakes by particular Occupy groups, and the misrepresentation of the movement by the mass media (Bray 2012; Gitlin 2012; Juris, Ronayne, Shokooh-Valle, and Wengronowitz 2012; Kim 2011). Yet, we are most interested in the cause that is conspicuously absent from the case: partisan politics. Unlike the Tea Party, Occupy was neither instigated nor demobilized by partisan or election-related events.

Occupy was not reacting to the gains or losses of a particular political party. The protest cycle represented in Figure 7.4 appears to be independent of partisan influence, as is expected in $H_{7.1}$ for cases of low party-movement overlap. The patterns reported in this section suggest that variations in the degree of overlap between a social movement and a political party may affect the timing of its mobilization: Greater overlap leads to correspondence between partisan events and the protest cycle; lesser overlap leads to independence between partisan events and the protest cycle.

PARTISANSHIP AND THE EVOLUTION OF MOVEMENTS

By early 2012, both the Tea Party and Occupy organizations had reached sustained, but diminished, levels of grassroots mobilization. Large demonstrations no longer appeared to be high on the agenda of either movement. Leaders in both movements were faced with the question of what to do next. Should activists give up on the cause? Should they try to revitalize their grassroots protests? Or, should they follow another path, perhaps increasing their engagement with political institutions? Our expectation in $H_{7.2}$ is that the Tea Party and the Occupy movement should lean in different directions on this question. Because the Tea Party has a relatively high degree of overlap with the Republican Party, we expect it to trend toward greater involvement in political institutions. Conversely, the relatively low degree of overlap between Occupy and the Democrats predicts a trend away from institutional involvement.

In order to gain insight on how activists in both movements thought about these issues, we asked our interview respondents whether the movement should "continue to stage protests, demonstrations, rallies, or public gatherings of its supporters." Activists in the two movements leaned in significantly different directions on this question ($p \leq 0.010$). In the Occupy movement, there was a strong preference toward continuing demonstrations, if possible, with 75 percent of respondents favoring this option. Tea Partyers, on the other hand, were somewhat more inclined to see the rallies come to an end, with only 41 percent favoring their continuation. Activists in the two groups offer alternative visions of the next steps for their movements.

In the Occupy movement, most respondents wanted to see the resumption or continuation of grassroots events. Those who did not think that the rallies should continue tended to believe that rallies had outlived their effectiveness. A respondent from Lake Worth, Florida, opposed continued demonstrations because "Occupy has faded into obscurity. We've lost our momentum." Others, such as a respondent from Grand Terrace, California, wanted the movement to shift toward "alternative forms of civic engagement." An Occupier from Reading, Connecticut, proposed that the movement's experience providing "food service and disaster relief after Hurricane Sandy" was a good example of what Occupy might do instead of holding rallies. Only one respondent – from Billings, Montana – proposed that trying to get candidates elected to office was a better use of the movement's energies than were grassroots demonstrations. Thus, the prevailing sentiment of the Occupy activists we interviewed was to maintain an emphasis on noninstitutional tactics.

In the Tea Party movement, a sizable minority of respondents favored the continuation of grassroots demonstrations. They cited these events as a way to keep up morale in the movement, release emotional energy, and show the world what the Tea Party is really about (contrary to the portrayals of the movement in the media). The more prevalent view, however, was to describe demonstrations as something that the movement had "outgrown." Along these lines, a respondent from Salt Lake City, Utah, explained, "At first, the rallies were really great. But it got overdone. And now we've outgrown that. Now we have to spend more time educating the public about Tea Party beliefs and values." An activist from Memphis, Tennessee, proposed, instead, that the Tea Party turn its attention to the legislative process at the state level. A Tea Partyer from Springfield, Nebraska, stressed that "now is the time to work with candidates." Thus, although many Tea Party activists saw value in demonstrations and wanted them to continue, the vision in the broader movement was to work more closely with formal political institutions.

Given the different views of activists within the movements about working inside or outside formal institutions, we imagine that the movements followed different paths vis-à-vis the party system. $H_{7.2}$ predicts that the Tea Party movement evolved *toward* the Republican Party, while the Occupy movement evolved *away* from the Democratic Party. To assess this expectation, we analyzed all newspaper articles about the Tea Party and Occupy movements published in the United States in the first three to four years of their existence (Newsbank 2013).[10] Through a computer-assisted content analysis, we determined the percentage of articles on the Tea Party that also referenced the Republican Party, as well as the percentage of articles on the Occupy movement that also referenced the Democratic Party.[11] This percentage is a measure of the degree to which the media associate the parties and movements with one another. While we acknowledge that newspaper analysis is an imperfect reflection of what is actually occurring in the movements (Earl, Martin, McCarthy, and Soule 2004), we believe that it is a good indicator of the nature of public discourse on the movements.

---

[10] We searched for the term "Tea Party" between January 2009 and December 2012. This search likely contained some false positives, since newspapers may write about tea parties (social events) that have nothing to do with the Tea Party (a political movement). We searched for the terms "Occupy Wall Street" and "Occupy movement" between September 2011 and June 2014. We identified 294,468 articles on the Tea Party (an average of 6,135 per month) and 54,231 articles on the Occupy movement (1,595 per month).

[11] Specifically, we searched the words "Republican" and "Democrat" or "Democratic." Since the Tea Party analysis contains a small percentage of false positives (e.g., events where people get together and drink actual tea), our estimates of the percentage of Republican mentions are slightly biased downward.

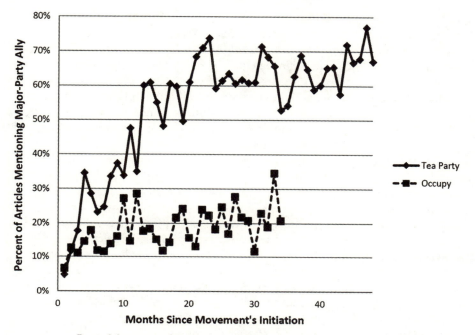

FIGURE 7.5. Party-Movement Associations in Newspapers

Figure 7.5 tracks the percentage of comentions of parties in movement-related articles for the first forty-eight months of the Tea Party's existence (beginning in January 2009) and for the first thirty-four months of the Occupy movement's existence (beginning in September 2011). The results show that both movements started out relatively low in terms of party-movement association. After three months, the Tea Party was associated with the Republican Party in 18 percent of newspaper articles, while Occupy was associated with the Democratic Party in 11 percent of newspaper articles. Both movements initially grew in the degree to which they were associated with their nearest major-party ally. After one year, the Tea Party was associated with the Republican Party 35 percent of the time, while Occupy was associated with the Democratic Party 29 percent of the time. However, at this point, the two movements diverged. The Tea Party became much more closely associated with the Republican Party. For the second through fourth years of the Tea Party, an average of 63 percent of newspaper articles mentioning the Tea Party each month also mentioned the Republican Party. In contrast, the Occupy movement remained dissociated from the Democratic Party. By June 2014, about 20 percent of articles mentioning Occupy also mentioned the Democratic Party.

Although not a perfect reflection of what transpired within the movements, the results of the newspaper content analysis reflect the divergent paths that the Tea Party and Occupy took when their grassroots presence began to diminish, as anticipated in H$_{7.2}$. Tea Party activists channeled their time and resources into molding the direction of the Republican Party. They struggled to influence whom the party nominated for public office, to have their preferred candidates elected, and to insist that those candidates serve the Tea Party's agenda once in office. Their movement was increasingly inside the Republican Party, rather than outside the party. On the other hand, Occupy splintered in many directions once maintaining occupations of public places became infeasible. Some Occupy groups continued to function and worked to make a difference in their local communities. But, without strong ties to a political party, Occupy faded from the national stage.

The partisan evolution of the Tea Party and Occupy movements reflects the dominance of partisan identities over movement identities. Within the Tea Party, the shift away from demonstrations and toward involvement in primaries and the legislative process transferred the locus of movement activity from free spaces created by movements toward institutional arenas dominated by party elites. For example, in twenty-eight states and the District of Columbia, voters will be required to register as Republicans in order to participate in Republican primaries and/or caucuses during the 2016 presidential election cycle (Green Papers 2013). Such rules exclude (or at least decrease the likelihood of) participation by independents and libertarians, who are important constituencies within the Tea Party. Thus, by accommodating a refocus on Republican electoral politics, Tea Parties disempowered some of their constituents and consequently narrowed their own bases of support. Moreover, channeling politics into the legislative and electoral arenas moves political competition to arenas where established party actors hold the purse strings on the financial resources necessary to participate successfully.

Tea Party activists recognized the increasing prevalence of Republican identifiers in the Tea Party and the political consequences of that change. Greater Republican involvement in the Tea Party occurred with a deepened expectation that the Tea Party would serve the ends of the Republican Party. An activist from Las Vegas, Nevada, observed:

Especially in the last year [2012–2013], I have seen more and more influence from the Republican Party, either in people from the Republican Party starting Tea Parties and becoming affiliated with Tea Party Patriots, or members of those Tea Parties who expect the Tea Party to adhere to Republican ideals pressing those issues during our meetings. More and more people expect the Tea Party to support candidates in Republican primaries, and we've had those debates during our national meetings.

She continued by asserting this trend was the result of a strategy of local Republican Party elites:

The people here in our county who are on the Republican Central Committee made a very deliberate decision to start Tea Parties, and to call them "Tea Parties," and try to run them from behind the scenes as a wing of the Republican Party without coming right out and saying, "We are the Republican Party operating a Tea Party." . . . They definitely wanted to get their foot in it.

From the perspective of this activist, involvement by Republican-identified actors meant that the mechanisms of party discipline were more deftly extended to Tea Party organizations.

The trends toward a more Republican-identified Tea Party and a more Tea Party-identified Republican Party – as suggested by $H_{7.2}$ – are likely a mixed blessing for the party and the movement. The expanded Tea Party involvement in the Republican Party helps to keep the Republican grassroots vibrant and mobilized but may simultaneously move the Republicans away from the median voter. The Tea Party is likely to benefit from greater attentiveness by Republican politicians but also becomes more vulnerable to the possibility that many of its issues may not receive any attention if they do not have the blessing of Republican elites. The federal government shutdown and debt default crisis of fall 2013 is an example of how greater engagement by Tea Party activists brought about Republican Party action on the Affordable Care Act and mounting government debt but also illustrates how partisan action on move-ment causes may lead to public backlash that weakens both the party and the movement.

The dominance of partisan identities over movement identities operated differently for the Occupy movement than it did for the Tea Party movement. Specifically, partisan identities worked to keep people out of the Occupy movement, undermining its quest for critical mass. Occupiers were perpetually concerned that the Democratic Party would try to co-opt the movement. An activist from Canton, Ohio, vocalized this perspective:

MoveOn.org started using the Occupy name – since no one's got copyright over it – they wanted to start Occupy groups around "structurally deficient bridges" and whatnot, which of course was basically fitting into the president's plan to revamp infrastructure as part of an effort to revitalize the transportation industry. So, basically, you have the Democratic Party trying to corral the Occupy movement in the same way that Fox News and the Republican Party tried to corral the Tea Party movement.

He continued that once the Democrats realized that they could not co-opt Occupy, they moved to crush the movement:

And because they couldn't corral the Occupy movement, very liberal Democratic mayors in many big cities – Portland, Oakland, Los Angeles – ordered these right-wing-style paramilitary actions with their police forces to crush the Occupy encampments in their cities.... And some of them, in a way, benefitted from the removal of Occupy encamp-ments because there was very little support in those major cities for having physical encampments in the downtown areas. Democrats wanted to have the Occupy movement as long as it benefitted their cause. But once they realized that it didn't benefit their cause, they wanted to try to find a way to remove it and move on.

To guard against these possibilities, Occupy groups rebuffed partisan actors, such as MoveOn, in their attempts to participate in the Occupy movement. By ostracizing partisans, Occupy guaranteed that it would not be co-opted. At the same, these decisions were costly to the movement: Occupy ensured that it would be excluded from resources and alliances that could have advanced its cause. That is, by rejecting affiliations with partisans, Occupy amplified the relevance of partisanship to the movement; it prevented strong partisans from being active contributors to Occupy. Partisan identities trumped movement identities for those who did join Occupy. Thus, antipartisanship had the effect of drastically narrowing Occupy's supportive coalition.

THE ANTIWAR, TEA PARTY, AND OCCUPY MOVEMENTS IN COMPARISON

Examining the Tea Party and Occupy movements, and their relationships with the Republican and Democratic Parties, generates useful benchmarks for deciphering the interaction between the antiwar movement and the Democratic Party after 9/11. From this comparison, it is apparent that the antiwar-Democratic relationship is an intermediate case among these three party-movement pairs. The antiwar movement was more closely connected with the Democratic Party than was the Occupy movement, but it was considerably less bonded than were the Tea Party and the Republican Party. Thus, we believe that it is reasonable to conclude that our conception of the party in the street extends beyond the antiwar-Democratic case. The concept may require adaptation to alternative contexts, but it should serve as a useful lens in examining other social movements and political parties in the United States.

When compared with the Tea Party and Occupy movements, the antiwar movement had an intermediate degree of overlap with its closest major-party ally. At the peak of party-movement synergy after the 2006 congressional midterm elections, slightly more than 50 percent of antiwar activists identified as members of the Democratic Party (see Figure 4.3). The results of our interviews with Tea Party and Occupy activists reveal that the Tea Party had a somewhat higher level of partisan fidelity (58 percent), while Occupy had a lower level of fidelity (30 percent). The antiwar movement differed notably from Occupy in that the antiwar movement embraced lobbying and electoral involvement, whereas Occupy did not. The antiwar movement could be considered to be roughly on par with – if not superior to – the Tea Party movement with respect to lobbying and legislative work. The Tea Party and antiwar movements both sparked the creation of legislative caucuses, sponsored grassroots lobby days, hired professional lobbyists, and championed signature legislation (which mostly failed to become law). In the electoral arena, the antiwar movement and the Tea Party can each reasonably claim to have helped to swing the balance of power in one congressional election (2006 for the antiwar movement and 2010 for the Tea Party movement).

The Tea Party was unambiguously more aggressive than the antiwar movement in sponsoring candidates and attempting to influence party primaries. There are several notable cases of antiwar-movement-inspired candidates – Ned

Lamont's attempt to unseat incumbent Democrat Joe Lieberman in the 2006 U.S. Senate election in Connecticut (Pirch 2008), Cindy Sheehan's bid to defeat Democrat Nancy Pelosi in the 2008 election for California's 12th district of the U.S. House of Representatives (Ewers 2008), and various antiwar candidates who sought the Democratic nomination for the presidency in 2004 and 2008 (e.g., Howard Dean, Dennis Kucinich, Barack Obama). Yet, antiwar electoral efforts do not compare to the pervasive attempt by the Tea Party to remake the Republican Party through the primary process. Tea Party-affiliated organizations endorsed at least 201 Republican candidates in the 2010 Republican primaries, of whom 74 percent were nonincumbents (Bailey, Mummolo, and Noel 2012, p. 773). Tea Party organizations made across-the-board moves to become players in the Republican Party in ways that the antiwar movement never did in the Democratic Party.

The protest cycle of the antiwar movement (see Chapter 2) bore some similarity to the protest cycle of the Tea Party. Both the antiwar movement and the Tea Party saw grassroots participation in their causes plummet after congressional elections that appeared to respond to their concerns. In both cases, the removal of a partisan threat served to pacify the movements. Antiwar protests, however, persisted somewhat longer than did Tea Party protests. While the Tea Party grass roots were appeased by a congressional victory alone, antiwar protests did not abate fully until a Democrat was elected president. We can only speculate as to the reasons for this difference. It could be the antiwar movement was fixated on President Bush – as the commander in chief of the armed forces – while the Tea Party was more content to stop the progress of new legislation, which was closer to their substantive grievances (on taxes, spending, debt, and health care). The Occupy movement, on the other hand, appears to have had little correspondence with partisan rhythms. The mobilization of the antiwar movement post 2008 somewhat resembles Occupy. This correspondence may result from a rise in antipartisanship in the antiwar movement after 2008 (see Figure 4.3), which placed the antiwar and Occupy movements on par with respect to this factor.

The evolution of the antiwar movement similarly follows an intermediate path when compared to Occupy and the Tea Party. If we were to regenerate Figure 7.5 to include party-movement associations for the antiwar movement and the Democratic Party from January 2003 through December 2006, we would find that the antiwar movement tracked the Tea Party in the early months of its existence but then followed the Occupy movement as the movement evolved beyond its first year.[12] As is the case for the Tea Party and Occupy, antiwar-Democratic associations trended upward in the first year of the movement. After thirteen and fourteen months, antiwar-Democrat

---

[12] We identified 12,133 articles mentioning the "antiwar movement" or "anti-war movement" during this period.

associations in newspaper articles rose to an average of 60 percent, matching Tea Party levels at that stage of the movement and far surpassing the highest threshold reached by the Occupy movement. Nevertheless, antiwar-Democratic associations settled into an average of about 28 percent in the second through fourth years. This level was below the rate of Tea Party-Republican association, but above the rate of Occupy-Democratic association.

In all three movements, we find that partisan identities trump movement identities, though the form of dominance varies from case to case. The antiwar movement and the Democratic Party appeared to work together for a time, until the movement was abandoned by the party. In this case, movement identities were trumped simply because partisans lost interest in the movement's cause, or perhaps because they believed that the problem (i.e., war in Iraq and Afghanistan) was being adequately addressed. For Occupy, partisan identities trumped movement identities by discouraging many of Occupy's potential supporters from working with it. The dearth of resources and support likely cut short Occupy's protest cycle and muted its visibility and political impact. For the Tea Party, partisan identities narrowed the movement's terrain and redirected its energies to arenas where the rules are defined by the party. The ultimate effects of the Tea Party movement inside the Republican Party are likely to be realized over the coming decade.

The evidence presented in this chapter documents three social movements that are deeply affected by relationships with major political parties. The party in the street varies in the extent to which it matters for the politics of each of these movements. At this point, it is essential to situate these observations within the broader context of contemporary American politics. To what extent is the party in the street affected by partisan polarization among masses and elites in the United States? Are there any strategies that movements and parties can use to cope with the fluctuating identities of their participants? What are the next steps for research in this area? We address these questions in the next chapter – the concluding chapter of the book.

8

Social Movements in a Polarized America

This book is about the formation and dissolution of an alliance between a social movement and a political party during a time of high partisan polarization. The story of this alliance is not about back-room deals among elites who negotiated a partnership and then eventually betrayed their allies. In contrast to prior research on party-movement alliances, ours is a story about a multitude of participants in a movement and a party who separately shifted their attention and effort among causes in light of developing political events. In telling this story, we emphasize how macrolevel outcomes were a consequence of these individual-level behaviors. The shifts were driven in part by intersectional identities that were critical lenses through which actors interpreted events and decided where to focus their energy. The fact that partisan identities tended to be stronger and more enduring than their intersecting movement identities led the party in the street to serve the interests of the party over the interests of the movement. In the case of the antiwar movement and the Democratic Party after 9/11, this pattern played out through the behavior of grassroots activists, advocacy organizations, and members of Congress.

We document the collapse of the antiwar movement after the election of President Barack Obama. Key to our argument is that this collapse was led by *Democratically identified* individual activists, organizations, coalitions, legislators, and funders. Of course, Democrats were not the only ones who left the movement. The movement declined for a variety of reasons, such as activist burnout from years of protest and the scarcity of funding after the global financial crisis of 2008–2009. But the fact that these declines occurred disproportionately among Democratically identified sources lends strong support to our partisan identification theory of mobilization. In contrast to prior research on social movement mobilization, ours helps to explain how partisan identifications shaped actors' interpretations of ambiguous U.S. foreign policies, how they allocated energy to antiwar movement goals, and why they shifted attention to other policy issues, such as health care.

Perhaps the most compelling piece of evidence we encountered in our research is that the decline of the antiwar movement began in earnest before Obama's nomination or election. Grassroots mobilizations diminished considerably after substantial Democratic gains in the 2006 congressional midterm elections. Surprisingly, the movement's downturn coincided with the initiation of "the surge" by President Bush, a policy that clashed with the public's growing apprehension about war in Iraq. We would have expected the execution of this antagonistic policy to reinvigorate the antiwar ranks. Yet, the magnitude of protests slid even as antiwar organizations redoubled their efforts to grow the movement. As explained in Chapter 4, anti-Republican sentiments became significantly less important motivators for movement participation, we argue, because of the reduced partisan threat from Republicans in Congress. The Tea Party experienced an analogous decline in grassroots mobilizations after the Republican Party recaptured a majority in the House of Representatives in the 2010 congressional midterm elections. These changes were consistent with our hypothesis that the reduction of partisan threat undermined the movements' abilities to attain critical mass in the streets.

In this concluding chapter, we reflect on the general lessons that should be drawn from our analysis. The antiwar movement after 9/11 was deeply influenced by an era of political polarization in which Democrats and Republicans became increasingly isolated from one another politically and socially. Examination of the Tea Party and Occupy Wall Street movements demonstrates that variation in the overlap between social movements and political parties – that is, in the size of the party in the street – matters for the unfolding of party and movement activism over time beyond our focal case. What does our analysis say more generally about political parties and social movements? How might the party in the street work differently across historical eras? What have we learned that should inform the strategies of political parties and social movements? How should our results inform future scholarly research?

THE IMPLICATIONS OF PARTISAN POLARIZATION

Partisan polarization means that, among other things, self-identified Democrats and Republicans tend to be sorted into ideologically homogeneous groups in which they take similar positions on an array of issues. For example, Democrats usually support broad reproductive rights for women, the regulation of firearms, greater taxation and social spending, and relaxation of immigration restrictions. In contrast, Republicans often advocate restrictions on access to abortion, protection of rights for gun owners, lower taxes and social spending, and tighter immigration restrictions. Crossover between these categories is relatively rare, making prolife Democrats and antigun Republicans relatively uncommon, for instance. When new issues arise, partisans generally pick up cues about which position to take from elites within their own political party and use partisanship as a filter with which to interpret emerging information about the issue. The Iraq War is a case in point. More so than for any American war since the advent of scientific polling, public opinion was divided such that self-identified Democrats were likely to oppose the war, while self-identified Republicans tended to support it (Jacobson 2010). Although opinion on the war in Afghanistan was not as polarized as was opinion on Iraq, opposition to that war was also substantially more likely to be expressed by self-identified Democrats than by self-identified Republicans.

Partisan polarization of opinion about war after 9/11 meant that there was relatively little organized opposition to war from self-identified Republicans. We estimate that only about 1 percent of antiwar demonstrators were Republicans. Republican-identified organizations rarely joined coalitions against the wars. Republican legislators sometimes took antiwar positions in Congress, but they did so at the periphery of other antiwar efforts, rather than in a sustained and focused way. Representative Ron Paul of Texas advanced antiwar positions during his 2008 campaign for the Republican presidential nomination, but he and his supporters remained on the fringe of both the Republican Party and the antiwar movement.[1]

The absence of sizable Republican opposition to the wars was detrimental to the antiwar movement. Expanded Republican involvement could have aided the movement in a number of ways. First, it could have helped to counter the perception that the antiwar movement was driven entirely by partisan-motivated enmity for President Bush. As long as the antiwar movement consisted mostly of Democrats, independents, and members of minor parties, it was easy to paint the movement merely as opportunists seeking to score points against a president whom they disliked for other reasons. The presence of Republicans at rallies would have been a signal that the movement entailed more than mere partisanship. This signal might have caught the attention of the news media and other elites, leading them to subject the wars to more intense scrutiny.

Second, a Republican presence in the antiwar movement could have broadened the dialogue regarding the war by expanding the range of arguments accessible to the public. As it was, the movement mostly advanced leftist and liberal arguments, such as that war harms innocent people; government funds should be spent on human needs instead of war; war propagates imperialism; the United States went to war mainly to guarantee the flow of oil from the Middle East; the wars were based on government lies; war harms the environment; the costs of war disproportionately affect the poor both in the United States and in the nations that it is at war with; and the wars were

---

[1] Paul received only 5.54 percent of the popular vote in the Republican primaries and was rewarded with only thirty-five delegates, amounting to 1.6 percent of the total (Real Clear Politics 2008).

an attack on Arab and Muslim peoples that tarnished the reputation of the United States around the world, thus fostering rather than curtailing the problem of terrorism. Republicans and conservatives might have additionally highlighted arguments such as that wars are expensive and must be paid for either with higher taxes or more debt; the aftermath of wars requires that the military undertake extensive nation-building operations and create improper foreign entanglements; war degrades the capacity of the U.S. military, especially the National Guard; and wars put too much power in the hands of the federal government, which tends to mishandle complex policies. Amplification of these arguments could have increased pressure on policy makers to avoid or shorten the wars.

Third, greater partisan diversity within the antiwar movement might have insulated the movement somewhat against drastic swings in support as the control of government vacillated from party to party. If some Democrats left the movement when a Democratic president assumed office, then the movement could have continued with support from its Republican base. If some Republicans left the movement when a Republican president assumed office, then the movement could have continued with support from its Democratic base. A greater diversity of supporters might have generated a more robust movement.

During less polarized times, it may be easier for social movements to attract supporters from multiple political parties. In her reevaluation of the woman suffrage movement in the United States, for example, Corrine McConnaughy (2013) explains that the state-driven political strategy of the movement meant that it had to collaborate with different parties, depending on the peculiar political circumstances of the state in question. In some states, the movement allied with the Democrats; in others, with the Republicans; and in still others it took the tack of a third party movement. Had the movement wedded itself to a single political party or a unified political strategy, it might not have been able to win some level of voting rights for women in more than three-fourths of the states or ratification of the 19th Amendment in 1920. There is no guarantee, however, that a movement that begins as a nonpartisan or bipartisan movement will remain so. For example, the labor movement originated on a nonpartisan basis but eventually forged strong ties with the Democratic Party (Greenstone 1969). Along these lines, Doug McAdam and Karina Kloos (2014) argue forcefully that mobilization by, and countermobilization against, the social movements of the 1960s contributed to pushing the parties into their current polarized state.

In a time of polarization, Democratic and Republican activists in the same movement would be unlikely to get along very well. Even if they could agree to work together on the issue of war, they would find that they disagreed on innumerable other issues ranging from national health insurance to charter schools. Beyond issue disagreements, they would hold divergent cultural attitudes on sexuality, marriage, religion, and other topics (Polletta 2002).

Personal clashes among activists would make routine collaboration problematic, as meetings could easily be sidetracked by disputes on unrelated topics. Coalitions of Democratic- and Republican-identified organizations might have trouble agreeing how to frame their messages and what tactics to use. Even if Republican-identified organizations consented to work with mainline peace organizations – such as UFPJ, Veterans for Peace, and Peace Action – they would almost certainly resist partnering with the socialist and communist organizations that are mainstays of the movement – such as the International Socialist Organization, the ANSWER Coalition, and World Can't Wait – which they view as "un-American." Because of these organizational challenges, any substantial Republican participation in the antiwar movement would have to be coordinated through coalitions that were disconnected from the liberal/leftist coalitions that actually led the movement. Thus, any genuinely bipartisan antiwar movement would likely be even more fragmented and uncoordinated than the actual movement after 9/11.

Partisan polarization creates conditions under which it is difficult or impossible to build a mass movement that draws significant support from partisans in both major parties. We find that this is true not only of the antiwar movement, but also of the Tea Party and Occupy Wall Street. Polarization does not mean that all of the supporters of a movement are self-identified partisans of a single party, as many of the movement's supporters are nonpartisan or aligned with minor parties. But it does mean that few if any activists in the movement are likely to identify with the more ideologically distant major party. The consequence is that, in an era of partisan polarization, social movements risk experiencing severe fluctuations in support concomitant with variations in partisan success. The less polarized the political system is, however, the less pronounced these risks are likely to be. Partisan polarization amplifies the risks of the party in the street to movements but reduces the risks of the party in the street to parties.

STRATEGIES FOR SOCIAL MOVEMENTS

Any social movement that seeks to bring about social change in the United States must confront the dominant role that political parties play in the American political system. There is no one right way for them to do so. This research demonstrates that parties present movements with risks that they must weigh against the potential benefits of working with parties. One of the most significant risks is that if movements draw their supporters largely from the ranks of a single political party, then those supporters may well abandon the movement at a critical time, if supporting the movement is no longer convenient for the party. On the other hand, partisanship may help the movement to grow at critical times. Our research demonstrates that anti-Republican partisanship buoyed the antiwar movement, especially during the early and middle years of George W. Bush's presidency. Occasionally, parties may deliver on their promises and make the policy changes that movements have been pressing. How should these considerations affect the strategies of social movements?

We propose that movement leaders ask themselves a series of questions when crafting a strategy vis-à-vis political parties. First, does the movement seek minor, moderate, or major change in society, and over what period? Second, how much partisan polarization is there in the political system? Third, what are the resources of the movement and to what extent are they bound to partisan sources? Fourth, what is the current size of the party in the street and what is its potential size? Is there a low, moderate, or high level of overlap between the party and the movement? How easily could that change? That is, how much potential does the movement have to draw self-identified partisans into (or expel them from) its ranks? In this section, we consider these questions in the context of the antiwar, Tea Party, and Occupy movements.

The Antiwar Movement

The antiwar movement after 9/11 sought immediate change in major policies advanced by the Bush administration. It did so during a period of extraordinarily high partisan polarization. It mobilized a party in the street that varied in size over time but had the potential to approach the size of the Democratic Party itself. As it was not tied closely to an occupational or industrial group, the antiwar movement was severely lacking in resources. For example, it could not rely on its supporters to pay sizable dues to the movement, as is the case in the labor movement. It received small contributions from its supporters but could not count on them for steady donations. When larger sums of money arrived in the movement's coffers, they were often from sources with strong partisan agendas, such as MoveOn. Under these conditions, what was the best strategy for the movement to confront the Democratic Party?

Despite the decline in Democratic support for the antiwar movement after 2007, working with the Democratic Party was still most likely the best strategy available to the movement. The movement did not have decades to change public opinion about the war; it wanted to stop the war *now*. The movement's best bet was to convince the Democratic Party to take a stand against the wars and then help its members be elected to office. In many ways, the antiwar movement followed exactly this strategy.

Nevertheless, the antiwar movement could have done more than it did to leverage the Democratic Party's potential to change U.S. policy in the Middle East. The movement made only limited use of primary challenges as a strategy to unseat intransigent Democrats in Congress. If the movement had run more of its own candidates in the 2006 and 2008 congressional elections, it might have had more leverage in advancing its approach to withdrawal. The movement might have also made greater use of lobbying after 2007, especially in 2009 and beyond. To be successful in pursuing these strategies, it would have had to do more to educate its supporters about the need for continued activism once the Democrats began to achieve electoral success. In doing so, the movement might have strengthened the identification of its supporters with the movement, so that they would have been more likely to resolve identity conflicts in its favor.

The antiwar movement could also have benefited from establishing a financial base that was independent of Democratically identified donors. The movement might have been able to broaden its appeal by adding conservative arguments against war to its discursive repertoire, even though doing so would also pose risks of backlash from the movement's liberal/leftist base. Taking these steps might have put the movement in a stronger position to push the party in its preferred policy direction, while securing greater autonomy for the movement.

The Tea Party Movement

The Tea Party movement sought immediate, intermediate, and long-term changes in national policies after the election of President Barack Obama. It sought to stop the enactment and implementation of the Affordable Care Act, a reduction of government spending and indebtedness, and a reorientation to a government with constitutional principles. It did so during a period of extraordinarily high partisan polarization. The size of its party in the street grew steadily over time as the Tea Party and the Republican Party became more closely associated with one another. Consequently, the intersectional identity of "Tea Party Republican" was strong. The movement was able to tap resources from some of party's key supporters, such as the Koch family, and to use the campaign finance system to its advantage. Under these conditions, what was the best strategy for the movement to confront the Republican Party?

The Tea Party initially began by relying on outsider tactics, such as staging protests and disrupting town hall meetings. These tactics enabled the movement to gain widespread attention and facilitated its growth. After the 2010 congressional elections, however, the movement reduced its reliance on outsider tactics and evolved toward working inside the Republican Party. It placed a premium on challenging incumbent Republicans in congressional primaries. In some cases, defeating incumbent Republicans in the primary contributed to a win by the Democratic candidate in the general election, as was the case in the contest for the U.S. Senate seat from Indiana in 2012. In other cases, Tea Party candidates won both primary and general elections, as was the case in the contest for the U.S. Senate seat from Texas in 2012. The Tea Party established caucuses in the U.S. House and Senate, helping it to become a force in congressional policy making. In September and October 2013, Tea Party supporters championed a partial shutdown of the U.S. federal government in an effort to eliminate the Affordable Care Act and stop an increase in the federal debt limit. While this strategy did not ultimately achieve its immediate objectives, it did demonstrate the growing influence of the Tea Party in Washington, D.C. It is hard to imagine that the Tea Party could have done much more to reshape the Republican Party between 2009 and 2014.

By mid-2014, the Tea Party appeared to be well on its way to capturing control of the Republican Party. Even if a Republican member of Congress does not subscribe to Tea Party positions, she or he must be cautious not to invoke its wrath, lest the movement organize a challenge to the member in the next primary election. The defeat of House Majority Leader Eric Cantor (R-VA) by a Tea Party–backed candidate (David Brat) in the 2014 primary election demonstrated how vulnerable any member of the Republican Caucus could be to the movement's ire (Martin 2014). The principal risk facing the Tea Party at this point is that it may overplay its hand and stimulate an organized challenge from moderate interests within the Republican Party. If that happens, a sustained battle within the Republican Party may undermine the party's ability to challenge the Democratic Party in federal elections, potentially moving policy away from the Tea Party's preferences, at least in the short term. Similarly, convincing its supporters that its policy goals can be accomplished quickly (for example, by threatening to shut down the government) entails the risk that its supporters may become disillusioned when they discover that the type of change they seek usually requires decades or more to accomplish. Further, by working so closely with the Republican Party, the Tea Party risks that it may be co-opted and lose much of its autonomy from the party. Given the substantial overlap between the Tea Party and the Republican Party, the Tea Party would probably be devastated if its activists believed that they had to choose between their Republican and Tea Party identities.

The Occupy Movement

The Occupy movement after 9/11 sought long-term changes in the structure of the American economy and society. Its policy goals were not always clear, yet the movement advocated broadly for a reduction in economic inequality, less power for corporations, and greater participatory democracy. It did so during a period of extraordinarily high partisan polarization. The Occupy movement had strong potential to form a party in the street with the Democratic Party, yet it deliberately and vocally rejected collaboration with the Democrats whenever possible. The movement received some resources through donations, but it eschewed forming the kinds of institutional structures that would have enabled it to expand its resource base. Under these conditions, what was the best strategy for the movement to confront the party system?

The core organizers of the Occupy movement saw collaboration with the Democratic Party as a serious threat to the movement's autonomy (Gitlin 2012). Thus, their strategy was to avoid working with the Democrats at all costs. This strategy allowed Occupy to retain purity in its message, especially given that the Democrats are closely allied with the corporate interests that Occupy seeks to undermine. Occupy's antipartisan strategy well served its participants' desires for self-expression (Smucker 2014). As long as self-expression is the movement's principal goal, then the movement should continue to maintain an antipartisan posture. On the other hand, if movement actors wish to influence policy change, then they may need to revise its purely anarchist orientation.

A first step for the Occupy movement might be to recognize that many of its supporters and potential supporters identify with the Democratic Party. By taking such a strong stand against the Democratic Party, Occupy cuts itself off from a key part of its support base. Instead, the movement might look for ways to recognize and incorporate the intersectional identity of "Occupy Democrats." A second step might be to inaugurate some institutional structures within Occupy. These structures might help to raise funds, employ staff, and regularize communication with Occupy supporters. While this suggestion is somewhat counter to the nonhierarchical ethos of Occupy, some minimal level of organization may be necessary to make any systematic progress toward the movement's long-term policy goals. A third step might be to forge alliances with genuine allies in the progressive community. While it may be that alliances with the Democrats and MoveOn are untenable, perhaps Occupy could partner with the Green Party and other political organizations whose agendas are not incommensurate with Occupy's vision.

General Lessons

The principal lesson of our analysis is that movements should be attentive to the ways in which intersectional identities of their supporters are likely to affect the pursuit of their goals. Since activists with dual identities may experience a shift in the salience of their identities in response to key events, they have the potential to sway the balance of power toward or away from the movement. Movements should weigh these risks while taking into account the nature of their policy goals, the overall degree of partisan polarization, and their access to resources.

While we stress the strategic implications of the party in the street during periods of high partisan polarization, the party in the street is relevant to movement strategies during times of low polarization as well. When polarization is relatively low, social movement leaders may be in a stronger position to threaten to switch their support from one political party to another. Such a threat is generally not as credible during periods of high polarization because party leaders may believe that the movement is essentially captured by the party (Frymer 1999). In the absence of polarization, it might be realistic for a movement's supporters to switch their partisan loyalties. In doing so, the party in the street would transfer energy, resources, and votes to the competing party. Under such conditions, the movement would be in a stronger position to make demands of the party and to insist that they be fulfilled in a timely fashion.

STRATEGIES FOR POLITICAL PARTIES

Any political party that seeks to govern in the United States must confront the ubiquity of social movements within its ranks. Movements may represent small and relatively inconsequential constituencies within the party, such as gays and lesbians inside the Republican Party. Or they may constitute core blocks of the party, such as the labor movement within the Democratic Party. Movements vary in the extent to which they have the potential to assist or challenge the party. What strategies should parties employ if they wish to reap the gains of movement activism while avoiding the costs?

We propose that party leaders ask themselves a series of questions when crafting a strategy vis-à-vis movements. First, does the movement seek changes that are in line with the party's current agenda, or does the movement aspire to take the party in a new direction? Second, could the movement realistically threaten to move its support to the competing major party or is it effectively captured? Third, are there ways that the party could restrict the resources available to the movement? Fourth, do many people within the party have views that are sympathetic with the movement's leaders such that they could be easily convinced to join the party in the street? Or is the movement on the fringe of the party? In this section, we consider the applicability of these lessons for the Democratic and Republican Parties.

The Democratic Party

The antiwar movement helped the Democratic Party to regain its vibrancy after two consecutive presidential election victories by the Republican Party in 2000 and 2004. Democratic gains in 2006 and, to a lesser extent, in 2008, may be partly attributed to a widespread antiwar sentiment in the American public (as we discuss in Chapter 2). In 2006 and 2008, the antiwar movement fit within the Democratic Party's agenda to criticize and delegitimize the Bush administration, though the party also sought to do so in a way that was not unpatriotic or disrespectful to the military. Even if the Democratic Party was hesitant to embrace the antiwar cause, it seemed highly unlikely that the peacenik crowd in the movement would readily bolt to the Republican Party, which had taken an unambiguous prowar position. While the movement suffered from a dearth of resources, it had the potential to appeal to the sympathies of a large swath of Democratic Party loyalists.

Many of the leaders in the Democratic Party were slow to endorse the antiwar movement in the immediate aftermath of 9/11, as a result of their perception of public sentiments supporting war. However, when insurgent violence began to increase in Iraq in 2005, Democratic Party leaders lined up with the antiwar movement. Importantly, massive antiwar rallies helped to demonstrate the salience of antiwar views in the public. Thus, from 2005 to 2008, many elites in the party supported the movement.

When Obama assumed the presidency in 2009, the Democratic Party could have faced a serious dilemma in interacting with the antiwar movement. If the movement had stayed highly mobilized – and had contested the president's decision to escalate the war in Afghanistan – then the Democrats could have faced serious discontent within their ranks. In such a circumstance, the party might have considered three options. First, the party could have capitulated to the movement and quickly reversed policy in Iraq and Afghanistan. This option could have been problematic if rapid and ill-planned withdrawals led to a spike in casualties and increased chaos in occupied regions. In this case, the party's effort to appease the movement could have led to crippling disapproval in the broader public. Second, the party could have tried to appease the movement by explaining the sensitivity of the policy situation and its desire to see the wars end as soon as it was practical. Third, the party could have simply ignored the movement, recognizing that it was unlikely to throw its support behind the Republican Party, though the Democratic Party could lose a key constituency in the upcoming elections. The party's actual response might be described as a hybrid of the second and third options. Nevertheless, the movement vitiated this dilemma for the party by demobilizing of its own accord. The Democratic Party did lose some backing because of its continuation of Bush's war policies, but we estimate this to have been only about 1 percent of its most loyal activists. President Obama may not have fully measured up to the vision of hope that he inspired in his 2008 campaign, but he ultimately did not need to confront massive antiwar-driven defection from the Democratic ranks.

The rise of the Occupy movement in the fall of 2011 also posed both risks and opportunities for the Democratic Party. The risks of the movement stemmed from the contentious and unpredictable nature of its tactics. The occupation of downtown spaces in many cities had the potential to lead to clashes with police, as well as possible health-and-safety harms to participants in an Occupy encampment. These concerns, along with the fact that the Occupy movement vehemently rejected collaborating with the Democratic Party, meant that party actors were only likely to lose from endorsing Occupy actions. Instead, Democratic politicians took the less risky approach of incorporating Occupy themes in their rhetoric. For example, party actors (such as President Obama) blended Occupy concerns about inequality and unjustly wielded corporate power into their talking points.

Still, the Democratic Party missed an opportunity to seize upon some of the grassroots organizing energy linked to Occupy. While hard-core Occupy activists were (and are still) unlikely to want to cooperate with the party, there were and are certainly more moderate actors connected to the movement that may be amenable to working on inequality-related policies with the promise of a more lasting institutional impact. MoveOn's efforts to approach Occupy in this way were clumsy at best (as we discuss in Chapter 7), but there may still be ways for local Democratic Party organizations (or their allies) to collaborate with Occupy sympathizers in a manner that harnesses the energy of the party in the street.

The Republican Party

The Tea Party was a much-needed burst of energy for the Republican Party after its demoralizing losses in the 2008 presidential and congressional elections. The near-filibuster-proof Democratic majority in the U.S. Senate was a harbinger of unwanted new liberal policies, which the Tea Party spoke out against. The Tea Party proposed that the Republican Party should place a much stronger emphasis on fiscal discipline than it previously had. Most of its supporters were committed Republicans, conservatives, and libertarians who were never going to defect to the Democratic Party, though they might realistically be expected to switch to minor parties or withdraw from the electorate altogether. The Tea Party had a resource base that was somewhat independent of the party and was regarded as too radical by many in the mainstream Republican Party.

The Republican Party leadership's strategy toward the Tea Party might best be described as appeasement. Republican leaders in Congress begrudgingly allowed repeated votes to repeal the Affordable Care Act. They also reluctantly permitted aggressive budgetary moves in 2011 for sequestration and a partial shutdown of the federal government in 2013. If the Republican leadership opposes these moves by the Tea Party, then it could face costly leadership challenges within Congress or in primary elections. Yet, maintaining the strategy of appeasement could hurt the party severely in national elections.

If the Republican Party leadership wished to reduce the influence of the Tea Party within its ranks, then it would face an uphill battle. Essentially, it would need to challenge the intersectionality between Republican and Tea Party identities. To do so, it might argue that many Tea Party stances are radical – not conservative – and thus harmful to the Republican Party. For example, tactics such as shutting down the government or threatening to default on debt only add to the growing debt by generating unnecessary shutdown costs and higher interest rates. To be effective, Republican leadership would also need to articulate an alternative, "moderate conservative" vision for the party. Such a strategy would be difficult to implement and, at a minimum, would require a charismatic spokesperson who could articulate that vision in clear and concise language. The Democratic presidential candidate Bill Clinton accomplished a similar feat in 1992 when he persuaded many actors in the Democratic Party to move to the center of the political spectrum on issues such as crime, trade, welfare, and fiscal discipline. If the Republican Party leadership were able to follow a similar model, it might be able to check the influence of the Tea Party within its ranks. We offer this strategy with the caution that any attempt to marginalize the Tea Party would likely be met with substantial, well-organized resistance.

Another possible opportunity/challenge for the Republican Party could arise from the resurgence of the Christian Right as an organizational force within the Republican Party. The Christian Right was a dominant faction within the party from at least the mid-1980s to the mid-2000s, so it is reasonable to anticipate that its prominence has not abated permanently. As research by Joseph DiGrazia

(2014) reveals, many individual Christian Right activists were drawn into the Tea Party movement. Yet because the Tea Party neglects themes that are closely identified with the Christian Right (such as the right to life, prayer in schools, and opposition to same-sex marriage), there may be opportunities for political entrepreneurs to rebuild the Christian Right or, perhaps, merge the two movements using hybrid organizations such as the Tea Party for Christians (2014; see also Heaney and Rojas 2014). The combination of these movements would likely push the Republican Party further away from the center of American politics. As a result, it may be wise for the Republican Party to develop rhetorical and organizational strategies that reinforce the separation of these movements.

General Lessons

The principal lesson of our analysis is that parties may be able to exploit the close identification that a movement's supporters have with the party. Some of the party's supporters may favor the movement over the party, but this group is likely to constitute a relatively small proportion of the party's members. The party may do so subtly by priming partisan identification when communicating with movement supporters. Or, it may do so more overtly by co-opting the movement's supporters by sharing power and resources within the party (Coy 2013, p. 281; Selznick 1949). The fact that the party holds an advantage, however, does not give it carte blanche in its relations with the movement. Movements are a dynamic force that has the potential to transform politics by reframing issues and shifting identities. If movements use this potential wisely, they may be able to outmaneuver parties, even though they are dwarfed by parties' support and resources.

During periods of low partisan polarization, the principal challenge for political parties is to persuade social movement actors to remain within the party fold and not to defect to the opposing party. One strategy for doing so is to actively appeal to the intersectional identities of movement actors, stressing the reasons why they have to be loyal to the party and to the movement. Other strategies would be to offer movement actors responsible positions with the party, to share the party's resources with the movement, and to enact the movement's policy agenda.

FUTURE INQUIRY INTO THE PARTY IN THE STREET

This book investigates the dynamic intersection between social movements and political parties. It does so by focusing on the shifting political involvement of activists, organizations, and legislators. This work breaks new ground in explaining why actors vary their attention between competing fields of politics. Yet, there is a need for more empirical research that tracks these dynamics over time and in other political contexts. Recent scholarship by Doug McAdam and Sidney Tarrow (2010) points to the importance of identifying and testing mechanisms that govern the reciprocal relationship between elections and social movements, such as the way that social movements introduce new forms of collective action and sometimes polarize political parties. Dana Fisher (2012) calls for more research that crosses disciplinary boundaries and covers the full ideological spectrum of activism. Stephanie Mudge and Anthony Chen (2014, pp. 320–1) emphasize the need for researchers to look more carefully inside parties, investigate their organizational structures, and situate them in the larger political system. In this penultimate section, we suggest three steps toward realizing these ambitions and consider the broader implications of this research.

First, in order to understand the party in the street's dynamics, it is essential to observe actors moving into and out of political domains. Along these lines, Hadden and Tarrow (2007) document the spillout of antiglobalization activists into the antiwar movement. Similarly, we observe the spillout of antiwar activists into the Democratic Party's other issue priorities, such as health care. These analyses are somewhat idiosyncratic, since they look only at the flow of actors from one specified area to another. Future research might benefit from following actors as they move among movements and parties more generally. For example, research might aim to identify individuals during their first experience with activism and then track them over several years of involvement. Such research would require significant methodological innovation, since prior research has not followed larger, representative samples of activists longitudinally. This approach could provide greater insight into what causes activists to switch between parties and movements.

Second, we have relatively little information about how elites in parties and movements think about and strategize toward the party in the street. To what extent is the emergence of intersectional identities – such as Tea Party Republicans – the result of the plans of party and movement leaders? To what extent do these identities emerge organically from evolving political events? How successful are elites in their efforts at strategic manipulation? Under what conditions is the party in the street captured as a result of these efforts and under what conditions does it maintain autonomy? Research in this vein would force scholars to address more explicitly how the competing organizational forms introduced by parties and movements shape the ways that elites strategize about reaching out to their diverse constituencies.

Third, it would be valuable to explore how agendas evolve from the party in the street and do or do not become policy. When does the party in the street succeed in getting its way over policy? Are there cases when the party in the street interferes with what otherwise might have been a policy success of the mainstream political party? Ideally, such an investigation would be conducted from a historical vantage point in which periods of both high and low partisan polarization could be considered. Research along these lines would have the potential to bridge the literature on agenda setting in political science (cf. Baumgartner and Jones 1993, 2015) with the literature on social movement outcomes in sociology (cf. Amenta 2006).

Each of the points of this research agenda would require more active collaboration between political scientists and sociologists. Remaining confined in disciplinary silos is antithetical to appreciating a phenomenon that principally involves crossing boundaries. Further interdisciplinary collaboration could help to illuminate how the party in the street becomes a locus for both the advantages and the pathologies of movements and parties as forms of political organization. Moreover, they would direct scholars to take organizational structures and organizing processes more seriously than is typically the case in the study of political parties and social movements (Mudge and Chen 2014). Such work would benefit from a strong grounding in the long tradition of scholarship in organizational theory (March 1997).

CONCLUSION

Social movements promise to give vibrancy to political parties, while parties have the potential to help movements reach their policy goals. In search of mutual benefit, partnerships often form between these distinct types of political organizations. These partnerships are complicated by the complex, intersectional identities of the actors who form them, as well as the evolved formal and informal rules that govern how parties and movements interact.

Political parties and social movements are ostensibly orthogonal forms of political organization. Still, political actors working in and with them may encounter considerable complementarities and trade-offs. The balance of risks from these intersections tends to favor parties, at least during an era of high partisan polarization. Indeed, strategic efforts by political actors to change this balance by creating new organizations and networks have the potential to set the stage for the next chapter of American political history.

The ability of political actors to manage the conflicting imperatives of political parties and social movements is challenged by the shifting identities of diverse actors. When identity shifts occur in the midst of an episode of contention, the motivations and policy goals of participants are likely to change. Thus, the basic parameters of the political situation may be modified in unexpected ways. As a result, participants may find that the consequences of their actions were not what they intended.

The interplay of political parties and social movements matters beyond realizing the interests of the actors involved in them. In many ways, it is at the heart of democratic practice in the United States. As Alexis de Tocqueville (1988 [1840]) noted long ago, Americans are "forever forming associations." Associating is a key way that they address problems and pursue their aspirations. Their associations are wide and multiple. Yet the way that associations affect one another – how they influence the behavior of political actors – is still ill understood. This book illuminates the consequences of party-movement intersections in one political context, but a multitude of other overlapping affiliations that shape the dynamics of American politics remain unexplored. Deepening our understanding of participatory democracy will require further probing into the ways in which political identification molds the views, involvement, and effectiveness of citizens, organizations, and legislators.

Epilogue

By the start of the Obama administration's second term, Bush's wars had nearly drawn to a close. American troops had withdrawn from Iraq but remained in Afghanistan. While some policies of the Bush years had been abandoned, others had continued and expanded. The Obama administration propelled the use of remote-control drone technology to new heights by conducting extrajudicial killings inside and outside war zones across the Middle East. The antiwar movement – once described as another "superpower" – could barely muster a few thousand protesters to contest drone strikes or aggressive U.S. foreign policies toward Libya and Syria.

When President Obama proposed launching missile strikes against Syria in August 2013, protests at sites around the United States were attended by only a few hundred people each. When we conducted protest surveys (analogous to those described in Chapter 4) at antiwar rallies on September 8 and 9, 2013, in New York, Washington, D.C., Chicago, and San Francisco, we found that only 19 percent of the participants were self-identified Democrats ($N = 227$). On the whole, Democrats would not turn out to protest their president.

As we finalize this book in the fall of 2014, the drumbeat to war has begun again, as President Obama announced plans for new airstrikes in Iraq to quell the rise of the Islamic State of Iraq and Syria (Cooper, Landler, and Rubin 2014). The anemic protests that characterized the antiwar movement in Obama's second term should perhaps be viewed less as a mark of the failure of the movement, and more a benchmark against which to evaluate the movement in the years immediately following 9/11. We believe that the overall mobilization of the movement should be seen as an extraordinary achievement. For all the fanfare received by the Tea Party and Occupy Wall Street, neither movement matched the antiwar movement in the size of its protests or the time frame over which they were sustained. For at least five years – from 2003 to 2007 – the antiwar movement was a major force in American politics.

The mass constituency of the U.S. antiwar movement has gone home. But it would be a mistake to see the movement as gone. Activists work every day to oppose military interventions around the world, to end the drone program, to free whistleblowers, and to terminate the surveillance state. They are supported by a cadre of organizations, such as UFPJ, ANSWER, Code Pink, World Can't Wait, and Peace Action. The antiwar movement is in abeyance. But it remains alive as it continues to train activists and to preserve the values of the movement.

While we wish that it were not so, there will likely be another day when masses of people swarm to the streets to condemn another ill-conceived war. When they do, they will confront political parties – Democrats, Republicans, and possibly others unknown to us today. We hope that this volume will offer activists of that day insight that might enable them to more effectively raise the voices of the people in the name of peace.

FIGURE E.1. Antiwar Activists Picket the White House, April 13, 2013 (Photo by Michael T. Heaney)

Appendixes

APPENDIX A.   SURVEYORS AND RESEARCH ASSISTANTS

SURVEYORS FOR 2004–2005 PROTEST SURVEYS

Marion Adams, Colleen Berndt, Jason Briggerman, Sylvia Broude, Alex Chisholm, Sun Choe, Michael Coleman, Brendon Daly, Clark Durant, Michael Heaney, Melissa Howe, Leslie Klein, Alexey Makarevich, Erin McLeod, Lynn Murphy, Clayton Nall, Hilary Packer, Vinay Patel, Ashley Peterson, Ryan Peterson, Elizabeth Pisares, Fabio Rojas, Elizabeth Rubenstein, Nathan Russell, Ramin Seddiq, Dominic Soon, Jacob Sumner, Aaron Tang, Leora Vegosen, Triyakshana Venkatraman, Melody Weinstein, Sylvia Woods, and Zhiyuan Yu.

SURVEYORS FOR 2007–2010 PROTEST SURVEYS

Luqman Abdullah, Elif Alp, Nicole Andersen, Andrea Anstett, Gavin Baker, Josiah Baker, Bob Bateman, Kate Bateman, Carl Bergquist, Erica Bormuth, Feler Bose, Andrei Boutyline, Michelle Brotman, Caroline Buddenhagen, Ahsan Butt, Luke Carman, Brena Cascini, Patricia Ceccarelli, Bob Childs, Laryssa Chomiak, Sarah Clayman Jim Cogley, Geoffrey Colon, James Curry, Casey Davidson, Laura Davidson, Nina DeJong, Jean-Louis Delayen, Ezra Deutsch-Feldman, Joe DiGrazia, Andrea Dinneen, Herbert Docena, Nathan Dollar, James Drembelas, Maria Dziembouslen, Anar Enhsaihan, Charleen Fed, Shawn Fennell, Lucila Figueroa, Rachel Fleishman, Sam Freund, Orin Frymer, Auriel

Gallimore, David Gastwirth, Ben Gebre-Medhih, Sholeh Geola, Rachel Girshick, Jill Gloekler, Kate Goff, Rayza Goldsmith, Shanthi Gonzales, Marie Gray, Colleen Hackett, Amy Hager, Aimee Hall, Susan Hanrahan, Alex Hartley, Michael Heaney, Alana Hecht, Vincent Heckard, Patrick Hogan, Megan Hoot, Nick Huober, Ricardo Hurtado, Matthew Jacobs, Sean Jahanmir, Erik Johnson, Ollie Khakwani, Rafael Khatchaturian, Leslie Klein, Michael Kramer, Erin Lamos, Courtney Lantzer, Dainia Lawes, Taehesk Lee, Liz Leicht, Justin Lepp, Shawn Lessard, Emi Lesure, Robert Lucas, Michelle Lueck, Jill Mailing, Leonard Major, Shana Marshall, Meb Marye, J. P. Mason, Agnes Mazur, Will McBride, Jessica McClain, Sean McClellan, James McConchie, Jonathan McKeller, Sandra Mendez, April Morton, Kristen Moussalli, Joseph Mulkerin, Ana Muniz, Ann Murphy, Philip Murphy, Clayton Nall, Laura Nelson, Hong Ngyuen, Tim O'Brien, Abigail Ocobach, Tom Ogorzalek, David O'Reilley, Chinyere Osuji, Ali Ozdogan, Josh Pacewicz, Alyssa Pappas, Matt Parker, Joanna Patenia, Joanna Patonia, Gonzalo Paz, Shanna Pearson, Ryan Polich, Matt Porta, Catherine Potter, Liza Prendergast, Sahana Rajan, Riham Ramadan, Erin Reed, Matt Reges, Laura Ridenour, Jeannette Roach, Lindsay Robinson, Fabio Rojas, Sarah Rose-Jensen, Benji Schechter, Kemyta Serrey, Monica Shattuck, Amanda Shigihara, Victoria Shineman, Pedro Silva, Stephanie Slade, Suzanne Smith, Chase Soha, Renee Souris, Evan Sparks, Alissa Stollwerk, Tamera Lee Stover, Andria Strano, Isaac Swaiman, Cary Tabora, Leigh Taylor, Jennifer Terrell, Roswell Thomas, Brett Thompson, Leora Vegosen, Joseph Waggle, Amanda Wall, Solongo Wandan, Alex Watts, Melissa Wells, Tabi White, Terrence Whitton, Zelena Williams, Dan Wang, Tiffany Wong, Chen-Yu Wu, Elise Yu, and Yael Zeina.

SURVEYORS FOR 2010 SOCIAL FORUM SURVEYS

Mary Akchurin, Michael Heaney, Minjoo Kim, Jack Masteller, Jessica McClain, Sahana Rajan, Fabio Rojas, Todd Schifeling, Jacob Smith, and Michael Sullivan.

RESEARCH ASSISTANTS FOR 2004–2005 (INDIANA UNIVERSITY)

Nicholas Rowland, Melissa Quintela, Ashley Peterson, Violet Yebei, Yasmiyn Irrizarry, and Jacob T. Sumner.

RESEARCH ASSISTANTS FOR 2007–2008 (INDIANA UNIVERSITY)

Matt Gougherty and Julie Panzica.

RESEARCH ASSISTANTS FOR 2008–2009 (UNIVERSITY OF FLORIDA)

Christopher Cartagena, Eric Netcher, and Matthew Newman.

RESEARCH ASSISTANTS FOR 2008–2009 (UNIVERSITY OF MICHIGAN)

Jaclyn Goldin, Adam Francis, and Jamie Wellinger.

RESEARCH ASSISTANTS FOR 2009–2010 (UNIVERSITY OF MICHIGAN)

Kate Balzer, Chelsea Carbary, Patricia Ceccarelli, Samah Choudhury, Jeanie Gong, Minjoo Kim, Emeralle Kirksey, Dayana Kupisk, Jill Mailing, Jack Masteller, Jessica McClain, Dori Moscowitz, Sahana Rajan, Riham Ramadan, Alison Shier, Vikram Singh, Jacob Smith, Alex Stankovich, Michael Sullivan, Thea Torek, Natalie Wengroff, Elise Yu, and Clare Zhang.

RESEARCH ASSISTANTS FOR 2010–2011 (INDIANA UNIVERSITY)

Matt Grace, Erica Thopmson, and Sean Buuck.

RESEARCH ASSISTANTS FOR 2010–2011 (UNIVERSITY OF MICHIGAN)

Sahar Adora, Charles Frank, Rayza Goldsmith, Katrina Gumbinner, Alex Hartley, Susannah Hope, Brigid Kilcoin, Rachel Klinghoffer, Brian Kobashigawa, Dayana Kupisk, Courtney Lantzer, Vicki Lau, Brian Pogrund, Erin Reed, Monica Shattuck, Michael Stern, Maria Trikolas, Erika Vijh, and Allison Yellin.

RESEARCH ASSISTANTS FOR 2011–2012 (INDIANA UNIVERSITY)

Erica Thompson, Lisa Carter, Peter Lista, and Karolina Gontarczuk.

RESEARCH ASSISTANTS FOR 2011–2012 (UNIVERSITY OF MICHIGAN)

Robert Dishell, Craig Kaplan, Kelsey Lee, Michelle Rubin, and Kendall Witmer.

RESEARCH ASSISTANTS FOR 2012–2013 (UNIVERSITY OF MICHIGAN)

Olivia Blanchette, Sandra Bortolin, Farid Damasio, Mackenzie Dewitt, Leslie Kang, Kristy Minielly, Skylar Elisberg, Elana Firsht, Elizabeth Ludwig, Michael Noeske, Christina Rowan, Kendall Russ, Serena Sana, Isabella Schiller, Vincent Sheu, Peri Silverman, Christopher Takahashi, and Stephen Zoski.

RESEARCH ASSISTANTS FOR 2013–2014 (UNIVERSITY OF MICHIGAN)

Amanda Block, Ian Chan, Caroline Chevat, Mira Friedlander, Ezekiel Harris, Olivia Hodgkiss, Nicole Joseph, Brandon Kassimir, Jake Lader, James O'Bryant, Jillian Robbins, Adam Rubenfire, Zachary Stapf, and Stephen Weidenbach.

APPENDIX B.   VARIABLE DEFINITIONS FOR VOTE CHOICE EQUATIONS

All numeric codes are indicated with square brackets.

VOTED FOR DEMOCRATIC CANDIDATE

For equations 2.6, 2.8, 2.10, and 2.12, the variable is based on the following question: "In today's election for U.S. House of Representatives, did you just vote for: Did not vote for U.S. House [o], The Democratic Candidate [1], The Republican Candidate [o], Other [o]."

For equations 2.7 and 2.11, the variable is based on the following question: "In today's election for U.S. Senator, did you just vote for: Did not vote for U.S. Senator [o], The Democratic Candidate [1], The Republican Candidate [o], Other [o]."

For equation 2.9, the variable is based on the following question: "In today's election for president, did you just vote for: Kerry [1], Bush [o], Nader [o], Other [o]."

For equation 2.13, the variable is based on the following question: "In today's election for president, did you just vote for: Barack Obama [1], John McCain [o], Other: Who? [o], Did not vote [o]."

CANDIDATE CHOICE

For equations 2.6 and 2.7, the variable is based on the following question: "Do you support or oppose the U.S. taking increased military action against Iraq to remove Saddam Hussein from power? Support [o], Oppose [1]"

For equations 2.8 and 2.9, the variable is based on the following question: "How do you feel about the U.S. decision to go to war with Iraq?

Strongly approve [1], Somewhat approve [2], Somewhat disapprove [3], Strongly disapprove [4]."

For equations 2.10, 2.11, 2.12, and 2.13, the variable is based on the following question: "How do you feel about the U.S. war in Iraq? Strongly approve [1], Somewhat approve [2], Somewhat disapprove [3], Strongly disapprove [4]."

POSITIVE ECONOMIC OUTLOOK

For equations 2.6, 2.7, 2.10, 2.11, 2.12, and 2.13, the variable is based on the following question: "Do you think the condition of the nation's economy is: Excellent [4], Good [3], Not so good [2], Poor [1]."

For equations 2.8 and 2.9, the variable is based on the following question: "Compared to four years ago, is your family's financial situation: Better today [3], Worse today [1], About the same [2]."

DEMOCRAT

For equations 2.6, 2.7, 2.8, 2.9, 2.10, 2.11, 2.12, and 2.13, the variable is based on the following question: "No matter how you voted today, do you usually think of yourself as a: Democrat [1], Independent [0], Republican [0], Something else [0]."

For equations 2.6, 2.7, 2.8, 2.9, 2.10, 2.11, 2.12, and 2.13, the variable is based on the following question: "On most political matters, do you consider yourself: Liberal [3], Moderate [2], Conservative [1]."

SEX/GENDER IS FEMALE

For equations 2.6, 2.7, 2.8, 2.9, 2.10, 2.11, 2.12, and 2.13, the variable is based on the following question: "Are you: Male [0], Female [1]."

RACE/ETHNICITY IS AFRICAN AMERICAN/BLACK

For equations 2.6, 2.7, 2.8, 2.9, 2.10, 2.11, 2.12, and 2.13, the variable is based on the following question: "Are you: White [0], Asian [0], Black [1], Other [0], Hispanic/Latino [0]."

AGE IN YEARS

For equations 2.6, 2.7, 2.8, 2.9, 2.10, 2.11, 2.12, and 2.13, the variable is based on the following question: "To which age group do you belong? 18–24, 25–29, 30–39, 40–44, 45–49, 50–59, 60–64, 75 or over [entered median of category]."

INCOME IN THOUSANDS OF DOLLARS

For equations 2.6, 2.7, 2.8, 2.9, 2.10, 2.11, 2.12, and 2.13, the variable is based on the following question: "2001 [2003 / 2005 / 2007], depending on the year] total family income: Under $15,000, $15,000–$29,999, $30,000–$49,999, $50,000–$74,999, $75,000–$99,999, $100,000 or more [entered median of category]."

APPENDIX C. DESCRIPTIVE STATISTICS FOR VOTE CHOICE EQUATIONS

Independent Variable	2002	2004	2006	2008
		Mean (Standard Deviation) [% Imputed]		
Opposed to Iraq War	1.0433	2.4985	2.7417	2.9160
	(0.2221)	(1.1880)	(1.1348)	(1.0312)
	[0.00]	[3.49]	[7.12]	[5.43]
Positive Economic Outlook	2.3131	2.0368	2.4621	1.5700
	(0.6816)	(0.7755)	(0.8210)	(0.6491)
	[0.00]	[3.85]	[0.07]	[4.04]
Democrat = 1	0.3864	0.3671	0.3821	0.4070
	(0.4695)	(0.4753)	(0.4755)	(0.4960)
	[1.01]	[4.04]	[7.35]	[1.38]
Liberal Political Ideology	1.8164	1.8629	1.8981	1.8889
	(0.6675)	(0.7101)	(0.6915)	(0.7094)
	[11.48]	[5.32]	[8.73]	[6.19]
Sex/Gender Is Female = 1	0.5126	0.5223	0.5174	0.5337
	(0.4955)	(0.4968)	(0.4969)	(0.4925)
	[1.03]	[0.41]	[0.59]	[0.62]
Race/Ethnicity Is African American/Black = 1	0.1202	0.8812	0.0945	0.1217
	(0.3065)	(0.3160)	(0.3030)	(0.3472)
	[1.75]	[1.31]	[1.70]	[2.13]
Age in Years	48.6843	47.3657	50.0350	46.9832
	(14.8508)	(15.9379)	(15.5220)	(15.8295)
	[1.01]	[0.76]	[0.88]	[0.75]
Income in Thousands of Dollars	59.5139	66.3853	74.7197	79.4239
	(34.1856)	(46.3151)	(49.5710)	(53.7413)
	[15.49]	[10.15]	[13.38]	[11.25]

APPENDIX D.   SOURCES FOR THE SIZE OF ANTIWAR PROTESTS, 2001–2012

SEPTEMBER 29, 2001

Organizer's estimate: 25,000 (ANSWER 2013). Media estimate: A few thousand (Crummy 2001). We resolved the conflict between the orders of magnitude of these estimates by splitting the difference between the estimates.

APRIL 20, 2002

Organizer's estimate: 100,000 (ANSWER 2013). Media estimate: 3,000–5,000 (National Public Radio 2002). We resolved the conflict between the orders of magnitude of these estimates by splitting the difference between the estimates.

OCTOBER 26, 2002

Organizer's estimate: 200,000 (ANSWER 2013). Media estimate: 100,000 (Walker 2002).

JANUARY 18, 2003

Organizer's estimate: 500,000 (ANSWER 2013). Media estimate: 200,000 (CNN 2003a).

FEBRUARY 15, 2003

Organizer's estimate: 375,000 (CNN 2003b). Media estimate: 100,000 (CNN 2003b).

MARCH 23, 2003

Organizer's estimate: 200,000 (ANSWER 2013). Media estimate: 125,000 (Fox 2003).

APRIL 12, 2003

Organizer's estimate: 30,000 (ANSWER 2013). Media estimate: 11,000 (DePledge 2003).

MARCH 20, 2004

Organizer's estimate: 100,000 (ANSWER 2013). Media estimate: 30,000–100,000 (Dobnik 2004). We resolved the conflict between the orders of magnitude of these estimates by splitting the difference between the estimates.

AUGUST 29, 2004

Organizer's estimate: 500,000 (United for Peace and Justice 2004). Media estimate: 500,000 (McFadden 2004).

JANUARY 20, 2005

Organizer's estimate: 10,000 (ANSWER 2013). Media estimate: Thousands (Staff 2005).

MARCH 19, 2005

Organizer's estimate: Tens of Thousands (ANSWER 2013). Media estimate: Tens of Thousands (Kunzelman 2005).

MAY 1, 2005

Organizer's estimate: Tens of Thousands (Abolition 2000, 2006). Media estimate: 60,000 (Hauser 2005).

SEPTEMBER 24, 2005

Organizer's estimate: 300,000 (United for Peace and Justice 2005). Media estimate: 100,000 or more (Featherstone 2005).

MARCH 19, 2006

Organizer's estimate: Tens of Thousands (United for Peace and Justice 2006b). Media estimate: Tens of Thousands (Frazier 2006).

AUGUST 6, 2006

Organizer's estimate: Thousands (Stop Bechtel 2006). Media estimate: None available.

SEPTEMBER 19, 2006

Organizer's estimate: 3,500 (United for Peace and Justice 2006a). Media estimate: No estimate.

JANUARY 27, 2007

Organizer's estimate: 500,000 (United for Peace and Justice 2007a). Media estimate: 100,000 (Woodward and Margasak 2007).

MARCH 20, 2007

Organizer's estimate: Tens of Thousands (United for Peace and Justice 2007b). Media estimate: Tens of Thousands (Schreiner 2007).

SEPTEMBER 15, 2007

Organizer's estimate: Tens of Thousands (ANSWER Coalition 2007). Media estimate: Several thousand (Barakat 2007). On the basis of our direct observation of the March on Washington on September 15, 2007, we judged that the organizer's estimate was more accurate than the media estimate. Hence, we coded this rally in the "tens of thousands."

OCTOBER 27, 2007

Organizer's estimate: Tens of Thousands (United for Peace and Justice 2007c). Media estimate: Tens of Thousands (Dearen 2007).

MARCH 19, 2008

Organizer's estimate: More than One Thousand (United for Peace and Justice 2008b). Media estimate: 2,200 (Associated Press 2008).

AUGUST 28, 2008

Organizer's estimate: Thousands (Wright 2008). Mediate estimate: 4,000 (Riccardi and Correll 2008).

SEPTEMBER 1, 2008

Organizer's estimate: None available. Media estimate: 10,000 (Forliti 2008).

JANUARY 1, 2009

Organizer's estimate: 150 (World Can't Wait 2009). Media estimate: "Few" (Associated Press 2009).

MARCH 21, 2009

Organizer's estimate: None available. Media estimate: Several Hundred (Staff 2009). On the basis of our direct observation of the March on the Pentagon on March 21, 2007, we judged that the media's estimate was too low and that an estimate of "thousands" is more accurate.

APRIL 4, 2009

Organizer's estimate: 10,000 (United for Peace and Justice 2009). Media estimate: Hundreds (Dobnik 2009). On the basis of our direct observation of the March on Wall Street on April 4, 2009, we judged that the organizer's estimate was too high and the media's estimate was too low. We coded this event as having "thousands" in attendance.

OCTOBER 17, 2009

Organizer's estimate: None available. Media estimate: 1,000 (Allday 2009).

NOVEMBER 7, 2009

Organizer's estimate: None available. Media estimate: None available. On the basis of our direct observation of the Black Is Back Coalition rally in Washington, D.C., on November 7, 2009, we coded this event as having "hundreds" in attendance.

DECEMBER 12, 2009

Organizer's estimate: None available. Media estimate: None available. On the basis of our direct observation of the End US Wars rally in Washington, D.C., on December 12, 2009, we coded this event as having "hundreds" in attendance.

MARCH 20, 2010

Organizer's estimate: Tens of Thousands (Associated Press 2010). Media estimate: Thousands (Associated Press 2010). On the basis of our direct observation of the antiwar rally in Washington, D.C., on March 20, 2010, we judged the media estimate to be more accurate than the organizer's estimate.

OCTOBER 16, 2010

Organizer's estimate: None available. Media estimate: None available. On the basis of our direct observation of the antiwar rally in Chicago, Illinois, on October 16, 2010, we judged the event to have "thousands" in attendance.

NOVEMBER 13, 2010

Organizer's estimate: None available. Media estimate: None available. On the basis of our direct observation of the Black Is Back Coalition rally in Washington, D.C., on November 13, 2010, we judged the event to have "hundreds" in attendance.

MARCH 19, 2011

Organizer's estimate: None available. Media estimate: More than 100 (Tucker 2011).

OCTOBER 7, 2011

Organizer's estimate: None available. Media estimate: None available. On the basis of our direct observation of the antiwar rally in Washington, D.C., on October 7, 2011, we judged the event to have "hundreds" in attendance.

MAY 20, 2012

Organizer's estimate: None available. Media estimate: Thousands (Peterson and Saphir 2012).

AUGUST 27, 2012

Organizer's estimate: None available. Media estimate: Hundreds (Kilkenny 2012).

SEPTEMBER 4, 2012

Organizer's estimate: None available. Media estimate: Hundreds (Democracy NOW! 2012).

OCTOBER 6, 2012

Organizer's estimate: None available. Media estimate: Hundreds (KGO 2012).

APPENDIX E.   LIST OF EVENTS FOR PROTEST SURVEYS

FIRST WAVE PROTEST SURVEYS

August 29, 2004, Protest outside the Republican National Convention, New York, New York

January 20, 2005, Protests outside the Presidential Inauguration, Washington, D.C.

March 19–20, 2005, Protests on the Second Anniversary of the Iraq War, Washington, D.C.; New York, New York; Fayetteville, North Carolina; Indianapolis, Indiana; Chicago, Illinois; San Diego, California; and San Francisco, California

May 1, 2005, Antinuclear rally in Central Park, Troops Out Now rally in Harlem, and May Day rally in Union Square, New York, New York

September 24, 2005, "End the War on Iraq!" rally, Washington, D.C.

SECOND WAVE PROTEST SURVEYS

January 27, 2007, March on Washington, Washington, D.C.

March 17, 2007, March on the Pentagon, Washington, D.C., and Arlington, Virginia

September 15, 2007, March on Washington, Washington, D.C.

October 27, 2007, National Mobilization against the War in Iraq, New York, New York; Chicago, Illinois; San Francisco, California

March 15–22, 2008, Five Years Too Many (on the Fifth Anniversary of the Iraq War), Los Angeles, Califiornia; Chicago, Illinois; Washington, D.C.; New York, New York; San Francisco, California

August 24, 2008, Rally outside the DNC, Denver, Colorado

September 1, 2008, March on the Republican National Convention, St. Paul, Minnesota

January 20, 2009, Protests outside the Presidential Inauguration, Washington, D.C.

March 21, 2009, March on the Pentagon, Washington, D.C., and Arlington, Virginia

April 4, 2009, March on Wall Street, New York, New York

October 5–17, 2008, Protests on the Seventh Anniversary of the War in Afghanistan, Washington, D.C.; Chicago, Illinois; Boston, Massachusetts; San Francisco, California

November 7, 2009, Black Is Back Coalition Rally, Washington, D.C.

December 2–12, 2009, Protests against the Escalation of the War in Afghanistan, New York, New York; Chicago, Illinois; San Francisco, California; Washington, D.C.

March 18–20, 2010, Protests on the Seventh Anniversary of the Iraq War, Chicago, Illinois; Washington, D.C.; San Francisco, California; Los Angeles, California; New York, New York

October 6–16, 2010, Protests on the Ninth Anniversary of the War in Afghanistan, San Francisco, California; New York, New York; Chicago, Illinois
November 13, 2010, Black Is Back Coalition Rally, Washington, D.C.

APPENDIX F. SURVEY WEIGHTS

	Responded	Declined	Response Rate	Survey Weight
Protest Survey First Wave				
White/Caucasian Males	909	153	85.59%	1.0231
Black/African-American Males	87	27	76.32%	1.1475
Latino/Hispanic Males	79	11	87.78%	0.9977
Asian Males	72	6	92.31%	0.9487
Other Males	78	1	98.73%	0.8870
White/Caucasian Females	1,123	108	91.23%	0.9600
Black/African-American Females	72	15	82.76%	1.0582
Latino/Hispanic Females	81	5	94.19%	0.9298
Asian Females	82	7	92.13%	0.9505
Other Females	59	3	95.16%	0.9203
Protest Survey Second Wave				
White/Caucasian Males	2,568	683	78.99%	1.0087
Black/African-American Males	267	135	66.42%	1.1996
Latino/Hispanic Males	236	76	75.64%	1.0533
Asian Males	137	42	76.54%	1.0410
Other Males	162	22	88.04%	0.9049
White/Caucasian Females	2,814	509	84.68%	0.9409
Black/African-American Females	197	62	76.06%	1.0475
Latino/Hispanic Females	221	36	85.99%	0.9265
Asian Females	153	45	77.27%	1.0311
Other Females	172	27	86.43%	0.9218
Social Forum Survey				
White/Caucasian Males	188	104	64.38%	1.0310
Black/African-American Males	44	32	57.89%	1.1466
Latino/Hispanic Males	37	20	64.91%	1.0227
Asian Males	21	12	63.64%	1.0432
Other Males	17	10	62.96%	1.0543
White/Caucasian Females	221	99	69.06%	0.9612

(cont.)

	Responded	Declined	Response Rate	Survey Weight
Black/African-American Females	64	43	59.81%	1.1098
Latino/Hispanic Females	32	15	68.09%	0.9750
Asian Females	36	14	72.00%	0.9220
Other Females	41	6	87.23%	0.7610
Democratic National Convention Survey				
Clinton Delegate Males	88	156	36.07%	1.0287
Edwards Delegate Males	2	2	50.00%	0.7420
Obama Delegate Males	74	147	33.48%	1.1080
Clinton Delegate Females	103	154	40.08%	0.9257
Edwards Delegate Females	4	2	66.67%	0.5565
Obama Delegate Females	100	168	37.31%	0.9943

Note: When subgroup information was missing for the protest surveys or the Social Forum survey (e.g., sex/gender was missing for a survey), weights were determined on the basis of available information (e.g., race/ethnicity only).

APPENDIX G.   SURVEY QUESTIONS

PROTEST SURVEY

Partisan Identification. Do you consider yourself to be a member of a political party? (circle one) [YES/NO] If "YES," which political party are you a member of?

Partisan Agreement. We are interested in knowing whether you tend to agree more with the Democratic Party or with the Republican Party. (Please check ONE) [Usually agree with Democratic Party; Sometimes agree with Democratic Party; Rarely agree either party; Sometimes agree with Republican Party; Usually agree with Republican party; Don't know]

Reasons for Attending Antiwar Protests (used to determine *Opposition to the Republican Party*). What are the most important reasons you came to this event?

Political Attitudes. How would you identify your POLITICAL ATTITUDES on the continuum from extremely liberal to extremely conservative? Please check ONE: [Extremely liberal; Liberal; Slightly liberal; Moderate, middle of the road; Slightly conservative; Conservative; Extremely conservative; Don't know]

Organizational Member. Are you a member of any civic, community, labor, or political organizations? (Circle ONE) [YES/NO] If "YES," which organizations are you a member of? (list as many as you can)

Sex/Gender. Circle your sex: [MALE / FEMALE]

Race/Ethnicity. What is your race/ethnicity? Circle as many as apply: [White/ Caucasian, Black/African-American, Latino/Hispanic/Mexican, Asian, Other]

Age. What is your age?

Level of Education. Could you please tell us the highest level of formal education you have completed? Please check ONE: [Less than high school diploma, High School diploma, Some college, Associate's degree or technical degree, College degree, Some graduate education, Graduate or professional degree]

Annual Income in Thousands of Dollars. Could you please tell us your level of annual income? (We are asking this question because studies show that level of income sometimes correlates with political attitudes.) Please check ONE: [$0 to $15,000 per year, $15,001 to $30,000 per year, $30,001 to $45,000 per year, $45,001 to $60,000 per year, $60,001 to $75,000 per year, $75,001 or MORE per year]

Months since September 2001. Calculation by authors.

SOCIAL FORUM SURVEY

Involved in Antiwar Movement. Have you ever been involved in the movement to prevent or end the U.S. wars in Iraq and/or Afghanistan? (CIRCLE ONE) [YES/NO]

Change in Antiwar Involvement. Since Barack Obama has been President of the United States, how has your level of involvement in the anti-war movement changed? (CHECK ONE) [My involvement in the anti-war movement has INCREASED SUBSTANTIALLY; My involvement in the anti-war movement has INCREASED SOMEWHAT; My involvement in the anti-war movement has STAYED THE SAME; My involvement in the anti-war movement has DECREASED SOMEWHAT; My involvement in the anti-war movement has DECREASED SUBSTANTIALLY]

Reasons for Reduced Antiwar Involvement. If you answered DECREASED SUBSTANTIALLY or DECREASED SOMEWHAT, then please check all of the reasons that you decreased your involvement in the anti-war movement. (CHECK ALL THAT APPLY) [Because of changes in my life, I have had LESS TIME for activism; I have FEWER FINANCIAL RESOURCES available to me for activism; I have received LESS ENCOURAGEMENT to participate from my friends; Barack Obama IS DEALING WITH THE PROBLEMS in Iraq and Afghanistan; Anti-war issues now seem LESS PRESSING THAN OTHER ISSUES; There have been FEWER OPPORTUNITIES for my involvement; Other]

Salience of Movement Identity. Some people closely identify with the term "activist," while other people do not think of themselves in this way. How important is the idea of being an "activist" to your personal identity? (CHECK ONE) [Being an "activist" is CORE to my personal identity; Being an "activist" is SOMEWHAT IMPORTANT to my personal identity; Being an "activist" is NOT THAT IMPORTANT to my personal identity; Being an "activist" is NOT PART of my personal identity; Being an "activist" is an idea that I REJECT; Don't know]

Self-Identified Democrat. Same as protest survey.

Dropped Democratic Party Identification. Have you ever considered yourself to be a member of a political party OTHER THAN the one that you listed in question 21 above? (CIRCLE ONE) [YES/NO] If YES, which OTHER PARTY were you most recently a member of? What YEAR did you leave that other party?

Political Attitudes. How would you identify your POLITICAL ATTITUDES on the continuum from LEFT to RIGHT? (CHECK ONE) [Radical/to the LEFT of extremely liberal/progressive; Extremely liberal/progressive; Liberal/progressive; Slightly liberal/progressive; Moderate, middle of the road; Slightly conservative; Conservative; Extremely conservative; To the RIGHT of extremely conservative; Don't know]

Sex/Gender. What is your sex/gender?

Race/Ethnicity. Same as protest survey.

Age in Years. What YEAR were you born?

Level of Education. Same as protest survey.

Annual Income in Thousands of Dollars. Same as protest survey.

Iraq Management. Since BARACK OBAMA has become President of the United States, how do you think that he has done in managing the situation in AFGHANISTAN? (CHECK ONE) [SIGNIFICANTLY IMPROVED the situation in Afghanistan; SLIGHTLY IMPROVED the situation in Afghanistan; MADE NO DIFFERENCE to the situation in Afghanistan; SLIGHTLY WORSENED the situation in Afghanistan; SIGNIFICANTLY WORSENED the situation in Afghanistan; Don't know]

Afghanistan Management. Which policy do you think Barack Obama should pursue in AFGHANISTAN? (CHECK ONE) [IMMEDIATELY WITHDRAW all troops; SOMEWHAT REDUCE troop levels; STAY THE COURSE and maintain troop levels; SOMEWHAT INCREASE troop levels; SUBSTANTIALLY INCREASE troop levels; Don't know]

Changing Involvement in Health Care Issues by Antiwar Activists. Thinking only of the PAST TWO calendar years since Barack Obama has been President (2009–2010), HOW ACTIVE have you been in the following issues? (CHECK ONE BOX PER ROW) Thinking only of the years when George W. Bush was President (2001–2008), HOW ACTIVE were you in the following issues? (CHECK ONE BOX PER ROW) [Aging Issues; Anti-War (outside Middle East); Anti-War (Iraq/Afghanistan/Iran); Arab-American Issues; Asian-American Issues; Black/African-American Issues; Civil Liberties-U.S.; Criminal Justice/Police Brutality; Disability Rights; Economic Justice-U.S. Economy; Education; Environment/Sustainability; Global Economic Justice/Globalization; Health Care; HIV/AIDS;

Housing; Human Rights-non U.S.; Immigration (not to U.S.); Immigration (to U.S.); Improving non-U.S. Political Institutions; Improving U.S. Political Institutions; Israel/Palestine; Labor/Workers' Rights-non U.S.; Labor/Workers' Rights-U.S.; Latino Issues; LGBT Rights; Mass Media Reform-U.S.; Native/Indigenous Peoples-non U.S.; Native/Indigenous Peoples-U.S.; Nuclear Proliferation; Opposing the U.S. Right Wing; Racism; Religion/Spirituality; Religious Freedom; Reproductive Freedom/Education; Transportation; U.S. Foreign Policy-Latin/South America; U.S. Foreign Policy-Africa; U.S. Foreign Policy-Cuba; U.S. Foreign Policy-Haiti; Women's Rights; Youth Issues] Options: [Not Active, Somewhat Active, Moderately Active, Highly Active]

DEMOCRATIC DELEGATE SURVEY

Participation in Antiwar Movement. Have you ever been involved in the movement to prevent or end the U.S. wars in Iraq and/or Afghanistan? Please check ONE: [No, I have never been involved in the anti-war movement; Yes, I have been involved in the anti-war movement]

Democratic Identification in Youth (by age 24). Some people identify with one political party for most of their lives. However, some people come to identify with a political party later in life. Please check ONE of the following which best describes your identification with the Democratic Party: [I first began to identify with the Democratic Party in my childhood (before age 18); I first began to identify with the Democratic Party during early adulthood (ages 18-24); I first began to identify with the Democratic Party in my mid-to-late 20s (ages 25–29); I first began to identify with the Democratic Party in my 30s (ages 30–39); I first began to identify with the Democratic Party in my 40s (ages 40–49); I first began to identify with the Democratic Party in my 50s or later (ages 50 on); I have never identified with the Democratic Party]

Participation in Non-War Social Movement Activism. While some people devote most of their political involvement to working with candidates and/or political parties, other people choose to work directly on political issues. For example, they may work to have a law passed or repealed, or to have the government change its policies in some way. Thinking of the past 10 years, how active have you been in working on each of the following political issues. For EACH ISSUE, please CHECK THE BOX that best describes your level of political involvement. [Criminal Justice Issues, Education Issues, Environmental Issues, Health Care Issues, Immigration Issues, Labor Issues, LGBT Issues, Peace/Anti-War Issues, Racial Justice Issues, Women's Issues, Other Issues (list)] Level of Political Involvement: [High, Moderate, Low, Not Involved]

Organizational Member. Same as protest survey
Sex/Gender. Provided by Democratic National Committee
Race/Ethnicity. Same as protest survey
Age in Years. Same as Social Forum Survey
Level of Education. Same as protest survey
Annual Income in Thousands of Dollars. Same as protest survey

APPENDIX H.   DESCRIPTIVE STATISTICS FOR ACTIVIST SURVEYS

H.I.   PROTEST SURVEY

	2004–2005 Unified Republican Control	2007–2008 Divided Government	2009–2010 Unified Democratic Control
	Mean (Std. Dev.) [% Imputed]		
Opposition to the Republican Party = 1	0.2309 (0.4192) [1.28]	0.1233 (0.3266) [3.62]	0.0125 (0.1023) [3.62]
Political Attitudes (1 = Extremely Conservative to 7 = Extremely Liberal)		1.7680 (0.7207) [41.57]	1.6262 (0.9845) [41.57]
Organizational Member = 1	0.5805 (0.4935) [0.00]	0.5098 (0.5000) [0.00]	0.6574 (0.4746) [0.00]
Sex/Gender Is Female = 1	0.5227 (0.4941) [1.87]	0.5118 (0.4973) [0.84]	0.4645 (0.4975) [0.84]
Race / Ethnicity Is White = 1	0.7994 (0.3967) [1.83]	0.8240 (0.3733) [1.44]	0.7626 (0.4135) [1.44]
Age in Years	38.3819 (16.3489) [0.68]	39.5345 (17.6911) [0.77]	40.2093 (18.6497) [0.77]
Level of Education (1 = Less than High School to 7 = Graduate degree)		4.8634 (1.8525) [3.73]	4.8048 (1.8227) [3.73]

(cont.)

	2004–2005 *Unified Republican Control*	2007–2008 *Divided Government*	2009–2010 *Unified Democratic Control*
		Mean (Std. Dev.) [% Imputed]	
Annual Income in Thousands of Dollars		3.1409 (1.8280) [7.99]	2.8146 (1.7362) [7.99]
Months since September 2001	43.5228 (3.4474) [0.00]	74.6878 (6.0010) [0.00]	99.4682 (5.4923) [0.00]

Note: Means were computed using survey weights. Standard deviations were computed using unweighted data. Complete-case imputations for the 2007–2008 and 2009–2010 periods were based on the full 2007–2010 dataset.

H.2.   SOCIAL FORUM SURVEY AND DEMOCRATIC DELEGATE
       SURVEY

	Social Forum	*DNC Delegates*
	Mean (Std. Dev.) [% Imputed]	
Salience of Movement Identity (5 = Activism core to identity, 1 = reject activism)	4.0295 (1.0749) [6.16]	
Self-identified Democrat = 1	0.2325 (0.4181) [13.32]	
Dropped Democratic Party Identification = 1	0.0860 (0.2804) [9.34]	0.0358 (0.18320 [N/A]
Democratic Identification in Youth (by age 24) = 1		0.9058 (0.3001) [0.27]

(cont.)

	Social Forum	DNC Delegates
	Mean (Std. Dev.) [% Imputed]	
Participation in Non-War Social Movement Activism		4.0945 (2.6603)
(Number of non-war social movements, 0 to 9)		[2.43]
Political Attitudes	8.3185	6.6626
(9 = Radical left, 1 = Radical right)	(0.9453) [12.52]	(0.9574) [2.70]
Organizational Member = 1	0.7916 (0.3969) [3.98]	0.8518 (0.3477) [2.70]
Sex/Gender Is Female = 1	0.5157 (0.4810) [7.16]	0.5263 (0.4973) [0.00]
Race/Ethnicity Is White = 1	0.7317 (0.4311) [5.86]	0.7375 (0.4407) [1.08]
Age in Years	38.2766 (16.6255) [3.98]	55.9717 (13.5129) [2.43]
Level of Education (1 = Less than High school to 7 = Graduate degree)	5.0698 (1.6865) [3.38]	5.8286 (1.4938) [0.27]
Annual Income in Thousands of Dollars	30.1949 (23.4383) [6.76]	66.9282 (22.5564) [2.70]

Note: Means were computed using survey weights. Standard deviations were computed using unweighted data. Both samples are of antiwar activists only.

APPENDIX I.   ANTIWAR LEGISLATION INTRODUCED IN CONGRESS, 2001–2013

107th Congress (2001–2003): H.Con.Res.473, H.Con.Res.518, H.J.Res.110, H.R.2459, H.R.2503, S.Con.Res.133.

108th Congress (2003–2005): H.Con.Res.101, H.Con.Res.296, H.Con.Res.392, H.Res.141, H.Con.Res.2, H.J.Res.20, H.J.Res.24, H.R.1673, H.R.2647, H.R.3132, H.R.3616, H.R.4825, H.Res.260, H.Res.629, H.Res.640, S.J.Res.9, S.Res.28, S.Res.32, S.Res.76, S.Res.479.

109th Congress (2005–2007): H.Con.Res.35, H.Con.Res.197, H.Con.Res.321, H.Con.Res.348, H.Con.Res.391, H.Con.Res.470, H.J.Res.55, H.J.Res.70, H.J.Res.73, H.R.3760, H.R.4232, H.R.4853, H.R.4983, H.R.5875, H.Res.82, H.Res.571, H.Res.635, H.Res.636, H.Res.637, H.Res.990, S.1756, S.1993, S.4049, S.Con.Res.93, S.J.Res.33, S.J.Res.36, S.J.Res.39, S.Res.171.

110th Congress (2007–2009): H.Con.Res.23, H.Con.Res.33, H.Con.Res.46, H.Con.Res.63, H.Con.Res.65, H.Con.Res.110, H.Con.Res.201, H.Con.Res.219, H.Con.Res.319, H.J.Res.18, H.J.Res.64, H.R.353, H.R.413, H.R.438, H.R.455, H.R.508, H.R.645, H.R.663, H.R.746, H.R.787, H.R.808, H.R.930, H.R.960, H.R.1263, H.R.1292, H.R.1460, H.R.1837, H.R.2031, H.R.2062, H.R.2237, H.R.2450, H.R.2451, H.R.2539, H.R.2574, H.R.2605, H.R.2929, H.R.2956, H.R.3071, H.R.3125, H.R.3178, H.R.3190, H.R.3863, H.R.3938, H.R.4156, H.R.5128, H.R.5499, H.R.5507, H.R.5626, H.Res.23, H.Res.41, H.Res.333, H.Res.625, H.Res.799, H.Res.1019, H.Res.1123, S.121, S.1077, S.1545, S.233, S.287, S.308, S.433, S.448, S.470, S.574, S.670, S.679, S.2633, S.Con.Res.13, S.Con.Res.2, S.Con.Res.4, S.Con.Res.7, S.J.Res.3, S.J.Res.15, S.J.Res.9, S.Res.302.

111th Congress (2009–2011): H.Con.Res.248, H.Con.Res.301, H.R.66, H.R.1052, H.R.2404, H.R.3699, H.R.5015, H.R.5353, H.R.6045, H.Res.417, S.3197.

112th Congress (2011–2013): H.Con.Res.107, H.Con.Res.28, H.Con.Res.51, H.Con.Res.53, H.Con.Res.57, H.Con.Res.58, H.J.Res.49, H.R.1212, H.R.1334, H.R.1609, H.R.1708, H.R.1735, H.R.2259, H.R.2278, H.R.2283, H.R.232, H.R.2757, H.R.6290, H.R.651, H.R.780, H.Res.292, H.Res.294, H.Res.331, H.Res.465, S.186, S.J.Res.14, S.J.Res.16, S.J.Res.18, S.Res.146.

APPENDIX J.   SCRIPT FOR INTERVIEWS WITH TEA PARTY AND OCCUPY ACTIVISTS

The following questions were treated as an interview guide and were adapted as needed depending on prior answers of the respondent.

1. In your opinion, what does the [Tea Party or Occupy] movement stand for?

2. In your opinion, what does it mean to be a member of the [Tea Party or Occupy] movement?

3. To what extent do you identify yourself as a part of the [Tea Party or Occupy] movement?

4. How did you initially become involved in the [Tea Party or Occupy] movement? What role do/did you play in it?

5. Do/did you work with any particular organizations (or affinity groups) involved in the [Tea Party or Occupy] movement? If so, which ones?

6. Have you been involved in social movements other than the [Tea Party or Occupy] movement? Which movements? What were the approximate times in your life that you participated in these movements and what did you do with them?

7. Have you ever been active in electoral politics? For example, have you ever volunteered to work for a campaign? Please elaborate on your past electoral involvement.

8. Where do you place your ideas on the left-to-right ideological spectrum? Are you to the left of extremely liberal, extremely liberal, liberal, moderately liberal, moderate, moderately conservative, conservative, extremely conservative, to the right of extremely conservative?

9. Do you consider yourself to be a member of a political party? If yes, which political party do you consider yourself to be a member of? To what extent do you identify yourself as part of the party? If not, is there a particular political party that you tend to agree with more than others? Which party is that?

10. (If pertinent) At what age did you begin to identify with this political party? What do you think led you to identify with it?

11. (If pertinent) Have you ever identified with another political party other than the one that you identify with today? If so, which party was that? Why did you disassociate yourself from it?

12. In your opinion, what does the Democratic Party stand for?

13. In your opinion, what does it mean to be a member of the Democratic Party?

14. In your opinion, what does the Republican Party stand for?

15. In your opinion, what does it mean to be a member of the Republican Party?

16. Do you think that the [Republican or Democratic] Party is doing what it should be doing to help the [Tea Party or Occupy] movement? Is the party doing too little, too much?

17. How important is it for the [Tea Party or Occupy] movement to promote candidates to stand for election in the [Republican or Democratic] Party? Do you think that the [Tea Party or Occupy] movement should promote candidates more often, less often, or at about its current level?

18. How important is it for the [Tea Party or Occupy] movement to continue to stage protests, demonstrations, rallies, or other public

gatherings of its supporters? Do you think that the [Tea Party or Occupy] movement should hold these events more often, less often, or about as often as it currently does?

19. What do you see as the relationship between the [Republican or Democratic] Party and the [Tea Party or Occupy] movement? For example, do you see the party and the movement as allied with one another, in conflict with one another, or some combination of the two? Do you see one of the two having the "upper hand" over the other? Please elaborate on your view.

20. Do you identify equally with the [Republican or Democratic] Party and the [Tea Party or Occupy] movement? Or do you consider yourself to be more closely connected with one or the other? (If pertinent) Which one are you closer to? Why?

21. What do you see as the relationship between the Republican Party and the [Tea Party or Occupy] movement? For example, do you see the party and the movement as allied with one another, in conflict with one another, or some combination of the two? Please elaborate on your view.

22. Do you think that there is a need for a new political party to address the concerns of the [Tea Party or Occupy] movement? Why or why not?

23. Is there anything about the [Tea Party or Occupy] movement, the [Republican or Democratic] Party, or the Republican Party which we have not asked, but which you would like to share?

24. [Interviewer records respondent's sex/gender without asking.]

25. What city and state do you live in?

26. How old are you?

27. What is your race/ethnicity?

28. What is the highest level of formal education that you have attained?

29. Are you married, single, or divorced?

30. Are you a member of a formally organized religious community? If so, what is your religious denomination?

31. Are you, or is anyone in your immediate family, a member of a labor union?

References

Abolition 2000. 2006. "Abolition 2000." Available online at: http://web.archive.org/web/20060101022426/; http://www.abolition2000.org/, accessed January 8, 2013.

Abramowitz, Alan I. 2009. "Viability, Electability, and Candidate Choice in a Presidential Primary Election: A Test of Competing Models." *Journal of Politics* 51(4): 977–92.

2010. *The Disappearing Center: Engaged Citizens, Polarization and American Democracy*. New Haven, CT: Yale University Press.

Abramowitz, Alan I., and Kyle L. Saunders. 2008. "Is Polarization a Myth?" *Journal of Politics* 70(2): 542–55.

Abrams, Dominic, and Michael A. Hogg, eds. 1990. *Social Identity Theory: Constructive and Critical Advances*. New York: Springer-Verlag.

Ackerman, Bruce and Oona Hathaway. 2011. "Death of the War Powers Act?" *Washington Post*. May 17. Available online at: http://articles.washingtonpost.com/2011-05-17/opinions/35263733_1_war-powers-act-james-stavridis-president-obama, accessed January 5, 2013.

Aday, Sean. 2010. "Chasing the Bad News: An Analysis of 2005 Iraq and Afghanistan War Coverage on NBC and Fox News Channel." *Journal of Communication* 60(1): 144–64.

Adbusters. 2011. "#OCCUPY WALL STREET." Available online: http://web.archive.org/web/20110818031558/; http://www.adbusters.org/blogs/adbusters-blog/occupy wallstreet.html?, accessed August 16, 2013.

Ainsworth, Scott H. 2002. *Analyzing Interest Groups*. New York: W. W. Norton.

Albert, Stuart, and David A. Whetten. 1985. "Organizational Identity." *Research in Organizational Behavior* 7: 263–95.

Aldrich, John H. 1995. *Why Parties? The Origin and Transformation of Political Parties in America*. Chicago: University of Chicago Press.

Aldrich, John H., Bradford H. Bishop, Rebecca S. Hatch, D. Sunshine Hillygus, and David W. Rohde. 2012. "Blame, Responsibility, and the Tea Party in the 2010 Midterm Elections." Paper presented at the 70th Annual Meeting of the Midwest Political Science Association, Chicago, April 12–15.

Allawi, Ali A. 2007. *The Occupation of Iraq: Winning the War, Losing the Peace*. New Haven, CT: Yale University Press.

Allday, Erin. 2009. "S.F. Anti-War March Smaller than Some Hoped for." *San Francisco Chronicle*. October 18. Available online at: http://www.sfgate.com/news/article/S-F-anti-war-march-smaller-than-some-hoped-for-3213165.php, accessed January 11, 2013.

Allen, Victoria Heavey. 2007. *Walking the Line: Social Movement Interest Groups and the Delicate Balance between Social Movements and Political Parties*. Ph.D. diss., Department of Political Science, The City University of New York.

Amenta, Edwin. 2006. *When Movements Matter: The Townsend Plan and the Rise of Social Security*. Princeton, NJ: Princeton University Press.

Americans Against Escalation in Iraq. 2008a. "Coalition Launches Nationwide, Multimillion Dollar Iraq/Recession Campaign." Available online at: http://web.archive.org/web/20080320044639/; http://www.noiraqescalation.org/press?id=0350, accessed July 2, 2013.

  2008b. "March to the White House." Available online at: http://web.archive.org/web/20080705025622/; http://noiraqescalation.org/, accessed July 2, 2013.

Anderson, Christopher J., and Silvia M. Mendes. 2005. "Learning to Lose: Election Outcomes, Democratic Experience and Political Protest Potential." *British Journal of Political Science* 36(1): 91–111.

Anonymous. 2011. Telephone interview with Michael T. Heaney, July 14.

Anonymous Former MoveOn Staff Member. 2010. Interview with Michael T. Heaney, September 10. Ann Arbor, MI.

Ansell, Chris, Sarah Reckhow, and Andrew Kelly. 2009. "How to Reform a Reform Coalition: Outreach, Agenda Expansion, and Brokerage in Urban School Reform." *Policy Studies Journal* 37(4): 717–43.

ANSWER Coalition. 2007. "March on Washington: A New Movement is Emerging." Available online at: http://www.answercoalition.org/national/past-events/demo-2007-09-15.html, accessed January 11, 2013.

  2013. "About Us." Available online at: http://www.answercoalition.org/national/pages/about-us.html, accessed January 7, 2013.

Arabic Media. 2013. "The Gulf Coalition (Allied) Countries during Gulf War I (1991)." Available online at: http://arabic-media.com/gulf_coalition.htm, accessed January 1, 2013.

Arceneaux, Kevin, and Stephen P. Nicholson. 2012. "Who Wants to Have a Tea Party? The Who, What, and Why of the Tea Party Movement." *PS: Political Science & Politics* 45(4): 700–10.

Armstrong, Elizabeth A. 2002. *Forging Gay Identities: Organizing Sexuality in San Francisco, 1950–1994*. Chicago: University of Chicago Press.

Armstrong, Elizabeth A., and Mary Bernstein. 2008. "Culture, Power, and Institutions: A Multi-Institutional Politics Approach to Social Movements." *Sociological Theory* 26(1): 74–99.

Arnold, Martin. 1966. "4,000 Picket Johnson in Antiwar Protest at Hotel: They Chant Peace Slogans as President Speaks at Waldorf-Astoria." *New York Times*, February 24: 16.

Associated Press. 2003. "Rumsfeld: No Immediate Iraq Withdrawal." *USA Today*. November 16. Available online at: http://usatoday30.usatoday.com/news/washington/2003-11-16-iraq-rumsfeld_x.htm, accessed December 31, 2012.

2008. "Police: 4 War Protesters Arrested in Chicago, IL." *The Associated Press News Service.* March 21.

2009. "Few Protesters Show Up for Obama's Inauguration." *The Associated Press News Service.* January 20.

2010. "Thousands Rally to Pull Troops from 2 War Zones." Available online at: http://www.foxnews.com/us/2010/03/20/thousands-rally-anniversary-invasion-iraq/, accessed January 11, 2013.

Austin, Allan W. 2012. *Quaker Brotherhood: Interracial Activism and the American Friends Service Committee, 1917–1950.* Urbana: University of Illinois Press.

Babb, Sarah. 1996. "'A True American System of Finance': Frame Resonance in the U.S. Labor Movement, 1866 to 1886." *American Sociological Review* 61(6): 1033–52.

Bailey, Michael T., Jonathan Mummolo, and Hans Noel. 2012. "Tea Party Influence: A Story of Activists and Elites." *American Politics Research* 40(5): 769–804.

Baker, James A., III, Lee H. Hamilton, and the Iraq Study Group. 2006. *The Iraq Study Group Report: The Way Forward – a New Approach.* Washington, DC: United States Institute of Peace.

Baldassarri, Delia M. 2011. "Partisan Joiners: Associational Membership and Political Polarization in the United States (1974–2004)." *Social Science Quarterly* 92(3): 631–55

Balser, Deborah B. 1997. "The Impact of Environmental Factors on Factionalism and Schism in Social Movement Organizations." *Social Forces* 76(1): 199–228.

Banaszak, Lee Ann. 1996. *Why Movements Succeed or Fail: Opportunity, Culture, and the Struggle for Woman Suffrage.* Princeton, NJ: Princeton University Press.

Barakat, Matthew. 2007. "Thousands of Iraq War Protesters March from White House to Capitol." *Associated Press Archive.* September 16.

Bartels, Larry M. 2002. "Beyond the Running Tally: Partisan Bias in Political Perceptions." *Political Behavior* 24(2): 117–50.

Bartle, John, and Samantha Lacycok. 2012. "Telling More than They Can Know? Does the Most Important Issue Really Reveal What Is Most Important to Voters?" *Electoral Studies* 31(4): 679–88.

Baumgartner, Frank R., and Bryan D. Jones. 1993. *Agendas and Instability in American Politics.* Chicago: University of Chicago Press.

  2015. *The Politics of Information: Problem Definition and the Course of Public Policy in America.* Chicago: University of Chicago Press.

Baumgartner, Frank R., Jeffrey M. Berry, Marie Hojnacki, David C. Kimball, and Beth L. Leech. 2009. *Lobbying and Policy Change: Who Wins, Who Loses, and Why.* Chicago: University of Chicago Press.

Becker, Brian. 2008. Interview with Michael T. Heaney, June 25. Washington, DC.

Beinart, Peter. 2008. "When Politics No Longer Stops at the Water's Edge: Partisan Polarization and Foreign Policy." Pp. 151–67 in Pietro S. Nivola and David W. Brady, *Red and Blue Nation? Consequences and Corrections of America's Polarized Politics.* Washington, DC: Brookings Institution Press.

Beisner, Robert L. 1970. "1898 and 1968: The Anti-Imperialists and the Doves." *Political Science Quarterly* 85(2): 187–216.

Benjamin, Medea. 2013. *Drone Warfare: Killing by Remote Control.* New York: Verso.

Bennett, Scott H. 2003. *Radical Pacifism: The War Resisters League and Gandhian Nonviolence in America, 1915–1963.* Syracuse, NY: Syracuse University Press.

Berejekian, Jeffrey. 1997. "The Gains Debate: Framing State Choice." *American Political Science Review* 91(4): 789–805.

Berelson, Bernard R., Paul F. Lazarsfeld, and William N. McFhee. 1954. *Voting: A Study of Opinion Formation in a Presidential Campaign*. Chicago: University of Chicago Press.

Bergan, Peter L. 2011. *The Longest War: The Enduring Conflict between America and Al-Qaeda*. New York: Free Press.

Berinsky, Adam J. 2009. *In Time of War: Understanding American Public Opinion from World War II to Iraq*. Chicago: University of Chicago Press.

Bernstein, Mary. 2005. "Liberalism and Social Movement Success: The Case of United States Sodomy Statutes." Pp. 3–18 in Elizabeth Bernstein, ed., *Regulating Sex: The Politics of Intimacy and Identity*. New York: Routledge.

Berry, Jeffrey M. 2003. *A Voice for Nonprofits*. Washington, DC: Brookings Institution Press.

Berry, Jeffrey M., and Sarah Sobieraj. 2014. *The Outrage Industry: Public Opinion Media and the New Incivility*. New York: Oxford University Press.

Biddle, Stephen, Jeffrey A. Friedman, and Jacob N. Shapiro. 2012. "Testing the Surge: Why Did Violence Decline in Iraq in 2007?" *International Security* 37(1): 7–40.

Black Is Back. 2011. "Endorsers." Available online at: http://web.archive.org/web/20111101120854/; http://www.blackisbackcoalition.org/nov5_endorsers.shtml, accessed July 2, 2013.

Black Voices for Peace. 2004. "President Bush: The Facts and the Lies." Available online at: http://web.archive.org/web/20041112090249/; http://www.bvfp.org/, accessed July 7, 2013.

Blee, Kathleen M. 2002. *Inside Organized Racism: Women in the Hate Movement*. Berkeley: University of California Press.

Boatright, Robert G. 2013. *Getting Primaried: The Changing Politics of Congressional Primary Challenges*. Ann Arbor: University of Michigan Press.

Bohan, Caren. 2008. "Obama Says Committed to Iraq Withdrawal Timetable." *Reuters*. July 22. Available online at: http://www.reuters.com/article/2008/07/22/us-iraq-idUSL0236543520080722, accessed January 3, 2013.

Borgatti, Stephen P., and Martin G. Everett. 1997. "Network Analysis of 2-Mode Data." *Social Networks* 19(3): 243–69.

Borgatti, Stephen P., Martin G. Everett, and Linton C. Freeman. 2011. *UCINet 6.289 for Windows: Software for Social Network Analysis*. Lexington, KY: Analytic Technologies.

Botetzagias, Iosif, and Wijbrandt van Schuur. 2012. "Active Greens: An Analysis of the Determinants of Green Party Members' Activism in Environmental Movements." *Environment and Behavior* 44(4): 509–44.

Bourdieu, Pierre. 1977. *Outline of a Theory of Practice*. Cambridge: Cambridge University Press.

Boyd, Andrew, and David Oswald Mitchell. 2012. *Beautiful Trouble: A Toolbox for Revolution*. New York: OR Books.

Bray, Mark. 2012. "Confronting the Many Men in Suits: Rethinking the 'Positive' Coverage of Occupy Wall Street." *Critical Quarterly* 54(2): 5–9.

Brock, William. 1968. *Pacifism in the United States: From the Colonial Era to the First World War*. Princeton, NJ: Princeton University Press.

Broder, David S. 2007. "A War the Public Will End." *Washington Post*, May 6. Available online at: http://www.washingtonpost.com/wp-dyn/content/article/2007/05/04/AR2007050401893.html, accessed November 19, 2012.

Browne, William P. 1990. "Organized Interests and Their Issue Niches: A Search for Pluralism in a Policy Domain." *Journal of Politics* 52(2): 477–509.

Burke, Peter J., and Jan E. Stets. 2009. *Identity Theory*. Oxford: Oxford University Press.

Burstein, Paul, and William Freudenburg. 1978. "Changing Public Policy: The Impact of Public Opinion, Antiwar Demonstrations, and War Costs on Senate Voting on Vietnam War Motions." *American Journal of Sociology* 84(1): 99–122.

Bush, George W. 2001. "Selected Speeches of President George W. Bush: 2001–2008." Washington, DC: White House Archives. Available online at: http://georgewbush-whitehouse.archives.gov/infocus/bushrecord/documents/Selected_Speeches_George_W_Bush.pdf, accessed January 4, 2013.

2007. "President's Address to the Nation." Washington, DC: The White House. Available online at: http://georgewbush-whitehouse.archives.gov/news/releases/2007/01/20070110-7.html, accessed May 18, 2012.

Cagan, Leslie. 2008. Interview with Michael T. Heaney, June 30. New York.

Campbell, Angus, Philip E. Converse, Warren E. Miller, and Donald E. Stokes. 1960. *The American Voter*. Chicago: University of Chicago Press.

Campbell, James E. 1982. "Cosponsoring Legislation in the U.S. Congress." *Legislative Studies Quarterly* 7(3): 415–22.

Caren, Neal, Raj Andrew Ghoshal, and Vanesa Ribas. 2011. "A Social Movement Generation: Trends in Protesting and Petition Signing, 1973–2006." *American Sociological Review* 76: 125–51.

Carmines, Edward G., Jessica C. Gerrity, and Michael W. Wagner. 2010. "How Abortion Became a Partisan Issue: Media Coverage of the Interest Group–Political Party Connection." *Politics & Policy* 38(6): 1135–58.

Carr, Chris. 1999. "Internet Anti-Impeachment Drive Yields Big Pledges of Money, Time." *Washington Post*. February 7: A9.

Carroll, Royce, Jeff Lewis, James Lo, Nolan McCarty, Keith Poole, and Howard Rosenthal. 2013. "DW-NOMINATE Scores with Bootstrapped Standard Errors." Available online at http://voteview.com/dwnominate.asp, accessed August 8, 2013.

Carroll, Royce, Jeff Lewis, James Lo, Keith Poole, and Howard Rosenthal. 2009. "Measuring Bias and Uncertainty in DW-NOMINATE Ideal Point Estimates via the Parametric Bootstrap." *Political Analysis* 17(3): 261–75.

Carsey, Thomas M., and Geoffrey C. Layman. 2006. "Changing Sides or Changing Minds? Party Identification and Policy Preferences in the American Electorate." *American Journal of Political Science* 50(2): 464–77.

CBS News. 2011. "700 Arrested at Brooklyn Bridge Protest." Available online at: http://www.cbsnews.com/2100-201_162-20114436.html, accessed August 18, 2013.

Center for Media and Democracy. 2007. "Out of Iraq Congressional Caucus." Available online at: http://web.archive.org/web/20070313105453/; http://www.sourcewatch.org/index.php?title=Out_of_Iraq_Congressional_Caucus, accessed July 29, 2013.

Center for Responsive Politics. 2013. http://www.opensecrets.org, accessed June 14, 2013.

Chandra, Kanchan. 2004. *Why Ethnicity Parties Succeed: Patronage and Ethnic Head Counts in India*. Cambridge: Cambridge University Press.

Chaudoin, Stephen, Helen V. Milner, and Dustin H. Tingley. 2010. "The Center Still Holds: Liberal Internationalism Survives." *International Security* 35(1): 75–94.

Cho, Wendy K. Tam, and James H. Fowler. 2010. "Legislative Success in a Small World: Social Network Analysis and the Dynamics of Congressional Legislation." *Journal of Politics* 72(1): 124–35.

Cho, Wendy K. Tam, James G. Gimpel, and Daron R. Shaw. 2012. "The Tea Party Movement and the Geography of Collective Action." *Quarterly Journal of Political Science* 7(2): 105–33.

Chochran, William G., and Gertrude M. Cox. 1957. *Experimental Designs*, 2nd ed. Oxford, England: John Wiley & Sons.

Chong, Dennis. 1991. *Collective Action and the Civil Rights Movement*. Chicago: University of Chicago Press.

Chun, Jennifer Jihye, George Lipsitz, and Young Shin. 2013. "Intersectionality as a Social Movement Strategy: Asian Immigrant Women Advocates." *Signs* 38(4): 917–40.

Cities for Peace. 2009. "Bring the Troops Home." Available online at: http://web.archive.org/web/20090907034117/; http://www.citiesforprogress.org/index.php?option=com_content &task=view&id=96&Itemid=62, accessed July 14, 2013.

Clarke, Harold D., Allan Kornberg, Thomas J. Scotto, Jason Reifler, David Sanders, Marianne C. Stewart, and Paul Whiteley. 2011. "Yes We Can! Valence Politics and Electoral Choice in America, 2008." *Electoral Studies* 30(3): 450–61.

Clemens, Elisabeth S. 1997. *The People's Lobby: Organizational Innovation and the Rise of Interest Group Politics in the United States, 1890–1925*. Chicago: University of Chicago Press.

Clerk of the United State House of Representatives. 2002. "FINAL VOTE RESULTS FOR ROLL CALL 455." Available online at: http://clerk.house.gov/evs/2002/roll455.xml, accessed September 19, 2011.

Clifton, Brett M. 2004. "Romancing the GOP: Assessing the Strategies Used by the Christian Coalition to Influence the Republican Party." *Party Politics* 10(5): 475–98.

CNN. 2003a. "Anti-War Demonstrators Rally around the World." *CNN*. January 18. Available online at: http://articles.cnn.com/2003-01-18/us/sproject.irq.us.protests_1_rally-inspection-team-iraq?_s=PM:US, accessed January 7, 2013.

2003b. "Cities Jammed in Worldwide Protest of War in Iraq." *CNN*. February 16. Available online at: http://www.cnn.com/2003/US/02/15/sprj.irq.protests.main/, accessed January 6, 2013.

CNN. 2006. "Bush, Dems Promise Cooperation as Senate Shifts." *CNN*, November 9. Available online at: http://www.cnn.com/2006/POLITICS/11/09/election.main/index.html, accessed May 10, 2012.

CNN Politics. 2002. "Top Bush officials push case against Saddam." September 8. Available online at: http://articles.cnn.com/2002-09-08/politics/iraq.debate_1_nuclear-weapons-top-nuclear-scientists-aluminum-tubes?_s=PM:ALLPOLITICS, accessed December 31, 2012.

CNN World. 2001. "Bush delivers ultimatum." September 20. Available online at: http://articles.cnn.com/2001-09-20/world/ret.afghan.bush_1_senior-taliban-official-terrorist-ringleader-osama-bin-mullah-mohammed-omar?_s=PM:asiapcf, accessed January 4, 2013.

Cohen, Cathy J. 1999. *The Boundaries of Blackness: AIDS and the Breakdown of Black Politics*. Chicago: University of Chicago Press.

Cohen, Marty, David Karol, Hans Noel, and John Zaller. 2008. *The Party Decides: Presidential Nominations before and after Reform*. Chicago: University of Chicago Press.

Coles, Roberta L. 1999. "Odd Folk and Ordinary People: Collective Identity Disparities between Peace Groups in the Persian Gulf Crisis." *Sociological Spectrum* 19(3): 325–57.

Collins, Patricia Hill. 2000. "It's All in the Family: Intersections of Gender, Race, and Nation." Pp. 156–76 in Uma Narayan and Sandra Harding, eds., *Decentering the Center: Philosophy for a Multicultural, Postcolonial, and Feminist World*. Bloomington: Indiana University Press.

Combahee River Collective. 1995. "A Black Feminist Statement." Pp. 232–40 in Beverly Guy-Sheftall, *Words of Fire: An Anthology of African American Feminist Thought*. New York: New Press.

Converse, Philip E. 1969. "Of Time and Partisan Stability." *Comparative Political Studies* 2: 139–71.

Conyers, John Jr. 2010. "Out of Afghanistan Caucus." Available online at: http://web. archive.org/web/20130213210920/; http://conyers.house.gov/index.cfm/afghanistan, accessed July 29, 2013.

Cooper, Helene, Mark Landler, and Alissa J. Rubin. 2014. "Obama Allows Limited Air-strikes on ISIS." New York Times, August 7. Available online at: http://www.nytimes. com/2014/08/08/world/middleeast/obama-weighs-military-strikes-to-aid-trapped-iraqis-officials-say.html, accessed September 20, 2014.

Cooper, Michael. 2008. "Palin, on Offensive, Attacks Obama's Ties to '60s Radical." *New York Times*, October 4. Available online at: http://www.nytimes.com/2008/ 10/05/us/politics/05palin.html?_r=1, accessed June 28, 2012.

Cordesman, Anthony H. 2008. "Victory and Violence in Iraq: Reducing the 'Irreducible Minimum.'" Washington, DC: Center for Strategic and International Strategy. Available online at: http://csis.org/files/media/csis/pubs/080227_irreducible.min-imum.final.pdf, accessed July 18, 2014.

Corrigall-Brown, Catherine. 2012. *Patterns of Protest: Trajectories of Participation in Social Movements*. Stanford, CA: Stanford University Press.

Cortright, David. 2004. *A Peaceful Superpower: The Movement against War in Iraq*. Goshen, IN: Fourth Freedom Forum.

2013. Telephone interview with Michael T. Heaney, June 26.

Costain, Anne N. 1981. "Representing Women: The Transition from Social Movement to Interest Group." *Western Political Quarterly* 34(1): 100–13.

Courser, Zachary. 2012. "The Tea 'Party' as a Conservative Social Movement." *Society* 49(1): 43–53.

Cox, Gary W., and Mathew D. McCubbins. 1993. *Legislative Leviathan: Party Government in the House*. Berkeley: University of California Press.

Coy, Patrick G. 2013. "Co-optation." Pp. 280–2 in David A. Snow, Donatella Della Porta, Bert Klandermans, and Doug McAdam, eds., *The Wiley-Blackwell Encyclo-pedia of Social and Political Movements*, Vol. I: A-E. Malden, MA: Wiley-Blackwell.

Craig, Stephen C., Michael D. Martinez, Jason Gainous, and James G. Kane. 2006. "Winners, Losers, and Election Context: Voter Responses to the 2000 Presidential Election." *Political Research Quarterly* 59(4): 579–92.

Crenshaw, Kimberlé. 1989. "Demarginalizing the Intersection of Race and Sex: A Black Feminist Critique of Antidiscrimination Doctrine, Feminist Theory and Antiracist Politics." *University of Chicago Legal Forum* 1989: 139–67.

Crummy, Karen E. 2001. "War on Terrorism: Protesters Call for Peace." *Boston Herald*. September 30: 5.

Davidson, Carl. 2008. Interview with Michael T. Heaney, December 13. Chicago.

Davis, Aaron C. 2011. "Iraq's Maliki Inches toward U.S. Troop Decision." *Washington Post*. May 11. Available online at: http://articles.washingtonpost.com/2011-05-11/world/35233028_1_troop-decision-sadr-maliki, accessed January 3, 2013.

Dawson, Michael C. 1994. *Behind the Mule: Race and Class in African-American Politics*. Princeton, NJ: Princeton University Press.

2001. *Black Visions: The Roots of Contemporary African-American Political Ideologies*. Chicago: University of Chicago Pres.

Dearen, Jason. 2007. "Thousands Protest Iraq War across U.S." *The Associated Press News Service*. October 28.

DeBenedetti, Charles. 1990. *An American Ordeal: The Antiwar Movement of the Vietnam Era*. Syracuse, NY: Syracuse University Press.

DeGregorio, Christine A. 1997. *Networks of Champions: Leadership, Access, and Advocacy in the U.S. House of Representatives*. Ann Arbor: University of Michigan Press.

Della Porta, Donatella. 2005. "Multiple Identities, Tolerant Identities, and the Construction of 'Another Politics': Between the European Social Forum and Local Social Fora." Pp. 175–202 in Donatella Della Porta and Sidney Tarrow, eds., *Transnational Protest and Global Activism: People, Passions, and Power*. Lanham, MD: Rowman & Littlefield.

Della Porta, Donatella, and Sidney Tarrow. 1986. "Unwanted Children: Political Violence and the Cycle of Protest in Italy, 1966–1973." *European Journal of Political Research* 14(5–6): 607–32.

Democracy NOW! 2003. "Peace Protests Continue despite President Bush's Dismissal of the Anti-War Movement as a Mere "Focus Group." February 20. Available online at: http://www.democracynow.org/2003/2/20/peace_protests_continue_despite_president_bushs, accessed June 30, 2012.

2012. "Ahead of Charlotte DNC, Hundreds Protest Corporate Giants in 'March on Wall Street South.'" Available online at: http://www.democracynow.org/2012/9/4/ahead_of_charlotte_dnc_hundreds_protest, accessed January 11, 2012.

Denselow, James. 2011. "The US Departure from Iraq Is an Illusion." *The Guardian*. October 25. Available online at: http://www.guardian.co.uk/commentisfree/cifamerica/2011/oct/25/us-departure-iraq-illusion, accessed January 3, 2013.

Department of Defense. 2006. "Quadrennial Defense Review Report." February 6. Available online at: http://www.defense.gov/pubs/pdfs/QDR20060203.pdf, accessed January 4, 2012.

DePledge, Derrick. 2003. "Anti-War Movement Faces Test as War Wanes." *USA Today*. April 13.

Desmond, Humphrey J. 1905. *The Know-Nothing Party: A Sketch*. Washington, DC: New Century Press.

Dewan, Shaila. 2006. "The Impetus for Changes: Voters Display Frustrations and Dissatisfactions." *New York Times*, November 8: P8.

Diani, Mario. 2009. "The Structural Bases of Protest Events: Multiple Memberships and Networks in the February 15th 2003 Anti-War Demonstrations." *Acta Sociologica* 52(1): 63–83.

Diani, Mario, and Ivano Bison. 2004. "Organizations, Coalitions, and Movements." *Theory and Society* 33(3–4): 281–309.

DiGrazia, Joseph. 2014. *The Tea Party Movement: Right-Wing Mobilization in the Age of Obama*. Ph.D. diss., Department of Sociology, Indiana University-Bloomington.

DiMaggio, Paul J., and Walter W. Powell. 1983. "The Iron Cage Revisited: Institutional Isomorphism and Collective Rationality in Organizational Fields." *American Sociological Review* 48(2): 147–60.

Dinas, Elias. 2013. "Opening 'Openness to Change': Political Events and the Increased Sensitivity of Young Adults." *Political Research Quarterly*. Published online first, February 14, 2013. Available at: http://prq.sagepub.com.proxy.lib.umich.edu/content/early/2013/02/14/1065912913475874.abstract, accessed February 22, 2013.

Disch, Lisa Jane. 2002. *The Tyranny of the Two-Party System*. New York: Columbia University Press.

Dobnik, Verena. 2004. "Major Protests Mark Iraq War Anniversary. *The Associated Press News Service*. March 21.

   2009. "Main St. Protests on Wall St." *Associated Press*. Available online at: http://www.thestar.com/business/article/613736–main-st-protests-on-wall-st, accessed January 11, 2013.

Dobson, Laurie. 2009. Telephone interview with Michael T. Heaney, December 16.

Dodd, Lawrence C. 1976. *Coalitions in Parliamentary Government*. Princeton, NJ: Princeton University Press.

Downs, Anthony. 1957. *An Economic Theory of Democracy*. New York: HarperCollins.

   1972. "Up and Down with Ecology – the 'Issue-Attention Cycle.'" *The Public Interest* 28: 38–50.

Dreier, Peter, and Christopher R. Martin. 2010. "How ACORN Was Framed: Political Controversy and Media Agenda Setting." *Perspectives on Politics* 8(3): 761–92.

Dreazen, Yochi J. 2011. "U.S. Troop Withdrawal Motivated by Iraqi Insistence, Not U.S. Choice." *National Journal*. October 22. Available online at: http://www.nationaljournal.com/u-s-troop-withdrawal-motivated-by-iraqi-insistence-not-u-s-choice-20111021, accessed January 3, 2013.

Duffy, Michael, and with Mark Kukis. 2008. "The Surge at Year One." *Time*. January 31. Available online at: http://www.time.com/time/magazine/article/0,9171,1708843,00.html, accessed January 3, 2013.

Duhalde, David. 2013. Telephone interview with Michael T. Heaney, July 22.

Earl, Jennifer, Andrew Martin, John D. McCarthy and Sarah A. Soule. 2004. "The Use of Newspapers in Studying Collective Action." *Annual Review of Sociology* 30: 65–80.

Edwards, Jason A. 2011. "Debating America's Role in the World: Representative Ron Paul's Exceptionalist Jeremiad." *American Behavioral Scientist* 55(3): 253–69.

Ehrlich, Judith, and Rick Tejada-Flores. 2000. *The Good War and Those Who Refused to Fight It*. Film. Berkeley, CA: Paradigm Productions.

Eisinger, Peter K. 1973. "The Conditions of Protest Behavior in American Cities." *American Political Science Review* 67(1): 11–28.

End US Wars. 2012. "Our Supporters Are Associated With." Available online at: http://web.archive.org/web/20121019065721/; http://www.enduswars.org/, accessed July 2, 2012.

Englehardt, Tom. 2006. "Permanent Bases in Iraq?" *Salon*. February 15. Available online at: http://www.salon.com/2006/02/15/tomengelhardt/, accessed January 1, 2013.

Erikson, Robert S., and Laura Stoker. 2011. "Caught in the Draft: The Effects of Vietnam Draft Lottery Status on Political Attitudes." *American Political Science Review* 105(2): 221–37.

Evans, Eldon Cobb. 1917. *A History of the Australian Ballot System in the United States*. Ph.D. diss., Department of Political Science, University of Chicago.

Ewers, Justin. 2008. "Cindy Sheehan Makes Last Stand against Nancy Pelosi." *US News and World Report*. November 4. Available online at: http://web.archive.org/web/20121026064422/; http://www.usnews.com/news/articles/2008/11/04/cindy-sheehan-makes-last-stand-against-nancy-pelosi, accessed August 21, 2013.

Fairclough, Adam. 1984. "Martin Luther King Jr. and the War in Vietnam." *Phylon* 45(1): 19–39.

Farber, David. 1988. *Chicago '68*. Chicago: University of Chicago Press.

Featherstone, Liza. 2005. "Make Levees, Not War." *The Nation*. October 10. Available online at: http://www.thenation.com/article/make-levees-not-war#, accessed January 8, 2013.

Feaver, Peter D. 2011. "The Right to Be Right: Civil-Military Relations and the Iraq Surge Decision." *International Security* 35(4): 87–125.

Federal Election Commission. 2013. "Official 2012 Presidential General Election Results." January 17. Available online at: http://www.fec.gov/pubrec/fe2012/2012presgeresults.pdf, accessed June 5, 2013.

Felbab-Brown, Vanda. 2005. "Afghanistan: When Counternarcotics Undermines Counterterrorism." *Washington Quarterly* 28(4): 55–72.

Feldmann, Glenn. 2009. "Southern Disillusionment with the Democratic Party: Cultural Conformity and 'the Great Melding' of Racial and Economic Conservatism in Alabama during World War II." *Journal of American Studies* 43(2): 199–230.

Fellowship of Reconciliation. 1917. "Statement of the Fellowship of Reconciliation." *The Advocate of Peace* 79(4): 113–15.

Festinger, Leon. 1957. *A Theory of Cognitive Dissonance*. Stanford, CA: Stanford University Press.

Fisher, Dana R. 2006. *Activism, Inc.* Stanford, CA: Stanford University Press.
   2012. "Youth Political Participation: Bridging Activism and Electoral Politics." *Annual Review of Sociology* 38: 119–37.

Fithian, Lisa. 2013. Telephone interview with Michael T. Heaney, June 25.

Fitzgerald, Kathleen J., and Diane M. Rodgers. 2000. "Radical Social Movement Organizations: A Theoretical Model." *Sociological Quarterly* 41(4): 573–92.

Fligstein, Neil, and Doug McAdam. 2012. *A Theory of Fields*. Oxford: Oxford University Press.

Ford, Glen. 2011. "The Phony Anti-War Movement." *Black Agenda Report*. May 4. Available online at: http://blackagendareport.com/content/phony-anti-war-movement, January 29, 2013.

Forliti, Amy. 2008. "Some Turn Violent in US Convention Protests." *The Associated Press News Service*. September 2.

Fouhy, Beth. 2011. "Occupy Wall Street and Democrats Remain Wary of Each Other." *Huffington Post*, November 17. Available online at: http://www.huffingtonpost.com/2011/11/17/occupy-wall-street-democrats-2012-election_n_1099068.html, accessed June 23, 2012.

Foweraker, Joe. 1995. *Theorizing Social Movements*. Boulder, CO: Pluto Press.

Fowler, James H. 2006a. "Connecting the Congress: A Study of Cosponsorship Networks." *Political Analysis* 14(4): 456–87.

2006b. "Legislative Cosponsorship Networks in the US House and Senate." *Social Networks* 28(4): 254–65.

Fox, Ben. 2003. "Tens of Thousands in U.S. Protest War." *The Associated Press New Service*. March 23.

Francia, Peter L. 2010. "Assessing the Labor-Democratic Party Alliance: A One-Sided Relationship?" *Polity* 42(3): 293–303.

Frazier, Joseph B. 2006. "Thousands around Globe Call for End of War." *The Associated Press News Service*. March 20.

Freeman, Jo. 1986. "The Political Culture of the Democratic and Republican Parties." *Political Science Quarterly* 101(3): 327–56.

1987. "Whom You Know versus Whom You Represent: Feminist Influence in the Democratic and Republican Parties." Pp. 215–46 in Marry Fainsod Katzenstein and Carol McClurg Mueller, eds., *The Women's Movements of the United States and Western Europe*. Philadelphia: Temple University Press.

Freeman, Linton C. 1979. "Centrality in Social Networks: Conceptual Clarification." *Social Networks* 1(2): 215–39.

Friedland, Roger, and Robert R. Alford. 1991. "Bringing Society Back In: Symbols, Practices, and Institutional Contradictions." Pp. 232–63 in Walter W. Powell and Paul J. DiMaggio, eds., *The New Institutionalism in Organizational Analysis*. Chicago: University of Chicago Press.

Frymer, Paul. 1999. *Uneasy Alliances: Race and Party Competition in America*. Princeton, NJ: Princeton University Press.

Fung, Archon. 2003. "Associations and Democracy: Between Theories, Hope, and Reality." *Annual Review of Sociology* 29: 515–39.

Gadarian, Shana Kushner. 2010. "Foreign Policy at the Ballot Box: How Citizens Use Foreign Policy to Judge and Choose Candidates." *Journal of Politics* 72(4): 1046–62.

Gallup. 2013a. "Afghanistan." Available online at: http://web.archive.org/web/20130424210002/; http://www.gallup.com/poll/116233/Afghanistan.aspx, accessed August 9, 2013.

2013b. "Iraq." Available online at: http://web.archive.org/web/20130523115513/; http://www.gallup.com/poll/1633/iraq.aspx, accessed August 9, 2013.

Gamson, William A. 1991. "Commitment and Agency in Social Movements." *Sociological Forum* 6(1): 27–50.

Ganz, Marshall. 2009. *Why David Sometimes Wins: Leadership, Organization, and Strategy in the California Farm Worker Movement*. Oxford: Oxford University Press.

Garcia, Stephen M, Avishalom Tor, and Tyrone M. Schiff. 2013. "The Psychology of Competition: A Social Comparison Perspective." *Perspectives on Psychological Science* 8(6): 634–50.

Garfinkle, Adam. 1995. *Telltale Hearts: The Origins and Impact of the Vietnam Antiwar Movement*. New York: St. Martin's Griffin.

Gartner, Scott Sigmund, and Garry M. Segura. 2008. "All Politics Are Still Local: The Iraq War and the 2006 Midterm Elections." *PS: Political Science and Politics* 41(1): 95–100.

Gelpi, Christopher. 2010. "Performing on Cue? The Formation of Public Opinion toward War." *Journal of Conflict Resolution* 54(1): 88–116.

General Social Survey. 2013. "GSS 1972–2010 Cumulative Datafile." Available online at: http://sda.berkeley.edu/cgi-bin/hsda?harcsda+gss10, accessed January 25, 2013.

Gerhards, Jurgen, and Dieter Rucht. 1992. "Mesomobilization: Organizing and Framing in Two Protest Campaigns in West Germany." *American Journal of Sociology* 98(3): 555–96.

Gervais, Bryan T., and Irwin L. Morris. 2012. "Reading the Tea Leaves: Understanding the Tea Party Caucus Membership in the US House of Representatives." *PS: Political Science and Politics* 45(2): 245–50.

Geys, Benny. 2010. "Wars, Presidents, and Popularity: The Political Cost(s) of War Re-Examined." *Public Opinion Quarterly* 74(2): 357–74.

Gillan, Kevin, Jenny Pickerill, and Frank Webster. 2008. *Anti-war Activism: New Media and Protest in the Information Age*. New York: Palgrave Macmillan.

Gillham, Patrick F., and Bob Edwards. 2011. "Legitimacy Management, Preservation of Exchange Relationships, and the Dissolution of the Mobilization for Global Justice Coalition." *Social Problems* 58(3): 433–60.

Gillham, Patrick F., Bob Edwards, and John A. Noakes. 2013. "Strategic Incapacitation and the Policing of Occupy Wall Street Protests in New York City, 2011." *Policing and Society* 23(1): 81–102.

Gitlin, Todd. 1981. *The Whole World Is Watching: Mass Media in the Making and Unmaking of the New Left*. Berkeley: University of California Press.

2012. *Occupy Nation: The Roots, the Spirit, and the Promise of Occupy Wall Street*. New York: HarperCollins.

Glauber, Bill. 2002. "Echoes of '60s Activism Resound at Peace Rally." *Chicago Tribune*, October 2. Available online at http://www.highbeam.com/doc/1G1-120056688.html, accessed July 12, 2011.

Goldstein, Kenneth M. 1999. *Interest Groups, Lobbying, and Participation in America*. Cambridge: Cambridge University Press.

Goldstone, Jack A., ed. 2003. *States, Parties, and Social Movements*. Cambridge: Cambridge University Press.

2004. "More Social Movements or Fewer? Beyond Political Opportunity Structures to Relational Fields." *Theory and Society* 33 (3–4): 333–65.

Goold, Bill. 2008. Interview with Michael T. Heaney, June 20. Washington, DC.

Goss, Kristin A. 2006. *Disarmed: The Missing Movement for Gun Control in America*. Princeton, NJ: Princeton University Press.

Goss, Kristin A., and Michael T. Heaney. 2010. "Organizing Women *as Women*: Hybridity and Grassroots Collective Action in the 21st Century." *Perspectives on Politics* 8(1): 27–52.

Gould, Roger V. 1995. *Insurgent Identities: Class, Community, and Protest in Paris from 1848 to the Commune*. Chicago: University of Chicago Press.

Green, Donald, Bradley Palmquist, and Eric Schickler. 2002. *Partisan Hearts and Minds: Political Parties and the Social Identities of Voters*. New Haven, CT: Yale University Press.

Green Papers. 2013. "Election 2016: Presidential Primaries, Caucuses, and Conventions." Available online at: http://www.thegreenpapers.com/P16/, accessed August 19, 2013.

Greenstone, J. David. 1969. *Labor in American Politics*. New York: Vintage Books.

Gregory Jr., Stanford W., and Jerry M. Lewis. 1988. "Symbols of Collective Memory: The Social Process of Memorializing May 4, 1970, at Kent State University." *Symbolic Interaction* 11(2): 213–33.

Gross, Neil. 2009. "A Pragmatist Theory of Social Mechanisms." *American Sociological Review* 74(3): 358–79.

Grossmann, Matt, and Casey B. K. Dominguez. 2009. "Party Coalitions and Interest Group Networks." *American Politics Research* 37(5): 767–800.

Gutierrez, Theresa. 2010. "Stop the War on Immigrant Workers: Teresa Gutierrez at the UNPC 7/23/2010." Available online at: http://www.youtube.com/watch?v=uYag-xoDKqXo, accessed July 3, 2013.

Habyariman, James, Macartan Humphreys, Daniel N. Posner, and Jeremy Weinstein. 2009. *Coethnicity and the Dilemmas of Collective Action*. New York: Russell Sage Foundation.

Hacker, Jacob S., and Paul Pierson. 2005. *Off Center: The Republican Revolution and the Erosion of American Democracy*. New Haven, CT: Yale University Press.

Hadden, Jennifer. 2015. *Networks in Contention: The Divisive Politics of Global Climate Change*. New York: Cambridge University Press.

Hadden, Jennifer, and Sidney Tarrow. 2007. "Spillover or Spillout? The Global Justice Movement in the United States after 9/11." *Mobilization* 12(4): 359–76.

Haddock, Geoffrey, and Mark P. Zanna. 1998. "On the Use of Open-Ended Measures to Assess Attitudinal Components." *British Journal of Social Psychology* 37(2): 129–49.

Hagan, John, Joshua Kaiser, Anna Hanson, Jon R. Lindsay, Austin G. Long, Stephen Biddle, Jeffrey A. Friedman, and Jacob N. Shapiro. 2013. "Correspondence: Assessing the Synergy Thesis in Iraq." *International Security* 37(4): 173–98.

Haines, Herbert H. 1988. *Black Radicals and the Civil Rights Mainstream, 1954–1970*. Knoxville: University of Tennessee Press.

Halchin, L. Elaine. 2004. "The Coalition Provisional Authority (CPA): Origin, Characteristics, and Institutional Authorities." April 29. Washington, DC: Congressional Research Service. Available online at: http://www.fas.org/man/crs/RL32370.pdf, accessed December 31, 2012.

Halstead Von Tyne, Claude. 1902. *The Loyalists in the American Revolution*. New York: Macmillan.

Hammond, Susan Webb. 1998. *Congressional Caucuses in National Policy Making*. Baltimore, MD: Johns Hopkins University Press.

Han, Hahrie. 2009. *Moved to Action: Motivation, Participation, and Inequality in American Politics*. Stanford, CA: Stanford University Press.

Hancock, Ange-Marie. 2007. "When Multiplication Doesn't Equal Quick Addition: Examining Intersectionality as a Research Paradigm." *Perspectives on Politics* 5(1): 63–79.

Hannan, Michael T., and John Freeman. 1989. *Organizational Ecology*. Cambridge, MA: Harvard University Press.

Hansen, John Mark. 1985. "The Political Economy of Group Membership." *American Political Science Review* 79(1): 79–96.

   1991. *Gaining Access: Congress and the Far Lobby, 1919–1981*. Chicago: University of Chicago Press.

Harvey, Anna L. 1998. *Votes without Leverage: Women in American Electoral Politics, 1920–1970*. Cambridge: Cambridge University Press.

Harvey, Frank P. 2012. *Explaining the Iraq War: Counterfactual Theory, Logic, and Evidence*. Cambridge: Cambridge University Press.

Hatic, Dana. 2013. "It Wasn't All Peace and Love for Obama." *Boston University News Service*. January 21. Available online at: http://bunewsservice.com/it-wasnt-all-peace-and-love-for-obama/, accessed January 31, 2013.

Hauser, Christine. 2005. "Anti-Nuclear Demonstrations Held in New York." *New York Times*. Available online at: http://www.nytimes.com/2005/05/01/nyregion/01cnd-protest.html?pagewanted=print&position=&_r=0, accessed January 8, 2013.

Heaney, Michael T. 2004a. *Identity, Coalitions, and Influence: The Politics of Interest Group Networks in Health Care*. Ph.D. diss., Department of Political Science and Irving B. Harris Graduate School of Public Policy Studies, University of Chicago.

2004b. "Outside the Issue Niche: The Multidimensionality of Interest Group Identity." *American Politics Research* 32(6): 611–51.

2006. "Brokering Health Policy: Coalitions, Parties, and Interest Group Influence." *Journal of Health Politics, Policy and Law* 31(5): 887–944.

2007. "Identity Crisis: How Interest Groups Struggle to Define Themselves in Washington." Pp. 279–300 in Allan J. Cigler and Burdett A. Loomis, eds., *Interest Group Politics*, 7th ed. Washington, DC: CQ Press.

2010. "Linking Political Parties and Interest Groups." Pp. 568–87 in L. Sandy Maisel and Jeffrey M. Berry, eds., *The Oxford Handbook of American Political Parties and Interest Groups*. Oxford: Oxford University Press.

2012. "Bridging the Gap between Political Parties and Interest Groups." Pp. 194–218 in Allan J. Cigler and Burdett A. Loomis, eds., *Interest Group Politics*, 8th ed. Washington, DC: CQ Press.

Heaney, Michael T., and Fabio Rojas. 2007. "Partisans, Nonpartisans, and the Antiwar Movement in the United States." *American Politics Research* 35(4): 431–64.

2008. "Coalition Dissolution, Mobilization, and Network Dynamics in the U.S. Antiwar Movement." *Research in Social Movements, Conflicts and Change* 28: 39–82.

2014. "Hybrid Activism: Social Movement Mobilization in a Multimovement Environment." *American Journal of Sociology* 119(4): 1047–1103.

Heaney, Michael T., and Geoffrey M. Lorenz. 2013. "Coalition Portfolios and Interest Group Influence over the Policy Process." *Interest Groups & Advocacy* 2(3): 251–77.

Heaney, Michael T., Seth E. Masket, Joanne M. Miller, and Dara Z. Strolovitch. 2012. "Polarized Networks: The Organizational Affiliations of National Party Convention Delegates." *American Behavioral Scientist* 56(12): 1654–76.

Herbert, Steve. 2007. "The 'Battle of Seattle' Revisited: Or, Seven Views of a Protest-Zoning State." *Political Geography* 26(5): 601–19.

Herring, George C. 2002. *America's Longest War: The United States and Vietnam, 1950–1975*. New York: McGraw-Hill.

Hetherington, Marc J. 2009. "Review Article: Putting Polarization in Perspective." *British Journal of Political Science* 39(2): 413–48.

Hilbe, Joseph M. 2007. *Negative Binomial Regression*. Cambridge: Cambridge University Press.

Hillyguys, D. Sunshine, and Todd G. Shields. 2008. *The Persuadable Voter: Wedge Issues in Presidential Campaigns*. Princeton, NJ: Princeton University Press.

Hirano, Shigeo, and James M. Snyder Jr. 2007. "The Decline of Third-Party Voting in the United States." *Journal of Politics* 69(1): 1–16.

Hirschman, Albert O. 1982. *Shifting Involvements: Private Interest and Public Action*. Princeton, NJ: Princeton University Press.

Hofstadter, Richard. 1969. *The Idea of a Party System: The Rise of Legitimate Opposition in the United States, 1780–1840*. Berkeley: University of California Press.

Holsti, Ole R. 2011. *American Public Opinion on the Iraq War*. Ann Arbor: University of Michigan Press.

hooks, bell. 1984. *Feminist Theory: From Margin to Center*. Cambridge, MA: South End Press.

Hopkins, Christopher Snow. 2013. "Anna Galland, 33, Leads MoveOn.org from Michigan." *National Journal Daily*. March 8. Available online at: http://www.nationaljournal.com/daily/anna-galland-33-leads-moveon-org-from-michigan-20130307, accessed July 6, 2013.

Horn, Steve. 2011. "MoveOn.Org and Friends Attempt to Co-Opt Occupy Wall Street Movement." *Truthout*. October 11. Available online at: http://www.truth-out.org/news/item/3870:moveonorg-and-friends-attempt-to-coopt-occupy-wall-street-movement, accessed August 18, 2013.

Howell, William G. 2003. *Power without Persuasion: The Politics of Direct Presidential Action*. Princeton, NJ: Princeton University Press.

Howell, William G., and Douglas Kriner. 2008. "Power without Persuasion: Identifying Executive Influence." Pp. 105–44 in Bert A. Rockman and Richard W. Waterman, eds., *Presidential Leadership: The Vortex of Power*. Oxford: Oxford University Press.

Howell, William G., and Jon C. Pevehouse. 2005. "Presidents, Congress, and the Use of Force." *International Organization* 59(1): 209–32.

Howell, William G., and Jon C. Rogowski. 2013. "War, the Presidency, and Legislative Voting Behavior." *American Journal of Political Science* 57(1): 150–66.

Hula, Kevin W. 1999. *Lobbying Together: Interest Group Coalitions in Legislative Politics*. Washington, DC: Georgetown University Press.

Hunt, Scott A., and Robert D. Benford. 2004. "Collective Identity, Solidarity, and Commitment." Pp. 433–57 in David A. Snow, Sarah A. Soule, and Hanspeter Kriesi, eds., *The Backwell Companion to Social Movements*. Malden, MA: Blackwell.

International ANSWER. 2001. "20,000–25,000 Rallied against Racism and War in Washington, D. C. on September 29, 2001." Available online at: http://web.archive.org/web/20011003191519/; http://www.internationalanswer.org/, accessed June 29, 2012.

2002. "International A.N.S.W.E.R. Coalition List." Available online at: http://web.archive.org/web/20040820132021/; http://www.answercoalition.org/endorsers.html, accessed July 2, 2012.

Iraq Moratorium. 2009. "Iraq Moratorium: It's Got to Stop! We've Got to Stop It!" Available online at: http://iraq-moratorium.blogspot.com/, accessed July 1, 2012.

Jacobs, Lawrence R., and Theda Skocpol. 2010. *Health Care Reform and American Politics: What Everyone Needs to Know*. Oxford: Oxford University Press.

Jacobson, Gary C. 2006. *A Divider, Not a Uniter: George W. Bush and the American People*. New York: Pearson Longman.

2010. "Perception, Memory, and Partisan Polarization on the Iraq War." *Political Science Quarterly* 25(1): 31–56.

2011. "The President, the Tea Party, and Voting Behavior in 2010: Insights from the Cooperative Congressional Election Study." Paper presented at the Annual Meeting of the American Political Science Association, Seattle, WA, September 1–4.

Jasper, James M. 1997. *The Art of Moral Protest: Culture, Biography, and Creativity in Social Movements*. Chicago: University of Chicago Press.

Jehl, Douglas, and Dexter Filkins. 2003. "The Struggle for Iraq: Troop Levels: Rumsfeld Eager for More Iraqis to Keep Peace." *New York Times*. September 5. Available online at: http://www.nytimes.com/2003/09/05/world/the-struggle-for-iraq-troop-levels-rumsfeld-eager-for-more-iraqis-to-keep-peace.html, accessed December 31, 2012.

Jenkins, J. Craig, and Craig M. Eckert. 1986. "Channeling Black Insurgency: Elite Patronage and Professional Social Movement Organizations in the Development of the Black Movement." *American Sociological Review* 51(6): 812–29.

Jennings, M. Kent, Laura Stoker, and Jake Bowers. 2009. "Politics across Generations: Family Transmission Reexamined." *Journal of Politics* 71(3): 782–99.

Johnson, Reinhard O. 2009. *The Liberty Party, 1840–1848*. Baton Rouge: Louisiana State University Press.

Jones, David R., and Monika L. McDermott. 2011. "The Salience of the Democratic Congress and the 2010 Elections." *PS: Political Science and Politics* 44(2): 297–301.

Jones, Jeffrey M. 2003. "Public Support for Invasion of Iraq Holds Steady: Fifty-Nine Percent in Favor of Invading Iraq." Washington, DC: Gallup. Available at: http://www.gallup.com/poll/7891/public-support-invasion-iraq-holds-steady.aspx, accessed October 27, 2012.

Juris, Jeffrey S., Michelle Ronayne, Firuzeh Shokooh-Valle, and Robert Wengronowitz. 2012. "Negotiating Power and Difference within the 99%." *Social Movement Studies* 11(3–4): 434–40.

Kahneman, Daniel P., Paul Slovic, and Amos Tversky. 1982. *Judgment under Uncertainty: Heuristics and Biases*. New York: Cambridge University Press.

Kamada, Tomihisa, and Satoru Kawai. 1989. "An Algorithm for Drawing General Undirected Graphs." *Information Processing Letters* 31(1): 7–15.

Kaplowitz, Michael D., Timothy D. Hadlock, and Ralph Levine. 2004. "A Comparison of Web and Mail Survey Response Rates." *Public Opinion Quarterly* 68(1): 94–101.

Karol, David. 2009. *Party Position Change in American Politics: Coalition Management*. Cambridge: Cambridge University Press.

Karpf, David. 2012. *The MoveOn Effect: The Unexpected Transformation of American Political Advocacy*. Oxford: Oxford University Press.

Katz, Milton S. 1986. *Ban the Bomb: A History of SANE, The Committee for a SANE Nuclear Policy, 1957–1985*. Westport, CT: Greenwood Press.

Katzman, Kenneth. 2012. "Iraq: Politics, Governance, and Human Rights." *Washington, DC: Congressional Research Service*. Available online at: http://www.fas.org/sgp/crs/mideast/RS21968.pdf, accessed January 3, 2013.

Katzman, Kenneth, and Jennifer Elsea. 2004. "Iraq: Transition to Sovereignty." July 21. Washington, DC: Congressional Research Service. Available online at: http://www.fas.org/man/crs/RS21820.pdf, accessed December 31, 2012.

Kessler, Daniel, and Keith Krehbiel. 1996. "Dynamics of Cosponsorship." *American Political Science Review* 90(3): 555–66.

Key, V.O. Jr. 1942. *Politics, Parties, and Pressure Groups*. New York: Thomas Y. Crowell.

   1948. *Politics, Parties, and Pressure Groups*, 2nd ed. New York: Thomas Y. Crowell.

KGO. 2012. "Hundreds March in SF to Protest Afghanistan War." *ABC*. October 6. Available online at: http://abclocal.go.com/kgo/story?section=news/local/san_francisco&id=8838279, accessed January 11, 2013.

Kilbride, Malachy. 2013. Interview with Michael T. Heaney, January 21. Washington, DC.

Kilkenny, Allison. 2012. "Hundreds of Activists Protest at the Republican National Convention." *The Nation*. August 27. Available online at: http://www.thenation.com/blog/169571/hundreds-activists-protest-republican-national-convention#, accessed January 11, 2013.

Kim, Richard. 2011. "The Audacity of Occupy Wall Street." *The Nation*. November 21: 15–21.

King, Martin Luther Jr. 1965. "How Long? Not Long!" Speech delivered in Montgomery, Alabama, March 25. Available online at: http://www.youtube.com/watch?v=TAYITODNvlM, accessed January 31, 2013.

Kingdon, John W. 1995. *Agendas, Alternatives, and Public Policies*, 2nd ed. Boston: Addison-Wesley.

Kirkland, Justin H. 2013. "Hypothesis Testing for Group Structure in Legislative Networks." *State Politics and Policy Quarterly* 13: 225–43.

Kitschelt, Herbert P. 1989. *The Logics of Party Formation: Ecological Politics in Belgium and West Germany*. Ithaca, NY: Cornell University Press.

Knowledge Networks. 2003. "Field Report: Pre-War Racial Differences Study." Menlo Park, CA: Knowledge Networks. Available online at: http://web.archive.org/web/20081120135426/; http://www.michaeldawson.net/wp-content/downloads/2003_Documentation.pdf, accessed July 7, 2013.

Koger, Gregory. 2003. "Position-Taking and Cosponsorship in the U.S. House." *Legislative Studies Quarterly* 28(2): 225–46.

2010. *Filibustering: A Political History of Obstruction in the House and Senate*. Chicago: University of Chicago Press.

Koger, Gregory, and Jennifer Nicoll Victor. 2009. "Polarized Agents: Campaign Contributions by Lobbyists." *PS: Political Science and Politics* 42(3): 485–88.

Kollman, Ken. 1998. *Outside Lobbying: Public Opinion and Interest Group Strategies*. Princeton, NJ: Princeton University Press.

Kolodny, Robin, and David A. Dulio. 2009. "Political Party Adaptation in US Congressional Campaigns: Why Political Parties Use Coordinated Expenditures to Hire Political Consultants." *Party Politics* 9(6): 729–46.

Kreiss, Daniel. 2012. *Taking Our Country Back: The Crafting of Networked Politics from Howard Dean to Barack Obama*. Oxford: Oxford University Press.

Kriesi, Hanspeter. 1995. "The Political Opportunity Structure of New Social Movements: Its Impact on Their Mobilization." Pp. 167–98 in J. Craig Jenkins and Bert Klandermans, eds., *The Politics of Social Protest: Comparative Perspectives on States and Social Movements*. Minneapolis: University of Minnesota Press.

Kriesi, Hanspeter, Ruud Koopmans, Jan Willem Duyvendak, and Marco G. Giugni. 1995. *New Social Movements in Western Europe: A Comparative Analysis*. Minneapolis: University of Minnesota Press.

Kriner, Douglas L. 2010. *After the Rubicon: Congress, Presidents, and the Politics of Waging War*. Chicago: University of Chicago Press.

Kunzelman, Michael. 2005. "Anti-War Protests Spill into Second Day." *The Associated Press News Service*. March 21.

Kupchan, Charles A., and Peter L. Trubowitz. 2007. "Dead Center: The Demise of Liberal Internationalism in the United States." *International Security* 32(2): 7–44.

Lalonde, Richard N., Janelle M. Jones, and Mirella L. Stroink. 2008. "Racial Identity, Racial Attitudes, and Race Socialization among Black Canadian Parents." *Canadian Journal of Behavioural Science-Revue Canadienne Des Sciences du Comportement* 40(3): 129–39.

Lapidos, Juliet. 2009. "One Ecstatic Inauguration Attendee, Two Ecstatic Inauguration Attendees: How Do You Measure a Crowd?" *Slate.* January 21. Available online at: http://www.slate.com/articles/news_and_politics/explainer/2009/01/one_ecstatic_inauguration_attendee_two_ecstatic_inauguration_attendees.html, accessed January 6, 2013.

Layman, Geoffrey C., Thomas M. Carsey, John C. Green, Richard Herrera, and Rosalyn Cooperman. 2010. "Activists and Conflict Extension in American Party Politics." *American Political Science Review* 104(2): 324–46.

Layman, Geoffrey C., Thomas M. Carsey, and Juliana Menasce Horowitz. 2006. "Party Polarization in American Politics: Characteristics, Causes, and Consequences." *Annual Review of Political Science* 9(1): 83–110.

Lazarsfeld, Paul F., Bernard Berelson, and Hazel Gaudet. 1948. *The People's Choice: How the Voter Makes Up His Mind in a Presidential Campaign*, 2nd ed. New York: Columbia University Press.

Leach, Darcy K. 2013. "Culture and the Structure of Tyrannylessness." *Sociological Quarterly* 54(2): 181–91.

LeBlanc, Judith. 2007. Interview with Michael T. Heaney, June 29. Atlanta, GA.
2013. Telephone interview with Michael T. Heaney, June 28.

Lee, Frances E. 2009. *Beyond Ideology: Politics, Principles, and Partisanship in the U.S. Senate.* Chicago: University of Chicago Press.

Leitz, Lisa. 2014. *Fighting for Peace: Veterans and Military Families in the Anti-Iraq War Movement.* Minneapolis: University of Minnesota Press.

Levendusky, Matthew. 2009. *The Partisan Sort: How Liberals Became Democrats and Conservatives Became Republicans.* Chicago: University of Chicago Press.

Levi, Margaret, and Gillian H. Murphy. 2006. "Coalitions of Contention: The Case of the WTO Protests in Seattle." *Political Studies* 54(4): 651–70.

Levy, Mark R. 1983. "The Methodology and Performance of Election Day Polls." *Public Opinion Quarterly* 47(1): 54–67.

Library of Congress. 2001. "Thomas." Available online at: http://thomas.loc.gov/cgi-bin/bdquery/z?d107:SJ00023:@@@X, accessed September 19, 2011.
2002. "Thomas." Available online at: http://thomas.loc.gov/cgi-bin/bdquery/D?d107:1:./temp/~bdOhx2:@@@X|/home/LegislativeData.php?n=BSS;c=107|, accessed September 19, 2011.
2011–2013. "Thomas." Available online at: http://thomas.gov/, accessed January 2011–July 2013.

Lichterman, Paul. 1995. "Piecing Together Multicultural Community: Cultural Differences in Community Building among Grass-Roots Environmentalists." *Social Problems* 42(4): 513–32.

Livingston, Ian S., and Michael O'Hanlon. 2012. "Afghanistan Index." Washington, DC: Brookings Institution. Available online at: http://www.brookings.edu/~/media/Programs/foreign%20policy/afghanistan%20index/index20121213.pdf, accessed January 2, 2013.

Lukas, J. Anthony. 1968. "Police Battle Demonstrators in the Streets." *New York Times*, August 29: 1.

Lynch, Frederick R. 2011. *One Nation under AARP: The Fight over Medicare, Social Security, and America's Future*. Berkeley: University of California Press.

MacAskill, Ewen. 2007. "Bush Rejects Congress Timetable for Iraq Retreat." *The Guardian*. March 28. Available online at: http://www.guardian.co.uk/world/2007/mar/29/usa.iraq, accessed December 31, 2012.

Madison, James. 1982 [1787]. "Federalist No. 10." Pp. 42–49 in Alexander Hamilton, James Madison, and John Jay, *The Federalist Papers*. New York: Bantam Books.

Malkasian, Carter. 2006. "Signaling Resolve, Democratization, and the First Battle of Fallujah." *Journal of Strategic Studies* 29(3): 423–52.

Mann, Robert. 2010. *Wartime Dissent in America: A History and Anthology*. New York: Palgrave Macmillian.

March, James G. 1997. "Administrative Practice, Organization Theory, and Political Philosophy: Ruminations on the Reflections of John M. Gaus." *PS: Political Science and Politics* 30(4): 689–98.

Martin, Jonathan. 2014. "Eric Cantor Defeated by David Brat, Tea Party Challenger, in G.O.P. Primary Upset." *New York Times*. June 10. Available online at: http://www.nytimes.com/2014/06/11/us/politics/eric-cantor-loses-gop-primary.html?_r=0., accessed July 19, 2014.

Marullo, Sam, and David S. Meyer. 2004. "Antiwar and Peace Movements." Pp. 641–65 in David A. Snow, Sarah A. Soule, and Hanspeter Kriesi, eds., *The Blackwell Companion to Social Movements*. Malden, MA: Blackwell.

Masket, Seth E. 2011. *No Middle Ground: How Informal Party Organizations Control Nominations and Polarize Legislatures*. Ann Arbor: University of Michigan Press.

Mason, R. Chuck. 2009. "U.S.-Iraq Withdrawal/Status of Forces Agreement: Issues for Congressional Oversight." Washington, DC: Congressional Research Service. Available online at: http://www.fas.org/sgp/crs/natsec/R40011.pdf, accessed January 3, 2003.

2011. "Status of Forces Agreement (SOFA): What Is It, and How Has It Been Utilized?" Washington, DC: Congressional Research Service. Available online at: http://assets.opencrs.com/rpts/RL34531_20110105.pdf, accessed January 4, 2013.

Maxwell, Angie, and T. Wayne Parent. 2012. "The Obama Trigger: Presidential Approval and Tea Party Membership." *Social Science Quarterly* 93(5): 1384–401.

Mayer, Kenneth R. 2001. *With the Stroke of a Pen: Executive Orders and Presidential Power*. Princeton, NJ: Princeton University Press.

Mayhew, David R. 1974. *Congress: The Electoral Connection*. New Haven, CT: Yale University Press.

McAdam, Doug. 1982. *Political Process the Development of the Black Insurgency, 1930–1970*. Chicago: University of Chicago Press.

1988. *Freedom Summer*. New York: Oxford University Press.

1989. "The Biographical Consequences of Activism." *American Sociological Review* 54(5): 744–60.

McAdam, Doug, and Karina Kloos. 2014. *Divided America: Racial Politics and Social Movements in Postwar America*. New York: Oxford University Press.

McAdam, Doug, and Ronelle Paulsen. 1993. "Specifying the Relationship between Social Ties and Activism." *American Journal of Sociology* 99(3): 640–67.

McAdam, Doug, and Sidney Tarrow. 2010. "Ballots and Barricades: On the Reciprocal Relationship between Elections and Social Movements." *Perspectives on Politics* 8(2): 529–42.

2011. "Introduction: Dynamics of Contention Ten Years On." *Mobilization* 16(1): 1–10.

McAdam, Doug, and Sidney Tarrrow. 2013. "Social Movements and Elections: Toward a Broader Understanding of the Political Context of Contention." Pp. 325–46 in Jacquelien van Stekelenburg, Conny Roggeband, and Bert Klandermans, eds., *The Future of Social Movement Research: Dynamics, Mechanisms, and Processes.* Minneapolis: University of Minnesota Press.

McAdam, Doug, Sidney Tarrow, and Charles Tilly. 2001. *Dynamics of Contention.* Cambridge: Cambridge University Press.

McAdam, Doug, and Yang Su. 2002. "The War at Home: Antiwar Protests and Congressional Voting, 1965 to 1973." *American Sociological Review* 67(5): 696–721.

McCain, John. 2007. "An Enduring Peace Built on Freedom." *Foreign Affairs* 86(6): 19–34.

2008. "The First Presidential Debate." *New York Times.* September 26. Available online at: http://elections.nytimes.com/2008/president/debates/transcripts/first-presidential-debate.html, access January 4, 2013.

McCall, Leslie. 2005. "The Complexity of Intersectionality." *Signs* 30(3): 1771–800.

McCarthy, John D., Clark McPhail, and Jackie Smith. 1996. "Images of Protest: Dimensions of Selection Bias in Media Coverage of Washington Demonstrations, 1982 and 1991." *American Sociological Review* 61(3): 478–99.

McCarthy, John D., and David Wolfson. 1996. "Resource Mobilization by Local Social Movement Organizations: Agency, Strategy, and Organization in the Movement against Drinking and Driving." *American Sociological Review* 61(6): 1070–88.

McCarthy, John D., and Mayer N. Zald. 1977. "Resource Mobilization and Social Movements: A Partial Theory." *American Journal of Sociology* 82(6): 1212–41.

McConnaughy, Corrine M. 2013. *The Woman Suffrage Movement in America: A Reassessment.* Cambridge: Cambridge University Press.

McFadden, Robert D. 2004. "Vast Anti-Bush Rally Greets Republicans in New York." *New York Times.* August 30. Available online at: http://www.nytimes.com/2004/08/30/politics/campaign/30protest.html, accessed January 8, 2013.

McLemee, Scott. 2007. "Party in the Streets." *Inside Higher Ed.* March 21. Available online at http://www.insidehighered.com/views/mclemee/mclemee136, accessed August 13, 2012.

McPherson, Miller, Lynn Smith-Lovin, and James M. Cook. 2001. "Birds of a Feather: Homophily in Social Networks." *Annual Review of Sociology* 27: 415–44.

Mearsheimer, John J. 2001. *The Tragedy of Great Power Politics.* New York: W. W. Norton.

Meckler, Mark. 2009. "Tax Day Tea Parties a HUGE Success." Available online at: http://web.archive.org/web/20090420020424/; http://teapartypatriots.org/, accessed August 17, 2013.

Melucci, Alberto. 1989. *Nomads of the Present: Social Movements and Individual Needs in Contemporary Society.* Philadelphia: Temple University Press.

Meyer, David S. 1990. *A Winter of Discontent: The Nuclear Freeze and American Politics*. New York: Praeger.

2007. *The Politics of Protest: Social Movements in America*. New York: Oxford University Press.

Meyer, David S., and Catherine Corrigall-Brown. 2005. "Coalitions and Political Context: U.S. Movements against Wars in Iraq." *Mobilization* 10(3): 327–44.

Meyer, David S., and Debra C. Minkoff. 2004. "Conceptualizing Political Opportunity." *Social Forces* 82(4): 1457–92.

Meyer, David S., and Nancy Whittier. 1994. "Social Movement Spillover." *Social Problems* 41(2): 277–98.

Meyer, David S., and Sidney G. Tarrow, eds. 1998. *The Social Movement Society: Contentious Politics for a New Century*. Lanham, MD: Rowman & Littlefield.

Meyer, Rachel. 2008. *Perpetual Struggle: Sources of Working-Class Identity and Activism in Collective Action*. Ph.D. diss., Department of Sociology, University of Michigan.

Miles, Stephen. 2013. Telephone interview with Michael T. Heaney, June 18.

Miller, Paul D. 2011. "Finishing the Job: How the War in Afghanistan Can Be Won." *Foreign Affairs* 90(1): 51–65.

Minkoff, Debra C. 1995. *Organizing for Equality: The Evolution of Women's and Racial-Ethnic Organizations in America, 1955–1985*. New Brunswick, NJ: Rutgers University Press.

Mische, Anne. 2008. *Partisan Publics: Communication and Contention across Brazilian Youth Activist Networks*. Princeton, NJ: Princeton University Press.

Monroe, J. P. 2001. *The Political Party Matrix: The Persistence of Organization*. Albany: State University of New York Press.

Morgenthau, Hans J. 1948. *Power among Nations: The Struggle for Power and Peace*. New York: Knopf.

Morris, Aldon D. 1984. *The Origins of the Civil Rights Movement: Black Communities Organizing for Change*. New York: The Free Press.

MoveOn. 2009. "Current Campaigns." Available online at: http://web.archive.org/web/20090714231219/; http://moveon.org/, accessed July 6, 2013.

2011. "Frequently Asked Questions about MoveOn and Occupy Wall Street." Available online at: http://web.archive.org/web/20111022201149/; http://www.civic.moveon.org/owsfaq/share.html, accessed August 18, 2013.

Mudge, Stephanie L., and Anthony S. Chen. 2014. "Political Parties and the Sociological Imagination: Past, Present, and Future Directions." *Annual Review of Sociology* 40: 305–30.

Müller von Blumencron, Mathias, and Bernard Zand. 2008. "The Tenure of Coalition Troops in Iraq Should Be Limited." *Spiegel*. July 19. Available online at: http://www.spiegel.de/international/world/spiegel-interview-with-iraqi-leader-nouri-al-maliki-the-tenure-of-coalition-troops-in-iraq-should-be-limited-a-566852.html, accessed January 3, 2013.

Munson, Ziad W. 2008. *The Making of Pro-Life Activists: How Social Movement Mobilization Works*. Chicago: University of Chicago Press.

Murakami, Michael H. 2008. "Divisive Primaries: Party Organizations, Ideological Groups, and the Battle over Party Purity." *PS: Political Science and Politics* 41(4): 918–23.

Murphy, Gillian H. 2005. "Coalitions and the Development of the Global Environ-mental Movement: A Double-Edged Sword." *Mobilization* 10(2): 235–50.

Mutz, Diana C. 2006. *Hearing the Other Side: Deliberate versus Participatory Democ-racy.* New York: Cambridge University Press.

Myers, Teresa A., and Andrew F. Hayes. 2010. "Reframing the Casualties Hypothesis: (Mis)Perceptions of Troop Loss and Public Opinion about War." *International Journal of Public Opinion Research* 22(2): 256–75.

Nah, Seungahn, Aaron S. Veenstra, and Dhavan V. Shah. 2006. "The Internet and Anti-War Activism: A Case Study of Information, Expression, and Action." *Journal of Computer-Mediated Communication* 12(1): Article 12. http://jcmc.indiana.edu/vol12/issue1/nah.html, accessed October 19, 2007.

National Assembly. 2008. "Endorsers of Open National Conference." Available online at: http://web.archive.org/web/20080513174102/; http://www.natassembly.org/, accessed July 2, 2013.

    2010. "United National Antiwar Conference Action Proposal Submitted by Confer-ence Co-Sponsors." Available online at: http://web.archive.org/liveweb/; http://northlandantiwar.blogspot.com/2010/06/action-proposal-to-be-discussed-at.html, accessed July 3, 2013.

National Election Pool. 2004. *National Election Pool General Election Exit Polls, 2004.* ICPSR 4181. Ann Arbor, MI: Inter-University Consortium for Political and Social Research.

    2006. *National Election Pool General Election Exit Polls, 2006.* ICPSR 4684. Ann Arbor, MI: Inter-University Consortium for Political and Social Research.

    2008. *National Election Pool General Election Exit Polls, 2008.* ICPSR 28123. Ann Arbor, MI: Inter-University Consortium for Political and Social Research.

National Peace Conference. 2010. "An Invitation From." Available online at: http://web.archive.org/web/20100503223306/; http://nationalpeaceconference.org/

National Public Radio. 2002. *Weekend Edition Saturday.* April 20.

    2009. "Transcript: Obama's Speech against the Iraq War." Available online at http://www.npr.org/templates/story/story.php?storyId=99591469, accessed July 13, 2011.

National Youth and Student Peace Coalition. 2007. "National Youth and Student Peace Coalition Member Organizations." Available online at: http://web.archive.org/web/20070701073734/; http://www.nyspc.org/members.html, accessed July 2, 2013.

    2008. "What Is NYSPC?" Available online at: http://web.archive.org/web/20081210074030/; http://www.nyspc.org/about.html, accessed July 2, 2013.

Nepstad, Sharon Erickson. 2004. "Persistent Resistance: Commitment and Community in the Plowshares Movement." *Social Problems* 51(1): 43–60.

Newey, Whitney K., and Kenneth D. West. 1987. "A Simple, Positive Semi-Definite, Heteroskedasticity and Autocorrelation Consistent Covariance Matrix." *Econome-trica* 55(3): 703–8.

Newnham, Randall. 2008. "'Coalition of the Bribed and Bullied?' U.S. Economic Linkage and the Iraq War Coalition." *International Studies Perspectives* 9(2): 183–200.

New Priorities Network. 2013. "About Us." Available online at: http://web.archive.org/web/20130605095440/; http://newprioritiesnetwork.org/about/about-us/.

NewsBank. 2013. "Access World News." Available online at: http://www.newsbank.com/schools/product.cfm?product=24, accessed January 7, 2013.

Nisbett, Richard E., and Timothy D. Wilson. 1977. "Telling More than We Can Know: Verbal Reports on Mental Processes." *Psychological Review* 84(3): 231–59.

Noakes, John, and Patrick F. Gillham. 2007. "Police and Protester Innovation since Seattle." *Mobilization: An International Quarterly* 12(4): 335–40.

Noel, Hans. 2013. *Political Ideologies and Political Parties in America.* Cambridge: Cambridge University Press.

Nownes, Anthony J. 2004. "The Population Ecology of Interest Group Formation: Mobilizing for Gay and Lesbian Rights in the United States, 1950–1998." *British Journal of Political Science* 34(1): 49–67.

Nyhan, Brendan, and Jacob M. Montgomery. 2015. "Connecting the Candidates: Consultant Networks and the Diffusion of Campaign Strategies in American Congressional Elections." *American Journal of Political Science, forthcoming.*

Nyhan, Brendan, and Jason Reifler. 2010. "When Corrections Fail: The Persistence of Political Misperceptions." *Political Behavior* 32(2): 303–30.

Oak, Robert. 2011. "Occupy Wall Street Goes Global." *The Economic Populist.* October 15. Available online at: http://web.archive.org/web/20111017075143/; http://www.economicpopulist.org/content/occupy-wall-street-goes-global, accessed August 18, 2013.

O'Connor, Karen. 1996. *No Neutral Ground? Abortion Politics in an Age of Absolutes.* Boulder, CO: Westview Press.

Obama, Barack. 2004. *Dreams from My Father: A Story of Race and Inheritance.* New York: Three Rivers Press.

    2007. "Remarks during South Carolina Democratic Debate, Orangeburg, South Carolina at South Carolina State University." April 26. Available online at: http://www.msnbc.msn.com/id/18352397/, accessed September 13, 2010.

    2008a. "Closing Arguments: A Presidential Super Dialogue." *MTV.* Available online at: http://www.mtv.com/videos/news/207164/6-of-10-the-military-is-just-one-way-to-serve.jhtml#id=1580846, accessed July 14, 2011.

    2008b. "The Democratic Debate in Las Vegas, College of Southern Nevada, Las Vegas, Nevada, January 15, 2008." Available online at: http://www.nytimes.com/2008/01/15/us/politics/15demdebate-transcript.html, accessed September 13, 2010.

    2008c. "The First Presidential Debate." *New York Times.* September 26. http://elections.nytimes.com/2008/president/debates/transcripts/first-presidential-debate.html, accessed January 4, 2013.

    2012. "Transcript: President Obama's Convention Speech." *National Public Radio.* September 6. Available online at: http://www.npr.org/2012/09/06/160713941/transcript-president-obamas-convention-speech, accessed January 4, 2013.

Occucards.com. 2013. "Republicrats: The Two-Party Duopoly." Available online at: http://www.occucards.com/images2/15-republicrats.pdfm, accessed August 22, 2013.

O'Hanlon, Michael E., and Ian Livingston. 2012. "Iraq Index." Washington, DC: Brookings Institution. Available online at: http://www.brookings.edu/~/media/Centers/saban/iraq%20index/index20120131.PDF, accessed January 2, 2013.

Oliphant, James. 2011. "Democrats Embrace Occupy Wall Street as GOP Strikes." *Los Angeles Times,* October 10. Available online at: http://articles.latimes.com/2011/oct/10/news/la-pn-occupy-democrats-20111010, accessed June 23, 2012.

Oliver, Pamela E. 1989. "Bringing the Crowd Back In: The Nonorganizational Elements of Social Movements." *Research in Social Movements, Conflicts, and Change* 14: 1–30.

Oliver, Pamela E., and Daniel J. Myers. 2003. "The Coevolution of Social Movements." *Mobilization* 8(1): 1–25.

Oliver, Pamela E., Gerald Marwell, and Ruy Teixeira. 1985. "A Theory of the Critical Mass, I: Interdependence, Group Heterogeneity, and the Production of Collective Goods." *American Journal of Sociology* 91(3): 522–56.

One Nation Working Together. 2010. "Mission." Available online at: http://web. archive.org/web/20100913035741/; http://www.onenationworkingtogether. org/pages/mission, accessed July 5, 2013.

Oruh, Chioma. 2009. Interview with Michael T. Heaney, December 12. Washington, DC.

Padgett, John F., and Paul D. McLean. 2006. "Organizational Invention and Elite Transformation: The Birth of Partnership Systems in Renaissance Florence." *American Journal of Sociology* 111(5): 1463–568.

Padgett, John F., and Walter W. Powell. 2012. *The Emergence of Organizations and Markets*. Princeton, NJ: Princeton University Press.

Panagopoulos, Costas. 2011. *Occupy Wall Street Survey Results October 2011*. New York: Fordham University, Center for Electoral Politics and Democracy.

Parker, Christopher S., and Matt S. Barreto. 2013. *Change They Can't Believe In: The Tea Party and Reactionary Politics in America*. Princeton, NJ: Princeton University Press.

Pearson, Richard. 1998. "Former Ala. Gov. George C. Wallace Dies." *Washington Post*. September 14: A1.

Peterson, Kyle, and Ann Saphir. 2008. "Thousands Protest in Chicago As NATO Summit Opens." *Reuters*. May 20. Available online at: http://www.reuters.com/ article/2012/05/20/us-nato-summit-protests-idUSBRE84I09X20120520, accessed January 13, 2013.

Petraeus, David. 2007. "Report to Congress on the Situation in Iraq." Available online at: http://www.defense.gov/pubs/pdfs/Petraeus-Testimony20070910.pdf, accessed January 3, 2013.

Pierson, Paul. 2004. *Politics in Time: History, Institutions, and Social Analysis*. Princeton, NJ: Princeton University Press.

Pirch, Kevin A. 2008. "Bloggers at the Gates: Ned Lamont, Blogs, and the Rise of Insurgent Candidates." *Social Science Computer Review* 26(3): 275–87.

Piven, Frances Fox. 2013. "On the Organizational Question." *Sociological Quarterly* 54 (2): 191–3.

Polletta, Francesca. 2002. *Freedom Is an Endless Meeting: Democracy in American Social Movements*. Chicago: University of Chicago Press.

2004. "Culture in and outside Institutions." *Research in Social Movements, Conflicts, and Change* 25: 161–83.

Polletta, Francesca, and James M. Jasper. 2001. "Collective Identity and Social Movements." *Annual Review of Sociology* 27: 283–305.

Polsky, Andrew J. 2012. *Elusive Victories: The American Presidency at War*. Oxford: Oxford University Press.

Powell, Colin. 2003. "Full Text of Colin Powell's Speech: US Secretary of State's Address to the United Nations Security Council." *The Guardian*. February 5. Available online at: http://www.guardian.co.uk/world/2003/feb/05/iraq.usa, accessed December 31, 2012.

Prior, Markus. 2013. "Media and Political Polarization." *Annual Review of Political Science* 16: 101–27.

Progressive Democrats of America. 2005. "Rep. Waters Creates New 'Out-of-Iraq Congressional Caucus.'" Available online at: http://web.archive.org/web/

20050620074120/; http://www.commondreams.org/news2005/0616-32.htm, accessed July 29, 2013.

Przeworski, Adam, and John Sprague. 1986. *Paper Stones: A History of Electoral Socialism*. Chicago: University of Chicago Press.

Public Law 110–28. 2007. *U.S. Troop Readiness, Veterans' Care, Katrina Recovery, and Iraq Accountability Appropriations Act*. May 25. Washington, DC: US Government Printing Office.

Rattinger, Hans. 1990. "Domestic and Foreign Policy Issues in the 1988 Presidential Election." *European Journal of Political Research* 18(6): 623–43.

Rayback, Joseph G. 1970. *Free Soil: The Election of 1848*. Lexington: University Press of Kentucky.

Real Clear Politics. 2008. "2008 Republican Popular Vote." Available online at: http://www.realclearpolitics.com/epolls/2008/president/republican_vote_count.html, accessed November 3, 2013.

Riccardi, Nicholas, and DeeDee Correll. 2008. "Protest Led by Iraq War Veterans Ends in Talk with Obama Liaison." *Los Angeles Times*. August 28. Available online at: http://articles.latimes.com/2008/aug/28/nation/na-protest28, accessed January 11, 2003.

Ringe, Nils, Jennifer Nicoll Victor, and Christopher J. Carman. 2013. *Bridging the Information Gap: Legislative Member Organizations as Social Networks in the United States and the European Union*. Ann Arbor: University of Michigan Press.

Roberts, Alasdair. 2012. "Why the Occupy Movement Failed." *Public Administration Review* 72(5): 754–62.

Robinson, Dan. 2011. "Obama, Maliki Hail 'New Chapter' for Iraq without US Troops." *Voice of America*. December 11. Available online at: http://www.voanews.com/content/obama-maliki-hail-new-chapter-for-iraq-without-us-troops-135449683/149460.html, accessed January 3, 2013.

Rodriguez, Dylan. 2012. "De-Provincialising Police Violence: On the Recent Events at UC Davis." *Race & Class* 54(1): 99–109.

Rojas, Fabio. 2007. *From Black Power to Black Studies: How a Radical Social Movement Became an Academic Discipline*. Baltimore: Johns Hopkins University Press.

Romano, David. 2006. *The Kurdish Nationalist Movement: Opportunity, Mobilization and Identity*. Cambridge: Cambridge University Press.

Rosenberg, Erik. 2008. *Future of NYSPC*. E-mail to the listserv of the National Youth and Student Peace Coalition, October 23.

Rosenblum, Nancy L. 2008. *On the Side of Angels: An Appreciation of Parties and Partisanship*. Princeton, NJ: Princeton University Press.

Rosenstone, Steven J., and John Mark Hansen. 1993. *Mobilization, Participation, and Democracy in America*. New York: Macmillan.

Rosenstone, Steven J., Roy L. Behr, and Edward H. Lazarus. 1984. *Third Parties in America*. Princeton, NJ: Princeton University Press.

Rupp, Leila J., and Verta A. Taylor. 1990. *Survival in the Doldrums: The American Women's Rights Movement, 1945 to the 1960s*. Columbus: Ohio State University Press.

Rycroft, Matthew. 2002. "The Secret Downing Street Memo." Available online at: http://web.archive.org/web/20051001070749/; http://downingstreetmemo.com/docs/memotext.pdf, accessed July 3, 2013.

Salisbury, Robert H. 1969. "An Exchange Theory of Interest Groups." *Midwest Journal of Political Science* 13(1): 1–32.

San Francisco Argonaut. 1892. "Third Party Tickets: Bubbles That Have Floated for a While on the Political Sea." *New York Times*, July 24: 4.

Santelli, Rick. 2009. "Rick Santelli's Shout Heard 'Round the World." Available online at: http://www.cnbc.com/id/29283701/Rick_Santelli_s_Shout_Heard_Round_the_World, accessed August 17, 2013.

Savage, Charlie. 2013. "Soldier Admits Providing Files to WikiLeaks." *New York Times*, March 1: A1.

Schattschneider, E. E. 1935. *Politics, Pressures and the Tariff*. New York: Prentice-Hall.
1960. *The Semisovereign People: A Realist's View of Democracy in America*. New York: Holt, Rinehart & Winston.

Schlozman, Daniel Aaron. 2011. *The Making of Partisan Majorities: Parties, Anchoring Groups, and Electoral Change*. Ph.D. diss., John F. Kennedy School of Government, Harvard University.
2015. *When Movements Anchor Parties: Social Movements, Political Parties, and Electoral Change*. Princeton, NJ: Princeton University Press.

Schlozman, Kay Lehman, Sidney Verba, and Henry E. Brady. 2012. *The Unheavenly Chorus: Unequal Political Voice and the Broken Promise of American Democracy*. Princeton, NJ: Princeton University Press.

Schnabel, Landon. 2014. "When Fringe Goes Mainstream Again: A Comparative Textual Analysis of the Tea Party Movement's Contract from American and the Republican Party Platform." *Politics, Religion, & Identity* 15(4): forthcoming.

Schreiner, Bruce. 2007. "War Protests Continue to Mark 4th Anniversary of U.S. Invasion of Iraq." *The Associated Press News Service*. March 20.

Schulzinger, Robert. 1997. *A Time for War: The United States and Vietnam, 1941–1975*. Oxford: Oxford University Press.

Schwartz, Mildred A. 1990. *The Party Network: The Robust Organization of Illinois Republicans*. Madison: University of Wisconsin Press.
2006. *Party Movements in the United States and Canada: Strategies of Persistence*. Lanham, MD: Rowman & Littlefield.
2010. "Interactions between Social Movements and US Political Parties." *Party Politics* 16(5): 587–607.

Seidman, Derek. 2010. *The Unquiet Americans: GI Dissent during the Vietnam War*. Ph.D. diss., Department of History, Brown University.

Selfa, Lance. 2008. *The Democrats: A Critical History*. Chicago: Haymarket Books.

Selznick, Philip. 1949. *TVA and the Grass Roots: A Study in the Sociology of Formal Organization*. Berkeley: University of California Press.

Shear, Michael D. 2012. "Influence of Palin and Tea Party Wanes in Early Contests." *New York Times*. February 2. Available online at: http://thecaucus.blogs.nytimes.com/2012/02/02/influence-of-palin-and-tea-party-wanes-in-early-contests/?scp=3&sq=sarah%20palin%20&st=cse, accessed June 21, 2012.

Simmel, Georg. 1955. *Conflict and the Web of Group Affiliations*, trans. Kurt H. Wolff and Reinhard Bendix. New York: Free Press.

Sinclair, Barbara. 2006. *Party Wars: Polarization and the Politics of National Policy Making*. Norman: University of Oklahoma Press.

Skinner, Richard M. 2009. "George W. Bush and the Partisan Presidency." *Political Science Quarterly* 123(4): 605–22.

Skinner, Richard M., Seth E. Masket, and David A. Dulio. 2012. "527 Committees and the Political Party Network." *American Politics Research* 40(1): 60–84.

Skocpol, Theda. 1997. *Boomerang: Health Care Reform and the Turn against Government*. New York: W.W. Norton.

Skocpol, Theda, and Vanessa Williamson. 2012. *The Tea Party and the Remaking of Republican Conservatism*. New York: Oxford University Press.

Skocpol, Theda, Ariane Liazos, and Marshall Ganz. 2006. *What a Mighty Power We Can Be: African American Fraternal Groups and the Struggle for Racial Equality*. Princeton, NJ: Princeton University Press.

Small, Melvin. 1987. "Influencing the Decision Makers: The Vietnam Experience." *Journal of Peace Research* 24(2): 185–98.

2002. *Antiwarriors: The Vietnam War and the Battle for America's Hearts and Minds*. Lanham, MD: SR Books.

Smith, Jackie. 2001. "Globalizing Resistance: The Battle of Seattle and the Future of Social Movements." *Mobilization: An International Quarterly* 6(1): 1–19.

Smith, Jackie, and Bob Glidden. 2012. "Occupy Pittsburgh and the Challenges of Participatory Democracy." *Social Movement Studies* 11(3–4): 288–94.

Smucker, Jonathan. 2014. "Can Prefigurative Politics Replace Political Strategy?" *Berkeley Journal of Sociology* 58. Available online at: http://berkeleyjournal.org/2014/10/can-prefigurative-politics-replace-political-strategy/, accessed November 12, 2014.

Snow, David A., and Sarah A. Soule. 2009. *A Primer on Social Movements*. New York: W. W. Norton.

Snow, David A., R. Burke Rochford, Steven K. Worden, and Robert D. Benford. 1986. "Frame Alignment Processes, Micromobilization, and Movement Participation." *American Sociological Review* 51(4): 464–81.

Sorauf, Frank J. 1980. *Party Politics in America*, 4th ed. Boston: Little, Brown.

Staff. 2005. "Inaugural Protests." *Washington Post*. April 16. Available online at: http://www.washingtonpost.com/wp-dyn/content/gallery/2005/04/16/GA2005041600451.html, accessed January 8, 2013.

2009. "Protesters Demand End to Wars in Iraq, Afghanistan." *CNN Wire*. March 21.

Staggenborg, Suzanne. 1986. "Coalition Work in the Pro-Choice Movement: Organizational and Environmental Opportunities and Obstacles." *Social Problems* 33(5): 374–90.

Stein, Jonathan. 2007. "John Murtha's "Slow Bleed" Plan to End the Iraq War Explained." *Mother Jones*, February 16. Available online at: http://www.motherjones.com/mojo/2007/02/john-murthas-slow-bleed-plan-end-iraq-war-explained, accessed November 19, 2012.

Stets, Jan E., and Peter J. Burke. 2000. "Identity Theory and Social Identity Theory." *Social Psychology Quarterly* 63(3): 224–37.

Stewart, Martina. 2012. "Tea Party Group Aims for 'Winning by Building, Building by Winning." *CNN*, June 19. Available online at: http://www.cnn.com/2012/06/19/politics/tea-party-group-building-organization/index.html, accessed June 23, 2012.

Stone, Geoffrey R. 2004. *Perilous Times: Free Speech in Wartime*. New York: W.W. Norton.

Stop Bechtel. 2006. "From Hiroshima to Yucca Mountain to the Middle East: Stop Bechtel." Available online at: http://web.archive.org/web/20070213115202/; http://www.august6.org/node/171, accessed January 11, 2013.

Stout, David. 2006. "Bush Predicts a Year of Progress in Iraq and Afghanistan." *New York Times*. January 4. Available online at: http://www.nytimes.com/2006/01/04/international/middleeast/04cnd-prexy.html?fta=y&_r=1&, accessed January 4, 2013.

Strolovitch, Dara Z. 2007. *Affirmative Advocacy: Race, Class, and Gender in Interest Group Politics*. Chicago: University of Chicago Press.

2012. "Intersectionality in Time: Sexuality and the Shifting Boundaries of Intersectional Marginalization." *Politics and Gender* 8(3): 386–96.

Stryker, Sheldon, Timothy J. Owens, and Robert W. White. 1990. "Social Psychology and Social Movements: Cloudy Past and Bright Future." Pp. 1–20 in Sheldon Stryker, Timothy J. Owens, and Robert W. White, eds., *Self, Identity, and Social Movements*. Minneapolis: University of Minnesota Press.

Students for a Democratic Society. 1962. "The Port Huron Statement of the Students for a Democratic Society." Available online at: http://coursesa.matrix.msu.edu/~hst306/documents/huron.html, accessed June 27, 2012.

Sundquist, James L. 1983. *Dynamics of the Party System: Alignment and Realignment of Political Parties in the United States*. Washington, DC: The Brookings Institution.

Sweet, Debra. 2008. "The Election and Our Responsibility." *World Can't Wait*. November 3. Available online at: http://www.worldcantwait.net/index.php/about-mainmenu-2/from-the-director-mainmenu-293/5133-this-election-a-our-responsibility, accessed January 12, 2013.

Taber, Charles S., and Milton Lodge. 2006. "Motivated Skepticism in the Evaluation of Political Beliefs." *American Journal of Political Science* 50(3): 755–69.

Tajfel, Henri, M. G. Billig, R. P. Bundy, and Claude Flament. 1971. "Social Categorization and Intergroup Behavior." *European Journal of Social Psychology* 1(2): 149–77.

Talbert, Jeffrey C., and Matthew Potoski. 2002. "Setting the Legislative Agenda: The Dimensional Structure of Bill Cosponsoring and Floor Voting." *Journal of Politics* 64(3): 864–91.

Tapper, Jake. 2007. "MoveOn.org Ad Takes Aim at Petraeus." *ABC News*. September 10. Available online at: http://web.archive.org/web/20070913050044/; http://abcnews.go.com/Politics/Decision2008/story?id=3581727&page=1, accessed July 7, 2013.

Tarrow, Sidney G. 1989. *Democracy and Disorder: Protest and Politics in Italy, 1965–1974*. Oxford: Oxford University Press.

1993. "Cycles of Collective Action: Between Moments of Madness and the Repertoire of Contention." *Social Science History* 17(2): 281–307.

2005. *The New Transnational Activism*. Cambridge: Cambridge University Press.

2011. *Power in Movement: Social Movements and Contentious Politics*, 3rd ed. Cambridge: Cambridge University Press.

2012. *Strangers at the Gates: Movements and States in Contentious Politics*. Cambridge: Cambridge University Press.

Taylor, Verta. 1989. "Social Movement Continuity: The Women's Movement in Abeyance." *American Sociological Review* 54(5): 761–75.

Taylor, Verta, and Nella Van Dyke. 2004. "'Get Up, Stand Up': Tactical Repertoires of Social Movement." Pp. 262–93 in David A. Snow, Sarah A. Soule, and Hanspeter Kriesi, Kriesi, eds., *The Blackwell Companion to Social Movements*. Malden, MA: Blackwell.

Taylor, Verta, and Nicole C. Raeburn. 1995. "Identity Politics as High-Risk Activism: Career Consequences for Lesbian, Gay, and Bisexual Sociologists." *Social Problems* 42(2): 252–73.

Tea Party for Christians. 2014. "About Tea Party for Christians." Available online at: http://teapartyforchristians.com/about/, accessed July 20, 2014.

Tea Party Patriots. 2013. "About." Available online at: http://web.archive.org/web/20130809044839/; http://www.teapartypatriots.org/about/, accessed August 13, 2013.

Theriault, Sean M. 2008. *Party Polarization in Congress*. Cambridge: Cambridge University Press.

Tiefer, Charles. 2006. "Can Appropriations Riders Speed Our Exit from Iraq?" *Stanford Journal of International Law* 42(2): 91–342.

Tilly, Charles. 1978. *From Mobilization to Revolution*. Reading, PA: Addison-Wesley.

Tobin, James. 1958. "Estimation of Relationships for Limited Dependent Variables." *Econometrica* 26(1): 24–36.

Tocqueville, Alexis de. 1988 [1840]. *Democracy in America*, trans. George Lawrence, ed. J. P. Mayer. New York: HarperPerennial.

Tracy, James. 1996. *Direct Action: Radical Pacifism from the Union Eight to the Chicago Seven*. Chicago: University of Chicago Press.

Trinko, Katrina. 2011. "McCain: Iraq Withdrawal a 'Serious Mistake.'" *National Review*. October 23. Available online at: http://www.nationalreview.com/corner/281029/mccain-iraq-withdrawal-serious-mistake-katrina-trinko, accessed January 3, 2013.

Troops Out Now. 2011. "Who We Are: The Troops Out Now Coalition." Available online at: http://web.archive.org/web/20110410034401/; http://troopsoutnow.org/statements/whoweare.shtml, accessed July 2, 2013.

Truman, David B. 1971. *The Governmental Process: Political Interests and Public Opinion*, 2nd ed. New York: Knopf.

Tucker, Eric. 2011. "Anti-War Protesters Arrested near White House." *Huffington Post*. March 19. Available online at: http://www.huffingtonpost.com/2011/03/19/anti-war-protesters-arrest_n_838031.html, accessed January 7, 2013.

Turner, J. C., R. J. Brown, and H. Tajfel. 1979. "Social Comparison and Group Interest in Ingroup Favoritism." *European Journal of Social Psychology* 9(2): 187–204.

Tyler, Patrick E. 2003. "A New Power in the Streets." *New York Times*, February 17: A1.

United for Peace and Justice. 2004. "Sunday, August 29: 500,000 Say No to the Bush Agenda!" http://web.archive.org/web/20040915002758/; http://www.unitedforpeace.org/, accessed January 8, 2013.

2005. "Three Days in September." Available online at: http://web.archive.org/web/20051006191146/; http://www.unitedforpeace.org/article.php?id=3111, accessed January 8, 2013.

2006a. "3,500 March against Bush War Agenda Outside U. N." Available online at: http://www.politicalaffairs.net/3–500-march-against-bush-war-agenda-outside-u-n/, accessed January 11, 2013.

2006b. "Telephone Press Briefing: 600+ Peace Activities Express Majority Opposition to Iraq War." Available online at: http://web.archive.org/web/20061230113943/; http://www.unitedforpeace.org/article.php?id=3213, accessed January 8, 2013.

2007a. "500,000 March for Peace – Call Congress Today!" Available online at: http://web.archive.org/web/20070214061514/; http://www.unitedforpeace.org//article.php?id=3507, accessed January 11, 2013.

2007b. "Grassroots Action Spotlight." Available online at: http://web.archive.org/web/20070220065548/; http://www.democracyinaction.org/dia/organizations/ufpj/blog/index.jsp?blog_KEY=345&t=, accessed January 11, 2013.

2007c. "October 27 National Mobilization to End the War in Iraq." Available online at: http://web.archive.org/web/20071022030856/; http://www.oct27.org/, accessed January 11, 2013.

2007d. Spread the Word about the January 27th Mobilization!" Available online at: http://web.archive.org/web/20070119114107/; http://www.unitedforpeace.org/article.php?id=3437, accessed May 10, 2012.

2008a. "United for Peace and Justice Member Groups." Available online at: http://web.archive.org/web/20081210104052/; http://www.unitedforpeace.org//article.php?list=type&type=27, accessed July 2, 2012.

2008b. "What Happened on March 19." Available online at: http://web.archive.org/web/20080408192130/; http://www.unitedforpeace.org/, accessed January 11, 2013.

2009. "10,000 March on Wall Street." Available online at: https://mail.quantumlinux.com/pipermail/hnet-bigmindmedia.com/2009-April/002914.html, accessed January 11, 2013.

2010. "UFPJ to Become a Network of Member Organizations." E-mail sent to UFPJ Listservs, February 9.

United National Antiwar Coalition. 2013. "UNAC Statements." Available online at: http://web.archive.org/web/20130310225641/; http://unacpeace.org/Action_Proposal.html, accessed July 3, 2013.

United Nations. 2001. "Agreement on Provisional Arrangements in Afghanistan Pending the Re-Establishment of Permanent Government Institutions." Available online at: http://www.un.org/News/dh/latest/afghan/afghan-agree.htm, accessed January 4, 2013.

United States Department of Defense. 2013. "Defense Casualty Analysis System." Available online at: http://web.archive.org/web/20130305094012/; https://www.dmdc.osd.mil/dcas/pages/casualties.xhtml, accessed August 9, 2013.

United States Department of State. 2007. "The New Way Forward." February. Washington, DC: Bureau of Near Eastern Affairs and the Bureau of Public Affairs. Available online at: http://2001–2009.state.gov/documents/organization/81600.pdf, accessed January 1, 2013.

United States Government Accountability Office. 2007. "Securing, Stabilizing, and Rebuilding Iraq." GAO-07-1195. Washington, DC: US GAO. Available online at: http://www.gao.gov/new.items/d071195.pdf, accessed January 1, 2013.

US Census Bureau. 2011. "Population – Race, Hispanic Origin." Available online at: http://www.census.gov/compendia/statab/2011/files/racehisp.html, accessed August 25, 2011.

US Election Atlas. 2013a. "1992 Presidential General Election Results." Available online at: http://uselectionatlas.org/RESULTS/national.php?year=1992, accessed August 18, 2013.

2013b. "1996 Presidential General Election Results." Available online at: http://uselectionatlas.org/RESULTS/national.php?year=1996, accessed August 18, 2013.

USLAW. 2012. "USLAW Affiliates." Available online at: http://web.archive.org/web/20120626223022/; http://uslaboragainstwar.org/article.php?id=16781, accessed July 2, 2013.

Vandenberg, Arthur. 1947. "America's Foreign Relations – Address by Senator Vandenberg." *Congressional Record* 93(January 13): 272–4.

Van Dyke, Nella, and Holly J. McCammon. 2010. "Introduction: Social Movement Coalition Formation." Pp. xi–xxvii in Nella Van Dyke and Holly J. McCammon, eds., *Strategic Alliances: Coalition Building and Social Movements.* Minneapolis: University of Minnesota Press.

Vasi, Ion Bogdan. 2006. "The New Anti-War Protests and Miscible Mobilizations." *Social Movement Studies* 5(2): 137–53.

    2011. "Brokerage, Miscibility, and the Spread of Contention." *Mobilization* 16(1): 11–24.

Vasi, Ion Bogdan, and Chan S. Shu. 2013. "Public Attention, Social Media, and the Spread of the 'Occupy' Movement in the United States." New York: Columbia University, Working Paper.

Voter News Service. 2002. *Voter News Service General Election Exit Poll, 2002.* ICPSR 3809. Ann Arbor, MI: Inter-University Consortium for Political and Social Research.

Voteview. 2012. "The Polarization of the Congressional Parties." Updated May 10, 2012. Available online at: http://www.voteview.com/political_polarization.asp, accessed December 16, 2012.

Walgrave, Stefaan, and Dieter Rucht, eds. 2010. *The World Says No to War: Demonstrations against the War on Iraq.* Minneapolis: University of Minnesota Press.

Walgrave, Stefaan, and Joris Verhulst. 2011. "Selection and Response Bias in Protest Surveys." *Mobilization* 16(2): 203–22.

Walgrave, Stefaan, and Rens Vliegenthart. 2012. "The Complex Agenda-Setting Power of Protest: Demonstrations, Media, Parliament, Government, and Legislation in Belgium, 1993–2000." *Mobilization* 17(2): 129–56.

Walker, Martin. 2008. "The Year of the Insurgents: The 2008 US Presidential Campaign." *International Affairs* 84(6): 1095–107.

Walker, William. 2002. "100,000 Protest Planned U.S. War on Iraq." *Toronto Star.* October 27.

Walsh, Declan, and Azam Ahmed. 2014. "Mending Alliance, U.S. and Afghanistan Sign Long-Term Security Agreement." *New York Times*, September 30.

War is a Crime. 2012. "Coalition Members." Available online at: http://web.archive.org/web/20121017183529/; http://warisacrime.org/coalition, accessed July 2, 2013.

Weaver, David A., and Joshua M. Scacco. 2012. "Revisiting the Protest Paradigm: The Tea Party as Filtered through Prime-Time Cable News." *International Journal of Press/Politics* 18(1): 61–84.

Weldon, S. Laurel. 2011. *When Protest Makes Policy: How Social Movements Represent Disadvantaged Groups.* Ann Arbor: University of Michigan Press.

Westheider, James E. 2008. *The African American Experience in Vietnam: Brothers in Arms.* Lanham: Rowman & Littlefield.

White House. 2001. "The Vice President Appears on NBC's Meet the Press." December 9. Available online at: http://georgewbush-whitehouse.archives.gov/vicepresident/news-speeches/speeches/print/vp20011209.html, accessed December 31, 2012.

    2007a. "Background Briefing by Senior Administration Officials." Available online at: http://georgewbush-whitehouse.archives.gov/news/releases/2007/01/20070110-1.html, accessed January 2, 2013.

2007b. "Fact Sheet: U.S.-Iraq Declaration of Principles for Friendship and Cooperation." Available online at: http://georgewbush-whitehouse.archives.gov/news/releases/2007/11/20071126-1.html, accessed January 3, 2013.

Whitlock, Craig. 2010. "U.S. Plans for Possible Delay in Iraq Withdrawal." *Washington Post.* February 23. Available online at: http://www.washingtonpost.com/wp-dyn/content/article/2010/02/22/AR2010022202933.html, accessed January 3, 2013.

Wilcox, Clyde, and Carin Robinson. 2011. *Onward Christian Soldiers? The Religious Right in American Politics*, 4th ed. Boulder, CO: Westview Press.

Williams, Daniel K. 2010. *God's Own Party: The Making of the Christian Right.* Oxford: Oxford University Press.

Wilson, James Q. 1962. *The Amateur Democrat: Club Politics in Three Cities.* Chicago: University of Chicago Press.

1995. *Political Organizations.* Princeton, NJ: Princeton University Press.

Wilson, Rick K., and Cheryl D. Young. 1997. "Cosponsorship in the U.S. Congress." *Legislative Studies Quarterly* 22(1): 25–43.

Win Without War. 2003. "Coalition Members." Available online at: http://web.archive.org/web/20030621084751/; http://winwithoutwarus.org/html/coalition.html, accessed July 2, 2013.

Wittner, Lawrence S. 2003. "The Forgotten Years of the World Nuclear Disarmament Movement, 1975–78." *Journal of Peace Research* 40(4): 435–56.

Woehrle, Lynne M., Patrick G. Coy, and Gregory M. Maney. 2008. *Contesting Patriotism: Culture, Power, and Strategy in the Peace Movement.* Lanham, MD: Rowman & Littlefield.

Wolbrecht, Christina. 2000. *The Politics of Women's Rights: Parties, Positions, and Change.* Princeton, NJ: Princeton University Press.

Wood, David. 2009. "Building Schools in Afghanistan: Not as Simple as ABC." *Politics Daily.* August 13. Available online at: http://www.politicsdaily.com/2009/08/13/building-schools-in-afghanistan-not-as-simple-as-a-b-c/, accessed January 4, 2013.

Woodward, Calvin, and Larry Margasak. 2007. "Crowds on Both Coasts Protest Iraq War." *The Associated Press News Service.* January 29.

Woolsey, Lynn. 2007a. "1/27/07 Antiwar Rally: Rep. Lynn Woolsey." *YouTube.com*, January 29. Available online at: http://www.youtube.com/watch?v=oRgfjo9UZUM, accessed May 10, 2012.

2007b. "Rep. Lynn Woolsey on Ending the Iraqi War." *YouTube.com*, January 27. Available online at: http://www.youtube.com/watch?v=WWgyyodZ7PM, accessed May 10, 2012.

Wootson, Cleve. 2012. "10 Protesters Arrested on DNC's Last Day." *Charlotte Observer.* September 6. Available online at: http://www.charlotteobserver.com/2012/09/06/3509951/10-arrested-on-conventions-last.html, accessed January 7, 2013.

World Can't Wait. 2009. "January 2009 Archives." January 25. Available online at: http://www.sfbaycantwait.net/2009/01/#000433, accessed January 11, 2013.

Wright, Ann. 2008. Interview at 44:16 in *The Activists: War, Peace, and Politics in the Streets.* Documentary film. Atlanta, GA: MeloFilms. Available online at: http://vimeo.com/49732898, accessed January 13, 2013.

Yeo, Andrew. 2011. *Activists, Alliances, and Anti-U.S. Base Protests.* Cambridge: Cambridge University Press.

Yeshitela, Omali. 2009. "Black Is Back Coalition for Social Justice, Peace and Reparations (Omali Yeshitela)1." http://www.youtube.com/watch?v=WMtJ7JZOELg, accessed August 25, 2011.

Yoho, James. 1995. "Madison on the Beneficial Effects of Interest Groups: What Was Left Unsaid in Federalist 10." *Polity* 27(4): 587–605.

Zald, Mayer N., and Roberta Ash. 1966. "Social Movement Organizations: Growth, Decay and Change." *Social Forces* 44(3): 327–41.

Zaller, John R. 1992. *The Nature and Origins of Mass Opinion.* Cambridge: Cambridge University Press.

Zelizer, Julian E. 2010. *Arsenal of Democracy: The Politics of National Security – From World War II to the War on Terrorism.* New York: Basic Books.

Zelney, Jeff, and Kate Zernke. 2006. "Democrats Take House: White House Concedes Defeat; Senate Is Tight; Spitzer in Rout; Menendez and Lieberman Win." *New York Times*, November 8: A1.

Zinn, Howard. 1997. *A People's History of the United States*, Teaching ed. New York: New Press.

Zuez, Dennis. 2010. "The Movement against Illegal Immigration: Analysis of the Central Node in the Russian Extreme-Right Movement." *Nations and Nationalism* 16(2): 261–84.

Index